BLOWTORCH

President Lyndon B. Johnson, right, meeting with Robert Komer on November 16, 1967, in the Oval Office *(LBJ Library photo by Yoichi Okamoto, White House Photo Office Collection)*

BLOWTORCH

Robert Komer, Vietnam, and American Cold War Strategy

by FRANK LEITH JONES

NAVAL INSTITUTE PRESS
ANNAPOLIS, MARYLAND

Naval Institute Press
291 Wood Road
Annapolis, MD 21402

Library of Congress Cataloging-in-Publication Data
Jones, Frank Leith.
  Blowtorch : Robert Komer, Vietnam, and American Cold War strategy / by Frank Leith Jones.
     pages cm
  Includes bibliographical references and index.
  ISBN 978-1-61251-228-0 (hbk. : alk. paper) — ISBN 978-1-61251-229-7 (ebook) 1. Komer, Robert, 1922-2000. 2. National security—United States—History—20th century. 3. United States. Military Assistance Command, Vietnam. Civil Operations and Rural Development Support—Biography. 4. Vietnam War, 1961-1975—United States—Biography. 5. United States—Armed Forces—Vietnam—Civic action. 6. Intelligence officers—United States—Biography. 7. National Security Council (U.S.)—Officials and employees—Biography. 8. United States. Dept. of Defense—Officials and employees—Biography. 9. United States—Military policy—Decision making. 10. Cold War. I. Title. II. Title: Robert Komer, Vietnam, and American Cold War strategy.
  UA23.J645 2013
  355.0092—dc23
  [B]
                              2012044954
⊗ This paper meets the requirements of ANSI/NISO z39.48-1992 (Permanence of Paper).
Printed in the United States of America.

21 20 19 18 17 16 15 14 13   9 8 7 6 5 4 3 2 1
First printing

To SHARON

CONTENTS

ACKNOWLEDGMENTS

Supreme Court Justice Felix Frankfurter once remarked that gratitude is "one of the least articulate of emotions, especially when it is deep." In writing this book, I have incurred many debts that I can never repay, but it is a pleasure to express my gratitude to the many people who helped me in this enterprise. They opened doors and guided my path over the past several years, and without them, I would not have been successful.

I want to thank my current and former colleagues at the U.S. Army War College for their support, encouragement, guidance, and interest in my work: Boone Bartholomees, Jim Embrey, Len Fullenkamp, Nat Freier, Jim Helis, Mike Neiberg, Charles Van Bebber, Tony Williams, and Rich Yarger. I am particularly grateful to Paul Kan and Janeen Klinger, who refined my thinking about the intricacies of international relations theory and its application to U.S. foreign policy. I also want to thank four outstanding scholars—Anthony Joes, Richard Immerman, Richard Hunt, and Andrew Preston—for their counsel and their willingness to work with me and to share their thoughts regarding the Vietnam War, the Kennedy and Johnson administrations, and the role of strategists in envisioning the implementation of U.S. foreign policy during the Cold War. Philip Nguyen (Ngyuyen Ky Phong), a valued friend and a historian of the Vietnam War in his own right, pointed me to useful bibliographic sources and served as an essential sounding board for my ideas.

I am also thankful for the assistance I received from librarians, archivists, and historians who guided my research, suggested possible sources of information, and helped me navigate the bureaucratic mazes that can often impede progress. In particular, I appreciate the help of Bohdan Kohutiak and the staff at the U.S. Army War College Library, David Keogh and the staff at the U.S. Army Military History Institute, Regina Greenwell and staff at the Lyndon Baines Johnson Presidential Library, Stephen Plotnick and the staff at the John F. Kennedy Library, Susan Lemke and the staff at the National Defense University's library, and Dale Andrade at the U.S. Army Center of Military History. I also received skilled and efficient assistance from the staffs at the Library of Congress and the libraries of Georgetown University, the George Washington University, Penn State University's Dickinson School of Law, and Harvard University as well as those at the Albert F. Simpson Historical Research Center at Air University, the Office of the Secretary of Defense Historian's Office, the U.S. Senate Historian's Office, and the publications staff at the RAND Corporation. I want to express my appreciation to the Lyndon Baines Johnson Foundation for providing a Moody Grant, which allowed me to conduct extensive research in the Johnson archives.

Several people who knew Robert Komer graciously gave me time from their schedules to speak with me. Douglas Komer, Robert Komer's son, was of invaluable help and provided me a copy of his father's unpublished memoir. Several others shared their recollections with me or furnished useful background information about the periods of Komer's government service, including George Allen, Francis Bator, Richard Boverie, Harold P. Ford, Hank Gaffney, P. X. Kelley, David Newsom, William Odom, Harold Saunders, Michael Sheridan, Christopher Shoemaker, Walter Slocombe, James A. Thomson, and Peter Swartz.

Parts of this book were published previously in *Parameters* and *Imperial Crossroads: The Great Powers and the Persian Gulf.* I thank the editors of these publications for allowing me to reproduce some of the material here. I am especially indebted to Jeffrey Macris, the editor of the latter, for recommending me to the Naval Institute Press. At the Naval Institute Press, I am fortunate to have Adam Kane as both my advocate and as an accomplished editor of this work. He read the manuscript with a vision of what it could be, and with his encouragement, it improved incalculably. Also at Naval Institute Press, I want to thank Claire Noble and Marlena Montagna for guiding me through the marketing and production processes, and Julie Kimmel, who as copy editor not only improved my prose but also pressed me to clarify my thoughts and arguments.

Lastly, I owe my wife, Sharon, a depth of thanks that cannot be measured or repaid. She is a superb reader and editor, sometimes my toughest critic, but she always wanted what was best for me as I labored on this manuscript. I appreciate her patience and efforts on my behalf, large and small, without which this book would not have been realized.

INTRODUCTION

*I*n March 1996 the historian Douglas Brinkley, a thirty-five-year-old professor at the University of New Orleans and the author of three books, including biographies of two giants in American Cold War history, Secretary of State Dean Acheson and the first secretary of defense, James Forrestal, strolled into the lobby of the Cantigny Conference Center in Wheaton, Illinois. He was there to participate in a conference on the Vietnam War sponsored by the U.S. Naval Institute and the McCormick Tribune Foundation. The next day he would chair a panel titled "Lyndon Johnson's War," named for the title of a book that one of the panelists, Professor Larry Berman, had written to substantial critical acclaim.[1]

As a young scholar from a different generation, Brinkley felt that one of the benefits of such a conference was the opportunity to meet for the first time the men whose memoranda and memoirs he had been reading for years as part of his research. He soon spied one of the officials who had been intimately involved in the formulation and implementation of U.S. policy during the Vietnam War—Robert W. Komer. The septuagenarian Komer was a participant on Brinkley's panel, so the professor strode over to introduce himself. After making his introduction, Komer replied, "So you're the ass who's moderating me tomorrow." Brinkley was "taken aback a little bit" by this pugnacious and rude response, but the reason for it soon became apparent. Komer told him that he had just learned that Brinkley expected him to give a speech at tomorrow's panel. He was not prepared to give a formal address on such short notice, and he held Brinkley personally responsible for not informing him of this requirement beforehand. After all, Komer snarled, he had not heard from Brinkley since he first contacted him about serving as a panelist. The conversation ended abruptly with that remark, but the exchange did not end there.[2]

The following day Brinkley had his say as the panel chair. After thanking the sponsors of the conference for the opportunity and commending them for convening a forum on the Vietnam War that would examine the latest scholarship, Brinkley proceeded to tell the audience about his encounter with Komer the previous day. If his recounting of the incident was a maneuver to shame Komer publicly, it was a failure. Komer would have the last word and did so as the opening panelist. He began by remarking that now that Brinkley had confessed, he could tell the rest of the story. Then he scolded Brinkley for being an inferior moderator. Komer admitted to the audience, however, that he had not prepared remarks even after learning of his responsibility. He was enjoying the hospitality of the conference too much. He had a couple of rum and tonics before dinner, followed by wine with dinner, and then a few more drinks after dinner. He had been in no shape to write a speech after all that, so he had jotted down some notes on a small telephone pad the hotel furnished when he awoke that morning. Then Komer made a confession of his own: he could not read his own handwriting. The audience laughed, and Komer launched into a rambling, often vague discussion of Lyndon Johnson and a dozen other topics.[3] It was a distressing valediction for a man who had once been at the pinnacle of political power.

Anyone in the audience who witnessed Komer's performance would have perceived him as a fumbling, peevish old man, nearly inarticulate and unable to focus on the matter at hand. However, as many of the scholars and Vietnam-era civilian policymakers and generals in the audience knew, the real Komer was the one Brinkley had met in the lobby the day earlier—prickly, irascible, and abrasive, but always in command, always willing to speak without reservation, his thoughts expressed directly, interlaced with curses and profanity. Brinkley had learned firsthand another feature of Komer's personality, which Komer's colleague McGeorge Bundy, the national security adviser to President John F. Kennedy and President Lyndon Baines Johnson, once remarked upon—he had an "exemplary instinct for the jugular."[4]

This book is an attempt to recover a man's career as an influential national security professional during a crucial period of the twentieth century—the Cold War. Komer is a member of a group of officials often lost in the biographies of presidents and cabinet officers or the political and administrative histories of presidential administrations: "second echelon" officials who were the authors and implementers of American foreign policy during this era.[5] In a more exact and focused sense, this book is "history from the middle."[6]

History has largely ignored Robert Komer. Perhaps his association with an unpopular war as an adviser to President Lyndon Johnson and as head of U.S. counterinsurgency efforts under Gen. William Westmoreland in Vietnam explains the omission. Perhaps his brash self-confidence, which earned him many enemies, accounts for it. His moniker, "Blowtorch," was an apt description of his aggressive personality. U.S. ambassador to South Vietnam Henry Cabot Lodge Jr. conferred the nickname on him, relating to a group of newspaper reporters that Komer's resolute determination to have the direction of his superiors carried out was akin to having a blowtorch aimed at the seat on one's pants.[7] Nonetheless, because he was such a colorful character, Komer assumes a number of cameo roles in various books, often reduced to caricature, a self-important sycophant, or a person so outlandishly optimistic that he is of no importance other than to serve as comic relief or a symbol of American hubris.[8]

The facts are far different, but two difficulties confront the biographer in recovering Komer's life and work. He left no cache of letters, diary, or journal of his experiences, and his unpublished memoirs are lifeless. As a longtime member of the U.S. intelligence community, his secretiveness is understandable, and he was not a man given to philosophical musings. We attain only a glimpse of his personality and activities through the numerous interviews that historians and journalists conducted with him, principally covering his responsibilities concerning the Vietnam War, and what others said about him. It is only in the official memoranda, cables, and other government documents as well as the books and articles he wrote where his voice is clearest.

The other difficulty in recovering Komer's career is that he assumed multiple roles during the Cold War in which he had a major influence on U.S. national security policy and strategy in addition to shaping public discourse on defense matters. In this respect, he differs from many of his contemporaries. The historian John Prados argues that most of the leading national security officials of the 1960s—and this contention is likely true of the entire Cold War period—were administrators, not innovators and initiators.[9] Fewer still were strategists.

McGeorge Bundy, as an example, seldom operated based on a carefully thought-out diplomatic strategy. Kennedy and Johnson's secretary of defense, Robert McNamara, in his exuberance over the Kennedy administration's staring down the Soviets during the Cuban missile crisis as the two nations stood on the brink of nuclear Armageddon, went so far as to declare, "There is no longer such a thing as strategy; there is only crisis management."[10] Apocryphal or not, this remark is the utterance of a technician, for as Gen. John Galvin pointed out, a strategist comprehends the complexity of the international environment and the human dimension, "appreciates the constraints of the use of force," and discerns "what is achievable and what is not achievable by military means."[11]

Presidents were often of a similar cast. Kennedy and Johnson, the two presidents Komer served directly, did not evince an interest in strategy, approve an overarching strategy, or even direct that a major review of U.S. strategy be conducted. Jimmy Carter, in whose administration Komer served, was another president without a larger, strategic design.[12] This is not surprising. As Colin Gray observes, "The politician is a person untrained in strategic analysis."[13]

Komer is also an exception to Prados' contention. His strategic vision is most perceptible in his proposals regarding U.S. policy toward the so-called neutralists, the states that did not align themselves ideologically with the United States or the Soviet Union. In sharpening this vision, Komer was unlike many of his colleagues, some of whom have been accused of not questioning the basic American ideological design for the Cold War: "that the world was divided into two basic hostile camps; that the 'free world' was the area synonymous with U.S. strategic interests; that every 'outpost of freedom,' no matter how insignificant in itself, must be denied to the Communists or the entire free world would be threatened."[14] Komer was not a cold warrior in the pejorative meaning of that term; he did not see the strategic environment in simplistic, bipolar, and Manichean distinctions.

As a strategist, he had to be cognizant of American strategic culture and its values and ideals to create a strategy consistent with national experience so that it achieved the domestic consensus necessary for political backing. Thus, he was a pragmatist. As the fabled strategist Bernard Brodie noted, pragmatism is a habit of thinking, and since strategy is "essentially the pursuit of success in certain types of competitive endeavor, a pragmatic approach is the only appropriate one. Thus, one weighs a strategic concept or idea by investigating as thoroughly as possible the factors necessary to its successful operation, as well as the question whether those factors do in fact exist or are likely to exist at the appropriate time. This inevitably involves one in a good deal of detailed study, preferably over a whole range of relevant and important variables—political, technological, geographic, etc."[15]

No doubt, in subscribing to such an approach, fraught with the challenge of discerning the topography of the constantly changing global environment, its threats, and opportunities, Komer made mistakes in perception and, consequently, in the advice he furnished presidents and other officials on policies to advance U.S. national interests. This flaw lies partially within the strategy-making process itself, relying as it does on human agency with all the frailties inherent in such an enterprise. Furthermore, as one practitioner-scholar has noted, "The impediments to even adequate, let alone superior, strategic accomplishment are so numerous and so potentially damaging that there is little room for skepticism over the proposition that the strategist's profession is a heroic one."[16]

Historians and political scientists sometimes forget that policy and the plan to execute it, that is, a strategy, occur in a setting fraught with chance, uncertainty, contingency, and an imperfect ability on the part of governments to mold or direct results. They examine the outcome of foreign policy decisions, shaped by such a vision, and with hindsight bias, state categorically that the senior officials should have realized the likely outcome or that based on the facts available it was doomed to failure. But not to act or to grasp an opportunity is to accept the status quo, to take no risks in an intrinsically unstable international system in which the vital interests of the nation are at stake is not simply negligent or mere carelessness and disregard, it is reckless and irresponsible, a dereliction of duty.

Robert Komer never neglected his duties, as that would have undermined his very conception of himself as a professional. He was a capable, imaginative, and successful practitioner of the strategic art, a distinct discipline that U.S. Army lieutenant general Richard Chilcoat broadly defined as "the skillful formulation, coordination, and application of ends (objectives), ways (courses of action), and means (supporting resources) to promote and defend the national interests." Chilcoat emphasized that masters of the strategic art not only understand the interrelationships among the domains of strategy (military, diplomatic, economic, and informational), but by employing skills developed "during the course of a lifetime of education, service and experience," they "can competently integrate and combine the three roles performed by the complete strategist: strategic leader, strategic practitioner, and strategic theorist."[17] According to Chilcoat, the strategic leader furnishes vision and focus as well as inspires or influences others to think and act. The strategic practitioner formulates and implements strategic plans derived from policy guidance, "employs force and other dimensions of military power, and unifies military and nonmilitary activities through command and peer leadership skills." Finally, the strategic theorist develops strategic concepts but also "teaches or mentors the strategic art," influencing others through his ideas and treatises.[18]

From 1947 to 1981, with the exception of an eight-year interval, Komer held a number of significant government positions, including several high-ranking offices. These appointments, signifiers of trust and confidence, are also indicative of his capacity to enter the inner circles of government and make himself essential to presidents and other senior officials. He achieved a reputation as the person who could formulate a strategy that would harness the elements of national power to achieve policy objectives and then vigorously and doggedly pursue its implementation. His experiences, both in war and peace, as well as his education and a demanding course of self-study give lie to the estimation that he was merely a self-promoting "paper pusher" or pompous buffoon. In that eight-year hiatus from government work and after his public service, he became a leading defense intellectual, teaching undergraduate and graduate students, lecturing, and writing numerous articles and essays, opinion pieces, and two books. These accomplishments merit him being designated a master of the strategic art.

PART ONE

TOWARD *the* NEW FRONTIER

CHAPTER 1

A Man of Proper Ambition

"*J*oe, you must become an expert on one country," Robert Komer advised his Harvard College friend and junior Central Intelligence Agency (CIA) colleague Joseph Burkholder Smith as they sat together for lunch in 1951. Smith, who had recently joined the agency, had been reading pile after pile of intelligence reports about Southeast Asia, the region covered by the division in which he worked, but he had no area expertise, could not prioritize what he was learning, and felt overwhelmed by his duties. "The trouble around here," Komer continued, "is that there is simply not enough solid, genuine expertise. Once you've established yourself a reputation as such an expert, you'll be on the way to the top."[1]

Komer had already found his place and established a reputation as an intelligence analyst of formidable intellect, a superbly quick writer, and an energetic debater—brash and uncompromising. His superiors on the National Estimates Staff, the brain trust of the deputy director for intelligence, viewed the analytical skills of their youngest staff member as more valuable than his occasional lack of congeniality.[2] The staff's job was to write intelligence estimates for the president on the most critical national security issues, ones that the president was interested in or should be. They collected data from the State Department, the military services, and Defense Department experts, but the final product, in all but special cases, was theirs. Their products were to be enlightened and objective analyses, designed to help the president choose a course of action or make policy.[3]

As Smith sat across from Komer and listened, he thought the analyst job suited Komer. Komer was never reticent about giving his friends his own explanations of Hitler's every move while they lounged around Cambridge waiting for their draft boards to offer them an opportunity to experience the war more intimately. Smith later wrote, "It might be said that Bob was a born estimator of situations."[4] He was not alone in that assessment, for already in Komer's brief career, all sorts of people found his views indispensable. He had traveled a long way from those undergraduate discussions, farther than Smith imagined.

———————————

Robert William Komer was born in Chicago, Illinois, on February 23, 1922, but he grew up in Clayton, Missouri, a western suburb of Saint Louis. He was the first child of Nathan Adolph and Stella Deiches Komer.[5] Clayton had been incorporated in 1877, when Saint Louis separated from its countrified neighbors. With that severance, the town became the new county seat of Saint Louis County, and by the turn of the century, it had begun its transformation from forest and farmland to a small town that continued to grow, especially after the trolley service arrived in 1895. In 1913 Clayton was chartered as an incorporated city, and prominent Saint Louis families began to flee the crowded environs of the city, now the sixth largest in the United States. Others soon followed, and between 1920 and 1925 Clayton's population swelled from about three thousand residents to more than seven thousand. By the end of the decade, the value of real estate in the city had tripled.[6] This population growth and increase in wealth was evident to the entrepreneurial Nathan, and in 1924 he moved his family from Chicago to Saint Louis to establish himself as the president of a small manufacturing firm, Lockwoven Company, which specialized in burial garments and funeral supplies in nearby Overland.[7]

Komer's childhood and adolescence is largely a mystery, as he seemed to prefer. His unpublished memoirs do not address this formative period of his life. It is as if that period was unimportant or he only sought escape from it. Perhaps even then he was practiced in the art of keeping secrets, revealing only what he wanted to divulge. Thus, his early life must be puzzled out from fragmentary evidence—official government documents and the few references he makes to his family life in other sources. What does seem apparent is that Komer began plotting at an early age his flight from the small city of corporate executives, merchants, and lawyers and, more importantly, from his father's aspiration for his son to succeed him, a man with whom Komer never identified, in the family business. It is clear that Komer did not share the view of an older, former area resident, the poet T. S.

Eliot, who claimed that Saint Louis affected him "more deeply than any other environment has ever done. . . . There is something in having passed one's childhood beside the big river, which is incommunicable to those people who have not." Eliot believed the city instrumental in forming his literary vision.[8] Komer let it serve as the catalyst for liberating himself from familial constraints.

The Komer family, which later included a sister, Margaret, known as Peggy, while prosperous and respectable, lived modestly. Thus, not wealth, an upper-class upbringing, or ancestry brought Komer to prominence. It was not physical prowess on the athletic fields either. He was unprepossessing, of medium height and slender build, with a noticeably large forehead, glasses, and often a puckish smile. His academic abilities distinguished him. Throughout his school years, his teachers rated him highly in originality, dependability, diligence, and leadership. He ranked thirty-first in a class of 119 students and graduated in 1938 at the age of sixteen from Clayton High School. He had completed the full four years of high school in three and a half. His college aptitude examination scores placed him in the 99th percentile and easily assured him a place in the freshman class at Washington University in Saint Louis. He lived at home and commuted the few miles to campus. This circumscribed life of study, achieving excellent grades, and working in his father's factory lasted two years, his parents believing he was too young to leave home. He applied to Harvard as much for its reputation as for its connection to Washington University, which had been founded by a prominent Saint Louis merchant and the Unitarian pastor, civic leader, and Harvard graduate, William Greenleaf Eliot,[9] T. S. Eliot's grandfather. With a Harvard acceptance letter in hand, he made good his independence, more than a thousand miles from his father's control.

———————

The Robert Komer who stepped into Harvard Yard in Cambridge, Massachusetts, in the fall of 1940 on an academic scholarship was serious and scholarly, the right fit for an institution that had undergone a significant transformation since the installation of James B. Conant as president seven years earlier.[10] When he assumed the presidency, Conant's goal was to create a "new Harvard," for he believed the social character of the institution had become increasingly "Brahmin," dominated by the social and economic elite of New England and New York—"socially snobby" and not "seriously intellectual." He aimed to make Harvard a meritocracy by attracting the most capable and intellectually superior students and faculty throughout the country.[11]

Three years into his presidency, Conant and his colleagues were combing the country for gifted and ambitious students to be part of the new intellectual aristocracy, promoting a "National Scholarships" policy to increase geographic diversity in both the undergraduate and graduate schools.[12] This was the environment in which Komer, a Jewish middle-class midwesterner, now found himself, the result of his exceptional intellect, superior test scores, and Conant's belief in drawing the best students to Harvard regardless of socioeconomic status.

Komer flourished at Harvard. He credited the institution for his intellectual development and his character, but he would never reminisce about his alma mater with fondness or gratitude. He was, however, an eager participant in his Harvard experience, involved in several extracurricular activities: he was associate editor of the *Harvard Guardian*, a magazine devoted to the social sciences; news commentator for the *Harvard Crimson*, the daily student newspaper; and a member of his residential house swimming and debating teams.[13] These pursuits were critical in building skills, such as writing, public speaking, and the art of persuasion, that would later benefit his career. Still, as a Jewish student, he was an outsider in social circles. Norman Mailer, who was a contemporary of Komer's at Harvard, recognized the underlying prejudice of the Harvard student body: "It would have been unthinkable . . . for a Jew to be invited to join one of the so-called final clubs like Porcellian, A.D. Club, Fly, or Spee."[14]

History attracted Komer as a field of study, and the department provided the opportunity to learn from some of the leading professors of the day: William Langer, an authority on European diplomatic history; Sidney Bradshaw Fay, famous for his comprehensive examination of the origins of World War I; and William Scott Ferguson, the distinguished scholar of ancient Greece. As an honors student, in his senior year, Komer was required to write a thesis on a contemporary subject. Komer selected the role that British prime minister Lloyd George and Winston Churchill played as strategists in World War I. He contended that these two political leaders were better strategic thinkers than the military officers who served under them and that they had the vision to conceive strategies that might have avoided the stalemate on the western front.[15]

"War is the continuation of policy by other means," wrote the twenty-year-old Komer in the opening sentence of his study, quoting from the

Prussian theorist Carl von Clausewitz's principal work *On War*. In this remarkable and precocious 170-page analysis, titled "Civilian Strategists in the Great War: Lloyd George and Churchill and the Conduct of the War," Komer set out two goals: to view the war through "the eyes of civilian war leaders," men who had their own ideas on how to prosecute the war, and to ascertain their influence on the military. His interpretive analysis was to be a "scientific study of the art of human conflict," using contemporary documents and avoiding postwar apologies. Such a study, he maintained, was particularly relevant given "the war in which we are now engaged." He also betrayed his biases. Espousing a view that would later have ramifications for his relations with military leaders, Komer stated, "One cannot study military history without becoming a bit prejudiced against the ineptitude of professional soldiers." However, he added, this assertion was "not a condemnation of all generals and an exaltation of all statesmen"; his research was an examination of particular generals and particular statesmen. Specifically, it was an assessment of Lloyd George and Churchill as strategists, not politicians.[16]

Komer's reliance on Clausewitz was noticeable in the beginning of his work, in which he equated modern war with total war, but he also conducted a historical survey of strategy with reference to the Greeks, the Romans, and such luminaries as Hannibal and Marlborough. He returned to Clausewitz in discussing the impact of the Industrial Revolution, popular government, and mass armies on conflict, adding his own thoughts on the role of weaponry and the influence its continuing sophistication had on warfare. He remained convinced that in the era of total war, it was, not military leaders such as British field marshal Douglas Haig and certainly not his French counterpart, General Joseph Joffre, but the civilian leaders, Clemenceau, Lloyd George, and members of his cabinet, who organized a nation, particularly its economy, for war and made the strategy of attrition possible. However, in his view, attrition was an unsound strategy; in fact, it was not a strategy but "brute force, crude, hard and costly."[17]

Conducting campaign analyses of the Dardanelles, the Balkans, Italy, and Palestine and Mesopotamia, Komer argued that Lloyd George and Churchill recognized a superior strategy, although its execution was often flawed. British strategist Basil Henry Liddell Hart had called this strategy the indirect approach in his 1941 book *The Strategy of Indirect Approach*, which Komer combed extensively. However, even as a disciple of Liddell Hart, Komer asserted that successful strategy also relied on the civilian leader's ability to formulate a grand strategy, using all the elements of national power, not only the military, but also the economic, political, both foreign and domestic, and as he termed it, sociological instruments. "Grand strategy," he concluded, "is not the product of professional education but rather of a broad understanding of mankind and men. It demands a compound of two qualities, the vision and imagination to devise plans and the determination and initiative to carry them into effect." It also entailed, he believed, an ability to see the major issues and paint broad outlines and to realize the full implication of total war: "every resource and sinew must be strained to the utmost for victory." He ended his study by agreeing with an observation attributed to Clemenceau: "Modern war is too serious a business to be entrusted to soldiers."[18] The study earned him honors in his major. He graduated in 1942, magna cum laude, Phi Beta Kappa, a good writer, a better thinker, and sure of himself and his faculties. His temperament manifested itself in turns as ebullient, enthusiastic, sometimes obstinate, and often impatient. The war he was about to enter would temper his enthusiasm, as would the tragic fact that his college class would lose more classmates in war than any class in Harvard's history.[19]

––––––––––––

With the United States now plunged into another global conflict, Komer recognized the uncertainty of his immediate future. He was likely to become a soldier, no matter how he felt about entrusting generals with the business of war. Nonetheless, before graduating he applied for admission to Harvard Law School and Harvard Business School and gained admittance to both. In the fall he enrolled in the Business School, which had survived its lack of enrollments during the Depression.[20]

Twenty-five years after he graduated from Harvard College, Komer implied in the Class of 1942 Anniversary Report that he pursued graduate studies at the Business School to become a "future captain of industry."[21] The truth was more prosaic. Komer had first enrolled in Harvard Law during the summer semester but withdrew because he was not interested in the difficult curriculum and the school did not have an officer-training program, which he considered vital because of his immediate eligibility for military service.[22] The business school's dean, Wallace B. Donham, had secured an Army Quartermaster Corps officer training unit at the school and arranged with the Navy to train its Supply Corps officers there as well. Both of these training opportunities were available while Donham pressed to maintain the civilian master of business administration (MBA) degree program. Komer enrolled as an MBA student and an officer candidate in the Army Reserve program in September 1942.[23] His decision to matriculate in the Business School delighted his father as he considered it better training for his son's eventual place at Lockwoven. The Army had other ideas, however, and in April 1943 it called Komer to active duty.[24]

Although the eventual summons was expected, it still jarred him as he had hoped to be able to complete the two-year master's degree curriculum. Another discovery was even more disquieting. The Army, he learned after completing basic training, no longer needed Quartermaster Corps officers, and so he entered active service as Private Komer, assigned to the Military Intelligence branch. Although he wanted a commission, he believed that at least the Army had the good sense to put him in intelligence work because of his knowledge of French, which he spoke fluently, and his proficient German.[25]

Assigned to the Military Intelligence School at Camp Ritchie, located in the mountains of central Maryland, in August 1943, Komer received training in intelligence and for his prospective assignment as a French interpreter. Within four months, however, he had received orders to report immediately to the G-2 (Intelligence) division of the Army General Staff at the newly constructed Pentagon in Arlington, Virginia. There Komer discovered that the Army had recently established a historical branch within that staff division. The branch's primary responsibility was to write and publish brief studies of particular military operations as lessons learned. These studies would eventually be published in a comprehensive historical narrative of the service's role in the war. Komer's superiors also informed him of his assignment to the first combat historical team deploying to Italy as part of the U.S. Fifth Army.[26]

Komer arrived at Fifth Army headquarters, the old royal palace at Caserta, Italy, in the autumn of 1943. Just before Christmas, his commanding officer told him that he would work on the history of an upcoming operation: the amphibious landing at Anzio, on the west coast of Italy. The purpose of the landing was to hasten the capture of Rome by breaching the Winter Line, a series of German fortifications that ran across Italy, and ending the stalemate in the Italian campaign.[27] It would be his first combat experience, and like any other soldier, he had no concept of what he was about to confront. In the interim, he began collecting information for the operational history he was to write.

On January 22, 1944, VI Corps under Maj. Gen. John Lucas landed at Anzio with what the U.S. Navy's official historian would call a "modest force." Although the landings surprised the Germans and went practically unopposed, the operation had been mounted hurriedly, and Lucas' orders regarding his immediate operational objectives were vague. Further, Lucas failed to exploit the surprise he attained by moving forward and instead consolidated his position.[28]

Komer arrived on the beachhead with elements of the 1st Armored Division shortly after the initial assault. He began to take notes from his own observations. However, his work was made more difficult when, within four days after the landings, the German commander in Italy, Field Marshal Albert Kesselring, reacted and had sufficient forces to surround the Allied forces.[29] The German plan was to initiate a counterattack and wipe out the Allies, who, trapped on all sides with their backs to the sea, had no place to go.[30]

By the second week, the situation was grim, particularly on the beach, marked with craters from nearly continuous German shelling from artillery in the Alban Hills and the Luftwaffe's strafing and bombing. The Allied soldiers dug into the beach, and while foxholes offered some protection from the barrages, it was such a small area that "no one in it was safe." Some soldiers wounded on the front lines were later killed by shells that hit the field hospital. Others, who had been sent to the rear to rest, soon requested return to the front because it was deemed "safer."[31] Komer found himself seeking such safety, interviewing units on the front lines and then returning to the rear to type his reports.

In London, British prime minister Winston Churchill now had doubts about the operation he had championed. Impatient with the bogged-down Allied forces at Anzio, he privately commented, "I thought we were landing a Tiger cat; instead all we have is a stranded whale."[32] Komer, however, was getting a firsthand understanding of what Clausewitz meant when he wrote, "Everything is simple in war, but the simplest thing is difficult."[33] The nightmare lasted four months, until, on May 25, VI Corps, now heavily reinforced, broke through the German defenses and joined up with the Fifth Army's II Corps to begin the Allies' victorious advance on Rome.[34]

Komer celebrated his twenty-second birthday in this cruel setting, but nearly fifty years later, he called Anzio a formative experience and credited it with making him less susceptible to panic during stressful situations. He was proud that he had been at Anzio, and in his government career, he would find occasion to let military officers know it, in case they supposed that as a civilian he lacked appreciation for what combat was like or the values the military held dear. To colleagues, when confronted with a challenge that seemed daunting, he would declare, "If I survived Anzio, I can survive anything."[35] His declaration was not hyperbole or bravado, but simply the truth. Anzio cost the Allies heavily—7,000 dead and 36,000 wounded or missing in action.[36]

Komer's ability to carry out his assignment under these severe conditions earned him a promotion to technician fourth class (equivalent to a sergeant but without command authority), and he continued his writing project through the summer of 1944. His work resulted in the first account of the campaign by Komer and his coauthor, Capt. John Bowditch. The narrative later served as the basis for the official history, *Anzio Beachhead*, printed by the Historical Division, War Department, for the *American Forces in Action* series, in 1949.[37]

Komer's superiors thought his work superlative. They awarded him a Bronze Star for meritorious service in 1944 and subsequently recommended him for a direct field commission. After a written examination, an interview by a board of officers, and a mandatory physical examination, he was commissioned as a second lieutenant on Christmas and assigned to the G-3 (Operations) section, Allied Force Headquarters (AFHQ). The assignment was short-lived, for beginning almost immediately after his arrival, he spent the next several months with the 34th Division on an officer exchange program. The divisional G-3, a lieutenant colonel who had been a newspaper editor in Iowa before the war and wanted publicity for the unit, put Komer's talents to use writing articles about recent operations, one of which *Infantry Journal* published under the lieutenant colonel's name. When the Germans surrendered in May 1945, Komer realized that he did not have sufficient points to return home and that war was still raging in the Pacific. By his calculation, he would not be discharged until late 1946. However, in November he received orders assigning him to the Army G-2 Historical Division in the Pentagon to write the official history of U.S. Army civil affairs in the Mediterranean theater of operations.[38] It would be his first book and one of the earliest published volumes of the Army's official history of World War II. He later used his research for an article on the subject, published in the scholarly journal *Military Affairs* in 1949.[39]

More importantly, this encounter with the historiography of the Army's role in the governance and civil administration of liberated and occupied areas would later influence his thinking about how the United States should use its military cooperatively in the developing world and, in particular, in directing political-military activities in Vietnam.

After his honorable discharge from the Army, as a captain, in May 1946, Komer waited to return to Harvard Business School to finish his degree. He spent the summer in Missouri, where his father trained him for future executive responsibilities by treating him as he had when he had been an adolescent working during summer vacations. Komer was made to "oil the machines and clean the floor and make boxes."[40] Nathan Komer's clumsy approach clearly backfired, solidifying his son's determination not to enter the family business after graduation.

Komer completed his master's degree in February 1947 with a concentration in foreign trade and resources and moved to New York to determine whether he wanted to work there. The venture was unsuccessful, and besides, he was courting a woman in Missouri. A potential way out of returning permanently to Saint Louis presented itself in April when "wartime intelligence colleagues" told him about a new agency, the Central Intelligence Group (CIG).[41] President Harry Truman established the CIG under an executive order on January 22, 1946, shortly after the World War II intelligence organization, the Office of Strategic Services (OSS), headed by the legendary William "Wild Bill" Donovan, was disbanded and only months before the National Security Act of 1947 established the Central Intelligence Agency, thereby creating a truly centralized intelligence agency.[42] After making inquiries with the agency's personnel office, Komer applied for a position and returned home to wait for a response.[43]

In his unpublished memoirs, Komer portrayed himself as a frustrated junior executive, the assistant sales manager of his father's company, learning the business under the tutelage of a more experienced man. Bored taking orders or marketing burial supplies, he chafed at the agency's plodding hiring process. He married Jane Doren Gleick, the daughter of a lawyer, who herself had been educated at the University of Missouri, a month after his return. The marriage took place in Temple Israel, a Reform congregation in Saint Louis.

Within a few weeks, his frustration with his prospects mounted, and he mailed several pestering letters to the agency's personnel director, making clear his continued interest in a position. The chief of the section responsible for hiring finally replied in July and assured him that CIG was still interested and that he was under consideration for a position as a foreign affairs analyst. The budget committee had to approve the hiring and other bureaucratic hurdles had to be cleared; the process would take another month or two.[44]

Finally, on October 1, 1947, Komer received a telegram from the newly formed Central Intelligence Agency informing him that his appointment had been approved. He sent his acceptance by telegram within days.[45] Two weeks later, accompanied by his new wife, he arrived in Washington, where he reported for duty at the old OSS headquarters, a complex of three multilevel brick buildings located on E Street in the northwestern section of Washington, D.C. Komer was initially assigned to the Office of Reports and Estimates (O/RE), the European section responsible for handling multilateral organizations, principally the United Nations. He soon learned that his superiors were not much interested in his portfolio, and during his tenure in that office, he wrote only a single major analysis, hardly an auspicious beginning to an intelligence career.[46]

Gen. Walter Bedell "Beetle" Smith saved Komer's career, indirectly. Truman selected Smith as the fourth director of central intelligence (DCI) on August 21, 1950.[47] One of Smith's immediate tasks was to conduct a major shakeup of the analytical process that the U.S. intelligence apparatus used. The rationale was that the CIA had failed to forecast the North Korean invasion of South Korea in June 1950 and the enormous Chinese involvement that autumn. In fact, the powerful *New York Herald Tribune* attributed five additional major analytical failures to the agency a month later.[48]

Smith, having served as Gen. Dwight Eisenhower's chief of staff during World War II and later as ambassador to the Soviet Union, had impressive credentials. He was prickly, talented, and said to be a most even-tempered man—always angry. He was also demanding and inventive. Less than two weeks after arriving at CIA headquarters in early October, he proposed there be a separate office in the agency to conduct national intelligence estimates, that is, intelligence projections. Additionally, based on recent experience and the conclusions of a report prepared by Allen Dulles, a former OSS operative and a future DCI, and two collaborators with

extensive intelligence experience, he believed that the quality of these estimates needed to be improved substantially. The national intelligence estimate (NIE), as Smith's innovation became known, would be of high quality
and sufficient in scope to address subject matter appropriate for national
security policy formulation at the highest level of government.

In November, Smith established the Office of National Estimates (O/
NE) and appointed Professor William Langer, Komer's former professor at
Harvard, to lead the new organization. Langer's wartime service had been
in OSS as the director of Research and Analysis, the self-named "Bad Eyes
Brigade." Sherman Kent, a history professor at Yale, that "great nursery of
spooks," as Godfrey Hodgson dubbed it, and who had served under Langer
at OSS, was named his deputy.[49] Smith had high expectations for the office:
"In his opinion it would be the heart of the CIA and of the national intelligence machinery."[50]

Langer had been Coolidge Professor of Diplomatic History at Harvard
when Komer studied with him.[51] Eloquent, with a nasal, singsong voice
and a slight lisp that made his Boston accent unique, Langer was "an aus-
tere man," "demanding and precise" but charming and amusing when the
situation demanded. As Sherman Kent remarked, "Langer was a driver" and
a perfectionist; he demanded the best, and if he felt cheated, he could be
"direct and disagreeable—very."[52] Langer was also a charismatic, worldly
man credited with thoughtful and bold visions. In 1944 he had argued for
a national system of intelligence, which he believed would be central to the
nation's security in the postwar period.[53] After Smith threatened a call from
Truman, Harvard begrudgingly granted Langer a leave of absence until
February 1952, with the firm understanding that at the end of his leave,
Langer would either return permanently or resign from his professorship.[54]

On Langer's arrival at the agency, he allegedly remarked that he wanted
only two people from the current CIA staff—Ray Cline, another former
student, Harvard PhD, Balliol College Fellow, and OSS Research and
Analysis staff member during the war, and Komer.[55] Langer tasked Cline,
now designated chief of the Estimates Staff, to identify a small professional
group of about thirty analysts, with "every man a broadly qualified intelligence officer and all capable of writing a review of evidence and a summary
of critical findings on a very broad strategic plane."[56] Langer personally
decided on each of the staff members, and Komer was one of the select.[57]
Smith had hired Langer to improve the quality of intelligence estimates,
which the professor did with the same intensity and rough handling as his

graduate students and the hapless researcher who Langer castigated for sloppiness because of a single typo in his paper had experienced.[58]

The function of the Estimates Staff was to draft the NIEs with contributions from the other intelligence agencies. The estimates would be reviewed by the Board of National Estimates, consisting of senior government and military officials and distinguished academics, which Langer chaired. If the board approved the estimates, then they would be passed to the Intelligence Advisory Committee, chaired by the DCI and consisting of the heads of the Federal Bureau of Investigation (FBI), the Department of State's Bureau of Intelligence and Research, the Atomic Energy Commission, and the armed services' intelligence agencies. Ultimately, the estimate was submitted to the National Security Council (NSC) for its use in policy deliberations and formulation.[59]

The interaction between the staff and board created a "rough and tumble" intellectual atmosphere. It set the serious, intense young men of the staff against the overbearing and authoritative views of the older board members as they debated the fifteen- to twenty-page draft estimates based on assembled intelligence from throughout the government and the analyst's best interpretation and judgment of the trend or pattern it portended.[60] The process required a thick skin, sophisticated analysis, clear-eyed objectivity, and an ability to tailor the product to meet the policymaker's needs. As O/NE matured as an organization designed to conduct long-range studies of foreign threats and capabilities, Komer's abilities did as well. Langer recognized his talents in preparing estimates and in September 1951 recommended him for a promotion, which took effect a month later. With Langer's departure in February 1952 to Harvard, Sherman Kent assumed responsibility for O/NE, and under Kent's tutelage Komer further advanced his understanding of strategic theory and the role of intelligence in helping formulate national security policy.

Kent was born into a wealthy California family with considerable commercial and political influence; his father served three terms as a member of Congress. In his own way, like Komer, Kent rejected the usual family interests and chose the academic life. He received his bachelor's degree from Yale in 1926 and a doctorate in history in 1933, and on completion of his PhD, he became a faculty member in that department. Kent was no tweedy Ivy League intellectual. He mixed scholarship with a flamboyant and boisterous

personality that filled a room; his showmanship was evinced by his ubiquitous red suspenders, a cheek swelled by a plug of chewing tobacco, off-color
quips, and a string of bawdy stories. As a colleague observed, he used the
"saltiest vocabulary ever heard in a Yale common room." His undergraduate friends called him "Buffalo Bill, the Cultured Cowboy," a nickname
his closest friends eventually shortened to "Buffalo." Yet, like Langer, he
was a serious scholar and a demanding professor who set rigorous standards
for his students' work, punished the slackers, and praised the enthusiasts.
World War II brought him another form of satisfying work; as a member of
the OSS, he demonstrated the rare aptitude for applying scholarly methods
to the production of intelligence analysis for the war effort.[61]

After his World War II experience and particularly the explosion of
the atom bomb, Kent became an ardent believer in the need for a literature of intelligence, a viewpoint he articulated in a 1946 *Yale Review* article
titled "Prospects for the National Intelligence Service." Yale granted him
an extension of his wartime leave of absence to become a faculty member
at the newly established National War College. In early 1947, with a grant
from the Guggenheim Foundation, Kent directed his time and energy to
the book he claimed he was compelled to write, published two years later as
Strategic Intelligence for American World Policy. It is considered one of the
most influential books ever published on intelligence analysis, and consequently, Kent is considered the preeminent practitioner of the craft of analysis in U.S. intelligence history.[62]

In essence, Kent gave Komer and the other staff members a disciplined
methodology for conducting the strategic intelligence analysis conveyed in
the estimate. The estimate, both speculative and evaluative, relied on the
fusion of large amounts of high-level foreign intelligence derived from various sources in a form both relevant and accessible to the pragmatic minds
of policymakers and strategists. This intelligence was vital to national interests, and therefore, the methodology began with an understanding of the
concepts of national power and strategy and a comprehensive worldview.
Specifically, for the intelligence analyst, this meant a thorough understanding of the strategic aims of other nations, particularly adversaries and potential opponents.[63]

Using this methodology, the analyst examined in detail the opponents'
strengths and weaknesses, which Kent called a nation's "strategic stature."

Specifically, Kent meant the "amount of influence" another nation "can exert in an international situation in which the United States has a grand strategic interest." This influence included a range of instrumentalities: moral suasion, propaganda, economic and political threats or inducements, threats of hostility, and ultimately, war. It included not just the means available to the adversary to wage war but also its potential for war. This potential could be measured by the resources that were available or that could be mobilized to undertake this objective. These components of national power included geography, population, natural resources, transportation networks, industrial capacity, political and social structure, and the "moral quality of the people and the kind of values for which they are prepared to make sacrifices" as well as the ability of the political leaders to plan, coordinate, and implement this mobilization of national power. The analyst then took this information, assessed the opponent's vulnerabilities and those of any other nations that were party to the situation, and provided the policymaker with an informed prediction of possible courses of action the opponent might take considering the adversary's historical pattern of foreign policy and, as could best be surmised, the opponent's own assessment of the situation.[64]

Kent never claimed that the methodology was infallible. He did believe, however, that intelligence analysis was a form of social science and that, no matter how imprecise, it was still a valuable tool. "The speculative evaluation or estimate," he wrote, "may not be exactly accurate, but if individual lives and the national security are at stake I would prefer the indexes of strategic stature, specific vulnerability, and probable courses of action as they emerge from this phase of strategic intelligence to the indexes afforded by the only alternative, i.e., the crystal ball."[65]

In Kent's view, such an analysis required a select group who mastered the subject matter; remained impartial in their assessments, particularly as new evidence surfaced; and were imaginative in the formulation of hypotheses, critical in the analysis of their own preferences or prejudices, and skillful in the presentation of conclusions.[66]

Komer was a member of this elite, and he thrived under Kent's high analytical standards and loose, "shirt-sleeved" management style. He was promoted and then appointed as head of O/NE's Western Europe and Africa Staff. A year later Kent selected Komer to lead the Middle East and South Asia Staff, which began Komer's long familiarity with that region, and in July 1954 Komer became the assistant to the chief of the Estimates Staff. He was now considered one of the CIA's up and coming intelligence officers by people both in and outside the agency. In a 1954 letter from Gen. Omar Bradley (Ret.) to Lt. Gen. Charles Cabell, the deputy director of central intelligence, Bradley commended Komer for his assistance on a special project, underscoring the analyst's ability to grasp fully the military and political significance of the issues. He concluded his praise by adding that Komer "bears observation as a man who has all the attributes and qualifications of a person certain to go far in anything he undertakes."[67] Komer's understanding of political-military affairs was also enhanced by his continued service as an Army Reserve officer assigned to the assistant chief of staff, G-3 (Operations), International Branch, in the Pentagon. He would retire from the Reserves as a lieutenant colonel in 1982.[68]

In June 1955 Komer was promoted to chief of the Estimates Staff, a job that the staff considered "onerous" and "detestable" since it was "chief of nothing." It amounted to "being a straw boss" among one's peers and organizing the estimates to make them responsive to the demands of the board.[69] However, the promotion was another indicator of Kent's confidence in Komer's abilities, and the latter proved particularly adept at the cunning and persuasive skills needed for this thankless task, although he occasionally generated friction. In Komer's fitness report for this period, Kent noted that Komer's eagerness to convince others, especially a policymaker, could prejudice the objectivity of his judgments. Nonetheless, Kent noted, "his versatility and ability as an estimator were remarkable and altogether overshadow his shortcomings." He also endorsed Komer's request to attend the National War College at Fort McNair in Washington, D.C., considered the armed forces' premier senior school. The mission of the college was, as it is today, to provide a course of study on national security affairs for selected personnel of the military services and other U.S. government agencies who would hold high-level policy, command, and staff functions as well as plan national security. In short, it was the "nation's graduate school for national security."[70] Komer's selection as one of the CIA's candidates was a significant privilege, denoting both achievement and potential, and he was accepted to attend the 1956–57 course of study.[71]

In late August 1956 Komer registered as a student at the War College. He would later remark that the name of the institution was misleading; he was disappointed that the students did not study war but mainly courses in anthropology, economics, sociology, and international affairs.[72]

Nonetheless, the ten courses he took and the lectures by distinguished academics and government leaders he heard provided him a historical and contemporary perspective on a number of important subjects, such as the global situation, the employment of national power, and the development of national security policy and U.S. military strategy.[73]

The highlight of the year was the class trip overseas, during which he had an opportunity to see Libya, Egypt, Lebanon, Turkey, Iran, Pakistan, and India firsthand and meet with political leaders and military officers in those countries. Additionally, he wrote a research paper titled "Toward a New Rationale for Foreign Military Aid," in which he argued that the program was based more on U.S. prestige than it was on defense priorities and that the funding level was insufficient. A faculty panel evaluated the paper as "Particularly Noteworthy" for oral presentation to the college as a whole. Only six papers were selected for this distinction. Vice Adm. E. T. Wooldridge, the commandant of the college, wrote to Allen Dulles, the DCI, that Komer was considered by the faculty to have "one of the most brilliant minds in the class." His performance had been outstanding in every respect and his presentation of his views had been articulate. The commandant also mentioned another trait: "While amiable, friendly and urbane, Mr. Komer has a strong and positive personality which gave the impression that he can combine forcefulness with a sense of humor, good judgment, powers of observation and tact."[74]

Upon graduation from the War College in June 1957, Komer returned to the CIA, where he became the head of the Soviet estimates group for a year and led several assessments, focusing primarily on military affairs. He was temporarily promoted to GS-16, then one of the three most senior executive levels of the civil service, known as "super grades."[75] After a year in this position, Robert Amory, the deputy director for intelligence (DDI), informed Komer that the CIA's representative to Eisenhower's NSC was vacant and he was appointing him to the position. Komer, who had earlier requested assignment to the NSC Secretariat or the other major policy analysis team, the State Department's Policy Planning Staff, was ecstatic.

He did not know much about the job, but Amory was a good person to work for. Komer noted that his new boss had an "inquiring mind, very strong views, but was always willing to listen to someone else, if he agreed, he did something about it." Komer moved to Amory's office with the title of assistant to the DDI. His principal duty was to serve as the NSC Planning Board alternate member (Amory was the principal and the other members were counterparts from other departments and agencies). The Planning Board was responsible for planning and drafting policy papers for decision by the NSC. Gordon Gray, President Dwight Eisenhower's special assistant for national security affairs, headed the group.[76]

Komer was now part of a small interdepartmental organization that wrote papers designed to integrate the manifold aspects of national security, debated the issue at hand vigorously, and recommended policy options to the president, the vice president, the secretaries of state and defense, the chairman of the Joint Chiefs of Staff, and the DCI. In the words of Gray's predecessor, Robert Cutler, the papers were to be "painstakingly prepared" over weeks, even months, and then tested in "the acid bath of the Planning Council" through a rigorous exchange of views, during its thrice-weekly meetings.[77]

The exchange of views among the planning assistants was stimulating, and Komer reveled in the details. He was also frustrated by the staid, unadventurous positions of his political masters in the Eisenhower administration. He pushed the board on several policy changes, including addressing the growing importance of nationalism in the Third World, particularly in Egypt. Joined by his State Department counterpart, he tried to initiate a "new look" at U.S. policy toward President Gamal Abdel Nasser but had no success.[78] Equally exasperating was the bureaucratic process with its numbing routine of painstakingly coordinating papers, rather than substance. The NSC system, Komer determined, was no longer the intellectual hub it had been under Cutler, who liked to "stir up the animals and had some very strong ideas." Instead, it had become a "shadow organization." He attributed this deterioration to a lack of leadership on Gray's part.[79]

In spite of these momentary setbacks and aggravations, Komer enjoyed the details of policy planning, and more importantly, Amory valued his work and deemed it successful, which compensated for the annoyances. Amory found Komer to be a "remarkably gifted officer who has an immense capacity for work and a really fine mind." He suggested that Komer's talents meant eventual slating for positions with more responsibility in the agency or assignment to the policy formulating echelons of the U.S. government.[80]

Amory's interest in the Planning Board's activities dwindled, and by mid-1959 he began to withdraw from participation gradually. Komer now found himself as the acting Planning Board member at least half the time, and then, ultimately, he became Amory's stand-in. Additionally, Amory wanted to broaden Komer's experience. This led to a detail to the

Department of State for five months to work on the Joint Disarmament Study Group, the Coolidge Committee, where he contributed his expertise on arms control and earned accolades from the study group chair.[81] As Amory noted in Komer's annual fitness reports for both 1959 and 1960, he had become highly esteemed by the senior members of the board, including Gray. His incisive views and superior intellect allowed him to make some original contributions, which led to his "conversion to permanent super grade" in August 1959.[82]

A little over a year later, with the election of John F. Kennedy as president, Komer's assignment with the Planning Board appeared to be over. McGeorge Bundy, Kennedy's special assistant for national security affairs, announced the new president's intention to abolish the Eisenhower administration's elaborate NSC structure, which had been under criticism from Senator Henry M. Jackson, a Democrat who served as chairman of the Senate Subcommittees on National Policy Machinery and on National Security and International Operations. Bundy stated that this structure was not what the new president wanted or needed. This information distressed Komer. "They had broken my rice bowl, they had eliminated my job," he wrote years later, but he also agreed that the system had become overly bureaucratic and hidebound in its policy analysis.[83]

One week before the inauguration, Komer wrote a memorandum to Bundy excoriating the current NSC system, specifically the Planning Board, as "sterile," "bureaucratic," laden with "badly written papers of unimaginative policy guidance" and with too strong an "emphasis on securing interagency consensus and coordination." The administration should avoid this "aimless activity" and undertake "forward thinking on basic national security policy issues."[84]

As an antidote to these deficiencies, he recommended establishing a small group of representatives from the essential national security bureaucracies, designed to "get important, substantive work done." This senior planning group would consist of assistant secretaries from State, Defense, and Treasury with Bundy as the chair. A CIA representative would serve as an adviser to the group, and other agencies, such as the U.S. Information Agency (USIA), the Bureau of the Budget, and the International Cooperation Administration, would be included as needed.[85]

Specifically, the group would address short-, medium-, and long-range issues relating to foreign policy and military and fiscal matters and would develop policy options. A small staff under the special assistant for national security affairs would write the papers, with contributions from others both inside and outside government, and the president and the other NSC members would use these papers as the basis for discussion. Once the president decided on a course of action, as contained in a summary of conclusions, it would become U.S. policy guidance, and the departments and agencies would periodically brief the NSC on their policy implementation, tied to the budget cycle.[86]

Komer also indicated that several issues, while not readily visible, were significant, and some of these needed the new administration's immediate attention. He provided a three or four sentence paragraph about each of these significant issues, including deterring the potential crisis between Indonesia and the Netherlands, a NATO ally, over West Irian (West New Guinea); reaching a new and tolerable relationship with Egyptian president Gamal Abdel Nasser; reviewing military aid programs; revamping the government's foreign economic aid approach; and exploring U.S.-India relations.[87] Komer thought he had done his duty by bringing these topics to Bundy's attention and could return to the CIA with a clear conscience.

"Midway upon the journey of our life I found myself within a forest dark, for the straightforward pathway had been lost." The opening words of Dante's epic poem *The Divine Comedy*, serve just as well for Komer at this point of his life. In early 1961, as Kennedy assumed the presidency, Komer was nearing forty, married with three children, and the son of a small businessman from a small suburb of Saint Louis, and he had ascended to the upper levels of government. He accomplished this without the East Coast preparatory school connections of many CIA officers, for the agency was very much an "old boys" establishment in its early years.[88] Even Komer's education at Harvard resulted from his aptitude, not his social connections. He readily acknowledged that the war and Harvard had shaped his career, and the patronage of three distinguished Harvard and Yale men, Langer, Kent, and Amory, propelled it.[89]

His last job only encouraged his ambition: savoring the experience of being at the center of political power. Now, he returned to the agency to assume an indistinguishable senior position, without the modicum of influence that the NSC staff position had provided. Although his memorandum to Bundy could be interpreted ostensibly as a policy handoff to his successors, more likely it was a scheme to be noticed and perhaps be asked to remain in some capacity.

Like his contemporary, Henry Kissinger, Komer's origins and upbringing would have normally barred him from Kennedy's cultured inner circle, but ironically, his varied government service made him particularly attractive and useful to the new administration. Kennedy's closest advisers recognized the value of having someone on the staff who knew the bureaucracy. It was as much this specialized knowledge as it was the "complex interplay between outsiders and insiders, prejudice and privilege, in the making of foreign policy" that Komer now used to advance his career.[90] As Komer commented, "All too few get to make the transition from observer to actor, and to realize the chance to relieve the accumulated frustrations of a decade's preparation." He was eager to secure a more prominent role in making foreign policy, not only to satisfy his sense of duty, but also to fulfill an urge to participate in the great events that shape the future.[91] His opportunity came in February 1961, when Kennedy's "New Frontier" beckoned in the person of McGeorge Bundy. In Komer, Bundy had found a man of proper ambition.[92]

CHAPTER 2

Pragmatic New Frontiersman

*M*c George Bundy, small boned and slender, sat behind a massive wooden desk in an equally enormous office in the Executive Office Building, adjacent to the White House. The former dean of the Arts and Sciences faculty at Harvard College was now President John F. Kennedy's special assistant for national security affairs. "Mac" Bundy had an incisive intellect, a disarming charm when he chose to use it, and a cool demeanor that belied his intense internal energy. Beside him, lounging in a leather chair was Bundy's deputy, Walt Whitman Rostow, an owlish and dapper man who had been a professor of economics at the Massachusetts Institute of Technology (MIT), a member of the so-called Cambridge River School of development economics, and an intimate of Kennedy since the 1950s. The two men stared at the third man in the room through their glasses.[1]

The subject of their intense gaze was Komer, who vaguely knew why Bundy had summoned him. It had something to do with the memorandum he had written concerning the foreign policy challenges the administration would confront in the coming months. Bundy told him over the telephone that he found the memorandum, which included many good ideas, intriguing. The response thrilled Komer. He had found it difficult to convince the NSC Planning Board to concentrate on some of the major policy problems the nation confronted beyond Europe. The rebuff became a source of "colossal and increasing frustration" to him. It had also made him realize he was a "frustrated policy maker."[2] However, Komer did not blame the failure entirely on the board; instead he blamed it on the institutional prerogatives of the bureaucracies, especially the Department of State. In his view, the State Department resented the NSC structure as an infringement on its prerogatives as primus inter pares in the field of foreign policy.[3]

Bundy broke the silence by telling Komer that he agreed with the views expressed in the memorandum and had forwarded it to President Kennedy, who had told his special assistant to follow up and analyze the problems Komer raised. Bundy had already vetted Komer with his older brother William, who was deputy assistant director of intelligence at the CIA and slated to be a deputy assistant secretary in the Defense Department. When Mac told his brother that he needed a few veterans for the NSC staff he was creating, some "middle-level doers" who knew how Washington worked, Komer was one of two people William Bundy recommended.[4] Bundy asked Komer if he would be interested in dealing with these problems as a member of the Kennedy White House staff. Komer snatched the opportunity and, two days later, moved into his new office overlooking the West Wing of the White House as a member of Bundy's staff.[5]

Bundy and Rostow had already divided the world between them, with particular attention to certain "hot spots," when Komer arrived at his new job. Bundy was responsible for Europe, particularly Berlin; Cuba and the other Western Hemisphere states; and the Congo. Rostow's loose responsibilities included Asia, especially Laos, Vietnam, and Indonesia, as well as "the developing world generally."[6] For the next several months, Komer would work closely with Rostow, but Komer appreciated Bundy's style: intellectually well organized, action-oriented, and probing. In Komer's view, Bundy had an "unerring instinct for what needed to be done"; he was "the high priest of feasibility."[7]

Komer also realized that given Kennedy's enthusiastic interest in world affairs and the activist National Security Council system that was emerging, the White House was where the nation's security policy and strategy would be fashioned. The trouble with the Departments of State and Defense, from Komer's perspective, was that in certain areas they were always looking for a policy without any risk, and thus, the result was no policy at all.[8]

Kennedy also considered the State Department mired in the status quo and slow to act. He likened working with State to putting a message "into a bottle, throwing it into the sea, and hoping it will wash up on shore someday." Nonetheless, Kennedy expected the department to carry out his direction with alacrity. He certainly did not view the Department of State as a place where new ideas would be formulated or decisions made. In selecting a secretary of state, Kennedy wanted "an experienced practitioner of international relations to carry out, not decide, foreign policy." He also wanted someone whose past utterances and actions would not foreclose bipartisan support for his foreign policies in Congress and among the American public, someone less well known and not ideologically rigid.[9] He found that person in Dean Rusk, the former head of the Ford Foundation.

As for the defense secretary, Kennedy appointed Robert McNamara, lately president of Ford Motor Company, for his management skills. McNamara was forceful enough to get his hands around what Kennedy perceived as an organizational mess in the Defense Department, to run it efficiently and assert civilian control over the military. The White House would handle major defense policy matters.[10] McNamara had his flaws. As the noted political scientist John Mearsheimer observed, "He was not a strategist, which was probably the most important requirement of his job," and was inexperienced and uneducated in international security issues and foreign affairs.[11]

If the president rejected the bureaucracy as the source of policy development, then strategic thinking had to occur in the White House. But it was also a rare commodity there. Kennedy and Bundy did not build an internal policymaking process to encourage strategy formulation, but instead "deliberately rubbed out the distinction between planning and operations," connecting Bundy's and his staff's role to the daily activities of the president.[12] Ironically, in his book *The Strategy of Peace*, Kennedy criticized Eisenhower's foreign policy as being reactive. "We move from crisis to crisis for two reasons: First, because we have not yet developed a strategy for peace that is relevant to the new world in which we live; and secondly because we have not been paying the price that strategy demands."[13] Kennedy found himself "consciously innovating, but without either a strong sense of strategic purpose or much success."[14]

While Kennedy valued innovation, he was not a strategic thinker or a planner but a politician who was used to a more improvisational, casual, and unruly way of thinking about issues.[15] He appeared to hold "no general conceptual outlook, no long-term view of American self-interest."[16] As James Reston, the *New York Times* columnist, observed, Kennedy "did not feel the need of some goal to help guide his day-to-day decisions and priorities. . . . It was only when I turned the question to immediate, tangible problems that he seized the point and rolled off a torrent of statistics."[17] Part of the problem, remarked Harris Wofford, a White House special assistant and associate director of the Peace Corps, rested with Kennedy's "spontaneous, unsystematic, ad hoc form of decision-making," often characterized by "jumping from point to point" and a failure in the early days of the administration to ask the right questions.[18] U.S. diplomat U. Alexis Johnson noted that Kennedy was unwilling to concern himself with long-range issues: "he liked to deal in hard realities . . . the immediate, specific issue that required decision at the time . . . without trying to look too far ahead."[19] This perspective was seconded by Assistant Secretary of State Harlan Cleveland, a Kennedy appointee: "The President would ask a very specific question about some little piece of the jigsaw puzzle but he gave no sense of having a view of the whole puzzle."[20]

The same was true for McGeorge Bundy and Walt Rostow. Bundy was a "brilliant bureaucrat," an "operationalist," but he did not think in broad strategic terms.[21] He had other liabilities as well. He may have been the "'boy wonder' Harvard dean" and the "paragon of the East Coast establishment," as Charles Maechling, a senior State Department appointee, observed, but his "foreign policy experience was negligible and his exposure to foreign cultures non-existent." The same was true of Rostow.[22] In fact, Rostow later described himself as well as many of his colleagues on the NSC staff as theorists with respect to national security issues. They arrived in Washington knowledgeable of economics, deterrence theory, and arms control. They also had organizational skills and the budgeting acumen needed to produce a rational force structure.[23] While these men knew limited war theory and defense economics, they were bereft of the skills necessary for formulating military strategy.[24]

This lack of strategic understanding was readily evident to knowledgeable observers. Within months of Kennedy taking office, the prominent international relations theorist Hans J. Morgenthau enumerated the shortcomings of Kennedy's "presidential government," one of which was his reliance on intellectuals in the process of policy formation. Not only were intellectuals often devoid of "practical wisdom," Morgenthau claimed, but they habitually lacked two other qualities indispensable to a "statesman": "a sense of limits—limits of knowledge, of judgment, of successful action—and a commitment to grand design, born of a sense of purpose that neutralizes the doubts arising from the awareness of limits."[25]

To Bundy's credit, he recognized the need for someone to fill this role of constructing a "grand design," and he made Komer the staff member responsible for all foreign policy planning on the NSC staff. Bundy also named him his second for all meetings of the group Komer had proposed in his January

1961 memorandum, now named simply the Planning Group.[26] The broad portfolio encompassed in this responsibility not only allowed Komer the opportunity to deal with any foreign policy issue worldwide, many of which he was familiar with, but it also had a second benefit. It allowed Komer to set the policy agenda by preparing Bundy and Rostow for the interdepartmental Planning Group meetings, which Bundy and George McGhee, the State Department's head of policy planning, chaired.

Komer may have been among like-minded men, such as Bundy and Rostow, with respect to how to organize the government's national security apparatus and the central role of the White House in policy formulation, but he did not share the worldview of his two superiors. He was not an "action-intellectual," a moniker bestowed on Kennedy administration officials who left academe to become Kennedy's closest advisers. He was also not a liberal internationalist like Rostow, who held that America had a weighty moral obligation to help improve the world through activism overseas. Kennedy shared this impulse as well as a disregard for the limitations of power.[27] These men of well-meaning ambitions aspired to replace Britain as the politico-military underwriter and moral leader of a world order based on liberal, democratic, and capitalist principles.[28] Rostow proclaimed that America's calling was to fashion, "no matter how long it may take, a world community in which men and nations can live at peace."[29] Komer, as Langer's student, would have likely recalled the words of France's famous eighteenth-century diplomat Charles-Maurice de Talleyrand-Périgord: "*Surtout, pas trop de zèle*" ("Above all, not too much zeal").

Komer also had no "cherished 'theory' to test." Pet theories can lead to evidence being misinterpreted to suit preconceived assumptions, as happened to Rostow, who perceived the world as wholly consistent with the thesis he presented in his book, *The Stages of Economic Development*, whereby all nations are motivated by economic self-interest in peace and war.[30] While Komer agreed with Rostow about the importance of the economic instrument in asserting national power and grasped its value in promoting development, he did not share Rostow's optimism that economic aid was a way to "create an environment in which societies which directly menace ours will not evolve."[31] Rostow and his former colleagues at MIT's Center for International Studies maintained that development would supersede traditional diplomacy, with its emphasis on alliances and treaties, by stabilizing governments and preventing revolts through precise intervention in a nation's modernization process.[32] Rostow believed such assistance would help developing nations through the stages of capitalist growth to sustained prosperity and modernization and thereby enlarge the noncommunist world.[33] It was a utopian vision, "a new day in which organized violence finally ends." An order attained through the distribution of American technology and practices throughout the globe, for the Rostovian creed maintained, "aggressive impulses diminish in technologically mature societies."[34]

Komer thought that Rostow's viewpoint relied on highly accurate indicators of when interventions should occur, to say nothing of taking into account the traditions and values of the society targeted for U.S. largesse. Komer held that economic assistance was just one of many tools available to the policymaker, but it was definitely not a scalpel. Nonetheless, he agreed with Rostow's belief that the United States could use its foreign aid programs where it had interests among the developing nations in Asia, Africa, and Latin America. As Komer remarked to Kennedy, "I daresay if we confined our aid to those countries who would use it 'effectively' (whatever this may mean), we could reduce the list of our clients considerably. . . . But in applying such criteria we would be opting ourselves out of shoring up, or otherwise influencing, a whole series of client states which, whatever their own internal weaknesses, it is in our strategic interest to help."[35]

For Komer, in the underdeveloped world, or the so-called periphery, other forces were in play, neither of which should be feared. As his White House colleague Arthur Schlesinger observed, one was nationalism, "the most potent political emotion of the age," and the other was nonalignment, a rejection of the U.S.-Soviet duopoly. In some regions, such as the Middle East and South Asia, maintaining economic and political stability was as vital as minimizing Soviet influence. Moreover, what history taught Komer and should have taught others was "how limited the superpowers were in their ability to order their allies and even to control client governments wholly dependent on them for economic and political support." Great powers often ended as prisoners of their clients.[36] Komer recognized the trap of becoming dependent on client states.

As for Bundy, he was a disciple of Henry L. Stimson, who had a long pedigree of public service, serving as secretary of war under two presidents and secretary of state under President Herbert Hoover. After World War II, Bundy had spent more than a year assisting Stimson with his memoir, *On Active Service*. As Stimson's protégé, Bundy absorbed the man's worldview, which was also grounded in the moralistic tradition of American foreign policy, a belief that U.S. diplomacy should foster constructive change in the world through its values and example as a state different from any other on the globe. This exceptionalist perspective had an idealistic and messianic force behind it, one that countenanced intervention, promoted global leadership, and advocated legalism through alliances, treaties, and agreements, supported by military might.[37] This perspective was based not on scholarly theory but on the conventions of the foreign policy elite epitomized by Stimson's Republican internationalism.[38] The younger Bundy clearly articulated this worldview after graduating from Yale in 1940, when he contributed a chapter to the book *Zero Hour*, which warned the world about the dangers of Nazism. "Let me put my whole proposition in one sentence," he wrote. "I believe in the dignity of the individual, in government by law, in respect for the truth and in a good God; those beliefs are worth my life."[39] Bundy, despite the "steely" public persona, was "given to strong feelings,"[40] which often ruled his policy prescriptions.[41]

Bundy also held that military power was indispensable to diplomacy; it was a "salve for America's foreign policy troubles."[42] The use of power by itself was too "crude." As Stanley Hoffman, one of his academic colleagues, noted, Bundy understood that power was important but that it must always be combined with idealism and not relegated to cost-benefit analysis, a cold calculation, a dependence on nuclear weapons to solve political problems, as it had been during the Eisenhower administration.[43] Additionally, Bundy deplored appeasement, whether in the form it took during the interwar period, that espoused by the "New Isolationists" of the Republican right in the 1950s, or that suggested by those who sought to compromise with the Soviets. Credibility, resolve, and commitment were his watchwords; these values characterized not only his worldview but also his perspective on how to handle what he believed to be the most significant menace confronting the United States and its allies—communism.[44]

Komer shared Bundy's anticommunism, but he had grave reservations about the use of force to solve international political problems and he was not troubled by appeasement or isolationism. World War II and Korea had largely banished those policy outlooks from any serious consideration in postwar U.S. foreign policy. While George Kennan, the former U.S. diplomat, saw the postwar debate over the conduct of U.S. foreign policy as a struggle between moralism and realism, driven by competitive self-interest,[45] Komer adhered to a third and often neglected strain in American foreign policy thinking—pragmatism. Komer stated clearly that his approach to national security was pragmatic; he was a participant in the policymaking process, not a theoretician or an armchair strategist.[46] He belonged to that group of government officials historian Eugen Weber, in a different context but still applicable, called "men of government" who recognized and dealt with problems in direct and empirical terms.[47] This was not, however, the pragmatism of the short-term view, the expedient, and the insubstantial examination of the second- and third-order consequences of a decision. It also should not be construed as a reference to Kennedy's political style or his resolve that the White House be perceived not as "soft or overly liberal but as a tough, pragmatic operation."[48] Instead, it was pragmatism as a philosophical stance deeply rooted in the American ethos of problem solving through experience and common sense.[49]

With respect to this pursuit of practical solutions, Komer's outlook was similar to some members of the foreign policy establishment of the period, such as Dean Acheson, who after his experience as assistant secretary of state for economic affairs in Franklin Roosevelt's administration had grown increasingly pragmatic in the "rough and tumble where principle and politics intersect."[50] In the postwar period, Acheson had come to realize that the United States could not act just as it wished; there were limits and opinions that it must acknowledge. These constraints meant that the best way to advance national interests was by applying a pragmatic approach within the framework of a broader concern wherein other states saw it to be in their interests to build or maintain a manageable international system.[51]

Komer had even more in common with Robert Bowie, who served as the assistant secretary of state for planning in the Eisenhower administration and the department's representative to the NSC's Planning Board. In particular, Komer shared with him a concern about the neglect of "the emerging issues of communism, Third World revolutionary nationalism, and post-colonial neutralism."[52] However, Bowie offered institutionalism, which emphasized international cooperation, conflict resolution through mediation, and reduction of the prominence of military force with greater weight on political and economic power and global economic interdependence, as an answer.[53] While Komer accepted the value of mediation in resolving conflict, particularly with regard to having the United Nations (UN) assist in preserving international peace, he saw the international organization largely as a "handy tool" and a mechanism for advancing U.S. interests.[54]

Additionally, Komer found the liberal internationalist or moral-legalistic strain in American foreign policy and the inclination toward exceptionalism disagreeable. As Langer's student, he understood the occasional need for elements founded in Otto von Bismarck's realpolitik: power has its purpose but also its limits; governments must retain sufficient flexibility to exploit options unfettered by ideology; and negotiation is a component of strategy.[55] From his reading of Clausewitz, he learned the necessity of taking society's ethical norms seriously, for behavior inconsistent with the "morality of the age" undermined the "standing, influence, and hegemony" of great powers.[56] In the longer term, great powers profited more by acquiring their allies' and third parties' admiration and legitimacy than they did from the types of short-term rewards that using unethical methods might achieve.[57]

Komer's acceptance of elements from these various schools of thought underscores how his pragmatic worldview was syncretistic, adaptive, and pluralistic; he believed in the necessity of "hard choices," which sometimes required policy decisions that resulted in conflict. The "rivalry of nations" and conflict between them was an indisputable facet of the international environment.[58] As a former intelligence analyst, he understood University of Chicago geographer Norton S. Greenberg's observation "Intelligence derives its raison d'etre from conflict. . . . Its goal at all times is neither maintaining peace nor provoking war, but preparedness for the latter."[59] In responding to this verity, Komer was Clausewitzian: war must be understood as a continuation of policy by other means, and the use of force should be calibrated to the objective sought.[60]

Further, Komer believed that the choice between the two schools of moralism and realism was a false dichotomy; foreign policy could not be worked out solely in terms of moral and legal prescriptions or exclusively in terms of objectives and limited interests, as Kennan declared.[61] Although he shared with Kennan the belief that "pursuit of abstractions" leads to problems,[62] the national interest required concrete definition and the formulation of unambiguous policy and well-fashioned strategy.

For Komer, U.S. national interests, a term presidents and their secretaries of state have called upon since the republic's establishment and that has delineated the broad purposes of U.S. foreign policy, defined the set of objectives that the nation strived for in the world. More specifically, for him, the "art of foreign policy" was "very simply the rational calculation of your interests and of the factors that affect your ability to achieve these interests, and then, on the basis of this, the construction of policy to that end." The assessment of national interests, he offered, required dispassion-ate analysis: "unless you can disassociate the practical hard facts with which you must deal, or the attitudes with which you must deal, from the emo-tional biases and prejudices of one kind or another . . . you cannot have a sensible approach."[63] Historically, these enduring interests consisted of defending the United States, ensuring economic well-being, attaining a favorable world order, and promoting American values, but for American policymakers in this period, such as Kennedy, U.S. world-order interests overshadowed the others.[64]

Thus, Kennedy's clarion call in his 1961 inaugural address that the United States was prepared to "pay any price, bear any burden, meet any hardship, support any friend, oppose any foe, to assure the survival and the success of liberty" was repugnant to Komer.[65] Such an ambitious declara-tion, while perhaps not to be taken literally, but certainly seriously, often led to interventionism, which could result in strategic overreach.[66] Again, Komer's guide was Clausewitz, who emphasized how Napoleon's hubris took form in unfettered ambitions to invade Russia, which led to disastrous overextension and, ultimately, defeat.[67] Kennedy's ideological language also diminished the importance of economic practicability and obliged the United States to become a sentinel for other nations, the "policeman of the world."[68] Although a relationship between interests and political rhetoric existed, ideology had a critical function in justifying a decision once it is made. Ideology played a secondary and lesser role in deciding the nation's objectives and the plan to achieve them.[69]

From Komer's perspective, not all interests had the same priority; there was a hierarchy of interests, with different intensities that changed from case to case. These distinctions mattered, for if an interest was vital—that is, if a dangerous threat to the nation existed—then the president should be prepared to use military force. If there was a dangerous challenge to U.S. interests abroad, the use of a nonmilitary instrument would be appropri-ate. If, however, the interest was peripheral, then the issue or problem was merely an irritant and perhaps diplomatic exchanges were the appropriate instrument. The most difficult job that a president and his foreign policy advisers grapple with is determining whether the issue they confront is vital or important.[70] This determination cannot be ascertained without under-standing the objectives of the policy to be implemented, the national instru-ments to be used, the risks and costs associated with its implementation, and most importantly, the issue's priority within the larger context of the administration's policy objectives.

Komer's goal was to minimize a tendency he found among some in the new administration to think that crisis should be an "instrument of policy."[71] A crisis mentality was evidence of misguided emotions, a fountainhead of heroics, a source of posturing, or machismo with an added dash of adrenalin. Equally disturbing was the inability of some to "disassociate the practical hard facts" with which policymakers must deal, or the attitudes with which they must deal, from emotional biases and prejudices of one kind or another.[72] Komer was well aware of how one element of Clausewitz's remarkable trinity—passion—could distort the calculation of interests. Irrationality was certainly a factor that had to be rationally considered, but it was "seldom approached without a high quotient of emotion."[73] The knack in formulating and executing policy was to supplant passion as a motive force with prudence and rational calculation.

———

It is with this worldview that a few days after becoming a member of the Kennedy administration, Komer called for a rational calculation by urging Bundy to initiate a basic policy review, which he believed would have three benefits. First, it would help provide a cohesive framework in which individual policies could be set and thereby avoid excessive inconsistencies and a lack of focus while giving some order of priorities. Second, it would force the new administration to "sit back and take a longer range view." Lastly, it would provide opportunity for the new team to address the crucial interrelationships between policies.[74]

Komer, supported by Robert H. Johnson, a Department of State employee who had served as part of the Eisenhower NSC apparatus, held that except for the beginnings of a "new look" at Western European affairs, U.S. policy had been largely static for the last several years.[75] Moreover, a world of nuclear stalemate, or at least one in which the Soviet Union would not flex its nuclear capability by launching an attack, meant that the areas requiring U.S. attention were in the periphery and more emphasis had been placed on nonnuclear deterrence and defense. Kennedy, fearful that the "periphery of the Free World" would be "nibbled away" through "indirect non-overt aggression, intimidation and subversion, internal revolution, increased prestige or influence, and the vicious blackmail of our allies," agreed with Komer's position, the position of deterrence.[76]

Komer proceeded to lay out for the administration four broad areas of strategic importance, areas in which he attempted to fashion U.S. policy and, ultimately, its grand strategy.[77] Two issues demanded immediate attention and were responsive to the levers of financial incentives and programs or policy modifications, whereas the others were thornier issues, strategic initiatives, which necessitated long-term approaches.

First, the developing world should not perceive U.S. foreign policy as supporting the continuation of colonialism by North Atlantic Treaty Organization (NATO) allies. Komer argued not only that the Europeans needed to confront reality, but that colonial warfare "soaks up NATO resources," which was an unnecessary diversion from European security.[78] The U.S. position must be "pragmatic" and clear: it would continue to support NATO, but it would not support the colonialism of its NATO allies, their attempt to maintain a hold on their "vestigial colonies." As Komer pointed out, world opinion was trending against these European states, and the loss of their colonies was unavoidable; the United States could not squander its goodwill in the "Afro-Asian world."[79] Further, such a perception only undermined U.S. interests in the developing world and provided the Soviets and Communist Chinese with an effective propaganda message, but equally important, such a stance, Komer believed, was contrary to U.S. values—the democratic principle of self-determination. Kennedy shared this policy position and had articulated it as a U.S. senator in a 1957 speech criticizing U.S. support of the French in the Algerian conflict. Kennedy stated that in taking such a position the United States had undermined its moral leadership and, in particular, its "leadership in the fight to keep the world free." He avowed, "The most powerful single force in the world today . . . is man's eternal desire to be free and independent."[80]

Komer believed that the most pressing issue the administration confronted in this respect was U.S. policy regarding West Irian, a subject which had simmered during the previous administration. The area was a remnant of the settlement that had led to Indonesia's independence from the Netherlands in 1949. At the time of the agreement, both parties decided to set the West Irian question aside and the Dutch maintained its presence there. Then, in the late 1950s, the Indonesian despot, President Sukarno, began a propaganda campaign over the territory, threatening to take it over by force and make it part of Indonesia. By the time the Kennedy administration came to office, Dutch and Indonesian relations had badly frayed because Sukarno was convinced that the Dutch presence was a threat to Indonesian security and was determined to expel them.[81]

In Komer's view, West Irian was a far more clear-cut "anti-colonialism" issue than the ongoing crisis in the Congo; it was one of "those thorny issues which have slid too long for any interim solution. We must bite the bullet, for this issue is heading toward a crisis, and the stakes involved, Indonesia's potential swing to a pro-Soviet stance, dictate cold *realpolitik*."[82] The Soviets recognized Indonesia as a "key piece of real estate," and with the aid of the Indonesian Communist Party, the largest outside the Soviet bloc, they would only gain influence.[83] Additionally, Komer asserted, "Indonesian nationalism will sooner or later run afoul of ChiComs [Chinese Communists] (of whom they are already scared), if only we play it right." In his view, Sukarno's "global orientation" did not make the Indonesian autocrat "necessarily pro-Communist" or incompatible with U.S. policy goals.[84] Instead, he believed U.S. strategic interests could be furthered in Southeast Asia by orienting Indonesia toward the West.

Komer's plan was to have the United States serve as an intermediary in a negotiated compromise to resolve this "teapot crisis" before it resulted in a war between a NATO ally and an emerging Asian power. He proposed that Indonesia secure early control of the area while the Americans fashioned measures to allow as much face saving for the Dutch as possible.[85] The State Department opposed his exercise in preventive diplomacy for several months because of Secretary of State Dean Rusk's personal dislike for Sukarno and the power of the agency's pro-Dutch European Bureau.[86] "The trouble with State," Komer complained in response, "is that it never thinks these problems through to the end." The administration could not afford an incremental approach to foreign policy, moving from crisis to crisis, he argued, but instead needed to pick a solid course of action after exploring a number of policy options.[87] Kennedy, however, chose to take a middle-of-the-road stance. Laos and Vietnam dominated the foreign policy agenda, and the president was concerned the Netherlands would quit NATO at a time, in mid-1961, when the Soviet Union was threatening West Berlin's security. Komer thought the Soviet threat in Berlin preposterous.[88] "Painful as it may be to accommodate a demagogue like Sukarno," he wrote to Kennedy, "Indonesia is a mighty important place. What is the value of holding mainland SEA [Southeast Asia] with a hostile Indonesia at its back?"[89]

After a couple of failed gambits at the UN in autumn that only embarrassed the United States and blunted its opportunity to gain political capital with the developing world by supporting Indonesia, Komer insisted that the administration take intelligent anticipatory action rather than remain passive and let the situation reach a crisis.[90] He had predicted that the UN approach would not succeed, as Indonesia would not back down on its demands. "Djakarta stands to win" one way or the other, he declared, and its purchase of Soviet weapons demonstrated its willingness to use force.[91]

Ultimately, as the likelihood of a clash between the two countries increased, Komer was able to begin a mediation effort with Ellsworth Bunker, an American who had served as an ambassador in the Eisenhower administration, acting as the mediator under UN auspices.[92] As Komer stated, "The real object of the exercise is not a bit of colonial debris, but Indonesia itself."[93] After five discouraging months, Bunker brokered a face-saving measure acceptable to both parties in August 1962, when the United States threw in its prestige and influence and used strong-arm tactics to get the agreement.[94]

While Bunker rightfully received praise for his patient and delicate orchestration of the successful outcome, a large measure of the triumph belongs to Komer. The success resulted from his strategic vision, or perception of the threats and opportunities, and his counsel and determination to implement a U.S. policy that the developing world would not construe as support of colonialism. He emphasized preventing Indonesia from strengthening its ties to the Soviet Union and, most importantly, preventing a war between a NATO ally and the largest, most populous, and wealthiest Southeast Asian state as both critical policy goals and investments in the future.

Komer not only guided this diplomatic success with substantial behind-the-scenes labor,[95] but as Howard Shaffer, Bunker's biographer notes, he also "played a major role in the development of U.S. West New Guinean policy."[96] Howard Jones, U.S. ambassador to Indonesia during this period, was even more admiring: Komer had a "feel for Asian affairs," and he repeatedly "saved the American government from over-reaching to Sukarno's excesses" by his "understanding response" to the issues in play.[97] Rostow had the final word two years later, when he called the event one of the crucial shifts in the balance of the Cold War, "opening improved relations between Indonesia and the West and frustrating Moscow's plans" to "disrupt this area and to align themselves and the local Communist" party by using issues that had powerful national attraction.[98]

———————

Komer's second urgent concern was the Soviet Union's growing emphasis on destabilizing pro-Western nations in the developing world through
subversion, that is, "indirect aggression." In fact, as Komer pointed out,
the growing Sino-Soviet schism had revolved largely around the issue of
how aggressive a revolutionary stance the two states should take.[99] This
divide became visible on January 6, 1961, when at the Moscow Meeting
of World Communist Leaders, Khrushchev promised his nation's support
for wars of national liberation, defined as local wars that began as uprisings
of colonial peoples against their oppressors and that expanded into guerrilla wars.[100] With several insurgencies already simmering around the world
in Laos, Vietnam, and Algeria, Khrushchev's words not only indicated an
intensification of what seemed to be a purposeful strategy to undermine
Western interests in the developing world, but also unwittingly functioned
as a call to arms for the presidential administration about to assume office
in a few weeks.

Kennedy seized on Khrushchev's speech as a prophetic warning. He
replied to the challenge in his inaugural address two weeks later. The concern was not, however, mere rhetoric. Kennedy took an intense interest
in communist revolutionary warfare, what he called "subterranean war."
His views were shaped by his study of communist support of insurgents
in ongoing conflicts, his 1951 visit to Vietnam where he concluded that
the war between France and the Vietnamese insurgents required use of the
political instrument of power, and most importantly, his views on Cuba,
an example of a successful communist guerrilla takeover. These were the
factors that helped frame Kennedy's worldview and his "sense of mission."
They also caused him to spur his staff and the bureaucracy to give this subject priority attention.[101]

For Rostow, Khrushchev's message was also deeply significant. As
Kennedy adviser Arthur M. Schlesinger would later write, "Guerrillas were
also an old preoccupation of Walt Rostow's."[102] Counterinsurgency was a
mechanism for controlling and moderating political transformation in the
developing world; the right mixture of political, economic, and military
techniques could harness change.[103] Further, the U.S. military could serve
as an elite vanguard to prod modernization along and build Third World
militaries that would protect against communist disruption so a "fledgling
industrial democracy," aided by U.S. economic assistance, could "take off."[104]

Rostow was soon spending considerable energy on the "guerrilla warfare problem," as Komer called it.[105] In mid-June Rostow sought Komer's

advice on the draft of a speech Rostow planned to give to the graduating class at the U.S. Army Special Warfare School, Fort Bragg, North Carolina. The speech would be a further articulation of the administration's response to Khrushchev. Komer thought it "a damn fine draft" but then made numerous comments and suggestions in the margin. Refining Rostow's policy pronouncement, Komer argued that two major themes deserved more attention than Rostow gave them. First, he reminded Rostow that guerrilla warfare required more than military measures and that the military had to understand this form of warfare to be a broad problem. Second, U.S. military guerrilla and counterguerrilla operations required "mobility, dash, and imagination quite different from normal military operations. Almost all of your great guerrilla leaders (e.g., Wingate, Marion, T. E. Lawrence) were atypical men." The U.S. military did not cultivate such leaders; therefore, it was imperative to search for such leaders in the military, leaders who could immerse themselves in the local culture and environment as well as develop training regimens that would build up a distinct esprit and provide special qualifications.[106] Rostow incorporated Komer's views, and on June 28 he delivered his remarks at the graduation ceremony.

While Komer credited Rostow with formulating the fundamental doctrine based on the ideas the latter raised in his Fort Bragg address, he continued to express concern to Rostow that the focus was primarily on the military instrument and not on "preventive medicine." In Komer's view, communist subversion succeeded because the situation was "ripe," that is, there had been a long preparation for covert intervention. Stressing precautionary measures in the initial preemptive phase would be less expensive in the end, minimize the risk of upheaval, and reduce the need for draconian measures to save the imperiled nation. Even such measures were not always successful since the critical issue was implementation.[107]

Meanwhile, after April's Bay of Pigs fiasco, an ill-conceived CIA-backed operation by Cuban exiles to overthrow Fidel Castro, Kennedy recalled Gen. Maxwell D. Taylor to active duty. The famed World War II commander and former Army chief of staff would serve as military representative to the president, a job that entailed advisory responsibilities in "intelligence and Cold War planning," which included fashioning the administration's counterinsurgency policy.[108]

Taylor knew of Komer's role in defining the administration's new counterinsurgency policy, so he solicited his views. Komer responded with a memorandum in which he again expressed his belief that the term "counterguerrilla" tended to narrow the focus to a military solution. He underscored his continuing concern that "preventive medicine to forestall a situation from ever reaching the stage of open warfare in the country-side" received little attention. He also argued that most of the situations in which the United States might be involved would be urban discord rather than rural insurgency. While the latter was certainly the case in Southeast Asia, it was not the case in other areas of the world, such as Iran and many Latin American countries. Iran and the Latin American states would continue to align themselves with the West as long as the United States provided military assistance and other aid. However, they were often unstable, and the administration needed to encourage internal reforms. Iran was the most visible example of this issue. Komer considered himself a heretic on Iran because he contended that there was "no definite correlation between economic development and political change in less developed countries." Providing aid would never be enough unless it was accompanied by political consensus.[109]

Nonetheless, while political, economic, and social measures were essential, Komer believed that the first line of active defense against subversion was usually the police, not the military. Instead of focusing on an Army counterguerrilla school, local police forces in underdeveloped areas should receive attention. Additionally, the Military Assistance Program (MAP), focused primarily on overt threats, required careful study as a means of enhancing counterguerrilla capabilities. The key was impeding subversion in its early stages.[110]

In mid-July a CIA-led interagency task force (the Counter-Guerrilla Warfare Task Force), formed earlier in the year, circulated a draft introductory chapter of its study. Rostow, a member of the group, asked Komer to fill out what the remainder of the document should cover. Komer laid out several areas that the study needed to address. The first was "knitting a resistant social fabric." He argued that there needed to be an enumeration of the steps considered necessary to create and maintain a political and socioeconomic environment hostile to rural insurgency or urban disorder. The second issue was "preventive medicine," that is, steps to take in the stage before open guerrilla warfare. A third area was military and police measures to cope with an active insurgency, followed by a discussion of how to convince the international community concerning the challenge of indirect aggression and legitimizing an adequate response. The remaining chapters should be devoted to "sealing off the disease" by isolating a guerrilla threat from outside support; encouraging counterguerrilla actions in adjacent enemy territory; and organizing and coordinating U.S. efforts to cope with this issue, ranging from education and propaganda to the coordination of police and military programs.[111]

Four months later, in the so-called Thanksgiving Day Massacre, which resulted in a presidential shake-up of the State Department's leadership, Kennedy removed Chester Bowles as under secretary of state for his poor performance as an administrator and his indiscretion in leaking to the press his opposition to the 1961 Bay of Pigs fiasco, and replaced him with George Ball. Kennedy also sent Rostow to State to replace McGhee as director of the Policy Planning Staff. Despite the distance from the White House, Rostow remained the major force behind the counterguerrilla warfare study, but Komer was now the principal White House staff participant and final arbiter of its contents, and the revised drafts represented his views.

The task force presented its final report, "Elements of U.S. Strategy to Deal with 'Wars of National Liberation,'" in December. Rostow urged Kennedy to approve its recommendations, including its key one—the creation of a high-level interagency committee to monitor and steer the national security community's counterinsurgency work, including the formulation of policy and doctrine.[112] A Joint Chiefs of Staff study, for which McNamara had been tasked, was also completed in December, and it too urged the president to establish an interagency steering committee.[113]

On January 18, 1962, Kennedy, who, according to General Taylor, was unsatisfied with the progress to date, approved a presidential directive that established the Special Group (Counterinsurgency or CI), with Taylor as the chair. Senior representatives from the Departments of State and Defense, CIA, U.S. Agency for International Development (USAID), and USIA; the chairman of the Joint Chiefs of Staff; Attorney General Robert F. Kennedy; and McGeorge Bundy would serve as members.[114]

Within two weeks of the Special Group's creation, Komer wrote Taylor and Bundy urging them to prevent funding cutbacks for police programs in developing nations, which he believed were "the first line of defense" in preventing subversion and indirect aggression. Funding for foreign police assistance programs under the Overseas Internal Security Program (OISP) was miniscule, about $30 million. Initiated by the Eisenhower administration, the program, Komer asserted, was an "orphan child" in USAID, and only the Special Group (CI) could protect it from dismantlement by the new agency leadership that deemed it of marginal value.[115]

Bundy took up the matter with Taylor personally, contending that the Special Group needed to pressure Fowler Hamilton, the USAID administrator, on police programs, as they were an essential element in the administration's counterinsurgency effort. Bundy also directed Komer to draft a presidential directive, which Kennedy signed on February 19, 1962. The directive instructed the head of USAID to reemphasize these programs as a means of "contributing to internal security and resisting to Communist-supported insurgency" and to consider giving the program autonomy in USAID so it would not be neglected.[116] Bureaucratic resistance prevailed for several months until ultimately, in November 1962, the administrator of USAID established the Office of Public Safety in the agency.[117] With that action, as well as Kennedy's subsequent directive in December 1962, the policy assistance program was rescued from bureaucratic obscurity and made a key feature of U.S. national security policy toward the developing world. Robert Amory, the old CIA hand, acknowledged that Komer's leadership had been instrumental in creating this independent office within USAID.[118]

By the end of the first two years of the administration, Komer's work ethic had made for mixed results. The long hours and demands of his job had inevitable impact on his family life. After nearly fourteen years of marriage and the birth of three children, he and his wife, Jane, divorced in April 1961; the marriage had been foundering for several months. He remarried in November of the same year to Geraldine Peplin, an Indiana native but now a Washington, D.C., area artist who exhibited in local galleries and was a member of the National Woman's Democratic Club. They would remain married until her death from cancer in 1996 at the age of seventy-one.[119]

As far as his career move was concerned, Komer had no regrets. He had established a solid and cordial relationship with Bundy, and although he and Rostow often held differing views, their relationship was suitably professional. Komer, however, had not gained the president's complete confidence, leading him to call himself a "New Frontiersman, Third Class."[120] Arthur Schlesinger viewed him as someone expert in dealing with the State Department and a strong ally in influencing Kennedy regarding policy.[121] In the national security bureaucracy, the belief was that Bundy worked from Komer's analyses and recommendations, and these marked out the position that went to the president. This influence disturbed some State Department personnel who felt that Komer was "staking out an increasingly large field and that he was, in a sense, establishing command of that field."[122]

Despite the centralization of policy planning in the White House,[123] Komer learned that policy innovation was a collaborative art. His contacts in the various departments and agencies were helpful in clarifying his views, but they also served as part of an informal policy formulation process. He was fortunate that the subcabinet officers he interacted with had a degree of autonomy in the development of policy provided their superiors retained confidence in them.

Although Bundy's "Little State Department" was an incubator of ideas and provided an entrepreneurial milieu, Komer viewed NSC staff operations as dysfunctional. Responding to Rostow's request for his views, Komer was characteristically blunt: "Essentially, you are running a two-man, self-contained operation, with the rest of us helping out here and there, offering a few ideas, but largely only grinding our gears. . . . You have a growing staff and a real management problem. . . . You are spread too thin." To fix this predicament, Komer recommended decentralization of responsibility, communication down the chain so the staff would know Bundy and Rostow's specific needs, and lastly, regional and functional assignments. In his view, there was no alternative. "We all can't be universal scholars."[124]

Bundy relented, and Komer's assigned portfolio included South Asia, portions of Southeast Asia, North Africa, and the Middle East.[125] Komer was now the vanguard of Kennedy's "New Frontier" foreign policy, which paid considerable attention to the "neutralists" or nonaligned states and the nationalists. In Komer's view, too much emphasis had been placed on the unproductive alliances of encirclement that the Eisenhower administration had created, "this sort of casting out into the outer darkness those countries which for one reason or another didn't feel they should be tied to Washington as opposed to Moscow."[126] The Southeast Asian Treaty Organization (SEATO), for example, was a "millstone" aimed at the imaginary threat of open aggression.[127]

As an alternative, Komer believed in engagement with the nonaligned states because he perceived that a "changing balance of power in the world" was occurring. This change demanded an approach that equalized obligations to existing allies and included outreach to the "Third World" as a confidence-building measure, what he perceived as a realistic "middle road."[128] He held that the Department of State's hands-off approach to sustained, formal interaction with these states, its belief that the Soviet Union was necessarily always pleased with the positions that these nations took or that all of them were anti-West, was wrongheaded. The idea was not to outbid the Soviets; the danger was that by not engaging, the United States was giving the Soviets an advantage.[129] Komer disdained those who "advocate 'tough' policies toward neutralists. . . . It was precisely such policies which helped influence those countries to accept Moscow offers in the first place."[130] The United States needed to maintain good relations with these states but not necessarily expect them to join the "western camp." Instead, it should attempt to influence the behavior of states such as Nasser's United Arab Republic or prompt states such as India to become countervailing forces against communism.[131] It was on these last points that Komer would devote a substantial part of his time with events providing the catalyst for doing so.

CHAPTER 3

Komer's War

*O*n September 19, 1962, Imam Ahmad, the monarch of Yemen, the man his subjects called "Big Turban," died at the age of seventy-one. That the imam died of natural causes was remarkable; he had been the target of numerous assassination attempts. Twice in his reign, he successfully fended off murderous rebellions by family members. He had beheaded or imprisoned his rival brothers. Still, the potential for intrigue remained in this repressive and backward country. Yemen's military elite, who had received advanced training in the modern states of Egypt, Syria, and Iraq, bemoaned the country's notorious reputation for squalor and despotism.[1] It was a Muslim theocratic state: slavery endured, adulterers were stoned to death, women were kept in seclusion, and possession of alcohol was a serious offense.[2]

In recent years, the old imam had feuded with the United Kingdom over the neighboring Aden Colony and the related British protectorates, and had turned to the Soviet Union for weapons and technical assistance. In 1958 he federated his kingdom with the United Arab Republic (UAR) of Egyptian president Gamal Abdel Nasser, but Nasser dissolved the relationship in 1961, after the imam wrote an offensive poem denouncing Nasser's socialism as contrary to Islam.[3] When Ahmad left the country for four months in 1959 to undergo medical treatment in Rome, his son, Crown Prince Saif-al-Islam Mohammed al-Sadr, became regent. During his father's absence, he initiated several reforms that the ruler repudiated when he returned home, sending his son into semiretirement.[4]

Now, upon his father's death, the crown prince assumed the throne. Yemeni religious leaders, tribal chiefs, and regional governors swore allegiance to the new monarch as the "Prince of the Faithful and Caliph of the Moslems." For his part, the new imam vowed to bring modernity to this small state at the tip of the Arabian Peninsula.[5] It was a short-lived declaration. A week later, the thirty-five-year-old monarch was under siege by a military faction led by Colonel Abdullah al-Sallal, which declared the establishment of the Yemeni Arab Republic (YAR). Artillery shells reduced the royal palace in the isolated capital of Sana to rubble, and although the ruler had reportedly died beneath the ruins, he escaped into the northern part of the kingdom, where loyal tribes rallied to him.[6] A civil war began, but a proxy war soon ensued as Egypt and Saudi Arabia vied for hegemony in the Arabian Peninsula.[7]

Seven thousand miles away, Komer sat in his Washington office in the Executive Office Building with its Empire décor and glass French doors overlooking the adjacent White House. He was preoccupied with other Middle East issues—certainly not Yemen. He later recalled, "This little crisis, of no importance in itself, was a sort of vortex which drew in the Egyptians," who wanted a successful UAR-supported revolution, but the consequences, Komer knew, went well beyond Yemen, that "little 14th century backwater."[8] The conflict could have severe ramifications for the U.S. policy he had devised and assiduously promoted for the Arab world.

In the nearly two years since Komer had joined Bundy's staff, he had become the foremost influence on U.S. policy toward the Middle East. He had filled a vacuum, as at the beginning of the Kennedy administration, the president and his principal policy advisers had decided to continue the modest policy that former secretary of state Christian Herter had initiated under President Eisenhower. There was little desire to place the Middle East at the top of a foreign policy agenda already packed with higher priority issues such as Berlin, Laos, and Cuba.[9] Komer had allegedly suggested during the Eisenhower administration that the United States cultivate a better relationship with Nasser, but "[Secretary of State John Foster] Dulles had peed on it."[10]

Komer was of two minds with respect to U.S. interests in the Middle East. He disagreed with the conventional wisdom that the Middle East was vital to U.S. interests. It was certainly important but not vital, as it had been for the British, who saw it as their lifeline to India. He saw no major overriding reason why the United States needed bases in the Middle East; they were not essential to the application of nuclear power against the Soviet Union. Even oil did not make the region vital to U.S. interests because only 3 percent of the oil that the United States consumed came from the region and U.S. trade with the Middle East was "piddling." Komer's more modest goal was to keep the Soviets out of the area, especially the northern tier of Turkey, Iran, Afghanistan, and Pakistan, by using local nationalism to achieve this end, which he considered a "much more flexible policy."[11]

He believed that the United States had learned to live with a degree of Soviet influence in neutralist or nonaligned countries, but he also stressed that the American commitment to Israel could not be jettisoned. According to Carl Kaysen, who replaced Rostow on the NSC staff, Bundy was uneasy about both Komer and Kaysen when it came to Israeli issues since they were Jewish.[12] Bundy's worries were misplaced; Komer increasingly became accepted, both inside and outside the Kennedy White House, as the person who fashioned U.S. policy in the Middle East.[13] He was a staunch advocate of an evenhanded policy as the only way to maneuver the "tortuous current of Middle East politics" in which the United States had important but not vital interest.[14]

In Komer's view, the United States had no choice but to pursue this policy of balance, which permitted it to continue to support Israel discreetly "while simultaneously maintaining tolerable relations with the Arab world." Such a policy could be attained with a small investment of U.S. power, supporting reform and modernization but doing so without using "our assistance for a crude political ploy." It was also essential to encourage the development of "viable political institutions, viable economic institutions, governments and economies . . . responsive to the growing needs and ambitions of their citizens." Living with local nationalism was also critical as long as it did not adversely affect U.S. interests, and that seemed unlikely. Nationalism, he contended, was essentially antithetical to communism, and the most important element from a strategic point of view was that the United States did not "thrust" Middle East leaders "into the arms of Moscow as we did in the period of the Aswan Dam-Suez period" (that is, the mid-1950s).[15]

In espousing such a position, Komer was stating the pragmatist agenda within the U.S. government regarding Middle East policy and with respect to nonaligned states in general. Komer, as one political scientist has noted, was the "quintessential representative" of this group of officials who were more "sensitive to divergent stimuli, pressures and considerations," ready to acknowledge and embrace shifting conditions and to examine them from a multitude of organizational and policy perspectives, tying together domestic and electoral considerations with strategic objectives and requirements.[16] As a strategist, Komer was well aware that the test of a sound strategy is not only its feasibility, but also its suitability, that is, whether it will achieve the desired end, and its acceptability, whether it was morally, legally, and politically viable.[17]

The second component of his policy approach was his belief that military power was the wrong tool because it contributed to arms proliferation or massive military assistance programs, which "perpetuated in much more dangerous form some of the mistakes that we [the United States] made in our own military policy in the aftermath of World War II." However, recognizing the deep commitment the United States had to the preservation of Israel, he believed it should be supplied arms to maintain a conventional deterrent. Once that prospect was lost, then the Israelis would be forced to seek a nuclear deterrent.[18]

The third element of his thinking was the value of giving assistance to the Arab world, principally Egypt. Food aid was crucial to Nasser and other leaders who could not fill the "bellies of the *fellahin*" (the peasant or agricultural worker). Keeping these populations well fed prevented them from getting restive since hunger and other deprivations usually meant that the leaders had to find outlets for the people's anger with the regime. Food aid, which the Soviets could not provide, gave the United States "leverage" in the Arab world, sent the signal that the United States was not against Arab aspirations, and most importantly, served to restrain the Arab states from attacking Israel.[19] Of the Arab states not aligned with the United States, Egypt was critical and influencing Nasser was essential. As Komer informed Rostow in June 1961 in response to an NIE that he believed bolstered his argument, "Nationalism will remain the most dynamic force in the Arab world and Nasser will remain its foremost leader."[20]

In September 1961, when a group of Syrian officers launched a successful coup d'etat leading to Syria's secession from the UAR, Komer pressed for a reappraisal of U.S. relations with Nasser. Five days after the secession, he observed, "I am convinced that recent events may present us with the best opportunity since 1954 for a limited marriage of convenience with the guy who I think is still, and will remain, the Mister Big of the Arab World. If we can turn Nasser inward, and get back on a friendly basis with him, it may not buy us much but it will certainly save us a peck of trouble that he can otherwise stir up for us."[21] By December Komer was still pressing for a "new initiative," and not in the more guarded fashion that the State Department was recommending in the aftermath of the coup. Instead, the United States needed to signal Nasser that it was "opening a new chapter, using as bait the very substantial aid we're probably going to give him anyway."[22] Komer labored under no illusions. As he told Kennedy, Nasser was a "charismatic neutralist leader whose ambitions and interests run athwart" of U.S. interests, but it was also apparent that with the Syrian coup that broke up the UAR, Nasser would turn inward to revive the Egyptian revolution because his nation was near bankruptcy. U.S. aid could be used to encourage him to focus on internal matters rather than on stirring up trouble elsewhere in the region.[23]

Komer also recognized that a solid relationship between the United States and the UAR would not occur quickly and would not "woo Nasser away from being a neutralist and nationalist (any more than Moscow could)." However, the relationship could become strong enough that Nasser would inhibit himself from taking actions that created problems for Suez transit—a vital line of communication—and oil flows. Nasser also had an interest in preventing undue Soviet penetration into the Middle East. Further, the Israelis favored turning Nasser's energies inward, although they recognized that strengthening the UAR might be at their expense. Regarding that anxiety, the United States, Komer clearly stated, had to make perfectly clear to Nasser that improved relations with him would not mean taking his side over the Arab-Israeli divide.[24]

Finally, Komer reasoned that such a policy initiative would not be costly in terms of financial commitment and certainly was worth the risk. Even if it failed, it would not drive Egypt further into the Soviet's embrace. To entice Nasser to listen required a changed approach with a sizable aid package; an emissary, someone with the president's ear, to begin the dialogue; and a visit to Washington by Nasser in early 1962. Then, if the interest in a new relationship were reciprocated, perhaps the United States would encourage a consortium for support of a major Egyptian development effort and contribute a substantial amount to that effort.[25] As Komer would characterize it in early 1962, economic assistance was "part of a long-term strategy toward an important neutralist state, still the most influential in the Arab world."[26]

Komer's ideas intrigued Kennedy, but the president expressed concern about "sweeping commitments." Komer responded that the potential gains from such a relationship were "intangible and long term, in fact a gamble," but the costs were minimal with the potential benefit of being able to modulate Nasser's policies and actions.[27] Kennedy also worried that Komer's approach or even the State Department's more modest proposal would raise domestic concerns; moreover, he was not persuaded that either approach would be productive. Instead, if unsuccessful, the gambit could be viewed as a New Frontier failure.[28]

After some intense lobbying by Komer, Secretary of State Dean Rusk, and Walt Rostow, now a State Department official, the president approved three steps: a multiyear food assistance agreement; offering Nasser a top economic planner for advice on development; and an exploratory visit by Chester Bowles, the administration's roving ambassador to the Third World.[29] Nonetheless, Kennedy remained cold to undertaking a full-scale discussion of future U.S.-UAR relations, including a Nasser visit, despite Komer's protestations that it was just as important as the meetings already held with other neutralists such as Yugoslavia.[30]

The stalemate continued for months, but Kennedy eventually weakened under Komer's persistent assaults and a receptive message from Nasser indicating that sending Bowles to Cairo and the potential for economic aid were understood as "tokens of good faith." Komer recognized that while small, cautious steps were acceptable to Kennedy, these tactics had to be "kept within the framework of a consistent long-term strategy and periodically evaluated for results." The long-range goal was UAR moderation on the Arab-Israeli issue. Kennedy, however, was not ready to invite Nasser to Washington as the price for a deeper dialogue.[31]

Nonetheless, to solidify its goodwill, the administration promised 400,000 tons of wheat, $51 million in development loans, and other aid in May 1962, made available under Public Law 480, Food for Peace. In response, the governments of Iran, Saudi Arabia, Jordan, and Israel complained about the U.S. largesse and remained unconvinced that helping Nasser would result in him being less "mortgaged to Moscow." Komer maintained that progress in overcoming ingrained UAR suspicion toward the West had been made, but more importantly, he cautioned Kennedy not to let minor irritants deflect the United States from its strategy.[32]

A more concrete sign that the strategy was working occurred in July, when Nasser sent a letter to Kennedy that recognized the aid as a sign of trust and confidence, as Komer claimed it would, and suggested a move toward cordial relations and new forms of cooperation.[33] Kennedy followed by extending personal courtesies to Nasser, such as contacting him when the administration sold Hawk antiaircraft missiles to Israel in 1962 because of the Defense Department's assessment that Israel had a valid requirement for these weapons for defensive purposes.[34] This considerateness, in Arthur Schlesinger's opinion, helped diminish any suspicions of U.S. intent in the region as well as "moderated Nasser's response to what he might otherwise have seen as unfriendly acts."[35] At the time, no one recognized it, but the summer of 1962 was the high point of what Komer called "a major experiment in the new Administration's policy of being more sensible toward the neutralists."[36]

By September 1962, this remote place named Yemen had Kennedy's attention and, consequently, Komer's as well. The Yemeni civil war not only drew in the Egyptians but also proceeded to engage the Saudis, who feared that if the Egyptians became involved in Yemen, they would be that much closer to overthrowing the House of Saud, the ruling dynasty. The Nasser-inspired Yemeni insurrection had all the elements that the regime feared: vulnerability of the kingdom to foreign invasion that its poorly disciplined and equipped military could not halt, potential peril of a revolt by the military if the king appeared weak, and discord within the royal family since some of the princes were living in exile in Egypt.[37]

Nasser's motives were a mix of the political and emotional. A short decisive triumph in Yemen would bolster his standing in the Arab world, counteract Saudi influence in the Arabian Peninsula, push the British out of their Colony of Aden and the related protectorate, and from a strategic standpoint, give him control of the Red Sea from the Suez to the Bab el Mandeb Strait. Finally, assisting the YAR leaders against the forces of reaction was the core principle of the Arab nationalist revolution, and not helping them sapped the energy of this objective, perhaps irretrievably.[38]

In the first week of October, Nasser sent five thousand troops to Yemen at the request of the revolutionaries who had obtained assurances of military support beforehand.[39] Meanwhile, the Saudis began using millions of dollars from their oil revenue to support the royalists, tribal leaders who were behind the new imam, and hire European mercenaries to plan, train, and operate with the royalist irregulars.[40] The potential for a Saudi-UAR conflict became more likely, and Kennedy grew increasingly sensitive to Jordanian and British complaints about the administration's pro-Nasser policy. Within weeks of the Egyptian intervention, Kennedy ordered Komer to find a way to tamp down the crisis, but without upsetting the newfound rapprochement with Nasser or alienating Great Britain and its two friends in the region, Saudi Arabia and Jordan. Further, the approach had to ensure that Nasser would not attack the Saudis.[41] If such an assault occurred, the United States would have to protect the Saudis, and the Kennedy administration would be in a fight with Nasser over Yemen, which had no strategic value.[42]

Britain had little interest in helping Kennedy obtain his objective. Its vital strategic interest was to maintain control of the neighboring Aden Colony, with its port and air base, which protected Persian Gulf oil as well as East Africa and served as an indispensable staging and communication connection with Asia. The British feared that if the UAR got a foothold in Yemen, it would inspire the Yemeni revolutionaries to foment trouble in Aden, which would undermine British power and stature in the region.[43] There was also Britain's concern about Yemen's long-standing claim to Aden, which the Yemenis called "occupied Yemen." Prime Minister Harold Macmillan remained steadfast in his opposition to the new regime, a position Komer considered narrow-minded and overly obsessed with Aden and Yemen.[44]

As the crisis accelerated after the coup, Komer met with Kennedy two or three times a week. The purpose was not to keep the president up to date—he was an avid reader of the daily intelligence—but to interpret the intelligence and to learn Komer's views as well as those of State Department officials. During the course of these meetings Kennedy coined the phrase, "Komer's War." This title became public when a journalist asked McGeorge Bundy a few questions about Yemen. Bundy could not resist and told the journalist, "When it [the war] goes well, we call it Komer's war, and when it goes poorly, we call it Talbot's [Assistant Secretary of State Phillips Talbot] war." This quip was published in a magazine article much to Komer's embarrassment.[45]

Komer, however, had concerns other than embarrassment, and one of them was walking the tightrope that Kennedy had erected for him. In October Komer wrote a memorandum to Kennedy informing him that the State Department wanted the president to sign the multiyear Food for Peace agreement with the UAR. Not only had the United States promised this agreement, but the UAR had also not openly complained about the Hawk offer to Israel and was genuinely supportive of an administration initiative, the Johnson Plan, to resettle Palestinian refugees living in the

West Bank and southern Lebanon. Komer warned the president that "this is one of those spots where nothing we do will be right" because approval would be perceived as U.S. support of Nasser's intervention in Yemen. He also weighed costs and benefits and ultimately recommended that the president approve the agreement because, in his view, "our Nasser policy is more important than that toward Yemen." More worrisome, however, was that Nasser might use the agreement to underscore that the United States backed the Egyptian leader despite Yemen. The Saudis and others would certainly interpret it that way. Nonetheless, Kennedy signed the agreement on Komer's advice but worried about the Saudi reaction. The president also directed that every effort should be made to ensure minimum publicity and asked that the UAR do the same.[46]

Kennedy's approval of the packages was a precarious step because later that day, Crown Prince Faisal ibn Abd-al-Aziz Al Saud, the Saudi Arabian minister of foreign affairs, visited the president at the White House. The message that Komer wanted Kennedy to give the crown prince on Yemen was that it was necessary to modernize this "oil-rich, non-country with a medieval regime and an incompetent king who is a drunkard." While many administration officials considered Faisal a political lightweight, Komer saw him as the chosen instrument; he believed the prince was the only person who might be able to influence the Yemeni monarch to reform, thus providing regional stability and preventing a disruption of oil production. Kennedy delivered the message.[47]

Meanwhile, Macmillan and his government, fearing an attack by the revolutionaries on the Aden Colony and Protectorate, held urgent meetings in early October and decided to take defensive measures.[48] The British also allowed arms to flow through the Aden Protectorate to royalist forces, and British military aircraft conducted nighttime missions to resupply these forces.[49] Despite Britain's concerns and its operations, Kennedy did not shift U.S. policy. But being in the middle did not suit Kennedy for long, and he asked Komer to devise a means of halting the civil war.

Komer worried that the Yemen crisis would result in a protracted war and possible escalation. If the United States joined the United Kingdom, Saudi Arabia, and Jordan, then it would undermine its new relationship with Nasser. If it supported the UAR, then it would offend its three friends. Komer recognized it was a gamble to trust Nasser, but he also believed conditions that both sides might find attractive could be created: the recognition of the YAR by all parties and the promise of aid; a UAR promise to desist in its war against Arab monarchies; a reassurance by Nasser and the YAR about Aden; and a rapprochement between the UAR and Saudi Arabia and Yemen with Faisal replacing King Saud. He also held that the United States would have to promote this agreement, serve as a mediator, and guarantee the provisions. His State Department colleagues found this approach sensible, but it was stillborn because Faisal stood by his commitment to the new monarch and believed that the royalist opposition could win.[50]

The State Department now urged caution in recognizing the YAR even if it reportedly had almost full control of the country. Robert Stookey, the U.S. chargé d'affairs in Yemen, made the case that recognition of the republican leaders would help prevent the country from coming completely under the influence of the UAR, but the cost of recognition weighed against it. It would anger two friends in the region, Jordan and Saudi Arabia, which would perceive recognition of Nasser's actions as providing him freedom of action in the Arab world. Komer argued even more strenuously than the Department of State for delaying recognition. He contended that the YAR leadership did not control the country and that guerrilla warfare could last for months. More urgently, recognition would undermine the "honest broker" role that was based on the principle of nonintervention by outsiders, eliminate a major point of advantage with the UAR, and infuriate not only our friends in the region but also Britain. Komer advocated delay until these three nations obtained the assurances they needed. He then refocused his attention on the disengagement plan.[51]

By the end of October, Kennedy, who had been distracted by the Cuban missile crisis, directed the State Department to write a letter for him to send to Faisal indicating that the United States intended to recognize the YAR, but reassuring Faisal of U.S. support for Saudi integrity. Faisal was so upset by the news that Kennedy wrote another letter to him, reassuring him of U.S. support. The United States informed Britain of its intent to recognize the new regime under certain conditions: if the Egyptians would agree to leave Yemen and the Saudis stopped aiding the royalists, the United States would recognize the new republic. The proposal only infuriated Macmillan.[52]

Komer, a month later, believed that the situation was more amenable to disengagement. The YAR was now in control of the country, and the UAR had agreed to reduce its presence in Yemen and offered "honeyed words" of reassurance that it would not attack Saudi Arabia or Aden. The key was to convince Faisal, who had become prime minister at the end of

October, to focus on internal reform, not a "vain fight in Yemen." Even the British recognized that the royalist cause was lost.[53] However, Komer did not expect Jordan to up the ante by sending aircraft to Saudi Arabia, which made Nasser "nervous" and threatened to escalate tensions. Further, he had severely misjudged Britain's position.[54]

An irritated Macmillan wrote Kennedy suggesting that the United States not recognize YAR until the UAR made a concrete agreement to the proposal. He further argued that recognition would "spread consternation among our friends throughout Arabia, and particularly in the Aden Protectorate where it could be assumed that Britain is not resolute enough to be dependable." Kennedy's response two days later was "discouraging." Macmillan observed, "So the Americans will risk paying the price [recognition] without effecting the purchase [Egyptian disengagement]."[55] Shortly thereafter, Macmillan scheduled a secure telephone call with Kennedy. The president asked Komer to meet him in the White House Situation Room and sit in on the conversation, as it was to be about two issues, one of which was Yemen.[56]

After a brief and cordial discussion of the first issue, the two leaders began a discussion of the Yemen situation, specifically, diplomatic recognition of the Yemeni Republic, and with several minutes of seesawing arguments, it was evident that neither man would budge on his position. Finally, Kennedy said to Macmillan, "You and I seem to be going around in circles. I've got my Yemen expert here. Why don't I put him on, and he'll explain to you why we don't think delay is such a good idea." Kennedy then handed Komer the telephone. Komer held the phone to his ear and then began making his argument to the prime minister. After a few minutes, Macmillan, perhaps tired from all the arguing, conceded that maybe the United States had a point. He then said plaintively to Komer, "Is the President still there? I presume he's gone." Komer replied no and indicated that the president was sitting next to him. In fact, Kennedy had been sitting there during the entire conversation, smoking a long, thin cigar and grinning broadly, as Komer debated with Macmillan.[57] It was a breakthrough moment for Komer. His relationship with Kennedy became personal, no longer somewhat distant with the patina of decorum. From that point on, Kennedy trusted Komer's judgment; he had become a full-fledged member of the team by mere serendipity.[58]

Komer continued to work diligently with State Department officials on a settlement plan. Less than a week after the telephone call, Komer sent a memorandum to Kennedy indicating that the administration was ready to initiate the disengagement plan. The UAR accepted the proposal but with the caveat that the announcement and the U.S. recognition of the YAR occur simultaneously. The YAR stubbornly opposed the plan, but Nasser believed he could convince them to go along. Faisal and King Hussein of Jordan were bitter and continued to urge against recognition unless the UAR withdrew all its forces. Komer's counterargument was for these two regimes to cease their involvement in the civil war lest they be deposed. He also felt that Macmillan's concerns had been addressed with a provision whereby the YAR would leave the Colony of Aden and the protectorate alone. It was a painful task to recognize the YAR, but in Komer's view, it was necessary to achieve a settlement and prevent escalation.[59] A few weeks later, after considerable negotiation with Nasser's government and the YAR, Komer informed the president that they had satisfactory declarations from both parties, with the YAR agreeing that it would "keep hands off Aden." The United States could proceed with recognizing the YAR as it was required to do as fulfillment of its part of the bargain. It did so on December 19, 1962.[60] It remained a controversial and unpopular decision among U.S. supporters in the area. Jordanian premier Wasfi Tel called it "a grave mistake," but that mild remark masked the bitter feelings of the pro-West monarchy and others.[61]

The decision was difficult for Kennedy but made easier when he coolly analyzed the situation: most of the European nations, except the United Kingdom, had recognized the republic; the UAR's interest in a settlement was promising; and recognizing the YAR might allow the United States to influence the new state regarding a settlement. Additionally, communist gains in the Middle East could be curbed by the promotion of internal reforms and the growth of enlightened governments, and Faisal, although discontent with the U.S. stance, had been kept in check.[62] Now the issue was to advance a potential disengagement scheme by using the UN as a mediator or forming a peacekeeping force under its auspices.

Then the plan came undone. Just weeks later Nasser negated all the previous U.S. efforts when his forces, perhaps encouraged by U.S. recognition of the YAR, bombed Najran, Saudi Arabia, on the Yemen border. The Saudis immediately demanded a new statement of U.S. support to the regime, a demonstration of U.S. strength in the area, provision of antiaircraft weapons and ammunition, and advice as to whether it should refer the matter to the UN. Komer recommended that the United States provide the first three and that the Saudis avoid bringing the issue to the UN.[63] On New Year's Eve Secretary of Defense McNamara asked the Joint Chiefs of Staff for their options and recommendations regarding U.S. military actions that could be taken to support policy in the Yemen situation. They replied by stating that U.S. response of this kind was like throwing gasoline on a fire. A political solution was preferable.

The UAR and its Yemeni allies continued to stir up the crisis, broadcasting appeals to the Saudi Arabian army, whose allegiance was in doubt, to depose the House of Saud. Additionally, some Jordanian pilots defected to the YAR. In response to these troubling developments, the administration dispatched an American oilman, an intimate of the Saudi monarch, to Riyadh as a secret envoy with instructions to persuade the king to undertake internal reforms as a means of shoring up his regime and to cease aiding the royalists. The mission failed, but it confirmed Washington's apprehensions. Kennedy demanded another approach to strengthen Faisal's shaky hold.[64]

In February President Kennedy convened a meeting to review U.S. policy on Yemen. Komer participated, as did under secretary of State for Political Affairs George McGhee, Phillips Talbot, Assistant Secretary of Defense Paul Nitze, and the chairman of the Joint Chiefs of Staff, Army general Earle "Bus" Wheeler. Komer's bold thinking set the tone for the meeting. His idea was to exchange the facade of American protection of Saudi Arabia for a Saudi commitment to cease support to the royalists and a U.S. pledge to build up Saudi air defenses. On that basis, the United States would pressure Nasser to withdraw his troops from Yemen, thereby ending the conflict. The U.S. mission, called Operation Hard Surface, would consist of "eight little planes" that would project a concrete image of American power.[65] Kennedy agreed to the concept and decided to send Ellsworth Bunker to Faisal as a special emissary with a presidential letter in hand that would offer him a "plate glass fighter squadron" if Faisal would agree to cease his support to the royalists. Nitze expressed the Defense Department's dismay at this approach. It was a risky venture, and it might actually provoke a war with the UAR. If that outcome occurred, the United States would be hugely unpopular with a number of Arab states. Further, the deployment of the squadron required better facilities than were present in Saudi Arabia, including radar to detect air threats. Komer, aided by Talbot, countered by pointing out that the United States had warned Nasser about bombings, but it turned out to be an empty threat. A squadron in Saudi Arabia would add credibility to the U.S. position. Talbot added that another sweetener would be to offer Faisal assistance in developing a capable air defense system for his country. Nitze agreed that this tactic had merit, but it had to be contingent on Faisal suspending aid to the royalists. The discussion continued with Talbot underscoring that the Bunker mission needed to dovetail with UN secretary general U Thant's decision to send UN assistant secretary general Ralph Bunche on a fact-finding mission to the region. Kennedy digested this information and directed that the Bunker mission should proceed. If Faisal accepted the proposal, then Nasser would be told that the squadron was a necessary step to get Faisal to stop supporting the royalists. Further, he agreed to send the squadron to Saudi Arabia but only for a few months; in actuality the United States would be prepared to keep it there longer if required. Komer suggested that Bunker inform Faisal that if he resumed gun running to the royalists after accepting the U.S. proposal, the squadron would be withdrawn, and Kennedy agreed. Yet Kennedy had little confidence that Faisal would accept these conditions.[66]

Kennedy wrote again to Macmillan urging the British to recognize the YAR. It could be potentially embarrassing to Britain; if the UN mediation effort was acceptable to all the other parties, recognition of the new republic would likely be a precondition for mediation. The president received a cool response because, nearly simultaneously, the YAR asked the British chargé in Yemen to leave the country. The British took offense, and Macmillan told Kennedy that his government could not recognize the YAR under those circumstances.[67]

As these events played out, the UAR conducted another bombing raid in Saudi territory. Komer informed Kennedy that Nasser justified the UAR attack as a means of halting Saudi arms flows to the royalists and not as an attempt to overthrow Faisal. Nasser added that the UAR would not conduct any bombing missions for a few weeks to give Bunker's mediation efforts a chance. Komer viewed this as a positive indication that Nasser did not want to alienate the United States, but U.S. ambassador to Egypt John Badeau misrepresented U.S. intentions by resting his argument for the cessation on Bunker's progress in mediation. Badeau's "pitch" worried Komer, for if the Bunker mission stalled, then Nasser could argue that he gave the process a chance and it failed. He could also resume bombing.[68] It was apparent to Komer that to convince the Saudis to cut off aid to the royalists, the administration would have to guarantee their security.

Bunker met with Kennedy in March and received his instructions to act as Kennedy's emissary. He would operate only at the pinnacle of the UAR and Saudi Kingdom governments, meeting with Nasser and Faisal.[69] Bunker left immediately for Saudi Arabia with Secretary of State Dean Rusk's cheerless good-bye resounding in his ears: "Be sure to tell Faisal that we will not be dragged into his little war in Yemen."[70] Kennedy played his part in preventing such a war too. He wrote to Faisal immediately, indicating that he was sending Bunker to meet with him and reassured him of the U.S. commitment to Saudi Arabia's integrity. Nonetheless, he also indicated that it was critical for the Saudis to disengage from Yemen, that a UN mediator would provide a face-saving mechanism, and that if the Saudis agreed to this approach, then the United States would consider stationing air defense in Saudi Arabia to deter UAR aggression.[71]

As March wore on, little progress toward disengagement was made; none of the parties had embraced the plan. Bunker was doing a wonderful job of explaining U.S. intentions to Faisal, but that was not the objective. Komer stressed that Faisal realized he was supporting the losing side and that Bunche, who had been dispatched to the region by Thant, was making progress in his talks with Nasser and YAR leader Colonel al-Sallal. Komer now laid out a new strategy for Kennedy. First, Bunker should keep the mediation efforts moving by traveling to Cairo and Sana. The impetus for a compromise would have to come from Bunker, who would have to shape the preliminary mutual disengagement agreement as the UN was acting too slowly. Perhaps after Bunker succeeded in developing a framework, the UN could assume responsibility. Second, Bunker should return to Riyadh to inform Faisal that his "conditions" for a UAR withdrawal could not be sold to Nasser and that he should accept a cease-fire pending further mediation efforts. Komer realized that the United States would almost certainly have to send an air squadron since it was a negotiating point for Bunker, but he worried about an indefinite military commitment.[72]

Bunker reported to Kennedy after his meeting in Riyadh that Faisal, lacking confidence in U.S. support, was in poor spirits. Bunker had stressed to the Saudi prime minister that it was difficult for the United States to help him when he was supporting the overthrow of a government it had recognized. By the end of the meeting, Bunker observed, Faisal was in a better frame of mind but had balked at the provisions of the U.S. disengagement plan, adding conditions of his own that Bunker characterized as unworkable. Faisal did indicate that he would receive Bunche. Bunker also reported on his earlier meeting with Thant and Bunche, and after listening to Bunche regarding his talks with Sallal and Nasser, Bunker believed that disengagement could work. Komer now remarked that the problem was getting the parties to agree simultaneously and especially keeping Nasser from attacking the Saudis during the mediation efforts.[73] The mediation efforts by Bunche and Bunker continued.

————————————

Kennedy watched the Bunker mission closely, with Komer reporting to him daily. Faisal remained concerned about U.S. commitment to the Saudi kingdom. The idea of sending a squadron to Saudi Arabia on a temporary basis surfaced again. The squadron would act as a visible sign of U.S. intentions and a deterrent to Nasser's aerial forays, if the Saudis would commit to the disengagement scheme. The fighter squadron would be deployed but without combat capability. It was a political gesture for which neither Faisal nor Nasser was any the wiser. Kennedy was intimately involved in the details of sending the aircraft and making decisions about the rules of engagement, as he was concerned about the potential for a U.S. fighter to be involved in combat with a UAR fighter. He knew that if that happened, it would ignite a Middle East conflict in which the United States would be involved directly. The Joint Chiefs of Staff remained wary; noting that one squadron was an insufficient force in case blows were exchanged. Kennedy and Secretary of Defense McNamara explained that the fighter aircraft were merely a sign of political commitment and that a larger force sent the wrong message and only increased the likelihood of creating a problem.[74]

Promising to send the squadron to Saudi Arabia proved to be a necessary lubricant for the disengagement scheme to work. Faisal agreed to the concept in principle, and Nasser signaled the same. For three weeks Faisal and U.S. ambassador to Saudi Arabia Parker Hart pleaded for the squadron, but Kennedy told Komer, "I don't want the squadron out there until after we are 99 percent certain it won't have to be used."[75]

Delays continued, but Bunker, after shuttling between Cairo and Riyadh for nearly a month, managed to broker an agreement in principle as the civil war was dying down. He informed Washington of his success on April 10, and Thant made a public announcement on April 30. The parties had to wait until Thant and the UN Security Council approved the measure. UN sponsorship of the Yemen disengagement plan lagged in the Security Council.[76] Meanwhile, Komer pressed the State Department to convey to Faisal through Hart to stop pushing supplies to the royalists. He opposed sending the planes to Saudi Arabia until Faisal complied with the agreed terms.[77] In June Thant finally realized that the Soviet Union was stalling on a Security Council resolution approving the plan. He subsequently issued his report indicating that he considered the disengagement plan to be in effect and that he was sending an advance party of the UN observer force to Yemen. The Security Council, with the Soviet Union abstaining, approved the Yemen mission's mandate for two months on June 10.[78] The UN observer force headed by Swedish general Carl van Horn, consisting of Yugoslav troops and Canadian airmen, arrived in Yemen three days later, with the "war in full swing," and began its operations along the Saudi-YAR border in early July.[79]

Komer was disappointed with how long it had taken to get a mediation effort. He believed that if the agreement had been signed in April and had not been delayed in the UN, the Yemen crisis might have ended by the middle of 1963. Kennedy had no recourse but to send the air squadron to Saudi Arabia, and he approved its deployment on July 3.[80] A week later Komer informed Kennedy that the situation was improving, "though it's folly to be too optimistic." The Saudis apparently had ended their aid to the royalists because they were concerned that the U.S. squadron would be withdrawn if they cheated on the bargain. Nasser, however, was not meeting his part of the bargain to withdraw troops. Badeau and Talbot pressured the UAR government representatives in Cairo and Washington, and Nasser responded that he would withdraw troops in August. Komer's reaction was negative—not quick enough—especially with the UN mission funded only through September 1. He continued to press the State Department to make U.S. views clear to Nasser and his representatives.[81]

Kennedy also summoned Egyptian ambassador Mostafa Kamel to the White House in late July to inform him that he expected a sign of good faith from Nasser.[82] August slipped into September with little progress on actual disengagement by both Nasser and Faisal, but the two leaders expressed a willingness to talk about a political solution in Yemen, which the United States promoted with the rationale that if they were talking, then "they'll at least be less inclined to start shooting." Weeks passed, and although both sides continued to convey an interest in disengagement, neither demonstrated a willingness to proceed.[83]

In mid-September Komer wrote a paper to clarify his thinking and advise Kennedy and Bundy on the way ahead. Komer stated the evident:

disengagement was not working. Nasser would not leave until the YAR was politically and militarily stable, but he was "trapped in Yemen" and "It's bleeding him." Saudi Arabia had reduced support but perhaps not eliminated it, and the United Kingdom continued to support the royalists. Thant was looking for a way out of the mess too. Komer recognized that there were various ways to influence the outcome, but no viable solution. As the State Department pointed out, there was no option but the middle course already taken. The United States was trapped. Komer concluded that he saw "no better prescription than sustained diplomatic pressure" on Nasser and Faisal, "repeated leaning on the UN to keep up its flagging energy, and no doubt continued presence of our eight planes (which we originally hoped to have out in sixty days or so)." On a positive note, the United States prevented the Yemen crisis from "blowing up into something far more painful." Komer believed that a deal could be worked out between Nasser and Faisal.[84]

Kennedy would not give up either, although the UN mission was unraveling, Nasser was stalling, and Faisal was furious because the UAR was not pulling out its troops. Komer advised Kennedy that if the UN withdrew, then the situation would regress to the point it had been five months previous.[85] On October 10, 1963, Kennedy signed a new presidential directive, which Komer drafted, that reiterated U.S. policy to work with all parties to effect the disengagement agreement and to prevent an escalation of the fighting. The Pentagon had been lobbying to remove the squadron from Saudi Arabia. The president quelled that effort by directing that the aircraft remain in place as evidence of U.S. steadfastness.[86]

A few days later a UN Security Council vote to renew the UN Yemen Observer Mission (UNYOM) almost came unglued when Yugoslavia considered pulling out its troops. Kennedy had to twist Yugoslav president Josip Tito's arm to keep them there, and the U.S. permanent representative to the UN, Adlai Stevenson, pressed the Canadians to do the same, which they did once Tito agreed.[87] Faisal whined about Egyptian attacks, and Kennedy again reaffirmed U.S. support if the Egyptians attacked Saudi Arabia, but he emphasized that the U.S. squadron would not be used for defensive measures.[88] The president also contacted Nasser again, scolding him for not disengaging and personalizing the message by pointing out that he was being criticized in Congress for the administration's Yemen policy.[89] On October 31, after Thant had earlier indicated that UNYOM would be withdrawn because of a lack of funding, the UN Security Council extended the mission for two months when Saudi Arabia and the UAR agreed to help finance it.[90]

The October decision ended the Kennedy administration's involvement in the Yemen crisis. It also concluded what Arthur M. Schlesinger Jr. called "one of Kennedy's most interesting experiments in foreign policy" and, equally, a failure to "turn Egyptian energies inward."[91] For Komer, despite his intense efforts, it was a personal setback in that he shared in the U.S. government's inability to direct Nasser's interest toward internal reform and cease his meddling throughout the region. The Yemeni crisis gradually eroded the basis for U.S. policy toward Nasser, and the Kennedy administration abandoned its plans for enlarged economic assistance in the face of Nasser's refusal to disengage and a congressional move to end U.S. recognition of UNYOM. Nasser's increasing reliance on Soviet arms and advisers also damaged the policy. Nonetheless, Komer consoled himself with the belief that although disengagement had not occurred, at least the strategy of preventive diplomacy averted a war between two important Middle East states.[92]

Recent analysts of the Kennedy administration's Middle East policy are less harsh in their assessment of its outcomes. Faisal actively sought the intervention of the Western powers in the Yemen civil war as a means of discrediting or even defeating Nasser to blunt the appeal of his republican and nationalist ideas in the Saudi kingdom. That the Kennedy administration chose to play the honest broker was not only an indication of its understanding of the political dynamics at play, and not communist subversion, but also a warning to Faisal to reform and modernize since the greatest threat was from internal division and not external causes. He heeded this counsel a month after meeting with Kennedy.[93]

Further, in assuming a balanced approach, the administration managed to retain cordial relations with Egypt. It recognized Nasser as the incontestable leader of the Arab world and, more importantly, as a means of influence in the region. In maintaining this relationship, Nasser did not become a wild card, bent on promoting Soviet interests to blossom in the "Arab East." Instead, the policy ensured that cheap oil continued to flow to a Europe dependent on its availability and kept the Israeli-Arab conflict in the so-called icebox, postponing war between Israel and the Arab states.[94] Although these accomplishments were fleeting and a qualified success,

Komer should be credited with fashioning a U.S. policy that not only was exceedingly different from that of its predecessors and its successor but also promoted U.S. interests.

Personally, Komer gained a closer relationship with Kennedy and, more importantly, the chief executive's trust, which was crucial to having credibility as other issues in Komer's portfolio arose. Komer was no longer simply a name on a memorandum or someone who occasionally attended meetings between Kennedy and his principal advisers. As Phillips Talbot, the assistant secretary of state for Near Eastern and South Asian affairs, acknowledged, "It was basically Komer in the White House counsels who would stake out the foreign policy position."[95] Komer was now the New Frontiersman the president contacted directly on policy matters associated with the Middle East and South Asia for the remainder of his term in office.

CHAPTER 4

"Our India Enterprise"

*J*ohn Kenneth Galbraith had difficulty sleeping despite his heavy use of narcotics. He understood President Kennedy's preoccupation with the Cuban crisis, but he had a full-blown calamity on his hands that had become extremely demanding for even this physically and intellectually imposing man. As U.S. ambassador to India, Galbraith, the former Harvard economist and Kennedy confidante, watched the Sino-India border dispute, which started as a string of skirmishes in early September 1962, grow into a major conflict by the end of October, and he had no instruction from Washington on what the U.S. policy stance was. Not a single telegram, letter, telephone call, or other communication of guidance had been received in New Delhi, he confided in his journal. Only one message had arrived from the Department of State informing him what not to say. He had not been idle, nor was he studying the situation as Foggy Bottom claimed it was doing. He had acted, sending cable after cable to Secretary of State Rusk about what steps should be taken. Yet he had no inkling as to whether anyone in Washington was reading them, let alone acting on them. The absence of communication meant that Galbraith was getting his military intelligence from the Indian newspapers.[1]

Discouraging reports filtered back to New Delhi from India's northern frontier. In a mere week, after heavy Chinese attacks on two fronts, the Indian troops' confidence had disintegrated. Currents of panic and fear surged through the upper levels of the Indian government; this led Indian defense minister V. K. Krishna Menon to wonder where the well-equipped Chinese forces would be stopped by Indian forces, if they were stopped at all. Prime Minister Jawaharlal Nehru called for all-out resistance, warning that India's independence was threatened, and ultimately declared a national emergency. In the Himalayas' thin, frigid air—at ten thousand feet or more of altitude—unconditioned soldiers shivered in summer uniforms for want of winter gear, wearing canvas shoes as their protection from the snow. The Chinese onslaught continued, Indian forces reeling from each blow were forced to fall back deeper into India.[2]

By late October 1962 Komer had begun hovering over the situation like an agitated wasp. He read Galbraith's cables and supported Carl Kaysen, the Harvard professor on academic leave who had replaced Rostow as deputy national security adviser, while the other members of the foreign policy team worried about initiating Armageddon with the Soviets over Cuba. Washington's response to the Chinese attack had been a strongly worded public statement indicating it "was shocked at the violent and aggressive action of the Chinese communists against India."[3] Komer knew, however, that now the administration would have to address the strategic value of India as a bulwark against Communist China, whose malicious criticisms of Kennedy had been constant since his inauguration.[4] He assessed the border conflict as "potentially one of the most critical events of the decade."[5] The favorable opportunity he had been waiting for to refashion U.S. policy toward India was at hand.

Kennedy's selection of Galbraith as ambassador set the tone for how his administration planned to conduct its relations with India. The president gave his confidante authorization to deal directly with the White House, a channel Galbraith used often because he considered communicating through the State Department like "fornicating through a mattress."[6] His occasional private letters to the chief executive became part of his campaign of bypassing the official network to strengthen U.S.-Indian relations, which was especially important given his prickly relationship with Rusk.[7]

On a daily basis, a hundred issues assailed Kennedy, and Galbraith's immediate influence on foreign policy formulation was minimal. Thus, Komer often acted as their interlocutor.[8] Nonetheless, Komer had ideas of his own. He had favored a reappraisal of South Asian policy since his days on the NSC Planning Board. He wanted a policy shift from primary support to Pakistan and very little for India to a more pro-Indian policy with greater aid for India. Although U.S. military assistance to Pakistan was designated for use against the Soviets to the north, Pakistan managed to use the aid primarily to reequip their forces deployed against India. Komer knew championing a policy change would not be easy, but he thought that if the United States had to choose between India and Pakistan, it should support the former. It was more crucial, he stated, "to support an India with 400 million people than Pakistan with a 100 million, divided into two parts, against a much larger India." Further, the Pakistanis were passionately anti-India and were constantly afraid that India would attempt to reunify the subcontinent. Komer thought the likelihood of such an attempt was non-existent. If it did occur, then the United States would have greater influence in halting Indian aggression if it had good relations with that nation. While India's neutralist policy and its official statements could be irritating, it was not anti-American.[9]

In December 1961, when the Department of Defense was considering the level of U.S. military assistance to Pakistan for the upcoming fiscal years, Komer decided to raise the issue of a more balanced policy approach. He reasoned that India and Japan were the only regional equals with sufficient economic and human potential able to stand up to Asia's emerging power, Communist China (that is, the People's Republic of China). He also grasped that his timing might be favorable. One of the major factors that made revision of long-standing South Asian policy possible was he had allies in place: Galbraith in India and Phillips Talbot, the assistant secretary of state responsible for the region, who was not Arabist but a man whose primary experience had been India.[10] Although these men favored the same end, they did not agree on the pace of the policy shift or the tactics to be employed.[11] The position of the Pentagon, however, was clear-cut; it was not pleased about Komer initiating a debate on this issue.

A month later Komer sent a memorandum to Bundy titled, "A New Look at the Pakistani Tie." Komer's opening words were a pugilistic burst: Pakistani president Mohammed Ayub Khan's recent démarche to Rusk was offensive, a patronizing lecture on how the United States should conduct its policy toward India. Komer argued that Pakistan's policy differences with the new administration on Afghanistan, Kashmir, and India demonstrated the need for a new approach to relations with Pakistan. Besides, Ayub's interest in an alliance with the United States was to keep the Afghans and Indians in check, not the communists in Asia: "he forces us into a position which runs contrary to our larger strategic interests in the area." Ayub held the tactical advantage, and the United States received little from the relationship except for intelligence facilities and paper commitments to the

Central Treaty Organization and SEATO. Komer granted that acting as an honest broker was a valuable role, but if choices had to be made, he favored supporting neutralist India because its interests coincided with those of the United States. India did not realize it yet, he observed, but China was forcing the Indians to move toward improved relations with the United States because simmering border disputes would ignite an eventual crisis. Pakistan, he continued, needs the United States more than the converse. He ended his thoughts as if he had just reviewed a scorecard, declaring that the United States "had better take a new look at our Pakistan relationship and ask whether we are giving too much and not getting enough in return."[12] Bundy did not acknowledge the memorandum, so Komer also sent a note to Kaysen with ideas on a Kashmir settlement, which he knew was an impediment to his policy goals.

For more than a decade India and Pakistan had argued over this area in the northwestern Indian subcontinent. The United States had supported Pakistan on resolving the Kashmir issue in the UN for several years. Komer viewed the quarrel over Kashmir as irresolvable because India, which occupied most of the area, was not going to accept a compromise. In a move that was surprising to many, Kennedy directed the State Department to discourage Ayub from action on the subject in the Security Council.[13] This development stunned the Pakistanis. However, it did not end U.S. involvement. Kennedy, desirous of bringing the two countries together to talk about a settlement, wrote Ayub and Nehru proposing that a U.S. diplomat act as a mediator. Pakistan accepted the invitation, but India demurred; Nehru preferred bilateral negotiations, as he did not want a third party to determine questions of Indian sovereignty.[14] Rebuffed, Kennedy discontinued his involvement in South Asian affairs.

The Kennedy administration certainly could not ignore India when the Chinese Communist aggression occurred in that late summer of 1962. On September 8, 1962, a small number of Communist Chinese troops crossed into Indian territory at a point in the North-East Frontier Agency (NEFA) near the border with Bhutan. Chinese intentions were initially confusing because as their forces attacked they shouted in Hindi, "Hindi-Chini Bhai-Bhai!" (Indians and Chinese are brothers). The Chinese moved toward the Indian military post at Dhola, about one to two miles inside Indian-claimed territory in the NEFA, but the Indian troops did not fire.

To the world, the Communist Chinese government claimed that its forces were "frontier guards" making a defensive attack against Indian aggression. The Indians asserted otherwise. The Chinese attackers then withdrew from Indian territory, but twelve hundred soldiers returned the next day. Again, the Chinese forces halted, but this time they dug in defensive positions. Nehru and Menon were convinced that the incursion was not serious, just another minor scuffle like others that had occurred periodically for nearly four years as the two nations made competing territorial claims in the northern frontier. Both men had planned overseas trips and left India unconcerned. Neither leader appreciated the extent of Chinese mobilization until October 20, when a massive number of Chinese troops poured into India. A rout soon ensued.[15] In the onslaught, elite units of the Indian Army's 4th Division were badly mauled,[16] giving lie to the Indian adage that when elephants fight, only the grass gets hurt.

Kennedy could not disregard Nehru's letter of appeal for help when it arrived a week later, especially when the prime minister dropped all pretense of nonalignment.[17] The Indian government also made requests for U.S. assistance through Ambassador Galbraith and the State Department for the urgent purchase of aircraft spare parts, military cargo aircraft, and communications equipment. As a gesture of India's good faith, U.S. military attachés, who had not enjoyed close relations with their counterparts, would be kept apprised of all developments.[18] The United States responded by providing its first military assistance on November 3.[19]

Komer worried the administration would let its preoccupation with the Soviets over Cuba distract it from the events along India's northern frontier. "Though we still see through a glass darkly," he wrote Talbot, "we may have a golden opportunity for a major gain in our relations with India. The sheer magnitude of India's reversal on the ChiCom [Chinese Communist] border may at long last awaken Delhi to the weakness of its position." He added that although delicate handling was required, the administration must be prepared to act quickly and not let the opportunity slip by. Not only was the Indian government frustrated, but it was perhaps bordering on despair and uncertain what to do next. It was clearly feeling out the United States and the Soviet Union regarding help. "The Indians seem to be relying largely on the Soviets to help bail them out" by intervening with the Chinese. This, Komer argued, was a misperception; "Sino-Soviet relations have reached a nadir." Komer also worried about Pakistan and thought the United States could do more to press Ayub not to take advantage of the situation by attacking the Indian army of occupation in Kashmir. Holding back might put Ayub in a better negotiating position for a peaceful settlement of this old nuisance. Further, the administration needed to signal clearly to Ayub that the United States would not back Pakistan against India. Nonetheless, Komer concluded that the "Sino-Indian conflict may have entered a stage whose long-term implications are fully comparable to those arising from Cuba. If necessary, we should force these on the top echelon, once we've decided how we ought to move."[20] It was, as Arthur Schlesinger Jr. wrote, "the opportunity to consolidate the American friendship with India."[21] The opportunity was enhanced when on November 7 Nehru, under pressure from his own political party and public opinion, fired Menon, who was viewed as partly responsible for India's inadequate military readiness. His dismissal eliminated Washington's main nemesis to closer relations.[22]

A week later the United States and India exchanged diplomatic notes, which established a formal basis for the military assistance that the United States had been providing for more than a week. The document indicated that the U.S. military assistance was to help India defend itself from "outright Chinese aggression."[23] A few days later Komer outlined for Kaysen how the United States should approach the Indians. He maintained that the Sino-India dispute presented two important ends for the United States: forcing India to reexamine its foreign policy and having the potential for promoting India-Pakistan reconciliation. He urged a thorough examination of long-term options instead of a frenzied response to the crisis.[24]

Komer also succeeded in convincing Kennedy to send a letter to Ayub to prevent Pakistan's remonstrance concerning the military aid offer the United States had made to India. Such a letter put the Pakistanis on the defensive and prevented them from squeezing the United States to get more aid or to force the administration to seek an Indian commitment on a Kashmir plebiscite. Komer underscored that the administration was in for a lengthy and painful dialogue with Ayub, but the Chinese attack justified a long-needed modification in U.S. policy. He believed that this policy adjustment could be achieved without losing Pakistan if it was handled properly. Again, he cautioned that the United States express "tolerant understanding but no give on our part, while the Paks readjust their thinking to the facts of life."[25]

Nonetheless, Komer expressed to Talbot his reservations about the approach the State Department was taking in its consultations with the British. The dominant theme appeared to be preventing the Sino-Indian confrontation from expanding so a "disastrous strain on the fragile Indian body politic or critical shortfalls in economic development" did not occur. Although Komer shared these concerns, he also noted that if they became the dominant features of U.S. thinking, they would overshadow the potential gains to the United States. The concern was not whether there was risk in escalation but that the whole affair would diminish before desirable changes in Indian and Pakistani attitudes developed. "Perhaps," he mused, "this view smacks too much of realpolitik," but he offered sound reasoning. The Chinese sought only limited territorial objectives, he argued, which was apparent from their various "peace" offers. They wanted the Ladakh area to protect the Aksai Chin road. Their tactical gains were largely an unpremeditated seizure of an opportunity: take as much of the territory that they believed they needed once they had "punched through the thin Indian crust." He doubted that the Chinese would move through the NEFA onto the plains of Assam, where they faced greater operational problems as well as world approbation. A wider U.S. perspective should prevail. He wrote, "Wars of this sort have often served as a national unifying force, a means of transcending local differences and focusing a nation's energies in a way not otherwise possible." The Indians as well as the Pakistanis needed to reassess their policies in light of the conflict. At a minimum, U.S. aid to India would gradually drive home to the Pakistanis that they could not rely on the United States to satisfy their demands on India. The Indians needed to understand that Pakistani-Indian strife is an "impossible luxury" in view of the greater Chinese threat. This change in perspective would take time to mature and so would the end of the Indian reliance on the Soviet Union. India had not shed all its illusions, which had been ingrained for generations. However, the United States should not be put off by the prospect of a substantial bill to modernize the Indian army. Komer wrote, "India is going to modernize anyway and (as Galbraith loves to point out) we'll be subsidizing it indirectly through our economic aid." His main point was that this episode needed to be used to create an atmosphere for the resolution of Pakistani-Indian differences and American leverage with both parties should be used to this end.[26]

Events moved quickly in Washington. At a meeting in the Oval Office a week later, discussion about the next steps that should occur ensued. Rusk wanted the British Commonwealth nations to weigh in with more aid and to take the lead. Secretary of Defense McNamara suggested that a small U.S. military mission be sent to India to assess the situation. The United States could not wait for the Commonwealth to act because, given the Chinese forces' vigorous attack, it might be too late. At the very least, the Indians needed U.S. C-130 cargo aircraft to move troops and supplies to the fighting. Komer added his voice, agreeing that providing the transport aircraft was critical as it might deter the Chinese by signaling U.S. willingness to get involved "in a big way." Finally, after several more minutes of discussion, Kennedy decided that the mission, led by Averell Harriman, assistant secretary of state for Far Eastern affairs, should go to Delhi to demonstrate support for India and as a signal of deterrence to the Chinese. Further, the United States would send some C-130s and the requested spare parts, and it would push the Commonwealth to get more involved.[27]

Meanwhile, Indian morale was flagging rapidly, and "General" Galbraith, as Komer nicknamed him, was having a hard time separating hope from reality. There was widespread alarm in Delhi on November 20 as rumors abounded about Chinese advances. Nehru asked the United States to provide an "air umbrella" of fourteen U.S. fighter squadrons to defend Indian cities. Galbraith disagreed with the request and instead proposed that ships from the U.S. Seventh Fleet in the Pacific be sent to the Bay of Bengal. Komer seized on the appeal. McNamara and the Navy were reluctant to send a carrier battle group to the Indian Ocean, but after considerable coaxing from Komer and others, a carrier deployed from the Sea of Japan.[28]

Komer also questioned the intelligence analyses of Chinese intentions. He assessed that the Chinese proposals demonstrated that they intended to end this affair on favorable terms instead of risking escalation. The risks were too great: combat operations on the plain of Assam made them vulnerable to Indian airpower and armor and put them on "the wrong end of a tortuous" line of communication; the Chinese did not want the United States and Great Britain to enter the conflict; and the Chinese could not count on Soviet support. The Chinese had the land they wanted. Komer told Bundy he would discuss this analysis with the State Department and hoped to achieve a consensus. If that occurred, then the administration would have to examine the implications for U.S. policy immediately.[29]

Komer's discussions with State Department personnel did not result in consensus. Consequently, he informed Bundy that the State Department's proposal was a settlement along the frontier that would provide security for India and avoid a large and intensive war. The State Department was too worried about the impact such a war would have on Indian economic prospects and its delicate political fabric. The Defense Department, with the exception of McNamara, was reluctant to envisage a major additional aid commitment, which it suspected might be at the expense of existing programs in Asia. Komer thought both viewpoints were too narrow.[30]

Administration officials, particularly the intelligence community, which had a communications intercept facility near Peshawar to monitor Soviet military activities, were also concerned about how Pakistan would react to the provision of U.S. aid to India. Komer summarized his views for the president: "The Pakistanis are going through a genuine emotional crisis as they see their cherished ambitions of using the U.S. as a lever against India going up in the smoke of the Chinese border war." The Pakistani government had expected the administration to consult with them on the assistance, but this expectation was transparently a delaying tactic. Komer offered that the Pakistani position should be treated with sympathy, but he urged equally strongly that there be "no give in our position." There was no need to apologize or to compensate Ayub, doing so would only be "postponing the long-needed clarification of our position." Komer counseled that Pakistan might move from words to action, but that depended on how willing Ayub was to jeopardize the relationship with the United States. Ayub would test the relationship, but Komer remained convinced that the Pakistanis understood that in the last analysis, they gained too much from the tie to do without it. This was not a foregone conclusion, but "if we can weather the current shock, we should be able to hold on to our assets in Pakistan, while still managing the sub-continent-wide policy toward which we aim."[31]

A week after he wrote the memo to the president, having considered the issue again, Komer thought the United States was "duty bound" to inform Ayub of the direction in which the administration was moving and that Kennedy should inform him personally, as anything less would be insulting. In a memorandum to Kaysen, he wrote, "We don't want to enter what may be a truly major policy enterprise with the key ally who can help us most standing disgruntled on the sidelines." He provided a draft letter for the president to send Ayub.[32]

None of the hand-wringing mattered, however, as events on the ground settled the issue. The Indian army, understrength, poorly equipped for the mountain climate and high-altitude warfare, with inferior weapons, and without sufficient communications equipment to maintain command and control, could not match the Chinese forces even with U.S. and British military assistance. On November 21 the Chinese, having obtained their military objectives, unilaterally declared a cease-fire and then withdrew two weeks later from the majority of the territory they had overrun. Nonetheless, China retained 2,500 square miles of captured real estate. A Chinese government spokesman said that India had been taught a lesson.[33]

Galbraith did not desist in his support to India once the crisis seemed to have passed. He pointed out to Kennedy that the Indians could not defend against a Chinese air attack and were worried about such an event. It was the reason that the Indians had withheld close air support from the army. Galbraith knew Indian anxieties had their basis in a Japanese air attack on Calcutta during World War II. Although it had been a trivial affair, it had caused psychological damage, which was what the Nehru government feared would happen again if hostilities between India and Communist China reignited. The administration decided that a series of joint U.S.-Indian air exercises would serve a useful purpose as a deterrent to the Chinese. Astonishingly, Kennedy had very little concern that the United States might be drawn into a conflict with the Chinese. He thought that although the United States did not have any treaty obligations to the Indians, the American public and Congress would be solidly behind the administration if intervention were necessary.[34]

Accordingly, Kennedy pressed his advisers for ways in which the United States and the United Kingdom could support the Indian government in the postcrisis period. A subcommittee of the NSC's Executive Committee, the small, high-level foreign policy operations group chaired by the president and set up to manage the Cuban missile crisis, was established to study various military and political recommendations and report to the president. Talbot chaired the group, which consisted of Komer and officials from the Office of the Secretary of Defense, USAID, and the Joint Staff. It made its first recommendations to Kennedy in early December, urging continued U.S. assistance to India over the next two to three months and notifying the president that it would explore the feasibility of an air defense package for India, consistent with the Harriman mission's assessment, and report its findings shortly.[35] Less than a week later the Joint Chiefs recommended to McNamara that the United States assist the Indians but minimally, providing radar systems in the near term and additional radar and air-to-air missiles to the Indian Air Force in the long term. The Joint Chiefs maintained that the British should take the lead for implementing an Indian air defense program.[36]

Galbraith continued peppering Washington with requests for assistance and policy recommendations before arriving for consultations with the president in advance of Kennedy's summit with British Prime Minister Harold Macmillan in Nassau later in December. Komer counseled that the situation called for delicate handling. First, it was not in U.S. interests to press too hard for a Kashmir settlement. It would only get the Indians' "backs up" at a time when the United States needed them to focus on China, and the administration should certainly not tie further military assistance to a settlement. Second, using the British as the mediator for a settlement was folly; the Indians did not trust them. Instead, only a "European type settlement (customs union, joint defense, etc.)" that upheld Indian sovereignty would likely be acceptable. Third, the air defense package was a sensible offer, but the British should not be credited with providing air squadrons while the United States provided low visibility items such as radar. Komer urged his superiors not to let the United States take a backseat to the British or some "wraith-like entity called the 'Commonwealth.'" He ended with his old theme: if the Sino-Indian clash ends too quickly, then the administration will not get a Kashmir settlement or bring to fruition the major shift in Indian attitudes that the United States wanted. The essential goal was to keep India's anti-Chinese nationalism in "full tide."[37]

A few weeks later Komer sent Kennedy another report of the interagency subcommittee that detailed matters requiring Kennedy's decision and then discussion when he met with Macmillan. Komer outlined the caution that the subcommittee members had articulated: Defense Department concerns about the expense of redeploying forces, the adverse effects of reallocating military assistance from other clients and the difficulty that approach may have in gaining congressional approval, and State Department's fear that the United States would be drawn into a Sino-Indian war. The departments wanted Britain to be out front, but Komer rightly pointed out that Macmillan had no appetite for such a role. Komer considered these cautious steps trifling when compared to the gift that China had bestowed, "a grand design," an opportunity to attain an eventual Kashmir settlement and India-Pakistan reconciliation, as well as a means of inducing India, with its aroused nationalistic fervor, to join the United States in the containment of China. With a Machiavellian flourish, Komer stated that it was "as much in our strategic interest to keep up a high degree of Sino-Indian friction as it is to prevent it from spilling over into a large-scale war." The United States had to stiffen the Indian spine and not allow Nehru's government to settle too quickly. Further, this was not the time to push for a compromise on Kashmir because neither side was ready and it might actually hinder progress. At the very least, it would divert Indian nationalist anger from China to Pakistan, and the former, he reminded the president, was the strategic priority. Komer recognized that his strategy was riskier than the subcommittee's proposal, but the stakes warranted it.[38]

Kennedy and Macmillan met in Nassau for three days just before Christmas, and although the South Asia situation was a topic, discussions about nuclear defense systems overshadowed it. The two leaders did inform Nehru, however, that they were willing to send a joint U.S.-UK team to Delhi to study strengthening India's air defense capabilities, which Komer had insisted was the main concern.

As the New Year started, Komer and Galbraith, although their rationales differed, continued to push for military assistance to strengthen the Indians. Galbraith worried about the reasonably substantial chance that the Chinese would renew attacks. Komer thought such a contingency was "highly unlikely" and "foolhardy." He held a broader perspective and argued that the administration's policy aims with India should be twofold.[39]

The first goal was to get the Indians to recognize definitively that their interests lay with the West. He held that the Indians did not need to change their official nonaligned posture, but they had to be clear in their own minds where they stood. It would have been easier to harness their nationalist fervor, but this already seemed to be spent. The second goal was to achieve a Pakistani-Indian reconciliation, which demanded a Kashmir settlement, but not ahead of helping the Indians to recognize the Chinese threat and not by allowing the Pakistanis to make unrealistic demands, which would only torpedo any chances.[40]

Komer was also troubled about Galbraith's "siren songs about Southeast Asia," which encouraged the Indians to believe that their quid pro quo for U.S. military aid would be vague promises to support U.S. containment efforts in that region. The emphasis, Komer contended, should be on "such gestures as a carrier visit, a promised air defense package and a high level of continued aid [which] have real political significance in terms of bucking up Indian morale" and providing them a sense of confidence about U.S. support if they took a hard line with the Chinese. The administration was walking a "fine line between such eagerness to help Delhi that it [India] concludes it is under no pressure to settle Kashmir, and making a settlement so much a precedent for any major aid that we divert Indian focus from the China issue." Komer did not want to appear bellicose, but he did not want to be too cautious and fail to exploit the situation.[41]

Komer followed this assessment with a letter to Galbraith, in which he welcomed Indian interest in "helping to contain Chicoms in Asia." "It is part of our grand design," he continued, "to engage India as well as Japan in sharing a burden, which we have had to carry almost single handed so far." He saw two kinds of help the United States needed from India: political and military. The former entailed India's support in the UN, the International Control Commission for Laos, and other international forums. The latter concerned developing gradually a defense arrangement, not as part of SEATO but something still undefined. Komer was still chary about a Kashmir settlement, but based on the Nassau discussions and Kennedy's interest, the United States could stress a linkage between providing assistance and progress on Kashmir. This approach was a limited and "one-time opportunity," to "remove the canker." Congressional hostility to U.S. aid to India and Pakistan remained a problem. "We will press the Paks hard as well," Komer promised, but Galbraith's efforts behind the scenes were also necessary to "keep Chicom threat visibly evident," which will "serve our long-term ends."[42]

Despite Komer's vision, the idea of long-term military aid to India continued to receive a chilly reception. The Defense Department agreed to send a small contingent of U.S. Army Special Forces soldiers to India to train units of the armed forces in guerrilla tactics and unconventional warfare but nothing more.[43] Komer and Galbraith remained undaunted. In late February the Indian government announced publicly that it would ask the United States, Britain, Australia, and Canada to provide air defenses in case of an attack by Chinese Communist aircraft. At a press conference, Kennedy tested his belief that the American public would support the United States coming to India's assistance if attacked by the Chinese. He confirmed to reporters that the Indians had requested air support in November. The United Kingdom and the United States had sent a mission to explore air security options with India, but the mission had not yet made any recommendations because it was still in the region. Kennedy then reiterated U.S. support for India and a willingness to be responsive to the Indian request for assistance, as "the balance of power in the world would be very adversely affected if India should lose its freedom."[44]

U.S. bureaucratic inertia was not the only impediment. The government of Pakistan vocalized its opposition and wanted the United States to use its military assistance to force a Kashmir settlement. The United States adopted this position, which left Nehru deeply distressed and politically vulnerable.[45] British diplomats, led by Duncan Sandys, the secretary of state for Commonwealth relations and colonies, and the British military took a similar stand, favoring a gradual increase in aid based on progress concerning Kashmir, although the United States suspected that the British lack of commitment stemmed from financial considerations and not political ones.[46]

India may have sensed U.S. wariness about helping because in late March 1963 Komer informed Kennedy that Indian sources were likely promoting scare tactics regarding a Chinese forces buildup. Komer did not let the matter end there. He urged Kennedy to approve a U.S.-UK air umbrella, which the Defense and State Departments agreed to recommend as a short-term step, in addition to long-term efforts, such as additional military aid beyond the $120 million emergency ceiling, assistance with Indian defense production, and UK-led upgrades to the Indian air force. In the meantime, Komer and Department of Defense leadership agreed to an air defense package.[47]

In April, Komer accompanied Walt Rostow on a trip to India and Pakistan to meet with senior officials about ongoing India-Pakistan talks on Kashmir. On their return, Rostow characterized the conversations as having a vision of a "stone wall" ahead. Both sides wandered irrationally in a political and psychological maze. Yet, the two envoys delivered the administration's message of exhortation and put pressure on the parties to find an acceptable path to a solution.[48] Komer followed up on Rostow's comments with a missive to Kennedy. He was not optimistic about a settlement and blamed the United States in part for the signals it had sent both parties. It was impossible to "stage-manage a difficult negotiation" this way. Given the emotional state of both Nehru and Ayub, the odds in favor of success were nearly zero.[49]

A day after Komer wrote his memorandum on the trip, Kennedy convened a meeting on India. Rusk and McNamara agreed that U.S. military aid to India should continue, but McNamara insisted on a small program, $300 million over three years as opposed to the Indian request for $1.6 billion over the same period, a figure that would have equaled all aid to Pakistan since 1954. The secretary of defense depicted the smaller program as realistic and said it would take two to three months to develop. Chester Bowles, the president's special representative on Asian affairs, argued the need to reassure the Indians of U.S. support. Kennedy expressed his skepticism that the proposed program would persuade the Indians. He also agreed with Bowles, that the time to act was now, not months from now. "India," Kennedy underscored, "is the important thing."[50]

Kennedy then wanted to know whether his advisers had reached a conclusion about an air defense package. McNamara; Paul Nitze, assistant secretary of defense for international security affairs; and Komer outlined the proposed air defense package, which would be at a small cost to the United States: $15 million for radar. Rusk suggested that the United States not make a commitment until he and Duncan Sandys returned from their trip to India and Pakistan. At first, Kennedy concurred, but then he changed his mind stating that he agreed that this step needed to be taken now. It was a less costly demonstration of U.S. commitment and less offensive to the Pakistanis. The United States would also fly its aircraft to India for exercises.[51]

In the following months Kennedy kept up the pressure on Rusk and McNamara with Komer egging the president on, advising Kennedy that the important policy goal was continuing and expanding ties to India.[52] Komer declared Rusk's cautiousness ("to play for time till Nehru dies") and support of "piddling aid" stemmed from a misguided fear of driving Pakistan to "irresponsible courses of action." This view was not only wrongheaded. It might result in saving money but "at the expense of a major strategic goal— that of bringing India into the non-nuclear Asian power balance. . . . The great danger is Indian backsliding. . . . Let's not end up this way (and still not get Kashmir); the stakes are simply too large." To this point, he added, "In short, can we hinge our South Asian policy to the fears of Pakistan?"[53]

Komer informed Galbraith privately of these roadblocks. He believed that Kennedy had reached the conclusion that the prospects for a Kashmir settlement were low, and he "seems determined not to end up with the worst of both worlds, i.e., no settlement and serious backsliding from India's present stance." In fact, the president made clear to McNamara and Rusk that the administration would take no steps that would "undermine our new relationship with the key nation in Free Asia." The battle over assistance to India would be fought repeatedly because, with the exception of the president, there was no eagerness to assume a major new commitment when the administration faced a "hell of a Congressional battle" over existing economic programs. "A few private words from you to the man you work for," Komer implored of Galbraith, "might be of considerable help here."[54]

On May 17 Kennedy met with Komer, Rusk, and Defense and State Department officials to decide the type of air defense exercise the United States would undertake with the Indians and the level of the military aid commitment. Kennedy pushed for a robust aid package because he did not want to waste the benefit of cementing the new relationship.[55] Komer boldly suggested the formation of an Indian Ocean task force; the idea intrigued Kennedy. Komer knew the merit of his arguments; it was a "powerful fillip," he was to recall later, "to the idea that we needed more power in the Indian Ocean area." There was a power vacuum in the region between the Suez Canal and Singapore. This wide arc from Egypt to Asia was considered a British responsibility, so the United States had no military assets there. However, the British were withdrawing from this area.[56]

Later, Komer laid out for Kennedy the value of a carrier task force with deterrent power in the Indian Ocean. First, it provided mission flexibility, operating off the coast of Africa, in the Persian Gulf, or in the defense of Pakistan, India, and Iran. It could patrol the choke point known as the Strait of Malacca. Second, if carriers were targets in a nuclear war against the Soviets in Western Europe, they had conventional applications elsewhere in the world.[57] Kennedy approved the concept and expressed his concern to McNamara about the slight U.S. military presence in the Indian Ocean. By attaining Harriman's backing, Komer also gained the support of the State Department, which now favored this idea because Komer fashioned his argument to suggest that Pakistanis would consider a carrier group in the Indian Ocean a reassuring signal of U.S. willingness to support Pakistan should the Indians attack them.[58]

Komer also secured the vice chief of naval operations' support when he contacted him. Adm. Claude Ricketts agreed that a carrier task force would give the United States credibility from the Red Sea to Indonesia. He assured Komer that the Navy could put a carrier presence into the Indian Ocean even if McNamara's ongoing effort to reduce the size of the Navy was realized; it was a matter of how long the task force would be on station—a permanent basis or a periodic three-month rotation.[59]

McNamara was certainly not enthusiastic about Komer's meddling, but he had no choice but to respond to the president. He directed the chairman of the Joint Chiefs to undertake an assessment in August, after Komer wrote a subsequent memorandum to Kennedy about the idea.[60] Komer's vision of a U.S. presence in the Indian Ocean could not be derailed. Finally, in October, the Defense Department agreed that an intermittent deployment of a carrier task force to the Indian Ocean was feasible. The deployment occurred the following year.[61]

By autumn, Komer recognized that the energy for closer U.S.-India relations had dissipated. It was not a policy change but a change in the circumstances that were now dictating relations between the two countries. Bowles, who had replaced Galbraith as ambassador in July, thought that he had become responsible for a broken program. Komer encouraged the president to "button up" the West's commitment to India when he and Macmillan met at Birch Grove in Sussex on June 30. The two leaders agreed to commit $100 million for military aid and a joint radar training exercise for an additional fiscal year.[62] A U.S.-Commonwealth Air Training Agreement was concluded in August, and air defense exercises were planned for later in November.[63] The Anglo-American commitments made Komer sanguine for a few months; he believed that by overcoming bureaucratic delays and British hesitancy, the administration had ended up with a military assistance package that represented a "sharp departure from Indian non-alignment, and a peg on which to hang" the next stage of U.S.-Indian ties in case the Chinese threat heated up again.[64] Nonetheless, Komer warned Bowles as early as September of the altered atmosphere and argued that neither the United States nor India could maintain the torrid pace of friendship that had been stimulated by the Chinese invasion a year earlier.[65]

Bowles did not have the policy influence or the relationship that his predecessor had with Kennedy, and many senior officials no longer took him or his prolix cables seriously, as he tried to prevent the slowdown in the "Indian end of the enterprise."[66] There were other blows as well. Pakistani-Indian talks over Kashmir had stalled; both parties rejected the possibility of a mediated settlement.[67]

Pakistan also successfully undermined the promising new relationship by highlighting the criticality of the U.S. intelligence facilities at Peshawar and threatening closer relations with China, which it had made more concrete with the Sino-Pakistani Border Agreement in March 1963 in return for Chinese recognition of Pakistan's right to control some parts of Jammu and Kashmir State. India also contributed to the cooling off by making policy changes that made it less likely to seek closer relations. It improved its ties to the Soviet Union, an association valued because of the military and economic aid that Moscow provided, but also because of the security it furnished against future Chinese military actions. It also increased military spending through an expansive five-year plan designed to boost the size of the military, improve the defense production base, and enhance the operational infrastructure. There was India's de facto acceptance of the border situation with China as well. These were understandable steps considering the outcome of the conflict and Washington's insistence that further military aid would be contingent on progress in resolving the Kashmir dispute with Pakistan—a tactic that soured the Indians who felt they were being taken advantage of during their weakened state.[68]

On November 13 Bowles met with the president and Komer to personally press his case about increasing military assistance to India. He received a hearing but no commitment.[69] It was the last time that the three would meet. Nine days later Kennedy was dead.

––––––––––––––

The prevailing assessment of the Kennedy administration's policy toward India is that it miscarried on questionable policy assumptions, flawed premises, and unrealistic expectations.[70] The shift should never have been attempted as the initiatives "were probably doomed" from inception and the administration's decisions were based on "global illusions."[71] However, policymakers must recognize, not acquiesce to, historical impediments and take advantage of the ripening moments when policy change is practical. To do otherwise, would result in a government paralyzed by an unwarranted belief in historical inevitabilities.

Komer in his role as Kennedy's adviser for South Asia is accepted as "of even greater importance" than other pro-India supporters—Galbraith, Talbot, and Bowles.[72] He fully appreciated India's desire to maintain strategic autonomy and envisioned a cooperative relationship, not an alliance, since he recognized that India believed the burdens of such an arrangement outweighed the advantages.[73] Komer also understood that closer relations with India would incense Pakistan; in one memorandum he wrote that the administration was "in for a rough time with the Paks, and JFK should be forewarned."[74] More importantly, he was not thinking about the near term, but the long view. The administration had to realize that it was "making a long-range politico-military investment" in India.[75] India was a future partner worthy of being wooed.

In pushing this initiative, he sought to eliminate the inherent weakness of Pakistan and India's insistence that Washington support one of them at the other's expense. Political scientist Stephen Blank calls this the insertion of a "hyphen into the relationship," whereby the United States must deal with both nations as if they were a single entity without a calculation based on interests and other factors.[76] Komer sought to decouple this "hyphenation" because it impeded closer relations with India.

Additionally, Komer appreciated that while the United States and India shared democratic values, this alone was not sufficient to build or nurture a bilateral relationship. Economic ties, through the sizable assistance that United States provided, and military cooperation with the West would go only so far. U.S. and Indian interests sometimes converged, but they were not congruent.[77] Instead, recognizing India's geopolitical significance, Komer sought to weaken India's relations with the Soviet Union and to amplify India's anxieties about Chinese hegemony to induce closer relations and uphold a durable balance of power in Asia. He also played to India's image of itself and its international and regional interests (such as security of its Himalayan border and the potential for war with China), believing that on the basis of its power potential and characteristics as a civilization, it deserved at some future point to be a major power. This role was also consistent with Nehru's personality and inclinations.[78]

Kennedy believed that the policy approach Komer recommended was a sensible one, in keeping with his philosophy that containment could be achieved outside of military pacts and that it was worth taking the small risk involved.[79] Ultimately, Kennedy's willingness to adopt a pro-India policy was not naive, misguided, or shortsighted. He, like Komer, understood the fragility of the U.S. position in South Asia when the Sino-India crisis first began.

On October 28, 1962, the administration learned that Soviet premier Nikita Khrushchev had signaled the removal of Soviet missiles from Cuba. Kennedy's hard-line position had been, as Macmillan told the House of Commons, "one of the great turning points in history."[80] That same day Bundy and Kaysen met with Kennedy and claimed that his plea to India and Pakistan to achieve a resolution over Kashmir would certainly be heeded now that the president looked "ten feet tall." "That will wear off in a week," Kennedy replied wistfully, "and everyone will be back to thinking only of their own interests."[81] He was right: from that day until his death, India, Pakistan, and the Kennedy administration worried about their own interests, as nations are prone to do.

PART TWO

LYNDON JOHNSON'S MAN

CHAPTER 5

Pacification Czar

*L*yndon Johnson loved an audience, especially a captive one, which is what he had. The White House press corps waited in an uneven arc before him in the Oval Office. Some reporters sat on the cream-fabric settees. Others stood beneath the fixed gaze of Henry Clay and Andrew Jackson's dark portraits. No one dared intrude beyond the presidential seal woven into the center of the pale green rug that lay before the president's mahogany desk, the proscenium of the stage.

The fragrance of cut flowers, tension, and a ragged silence hung heavy in the air. The time had not yet come for words, and the president sat behind his desk preparing for that moment, looking up occasionally to scrutinize the spectators. "Reporters are puppets," he once remarked. "They simply respond to the pull of the most powerful strings."[1] Then, at precisely 4:15 p.m., on Tuesday, March 22, 1966, with his aides in their places, the White House stenographers with their pencils and notepads at the ready, and all preparations complete, Lyndon Johnson pulled the strings and began the sixtieth press conference of his presidency: "I am ready if you have any questions."[2]

Komer felt the tug of the string as well. Appointed Johnson's interim national security adviser when Bundy left the White House at the end of February to head the Ford Foundation, Komer later recalled that period as "the most painful six weeks of my life."[3] Now, after responding to several reporters' questions, Johnson announced that Komer would assume a new position on the White House staff, a choice about which he had mused aloud to the head of White House personnel, John Macy, a few days before.[4] Johnson had earlier summoned Komer to the Oval Office to discuss his new role. "Bob," Johnson drawled when they sat together, "I'm going to put you in charge of the other war in Vietnam." Komer was unfamiliar with the term the "other war." "Mr. President, what's the other war in Vietnam? I thought we only had one." "Well," the president replied, "that's part of the problem. I want to have a war to build as well as to destroy. So I want to put you in charge of generating a massive effort to do more for the people of South Vietnam, particularly the farmers in the rural areas, and your mandate will be an extensive one. In fact, I wrote it myself." Komer declared that he was no expert in Southeast Asia. The president parried his feeble protest: "I've got too many people who claim to be long-standing experts. What we need is some fresh blood."[5] Komer knew that there was no argument he could muster to dissuade Johnson. Johnson's leadership style was simple: pick the "right man" for the job and the rest will take care of itself. Komer was the "right man" for this new job; he got things done.

———————

Johnson had asked Komer to continue as a member of the NSC staff shortly after Kennedy's death. The request was an appeal to Komer's pride and sense of duty. Johnson knew he needed Komer and other White House staff members; they were his link to Kennedy, and through this connection, he could gain support of other Kennedy constituencies to govern the nation. Continuity in the conduct of foreign affairs was essential until he was elected president in his own right.[6] It was difficult not to make a commitment in the presence of Lyndon Johnson, the "formidable bargainer," shrewd, convivial, assessing what people needed and what it would take to induce them to help him achieve his goals.[7] Komer pledged his support without hesitation.

The two men had first met in 1962, when President Kennedy sent then–Vice President Johnson on a goodwill tour of the Middle East. Kennedy and McGeorge Bundy selected Komer to accompany Johnson after the vice president said he would make the trip only if "one of Kennedy's people was at his elbow. I'm not going to be at the mercy of the State Department." Johnson believed that the career diplomats hated him. From the first stop on the trip, Beirut, Lebanon, Komer became inseparable from Johnson. The vice president told his personal staff that Komer was his senior policy adviser and that he would accompany him to all the important meetings. He did not want State Department personnel present at what he considered private meetings. He also introduced Komer to all the foreign officials as President Kennedy's Middle East expert.[8]

When the entourage returned to Washington, Johnson penned a personal note to Komer thanking him for his contribution in making the trip successful, particularly for giving him high-quality advice and for providing him with substance and not the banalities often offered for him to utter. Although Komer had been warned that Johnson was nearly inarticulate when it came to diplomacy and would likely put "his foot in his mouth," Komer found this not the case. Instead, he discovered that Johnson was receptive to his suggestions, an articulate envoy with an innate feel for the issues, and a quick study, and he informed Kennedy of the same after the trip. He also respected, admired, and genuinely liked Johnson and was pleased that the feeling was mutual. He ascribed his fondness for the vice president to his being a "Missouri boy" and "not part of the Eastern establishment," and to Johnson's receptiveness to his plain and, at times, earthy talk.[9]

————————————

Komer remained friendly with the vice president's staff, who invited him to dinner and other social events; the forced intimacy of the trip had only accelerated their acquaintanceship. Komer, for his part, made it a point to send them copies of his memoranda and other material on foreign policy issues that he thought the vice president would find of interest. In response, Johnson would call Komer and ask him his opinion on various issues.[10]

Komer's decision to remain in the White House after Kennedy's death was as much a gesture of allegiance to the presidency as an institution as it was to a particular person. "Washington is not a sentimental place," Ronald Steel has observed. "Respect resides with power,"[11] and Komer understood this dictum from his years of Washington experience. He also believed staying was what was demanded of him as a professional.[12] In taking that view, he realized that Johnson's national security apparatus might operate differently. On the evening of Kennedy's assassination, Komer and Phillips Talbot sat in the living room of Talbot's Washington, D.C., home "in a sentimental exchange of drinks and worry." The two of them were slowly anesthetizing themselves, recalling the experiences they shared during Kennedy's presidency and recognizing that Kennedy's death signaled an end of an era in American foreign policy. "You know," said Talbot, "one of the great things about the New Frontier was the President's own personal handling of the affairs in which you and I, Bob, were involved. He really was the Secretary of State." They both sensed that the latitude of action that they had and the presidential attention their issues received would not be the same under the new president.[13] They proved prescient.

Johnson was uneasy with the freewheeling staff style that Kennedy promoted, and so he restructured the White House with a middle tier of officials with whom he felt comfortable, primarily Johnson loyalists. He relied more on Rusk and McNamara and other people whose judgments he respected rather than on the NSC staff.[14] As one of his senior staff observed, "He had very definite views about relations between presidents and Cabinet officers, and about the difference between advice and pressure."[15] Komer also readily understood this difference between policy adviser and policymaker. His role as a presidential adviser was limited. It was to provide counsel to the chief executive, to provide context on issues, and to serve as a presidential staff officer. "LBJ was his own chief of staff," one of Komer's colleagues observed.[16] The president was free to accept or ignore advice; the latter, Komer noted, was more likely to be the case.[17]

Nonetheless, Komer's loyalty to Johnson was unwavering and out of this fidelity grew Johnson's confidence and trust in Komer. The personal relationship forged during the 1962 Middle East trip and subsequent events, such as Komer's handling of U.S. efforts in the 1965 India-Pakistan war, sealed a more than comfortable superior-subordinate rapport.[18] There was a personal affinity as well. Komer was similar to Johnson in that he would use charm and manipulation to achieve his ends and was not reluctant about browbeating someone if it was necessary to bend a person's will to his own to achieve success.

Komer was also one of the few Kennedy men that Johnson trusted.[19] The president, along with McNamara and the White House staff, considered him for a number of senior appointments. As many of Komer's contemporaries have remarked, Komer had a powerful, incandescent intellect, which was melded to his forceful personality, which some found "brash and intrusive."[20] The highest compliment Komer could ever pay anyone was to bestow the epithet "expediter." It was how he thought of himself. He was a person of action, who carried out his duties with speed and effectiveness, "a marvelous staff man," as McGeorge Bundy called him.[21] Because of these attributes, McNamara tried to poach Komer from the White House to be deputy assistant secretary of defense for international security affairs.[22] Johnson prevented this attempted plundering and made Komer, at Bundy's insistence, Bundy's deputy. In Bundy's view, Komer was one of the few men in government that Johnson could rely on for sound advice during a crisis.[23] Komer was also considered a potential candidate for ambassadorships to Turkey and Pakistan because of his "drive and imagination."[24] However, for more than two years after Johnson assumed the presidency, he showed little interest in Komer's portfolio except when the occasional flare-up required his attention or the issue concerned Israel, for which Johnson had a long record of support beginning from his tenure as Senate majority leader.[25]

Now Johnson had made Komer responsible for the other war in Vietnam when Komer had anticipated becoming Bundy's replacement.[26] For three years Komer had successfully stiff-armed Bundy on involvement in Vietnam policy; his excuse was that too many staff members were already tied up in Vietnam, and besides, someone had to watch the rest of the world.[27] He was purposely being evasive. Not only was he familiar with what was at stake there, he had a solid understanding of the nature of the warfare involved. But his reservations about getting involved in Vietnam policy ran deep. He was not convinced Vietnam was of vital interest to the United States.

He had first signaled his qualms a few weeks after Kennedy was inaugurated, when he sent a paper to Rostow titled "Forestalling a Crisis in South Vietnam." He argued that the United States had no feasible alternative but to support the president of the Republic of Vietnam (South Vietnam), Ngo Dinh Diem. Nonetheless, Komer contended, U.S. pressures on the leader to reform and his belief that the United States had been involved in a November 1960 coup attempt had shaken Diem's confidence in U.S. intentions. The key was to move quickly to restore Diem's confidence in the United States.[28]

At the same time, Komer emphasized that Diem must understand clearly that "internal Communist subversion is a problem which only he and his people can overcome; that it is as much a political and psychological as a military problem; and that which the US can do is only marginal to the total effort—the will, the initiative, and the determination must come from the Vietnamese." He also underscored that the United States needed to make a firm and public commitment to defend South Vietnam from overt aggression by North Vietnam. Such a commitment would likely reorient the training, deployment, and use of Diem's forces toward the major threat he faced—communist subversion and guerrilla warfare. "While first priority must be to meet the impending crisis . . . we cannot neglect the longer term viability of South Vietnam. . . . Hence let's not focus only on the immediate problem, but do some imaginative longer planning as well," wrote Komer.[29] A few months later, he again told Rostow that Diem needed to assume a stronger leadership role because it was his war and continued procrastination could prove fatal. Komer had believed that a public commitment on the part of the Kennedy administration would have been an unmistakable signal of its support.[30]

When the Joint Chiefs of Staff recommended the dispatch of American troops to South Vietnam in late 1961, "to provide a visible deterrent to potential North Vietnamese and/or Chinese Communist action" and to "indicate the firmness of our intent to all Asian nations,"[31] Komer was more flexible but still registered his reservations about the importance of Vietnam. "The point of installing token US forces before the event," he told Bundy, "is to signal our intentions to the other fellow, and thus hopefully avoid having to face up to the commitment of substantial US forces after a fracas has developed." He did not rule out the possibility of "something approaching another Korea," but he thought "the best way of avoiding" that end was "to move fast now before the war spreads to the extent that a Korea type commitment is required." He concluded that he was "no happier than anyone about getting involved in another squalid, secondary theatre in Asia." He saw involvement in the conflict in Vietnam as inevitable: "We'll end up doing so sooner or later anyway because we won't be willing to accept another defeat. If so, the real question is not whether but how soon and how much!"[32]

Almost three years later, in 1964, Komer took a different approach by suggesting the Johnson administration use its Vietnam policy to produce a rapprochement with China that would bring it within the realm of U.S.-Soviet peaceful coexistence.[33] However, even he conceded that Walt Rostow's case for reprisals against North Vietnam "seems to make more sense than it did previously." Reprisals were a radical step and could potentially widen the war, but "unless we ourselves move forward here we may find ourselves playing a losing defense game, while the Sihanouks, Sukarnos, Maos and DeGaulles nibble at our flanks."[34] Komer visualized "the war as a diplomatic problem for the United States" and not, as Rostow did, as "a tough but winnable war," a "necessary price to pay for improvements occurring elsewhere in the world."[35]

By early 1965 Komer's misgivings seemed clearer and definite. He was soon recommending to Johnson that he not spurn third-country peace initiatives.[36] When James Thomson, the NSC staff's Asian specialist, confided his own growing policy doubts about Vietnam to "an older colleague on the staff [Komer], he assured me that the smartest thing both of us could do was to 'steer clear' of the whole Vietnam mess; the gentleman in question had the misfortune to be a 'can-do guy,' however, and is now highly placed in Vietnam, under orders to solve the mess."[37]

Komer understood Johnson's determination to strengthen pacification as an element of U.S. policy in Vietnam. The president wanted to make Vietnam a showcase of economic, social, and political development in Asia. Pacification was the "Great Society" transplanted thousands of miles away. Komer recounted that Johnson "saw the 'other war' as largely being a sort of building of TVA [Tennessee Valley Authority] and REA [Rural Electrification Administration]." The president "felt that there should be a positive element on the war to build rather than destroy." He was "constantly breaking out of the confines of Vietnam as a war—and seeing it as a problem of winning hearts and minds. That was something he understood. He was quite conscious from the beginning that he had to do something about winning the allegiance of the Vietnamese."[38]

To that end, Johnson made a personal commitment to pacification when he met with Chief of State Nguyen Van Thieu and Prime Minister Nguyen Cao Ky of the Republic of Vietnam in Honolulu in February 1966.[39] Pacification had been "enthusiastically endorsed," not only by Johnson, "but, in the beginning, by a great number of dedicated men on Ivy League faculties and at places where organized thinking went on, like the Hudson Institute and the Rand Corporation."[40] Johnson was also not alone in recognizing the U.S. government's flawed organization to support pacification. Subcabinet officials from civilian agencies, the Department of Defense, and the U.S. mission in Saigon had met in January 1966 in a small Virginia town outside Washington, D.C., to discuss this topic, but they could not reach agreement on how to manage pacification more effectively in Washington or in Saigon.[41] The idea of a "Vietnam czar" in Washington surfaced soon after, but there was disagreement about where this person should work. The State Department wanted the person to be a special assistant to the secretary of state.[42] Chester Cooper, an NSC staff member, wrote an impassioned memorandum arguing that the person should work for the president in the White House because one bureaucracy cannot manage others at the same level and because the position would carry more power if the person worked for Johnson.[43]

Jack Valenti, a presidential aide and former Houston advertising executive, expressed concern about the lack of the LBJ brand on White House personnel. While Valenti thought highly of the holdovers from the Kennedy administration, men of uncommonly high talent, he recognized that they were not Johnson men. He favored Walt Rostow's appointment to replace Bundy as national security adviser and pushed Johnson to underscore to the public that a "new, hard-striking, imaginative, creative brain team" was working on national security. If Komer was assigned the Vietnam job, Valenti suggested, then "he ought to be given a title bespeaks exactly our aims so that every time his title is mentioned, it becomes a slogan: Special Assistant for Re-Construction in Vietnam."[44]

Valenti was not alone in his assessment of Komer as a potential "Mr. Vietnam." Before leaving Washington, Bundy wrote a memorandum to Johnson in which he framed the requirement for a Washington-based pacification czar who could support the presidential direction for the U.S. embassy in Saigon to take the lead in pacification. Bundy argued that someone—a person who valued "action to excuses, management to contemplation," and who reported directly to the president—needed to prod the bureaucracy. Johnson found Bundy's memorandum to be an excellent statement of the problem and asked Rusk, McNamara, and Bundy to provide him with names of potential candidates by mid-February. Bundy recommended several candidates, but Komer topped the list. The role, Bundy argued, would be "the best possible use of Komer. He has a very unusual combination of energy and experience, and his abrasiveness (which can be more accurately described as brashness) would be a positive asset in this particular assignment."[45]

Komer, in his position as acting special assistant for national security affairs, also weighed in on the Vietnam czar issue with a memorandum. Unaware of the discussions swirling around him, he too urged the president to locate the position in the White House and not the State Department. To do otherwise, he argued, was to downgrade the position to such a degree that it would make it "more difficult to for him [the appointee] to crack the whip as is intended." Besides, Komer reasoned, "if the position is situated in the State Department, then it would be even harder to find the right talent."[46] Komer may have sealed his fate without knowing it.

These arguments prevailed, and now Komer was responsible for carrying out the president's commitment in the face of bureaucratic resistance from the civilian agencies. Komer recognized that a conversation between the president and him would be insufficient to move the civilian bureaucracies to achieve the president's objective. Johnson's directive that he was to "manage and supervise," an authority McNamara wanted included, would have to be in writing for the bureaucracy to accept it.[47] Even then, the bureaucrats would challenge Komer's authority and cooperation may have to be forced, but a presidential directive was a necessity for him to have any chance of succeeding. He set about writing a document for the president to sign. In essence, Komer was writing his own job description.

Komer understood his mandate as a management problem subject to analysis, an input-output model, concepts he had learned at the Harvard Business School: synchronize existing U.S. civilian agency programs in Vietnam, identify existing gaps in civilian capabilities, develop new programs to eliminate those problems, as "it was the President's determination that the program be speeded-up, given priority over military operations and conducted with wartime urgency."[48] He recognized as well that the primary focus of his effort must be in Saigon, and not Washington, in order to implement the president's direction. There were two approaches to take. The more direct approach—and Komer always preferred the direct approach—was to work with Ambassador William Porter, Lodge's deputy, who in February had been designated to improve the management of U.S. support of the pacification effort as Komer's counterpart in Saigon and to use the authority the president had given them to overcome bureaucratic resistance in Saigon. In this approach, the mission would be both friend and foil. The indirect and secondary approach was to use his mandate to advantage with senior officials in Washington by having these officials instruct their field agencies to comply with Porter's or his guidance. One aspect was certain: Komer was not going to waste valuable time working through interagency committees in Washington. He believed in "intervening from the top to solve quickly certain specific problems that otherwise would be massaged by the bureaucracy for months on end."[49] He also consulted with McNamara, his strongest supporter, as to how he should approach the new job. McNamara told him it would be impossible to perform it from Washington and advised him to travel frequently to the field. He also promised to put U.S. military aircraft at Komer's disposal anytime he wanted to travel.[50]

By the end of March, Komer had completed and cleared with the relevant civilian agencies a presidential directive designed to centralize the management of pacification in Washington under his direction. State Department put up a fight, but Presidential Assistant Joe Califano and Press Secretary Bill Moyers convinced Rusk to yield. President Johnson signed this directive, National Security Action Memorandum (NSAM) 343, "Special Assistant for Peaceful Construction in Vietnam," on March 28.[51] Komer's handiwork not only ensured him extensive authority over seven civilian agencies, but also considerable say in the mobilization of military resources to support the president's pacification commitment.

The directive spelled out clearly Komer's mandate to carry out the responsibility for "the direction, coordination, and *supervision* [emphasis added] in Washington of U.S. non-military programs for peaceful construction relating to Vietnam."[52] The document also underscored the urgency with which the president wanted his commitment carried out and stated that Komer and his deputy, Ambassador William Leonhart, would ensure that the civilian pacification efforts were coordinated with military operations. Further, he would support the U.S. mission in Saigon on matters within his purview. Komer then administered a White House bureaucratic coup de grâce. He was to have direct access to the president at all times. He had divorced himself from the NSC staff; he would not report through the president's national security adviser.[53] Additionally, he would now join the president, Rostow, McNamara, and Rusk on Tuesdays when discussions on Vietnam policy and strategy were held around the lunch table.[54]

Komer then created an office with a small, select staff to assist him with his duties. In addition to Leonhart, Porter recommended a young foreign service officer, Richard Holbrooke, who had worked for him in Saigon. Holbrooke in turn recommended Komer hire Army lieutenant colonel Robert Montague. Montague had extensive experience in Vietnam; he had served as an adviser to a South Vietnamese army unit and on General Westmoreland's staff at U.S. Military Assistance Command, Vietnam, (MACV). Komer added two RAND Corporation employees to assist with economic issues, a Bureau of Budget employee to control agency allocation of funding for pacification activities, and two other staff members.[55]

In less than a week after Johnson's announcement and at the president's direction, Komer accompanied Bill Moyers and Deputy Secretary of

Defense Cyrus Vance to see firsthand how pacification was faring.[56] It was the first of seven trips to Vietnam Komer would make over the next year. He sent his initial trip report to the president at the LBJ Ranch in Texas, and it arrived on April 13. It began with a self-deprecatory statement that his views should "be taken with a grain of salt as coming from a one-week expert." Nonetheless, Komer's assessment was generally positive. He had established a close working relationship with Lodge, Porter, and General Westmoreland. He was also confident that the U.S. government could build an effective nonmilitary effort to complement the military's actions. Praising Porter for his initial efforts to coordinate the previously loosely aligned civil efforts, he agreed that the civil program was lagging significantly behind the military effort. Komer understood that military requirements had priority but cited a number of problems that were causing economic instability for South Vietnam. These issues needed immediate attention. The first was that civil-military competition for port space and inefficient USAID/Government of Vietnam (GVN) port operations were hindering the distribution of aid to the Vietnamese people, examples of vexations that precluded effective civil programs. Other concerns were pacifying the countryside and reining in inflation. He asserted that without resolving these issues, "all our other grand enterprises will go for naught."[57]

About a week later Komer followed the message with a lengthy report to Johnson, which included several pages for the president's "eyes only." In this more comprehensive analysis, Komer stated that with respect to the civilian programs and pacification, the United States could not take over the effort as it had done with the military side or even try "to do too much too soon." Such an approach would be self-defeating. While the GVN was feeble, strengthening its capability to govern must be the goal, using whatever leverage—persuasion, inducements, and pressures—the United States could apply. Spurring a socioeconomic revolution in a "non-country" during wartime would be impossible unless efforts were well planned and phased in properly. But more ominously, "pacification—not to mention a social revolution—would critically depend on whether we can set an at least marginally effective GVN." Komer recognized as well that Vietnamese elections, however conducted, would not be as democratic a process as Americans would expect. Nonetheless, the United States needed to be thinking of how to manage them in terms of having sensible elections laws and procedures, with adequate checks and balances in place. As he noted, the United States had a major stake in the country's political future.[58]

In private correspondence with Porter shortly after he wrote his report, Komer reiterated several points he had made to the president and stated that USAID administrator David Bell believed that Porter was not getting sufficient "higher level" support. Komer expressed his concern that Porter was being overloaded with too many assignments and that he had too few capable staff working for him.[59] Komer would continue to be concerned about the unity of effort required to harmonize military and civil operations, especially in the field. He was not the only one worried; McNamara had come to question whether Porter was up to the task. Komer, however, understood the pressures Porter was under because he felt them himself and characterized their jobs as "backbreaking." At times, the relationship between the two men could be contentious, but Komer urged Porter to recognize that like it or not, the only way they could succeed in their respective jobs was by working together. He even stated that Porter should use his messages as Komer intended—as "sticks" to move efforts forward. This use would be to Porter's advantage, as he could blame Komer for all the Washington directives. Further, these messages were sometimes disseminated to a wider audience to warn MACV and the Pentagon to provide assistance or stop resisting efforts at improved interagency operations.[60] The important point was to "get the show on the road." Saigon was the locus for action; Washington, where such matters resulted in "interminable discussions," was not.[61] The pressure was on both men to produce results, especially with respect to the GVN assuming more responsibility for pacification. Komer was under no illusions about how difficult it would be to make progress in this effort.

A month later Komer apologized to the president for the long period during which he had not provided him with a status report. He wrote, "If I have not been much in evidence, it is because I have been trying to operate full tilt—as a flood of traffic and resulting anguished screams will attest." Komer had already earned the moniker "Blowtorch" from Lodge and reveled in the appellation. He continued his message by providing a frank assessment to Johnson. The civil side was a "mess." Again, he pointed out the military's dominance in Saigon, the weak and apathetic South Vietnamese government, the inability of the U.S. civilian agencies to operate at the high tempo that war required, and Lodge's ineffectual leadership of the U.S. pacification effort. Komer argued that a military buildup would prevent a disaster but would not guarantee victory in a "political war." Further, he saw adverse side effects to the military buildup:

"anti-Americanism induced by the visible military presence and pressures of inflation." Yet, he remained determined that Porter and he would "bring order out of chaos on the civil side." He offered several recommendations that he knew the Pentagon would not find appealing. Lodge needed to insist on better balance between the military and civil efforts and press for military assistance, such as in-country airlift for moving USAID supplies to the rural areas and helping with the port congestion. Komer believed that eliminating the Viet Cong influence in the countryside and limiting inflation were the highest priorities. He urged the president to press these points on Lodge and support Komer's position in the inevitable fights with the Pentagon over them. In a private letter to Porter, Komer underscored that the president would tell Lodge directly that the civil side required more attention, especially from the GVN.[62]

The president acted as Komer requested when Lodge returned to Washington for consultations shortly after he made his second report, and Komer reiterated his concerns at an NSC meeting a few days later going as far as to say that pacification "has been out-run by our search and destroy capability" and that the U.S. military effort fueled anti-Americanism and caused runaway inflation in South Vietnam. If the United States is blamed for these effects, he warned, real harm would be done during the forthcoming election period in Vietnam.[63] Johnson was sympathetic to Komer's message. Speaking to reporters after the meeting, the president said that Lodge would spend time consulting with Komer and Rostow. He added that the problems in Vietnam were not solely military, but also political and economic, and that Komer would be responsible for leading the effort to address these additional concerns.[64]

Komer had the president's ear again when at a May 16 meeting on Vietnam, he recommended to Johnson that the Defense Department take steps to reduce the inflationary impact of military outlays and take over port operations from USAID, since the agency lacked the capability and training to perform this enormous logistical task. Johnson's response was simply to get "recommendations and let's move" on these points.[65] Komer subsequently sent a cable to Porter informing him of the president's direction.[66]

Komer understood Johnson's psychological need for information on the progress being made on pacification. He sent a flurry of memoranda to Johnson in May and June outlining the issues and his intended actions. The president's response was favorable: "Bob, I applaud you, good. Keep it up & Keep it Hot."[67] Johnson's words clearly indicated why the president had selected him, but Komer recognized the memoranda for what they were: merely a device to keep Johnson informed. Johnson never issued any orders from the memoranda or his trip reports, but then again, he never did so with any of the reports he received from other senior officials either. Although Komer met with the president once or twice a week in meetings alone or with others to discuss Vietnam matters, and attended relevant Tuesday lunch meetings with Johnson, Rusk, McNamara, and other selected advisers, when the agenda included pacification, Komer believed his job was to relieve the president of daily concerns about the subject, not badger him with questions or seek answers. He was essentially on his own.[68] Komer kept pressing Porter for more progress, and he kept the pressure on by sending Leonhart or other staff to Vietnam to see whether the "Komer priorities" were being initiated quickly enough.[69]

In weekly reporting cables to the president, Lodge included information on pacification efforts, but he was merely responding to what he knew to be Johnson's interest. In truth, Porter was devoting most of his energy to being the deputy chief of mission responsible for the U.S. mission's daily functioning, and not to pacification. Further, Porter, as deputy ambassador, had no alternative but to defer to Lodge's authority in all matters, including the pace at which pacification improvement occurred.[70] Westmoreland's feeble backing of the effort disturbed Johnson as well, so the president made clear his expectations to the general: "I've put the best man on my own staff to work on getting the civil side rolling and am solidly behind Komer and Porter in this. I know you will give them your fullest support and cooperation. They need all the help you can spare."[71]

By mid-1966 Komer had new ideas about pacification and decried the lack of bold thinking in Saigon. A U.S. Army study conducted at the direction of the Army chief of staff, Gen. Harold K. Johnson, influenced his point of view considerably. The study resulted from General Johnson's substantial misgivings about the conduct of the war, particularly Westmoreland's strategy of attrition, which Johnson believed would not achieve U.S. political and military objectives. He supported a counterinsurgency approach, a view largely shaped by his discussions with British officers involved in the Malayan insurgency as well as his own trips to South Vietnam.[72] The study, "The Program for the Pacification and Long Term Development in Vietnam" (PROVN), completed in March 1966, concluded that the key problems with the conduct of the war were the lack of a unified war effort and, in the case of pacification, insufficient interagency coordination. The study also recommended that pacification play a larger role in the execution of allied operations, particularly eliminating the Viet Cong infrastructure, and that the U.S. ambassador in Saigon be the single manager for all U.S. activities in Vietnam.[73] General Johnson made sure that Komer received a copy of the study, and he became an enthusiastic proponent both within Washington circles and, ultimately, in Vietnam. The head of the study group, Col. Thomas Hanifen, commented, "Komer took PROVN and rode it like a horse."[74] Another of the study group members, Lt. Col. Volney Warner, considered Komer to be "our champion."[75] Komer was determined to use whatever tools were necessary to fulfill his mandate; he readily conceded, "Most of my ideas have been borrowed liberally from the people and studies which impressed me—especially the PROVN Study."[76]

It was also clear to Komer that Lodge was not focused on any of the pacification initiatives that Komer and Porter considered necessary; the president wanted "action—not explanations—on the civil side." It was not that Johnson failed to acknowledge the difficulties inherent in pacification, but he expected Komer to "break the bottlenecks." The president also continued to urge Westmoreland to support the effort, underscoring his personal interest and the expectation that the general would give Komer and Porter all the help they needed.[77] Komer was increasingly convinced that there was no single key to success on the civil side other than better management and stepped-up activity along political, economic, and social fronts, including a vigorous anti-inflation program to stabilize the South Vietnamese economy and other economic reforms.[78]

Komer also stressed to President Johnson the need to generate a major positive effect in the near term because the civil effort was still "barely off the ground." Komer knew he was inviting resistance from the Pentagon, but to increase the urgency, pacification demanded that more civil logistics functions be turned over to the military; he was unimpressed with USAID's ability to perform its functions. Additionally, Porter's mandate required strengthening. He was too involved in the daily administration of the mission and could not devote sufficient time to pacification. He needed clear and unequivocal authority over civilian operations throughout the country. Most importantly, Westmoreland needed to devote fewer resources to search and destroy and more to clearing and holding the countryside. Finally, pushing the GVN to assume its pacification responsibilities could broaden the civil program. The codicil to this missive was a model of under-statement: "My program is not dramatic—but it will help win the war."[79]

Komer was convinced that the military could "win battles and prevent disaster." However, "they can't win the war." The reason was simple: they "can't pacify the countryside" and that was essential. This aim would be accomplished not only by securing the rural areas but also by political and economic development. Komer was leery of the GVN's commitment and had come to the view that "only leverage would work." If the GVN would not pursue the U.S. initiatives, then he would threaten suspension of aid. It was plain to Komer that "we've let the GVN lay down on the job, and that way lies disaster."[80]

Nonetheless, Komer perceived some progress during a visit to Vietnam in late June. After several days of traveling throughout South Vietnam, speaking with the ambassador and the GVN as well as sergeants and vil-lagers, he told the president he was "both an optimist and a realist." He was optimistic that Westmoreland's "spoiling operations" were having an effect on the Viet Cong, the civil side of the effort was finally under way, the GVN appeared more confident after containing the Buddhist bid for power over the past three months, and the economic situation was under control. At the same time, he was "sobered by the realization of how much further we may have to go." He questioned whether Westmoreland was accurately reading the intentions of the Viet Cong and North Vietnamese army (NVA). The general held the belief that the enemy was "committed to a classical Phase III Maoist strategy rather than reverting to guerrilla war." Too much attention was being paid to the Viet Cong main force; the war was more like a mosaic in that the phase of revolutionary war depended on the situation on the ground. In some locales, guerrilla war was being fought; in others, a more conventional fight was occurring; and in some areas there was a combination of both. Pacification was both the key and the problem; the United States and the GVN had not been able to capital-ize on the initiative that the military operations were providing by extend-ing control over the countryside. "Until we can get rolling on pacification in its widest sense," Komer concluded, "securing the villages, flushing out the local VC [Viet Cong] (not just the main force), and giving the peas-ant both security and the hope for a better future—we cannot assure a victory."[81] The GVN and the Army of the Republic of Vietnam (ARVN) were the weak links; they were not "pulling their weight." There needed to be additional emphasis on building units of the police field force and the revolutionary development (RD) cadre, which acted as an agent of social change in the rural areas, as well as regional forces/popular forces (RF/PF) capabilities. Until the United States stepped up its own pacification effort and galvanized the GVN and ARVN effort, everyone involved was just paying lip service to the notion that the conflict was a political one, a revolutionary war, with its civil dimension as important as its military one. The declared policy was not being carried out.[82]

In a press conference held the day Komer left Vietnam, Westmoreland remained upbeat. He told reporters that the United States and its allies were beginning to win the war militarily. The reporters noted it was the most optimistic public comment that Westmoreland had made to date. Westmoreland then added a note of caution. Victories in battle, while important, were not enough; political, social, and economic gains must occur as well, and these efforts were lagging the military effort.[83]

Not everyone shared Westmoreland's qualified optimism. By the summer of 1966, public and congressional support for the war was diminishing. The administration was concerned that unless this trend was arrested, it could result in increasing pressure on the United States to "win or get out." One response that Johnson considered was to make some major personnel changes. He raised with Rostow the idea of moving Komer to the State Department to replace William Bundy as assistant secretary for East Asian and Pacific Affairs.[84] This proposal underscored not only Johnson's trust and confidence in Komer, but also his belief that Komer had a substantial grasp on the political-military issues surrounding U.S. policy. The idea was stillborn. Komer was too valuable where he was.

Despite the president's favorable view, Komer had detractors in the civilian agencies and his trip reports sent some of them into a rage. At the CIA, George A. Carver, special assistant for Vietnam affairs, sent a memorandum to Director of Central Intelligence Richard Helms after Komer's second visit to Vietnam in late June that was a combination of bureaucratic backbiting and perceptive analysis. Carver accused Komer of having fundamental misconceptions about the nature of the war in Vietnam. He felt Komer was raising the president's expectations precipitously by giving the chief executive the impression that there would be quick and measurable results in the pacification area. Further, Carver contended that Komer's recommendations were counterproductive. While he agreed that securing the villages, eliminating Viet Cong influence, and providing the peasants with security were useful steps, Carver disagreed vehemently with the notion that additional resources and better management were the keys to winning the war. Carver's response also underscored an issue with which Komer was contending already—a concern about militarizing the pacification effort— but his remarks could alternatively be interpreted as demonstrating his worry that the CIA would lose control of its rural pacification program. CIA personnel were particularly upset with Komer's view that there should be a single manager for pacification running through the three-tier GVN governance system of regions, provinces, and districts, with MACV having broad supervisory authority over civilian agencies at the lower levels.[85] Carver's memorandum to Helms had the desired effect. Helms sent a reply to Komer outlining the CIA's concerns, but Johnson made no subsequent effort to rein Komer in or to weaken his recommended approach.[86]

Meanwhile, Komer again expressed his concerns about the civil agencies' capabilities. In another private letter to Porter, he characterized their activities as "farcical" when compared with the military's efforts. Lodge blamed the GVN for not giving pacification priority, arguing that the U.S. mission had organized the civilian agencies more effectively. Komer conceded that Lodge had a point. Some portion of the ARVN should be redirected toward pacification and in support of the RD cadre, while the U.S. Army should continue its large unit strategy against the Viet Cong main force and NVA units. Nevertheless, Komer was still unsatisfied with the mission's movement on pacification, and this attitude created friction between him and Porter.

Komer complained that in their recent exchanges Porter's correspondence had taken on a petulant tone; Porter saw the performance statistics Komer provided him as criticism. On the contrary, Komer replied, he was trying to keep Lodge and Porter informed about how these indicators were perceived by Washington officials. It was a warning shot. These officials believed that Saigon focused on unimportant issues while critical issues fell into neglect or were disregarded. As an example, USAID's inability to account for goods in the supply pipeline was not simply an issue of inventory control. It required an expansive view to understand that this deficiency might mask corruption as well as an inability on the agency's part to demonstrate where the supplies were going and what they would be used for once they arrived. For his part, Komer stated that he was not going to "sit back and watch a potentially major scandal develop" without letting his two Saigon collaborators know about the problem. Washington's responsibility was to ensure effective policy implementation and accountability.

As he pointed out, as special assistant his job was not to expedite "requests from Saigon for people and supplies. . . . This is not the conception the President had in mind in setting up our operation, nor the way I intend to play the game." Komer was apologetic about any enmity his actions or words may have triggered. "But as long as I'm in this job I'm going to do my best to get it done."[87] Hurt feelings aside, as the summer slipped away, Johnson's patience with Lodge's excuses for slow progress on pacification was almost at an end.

———————

Bundy's departure and Johnson's indecision about a successor resulted in Komer's appointment as the interim national security adviser. Jack Valenti had suggested Komer for the position, and Bundy recommended his "interim" status should be made permanent.[88] However, the interim appointment was not a vote of confidence on Johnson's part. He informed the departing Bundy, "Tell Komer that he is to sit in your chair and do what needs to be done of your job, but his is to be absolutely invisible. I do not want anybody to see or hear or know that Komer is in the chair." Komer was to be invisible in a position that Bundy had made visible, and he was also to do all the work that Bundy had done without it being clear to him whether the assignment was permanent or temporary and for how long. Komer recognized it as the typical Johnsonian ploy; the president was keeping his options open. Komer was a loyal lieutenant so he did as told.

Komer's role as a policy entrepreneur had ended when Johnson assumed the presidency because LBJ's management style, personality, mind, and character were substantially different from that of Kennedy and he did not wish the NSC staff to function as it had under the deceased president. Johnson had little interest in an activist foreign policy, most visible in U.S. policy toward India and Egypt during the Kennedy administration. H. W. Brand's comment that Johnson "did a fair job sweeping up the shards of his predecessor's policies" is a telling remark about Johnson's more traditional approach to foreign policy.[89]

Instead, Johnson saw Komer as the expediter Komer fancied himself. "My job," Komer told a *Fortune* magazine editor soon after he became the special assistant for pacification, "is to hold a blowtorch to these agencies, to expedite. I figure out *how* to expedite as I go along." The agencies certainly felt the heat. As one USAID official admitted, "Say we have an order for twenty trucks. For a while, maybe nothing happens. But when Komer gets interested, we move those twenty trucks."[90]

The president trusted the bumptious Missourian to promote his interests, to direct the other war. This trust translated into broad authority, discretion, and autonomy, although it was bounded by presidential directive and instructions. In becoming the special assistant for pacification, Komer became, as Ambassador William Porter described him, "President Johnson's man."[91] Komer was no longer advising a president, he was helping Johnson govern and lead.

CHAPTER 6

A New Thrust to Pacification

*P*resident Johnson's pledge of pacification on behalf of the U.S. government signaled a new period of U.S. involvement in Vietnam,[1] but he remained uneasy about pushing Lodge too hard on implementing his vow to the South Vietnamese leaders. Despite Komer's concerns about Lodge's leadership and lack of attention to the other war, which he expressed directly to Johnson, the president would not direct Lodge to ensure that Porter was dedicating his time solely to pacification as the president had intended. Instead, he instructed Lodge to submit proposals to improve GVN and U.S. management structure and to harmonize pacification efforts from Saigon to the district level. Johnson, likely making a political calculation, counseled Komer not to say or do anything that would adversely reflect on Lodge.[2] The president did not want his administration disparaging a Republican ambassador whom the chief executive had personally selected and whom many considered an expert on pacification and a potential Republican presidential candidate in 1968.

In August 1966 Komer, Holbrooke, and Montague wrote a paper that set out a course of action for pacification. By this time, Komer and his staff were clear on their ideas and from this point on, it was a matter of advocating their position to the president.[3] The paper represented a plan for sweeping American organizational changes that blended Komer's ideas on U.S. support for pacification. It came at a propitious time, for that same month, Lodge disclosed that he planned to resign his post in the spring of 1967 so he could enter the Republican primaries as a presidential candidate. This revelation presented Komer with an opportunity to reintroduce the issue of better management in Saigon and increased military participation in pacification.[4] The paper would be the mechanism. It would have far-reaching consequences, for "no other document so accurately forecast the future course of the U.S. pacification advisory program."[5]

The paper, titled "Giving a New Thrust to Pacification," began by focusing on what were considered the essentials, given that only a little more than half of the population was regarded as being under GVN control: security in the countryside and getting the peasantry involved in the struggle against the Viet Cong. It continued by arguing that success in Vietnam had to include the "village war," that is, pacification, by dismantling the Viet Cong infrastructure to counter local guerrilla capability and weapons of intimidation and terror. It then posed the question, "How can pacification be managed more effectively?" The paper provided three options: (1) give Porter operational control over all U.S. pacification activity, (2) retain the present civil-military dichotomy but strengthen the management structure, or (3) assign the responsibility for both civil and military pacification to Westmoreland, with an integrated civil-military staff element in MACV to manage the program, which would be run by a civilian deputy to the commander.[6] Thus, Komer suggested for the first time in writing that Westmoreland assume responsibility for pacification as a practical necessity in order to remedy the overlap and duplication of programs run by military and civilian agencies. Additionally, as Komer explained to historian Mark Moyar, he preferred placing pacification under Westmoreland's authority because the military could manage the logistics and provide the considerable personnel needed to execute the program, which the civilian agencies could not furnish.[7] Since the third option was Komer's favorite, his argument for it was the strongest.[8]

Komer was finally satisfied enough with the third draft of the memorandum to share the twenty-one-page paper with two men whose views he trusted, John McNaughton, assistant secretary of defense for international security affairs and a conduit to McNamara, and John Paul Vann, a retired Army officer who now worked for the USAID in Vietnam.[9] Komer had met Vann during his first trip to Vietnam and recognized him as both an original thinker on counterinsurgency and an experienced field operator.[10] He also had Leonhart take the paper to Saigon to get the views of Lodge, Porter, and Westmoreland. Lodge and Porter, as expected, wanted the status quo; Westmoreland was willing to assume responsibility, if directed, and he had already given a higher priority to pacification as Communist main forces began to avoid direct engagements with American forces. This was all

Komer needed to hear. He discussed the matter with McNamara when he realized that State Department and the mission were not going to support his views.[11]

Komer's interest was not solely organizational. He was equally concerned about how the pacification effort could be advanced in Vietnam. His review of CIA and Defense Department intelligence analyses led him to conclude that while the evidence was still somewhat fragmentary, there was enough to suggest that the Viet Cong was not as potent a force as was suspected. There appeared to be recruiting and supply difficulties as well as declining morale, which made the force more vulnerable to increased pressure against it. If that was the case, then pacification might not be as slow or painful a task as many predicted. There would also be a stronger case for increasing the emphasis and resources on several programs, such as the defection program, police manpower, and political and economic development, which in conjunction with the military effort could enhance local security and might even show substantial early results. Komer urged McNamara to push for a more complete picture of the Viet Cong strength.[12] He continued to champion this issue over the coming months with the CIA's Saigon station chief, John Hart, and in early 1967 Komer indicated that because conventional and unconventional warfare in South Vietnam were interdependent, successful conventional operations against Viet Cong main force units were having a deleterious effect on the guerrilla units employed in the other war.[13]

In September Komer and McNaughton talked McNamara into officially asking the president to place pacification under military leadership. The third option was strengthened and circulated as a McNamara proposal to the other agencies for concurrence.[14] The proposal was also discussed with Johnson, who believed that Komer and McNamara were right. CIA, USAID, and State condemned the proposal, although Komer tried to sway Richard Helms by sharing his reasons for supporting the proposal with him.[15] Komer sent a memorandum to McNamara as a formal response extolling the concept. The negative civilian reaction, however, led Johnson to hold off on implementing the proposal until the right psychological moment. The civilian agencies did not want their personnel in the field under military control, and the State Department was particularly concerned that military leadership of pacification would give the impression that the United States was establishing something akin to a military government. This could be interpreted as a step toward U.S. occupation.[16]

Komer made allies outside of government who could be helpful in promoting his approach in the press and in order to respond to the substantial criticism of pacification by the *New York Times*' Saigon correspondent, Charles Mohr. He was also hoping to shape the views of important opinion makers and experts. In mid-September he met with Sir Robert Thompson to discuss pacification, a meeting that also convinced Komer that his approach was right. Komer had read Thompson's RAND paper, "A Proposal for Coordinating Operations in South Vietnam," wherein Thompson, the British counterinsurgency expert famous for his work in averting Communist insurgency in Malaysia, outlined a strategy for Vietnam pacification and the importance of U.S.-GVN coordination. One point Thompson made forcefully to Komer was the importance of demonstrating early success by pacifying some areas that were relatively easy to manage, rather than concentrating on areas that were more difficult or spreading efforts too widely and thereby having insufficient resources to make a difference. Despite his many suggestions, Thompson, who was a longtime observer of the war, was complimentary of the efforts being taken to step up pacification.[17]

Komer needed all the help he could muster. Mohr eviscerated Komer for his unclassified, glossy, public relations report to the president on pacification, released in September. The article's lede told it all: "The rural pacification plan in South Vietnam is behind schedule, even on paper. When viewed with the coldest realism in the countryside, it is still further behind schedule." Porter tried to console Komer by saying that some U.S. personnel were obviously providing background information to Mohr and that he would clearly rather "play the negative than the positive aspects." Porter was confident that the president would understand that reality.[18] Years later Komer would admit that the report was one of the most embarrassing events in his Vietnam-related activities.

Meanwhile, Johnson and Walt Rostow, who had been appointed national security adviser earlier in the year, were interested in keeping the pressure on the GVN to play a larger role in pacification. Westmoreland had submitted a concept of operations in August in which he specified that in the coming year the U.S. military would work directly with South Vietnamese forces and U.S. civilian agencies on RD activities. Rostow viewed the plan as a favorable sign and a feasible approach, as did

Johnson, who remarked, "Let's get Komer to pick up & spark the inspiration." Although Westmoreland's plan pleased Komer, he acknowledged that maintaining the initiative would be difficult, which proved the case a month later when reports underscored the civilian agencies' inability to execute their part of the plan.[19] The evidence of Johnson's growing frustration with Vietnam was mounting; the war was becoming unpopular domestically and a lightning rod for international criticism. U.S. forces were not losing, but neither negotiations nor victory was at hand. LBJ would not back down. No matter how beleaguered or ensnared he felt, the war was in the nation's vital interest, and he could not abandon an ally or those who had died fighting for this aim.[20]

Johnson continued to indicate his interest in helping domestic and international audiences understand—what Komer called "beating the publicity drum"—that the United States was interested not only in fighting but also in putting South Vietnam on more solid political and economic footing. Rostow recommended a conference in October, this time in Manila, and invited the GVN as well as other troop-providing allies. Although the primary thrust of the conference was peace negotiations with the North Vietnamese, Rostow, supporting Komer's view of the military running pacification, also wanted a renewed commitment by Saigon, backed by the allies, to pacification and related issues, such as economic development, education, health, and agriculture.[21] Johnson agreed to the conference, although he believed that it "will probably accomplish little so we must consider how to keep the initiative in the period ahead."[22] Nonetheless, Moyers and the president managed the public relations facet of the meeting as a means to persuade the American public that 1967 would be a bellwether year whereby U.S. combat success would compel the North Vietnamese to the negotiating table.[23]

In preparation for the Manila conference, Johnson asked Komer to provide language for use in his speeches.[24] Komer thereby used the Manila conference, which he attended with the president and other senior U.S. officials, to surface his argument that the U.S. military must assume responsibility for pacification management since local security was critical. Only the ARVN and U.S. military could provide this essential ingredient, with the ARVN providing security for the RD cadres. The South Vietnamese government committed to the last point at this Manila conference, although the decision disappointed ARVN officers who considered their forces relegated to a less important mission.[25]

Komer also used the conference preparations to sway the president on a second issue. He argued that because the U.S. military had the organization, personnel, engineering resources, and logistical capability, it had to be involved in support of pacification.[26] In response, Johnson told McNamara, "I feel strongly that it [pacification] ought to go to the military,"[27] but he delayed making a final decision until McNamara along with Komer; under secretary of State Nicholas Katzenbach, who had recently replaced the dovish George Ball; and Gen. Earle Wheeler met with Lodge in Saigon in early October to discuss this new approach. By the time the party left Vietnam, McNamara, convinced that the large-unit operations and bombing would not lead to a victory by the end of 1968, was formulating a pessimistic report to Johnson. A revitalized and vigorous pacification program, he argued, held the most promising basis for conducting the war over a prolonged period, but with reduced risks and costs to the United States.[28]

Thus, Komer secured powerful allies. McNamara and Rostow were supportive, and the Joint Chiefs of Staff agreed that transferring pacification management to Westmoreland was likely the best approach; they were not optimistic that an effective civilian organization could ever be created and certainly not speedily.[29] The civilian agencies realized that the burden was on them to offer a better alternative and that Komer and McNamara had already convinced Johnson that pacification was not working and that only the military could do what was needed. Rusk objected strenuously, but his views did not win over the president. The CIA realized that the probability of changing the president's mind was slight, so it opted to attack any recommendations whereby it would lose control of its programs in country.[30]

Lodge opposed the change in concept, which caused Johnson to again relent temporarily and consider an alternative that Katzenbach proposed in a separate report to the president on the party's return from Saigon.[31] Katzenbach argued that the U.S. mission had made progress and that the best approach was to have the U.S. military and ARVN improve security while the civilian agencies were consolidated in a new organization known as the Office of Civil Operations (OCO), which Porter would run after being relieved of his day-to-day deputy ambassador duties.[32] Komer was perturbed by the State Department's counterploy. Johnson, although still dissatisfied, approved the scheme, wanted OCO established "soonest," and asked to see progress quickly. He set an unworkable deadline of 90 to 120 days for the new organization to demonstrate movement. Rusk notified Lodge on November 4 of the president's decision.[33] General Wheeler and General Johnson advised Westmoreland to prepare for the eventuality of assuming responsibility for pacification. Westmoreland, who considered OCO a "sop to the prideful creatures in the bureaucratic jungles of Washington and Saigon," believed that the president would disband it in ninety days. Consequently, he established the Revolutionary Development Support Directorate in MACV under the direction of Brig. Gen. William A. Knowlton.[34]

Komer informed Porter that the president's deadline was firm and that he had better "get on the stick." Johnson personally attested to this view by writing a letter to Lodge urging him to move quickly.[35] Komer also advised Porter by private correspondence that the perception in Washington was that there was an initial "head of steam," but the problem would be sustaining this initial momentum. Komer offered a few suggestions that included pressing for a pacification plan in which a "clear and hold" strategy would be accepted by MACV and the Republic of Vietnam Armed Forces (RVNAF) as an "indispensable prerequisite to the civil side of pacification"; GVN political and economic developments in the countryside could occur only in a secure environment. He also advised Porter to demonstrate progress on a few programs that would have a major impact on the rural areas and the GVN's image, such as local elections, land reform, and anticorruption drives. He needed to show visible progress within ninety days.[36]

Komer and his staff wrote the directive establishing the OCO, and then Komer sent Montague and Holbrooke to Saigon to assist with setting it up. The mission refused to take the short deadline seriously and moved at a "glacial pace," as Richard Holbrooke informed Komer after returning to Washington from Saigon.[37] The office was not established until November 26.[38] Komer understood that part of the problem was the RVNAF's reluctance to support pacification. He believed that this could be attributed to a lack of emphasis on the part of MACV and an unwillingness to institute a clear and hold strategy, a strategy that he considered a vital first step toward successful pacification. He urged Rusk to press Westmoreland on this issue when the two met in Saigon in December.[39]

Holbrooke, however, held a contrary view. He drew a connection between reducing the enemy's political base and building up support for the GVN as the two most important purposes of pacification. He argued that the State Department, his parent agency, was the problem because it was incapable of reshaping the very nature of the South Vietnamese government, which was critical to both purposes. Holbrooke believed that new civilian and military leadership and encouragement of the evolution of the political process, through such mechanisms as elections, was essential and that the programs Komer ran were the means of initiating this evolution in the political process.[40] While Komer was sympathetic to this view, he believed the emphasis should continue to be on better integrating U.S. efforts in Vietnam rather than on bureaucratic knife fights in Washington.

Nonetheless, Komer thought it necessary to maintain cognizance of all Vietnam issues because, with the exception of the air war and the negotiations track, which he believed was a diplomatic responsibility, all issues impinged on pacification to some degree. Komer had recognized months earlier that enhanced coordination of interagency efforts at the Washington level could yield improved effectiveness of U.S. efforts in Vietnam. On September 30 he had sent a memorandum to Moyers, who was part of the president's Tuesday Lunch Group along with McNamara, Rusk, and Rostow, proposing the establishment of a small "war council" to upgrade the management of all aspects of the war. He recommended that Katzenbach chair the group. In Komer's view, "the problem is how to organize at the level below the President or even Rusk and McNamara, who are also busy on so much else." The proposed group would meet biweekly and report directly to the president and the two secretaries in writing. The advantage of having Katzenbach chair the group was that because he was new to the job, he would be viewed as impartial; he did not have a "hawk/dove image problem yet." The council's membership would be limited to Katzenbach, Deputy Secretary of Defense Cyrus Vance, Rostow, and Komer—anything larger would be unwieldy.[41]

Not satisfied with this approach, Komer sent Moyers another memorandum the same day offering an alternative "Vietnam kitchen cabinet," run out of the White House with Moyers in charge. Komer argued that Rostow could not run the group—"he has the wrong image"—and Komer could not manage it because that would create friction with Rostow. "Besides," he remarked, "the whole virtue would be to give it to someone who has the President's constant ear." Moyers sent a memorandum to the president the same day in which he outlined Komer's original proposal. Komer, in his usual fashion, followed with a memorandum to the president less than a week later in which he restated the necessity of "*an effective subcabinet level mechanism in Washington to monitor performance*" [emphasis in the original].[42]

On November 15, at a Tuesday lunch meeting, Johnson directed that a group, chaired by Katzenbach and composed of Komer, Rostow, Vance, and a senior military officer, be formed to meet three times a week "on Vietnam and all its dimensions." Komer's subcabinet council, known as the "Non-Group" by its participants, began meeting in early 1967 in Katzenbach's office at the State Department building in northwest Washington nearly every Thursday at 5:00 p.m. Since the group met after usual business hours, the meetings had a relaxed and informal atmosphere, drinks were served, and although the subjects of discussion were known in advance, neither an agenda nor notes were kept. In addition to the principal members Komer had identified, General Wheeler was later added, and other members included William Bundy or his deputy, Philip Habib; Averell Harriman; and Richard Helms. McNamara attended frequently and on occasion so did Rusk, although technically both were not members.[43]

The Non-Group, in essence a lower-level version of the Tuesday Lunch Group, became a vehicle for the members, through their recommendations, to influence interdepartmental policy planning and implementation, particularly with respect to coordination among the relevant agencies, the flow of information, and the major issues and problems associated with the war, especially the bombing policy and pacification.[44] This is exactly how Komer intended to use the group: to move beyond management issues and begin to fashion a strategy that would link pacification to the wider military effort in Vietnam. Katzenbach described the strategy as Komer's "plans for 'Vietnamizing' the war."[45]

Soon after formation of the Non-Group, Rostow and Komer, in consultation with William Bundy, wrote a paper titled "A Strategy for the Next Phase in Vietnam," which Rostow forwarded to the president. In the paper, they proposed a strategy for compelling the North Vietnamese to the negotiation table, contending that while the enemy could not win, the United States had not yet forced its adversary to accept negotiations on U.S. terms by breaking the Communists' will. Two options other than occupying North Vietnam were available to the United States. The first was to bomb the North so heavily that it imperiled the country's political, social, or economic structure. Komer and Rostow rejected that option, arguing that it could result in Chinese intervention and exact a heavy political toll at home and in world opinion. The second option was to "produce a palpable process of political and military disintegration of the Viet Cong." Their assessment was that Viet Cong morale was declining, as evinced by desertion rates; the enemy was suffering from shortages of food and medical supplies; and the GVN had been successful in establishing itself as a viable government. Thus, Komer and Rostow believed that these vulnerabilities, if accelerated, could cause a split between the Viet Cong and Hanoi, which would be "a decisive step toward winning the war."[46] Their approach necessitated waging war on several fronts—political, social, economic, ideological, and psychological—in order for the United States and its South Vietnamese ally to succeed.

Their plan consisted of the following elements. The first objective was a dramatic and sustained appeal to the Viet Cong to desist from fighting and to collaborate in the development of a new South Vietnamese nation. Accomplishing this goal entailed an offer of amnesty, enhanced efforts to prompt the defection of Viet Cong leaders, increased psychological warfare activities to divide the Viet Cong from Hanoi, and an agreement to a constitution, followed by elections in which the Viet Cong, granted amnesty, could vote. The second major element would be accelerated pacification through unified U.S./GVN civil-military management, including an increase in the number of ARVN forces involved in pacification duties, a focus on pacification in key areas of South Vietnam, and an expansion of foundational pacification programs, such as RD cadres and police. Supplementing these two major thrusts were other activities, such as land reform and continuation of the bombing offensive in the North as a means of imposing a cost on Hanoi for continuing the war.

On October 5 Komer sent the president a memorandum that reiterated many of these same points and offered an enthusiastic appraisal: "We're doing much better than we think, we have at the end of September 1966, achieved some real momentum in Vietnam." He underscored that the steps Rostow and he had outlined in their earlier memorandum were critical to achieve a cumulative effect on Hanoi to "either force the enemy to negotiate or cripple his ability to sustain the war." The primary objective, he declared, was to achieve a "satisfactory outcome by the end of 1967, or at the minimum achieving such momentum that it will be clear to all—including the US public—that it is only a matter of time." This strategy, he believed, could be accomplished without further escalation in the bombing of the North or an increase in troop deployments beyond the level the president had already approved.[47] By offering this proposal, Komer hoped to blunt Hanoi's strategy of revolutionary war, which called for a protracted conflict that ate away at the adversary's political will.

While Rostow continued to push the Rostow-Komer strategy with the president, Komer turned his attention to bolstering McNamara's waning morale and setting out with more specificity the situation on the ground with a recommended plan for 1967. In a paper titled "Vietnam Prognosis for 1967–68," which he sent the secretary, he recommended that the Non-Group fashion a 1967 program for the president's approval. He outlined his reasons for a more optimistic appraisal: First, Westmoreland's "spoiling strategy," that is, the acceleration of search-and-destroy operations, had blunted any hopes Hanoi had of initiating its Phase III strategy. (Phase III focused on destruction of the enemy. At this phase, a substantial part of the guerrilla force had matured into regular conventional army units that could decisively engage with opposing government forces.) Second, Viet Cong and NVA losses from death or defection were occurring at a rate faster than could be replaced (a situation known as the "cross-over point" in the bureaucratic argot. Third, there may have also been a major psychological turning point among the population, as evinced by the 80 percent voter turnout for the September elections. In short, the election turnout indicated that the vast majority of the South Vietnamese population had confidence that the GVN and its U.S. ally were winning the war. Komer cautioned that these signs did not mean that the GVN and the United States would win the war; rather they signaled that "we're beginning to 'win' the war in Vietnam." The key was eroding the strength of the southern Communists through a successful pacification program, which included a better and more effective representative government, additional emphasis on defections, improved management and orchestration of U.S. programs, and prudent employment of the ARVN. Together, these elements would create a "bandwagon psychology" that would ultimately lead to a "successful outcome" by the end of 1967 or perhaps 1968. Again, Komer recognized that in the "fog of war," nothing is guaranteed, and this plan could be upset by a number of unknowns such as whether the South Vietnamese government remained intact and was not upended by other crises or increased infiltration of NVA forces.[48] One historian has remarked that because Komer suggested in this memorandum that there were few alternatives to the current strategy, but that the United States should continue its effort nonetheless, he thereby created an atmosphere that included a "curious mixture of gloom and optimism."[49]

The same day, Komer wrote a second paper, "A Strategic Plan for 1967 in Vietnam," which he forwarded to Rostow on December 10, with a cover note asking him to endorse his proposal and send it to the president. Rostow did so after making some minor edits, and Komer followed up with a note to Johnson stating that the paper was "a means of getting a clear focus on the all-out effort needed next year." He and Rostow recommended that the paper be issued as a presidential directive to emphasize its importance to Johnson and the clear assignment of responsibilities. The president agreed with Komer's proposal. He told Rostow that he thought the paper was good and that he wanted to discuss it further with them. On December 12 the paper, which was now titled "Strategic Guidelines for 1967 in Vietnam," was sent as a draft presidential directive to Rusk and McNamara with a cover note from Rostow indicating that the president wanted to issue a set of guidelines.[50] Komer's plan focused on seizing the strategic initiative, politically, militarily, and psychologically, from Hanoi for the United States and the GVN. He also wanted to lessen the ambiguity of U.S. political-military objectives. To accomplish both these goals he recognized that all the instruments of national power had to be employed and unity of effort enhanced.

In the paper's brief introduction, Komer stated that the deployment of substantial U.S. forces had significantly improved the military situation in Vietnam, but that was not sufficient. Instead, "it is imperative that we mount and effectively orchestrate a concerted military, civil, and political effort to achieve a satisfactory outcome as soon as possible" based on three strategic aims. The first was to maximize a satisfactory outcome by December 1967 or, if that end were not possible, to put the United States and GVN in a position to do so over a longer period. The second aim was to force Hanoi to negotiate, to weaken irreparably the Viet Cong/NVA so the North would relent, or to make it demonstrable that the war was being won by the United States and GVN. The final aim was to augment the bombing offensive and the main force campaign with increased efforts to pacify the countryside and "increase the attractive power of the GVN."[51] The last point stressed that to counter Hanoi's seizure of political power, an essential component of revolutionary warfare, the GVN had to be perceived as a viable and preferable political alternative.

Komer then stated that, because countering revolutionary warfare required assailing the enemy on several fronts, the achievement of these strategic aims rested on nine program areas, each of which included several facets. The two principal elements were a major pacification effort and increasing the anti–main force spoiling offensive. The remaining seven were (1) limiting infiltration from the North by using a more precise and effective bombing offensive focused on harassing infiltration routes; (2) implementing a major national reconciliation program; (3) creating a popularly based GVN; (4) implementing several of the commitments made at the Manila Conference, such as improving local government, initiating land reform, and rooting out corruption; (5) maintaining a viable civil economy and, in particular, preventing an inflationary spiral; (6) formulating a pre-negotiating and negotiating strategy; and (7) mounting a major information campaign to inform the U.S. electorate and world citizens regarding the war, including a way to measure progress in a credible fashion.[52]

Komer was offering a strategic plan that did not concentrate on the various options available to the United States but instead on a feasible, acceptable, and suitable counterstrategy designed to take possession of the strategic initiative rather than react to Hanoi. Further, he realized that the changing and "mosaic" nature of the war meant that the counterstrategy had to be flexible enough to address the phases in which the current conflict was being fought and to anticipate its future character.

Komer's effort went unrewarded. The Defense and State Departments, including the Joint Chiefs of Staff, the U.S. embassy in Saigon, the U.S. Pacific Command, and MACV, for a variety of reasons rejected the plan or recommended tepid revisions. The principal agencies could not even agree on the primary U.S. objective in the war. Some of the criticisms were obvious attempts at bureaucratic "turf protection," such as the military's concern about civilian intrusion into the field commander's operational role or concern about appearing weak when carrying out Komer's recommendation regarding contact with the Viet Cong, while others demonstrated complacency and an unwillingness to press for change. Because of these divisions among the principals, the directive was never issued; it died from a thousand bureaucratic cuts even after being modified. Ultimately, the White House believed that the "best approach to retain flexibility in Vietnam and at home was to allow the ambiguity and uncertainty to continue."[53]

Komer was roused from his strategist role to attend solely to pacification, his primary duty. Even after repeated visits in December and January by Komer and his staff, urging a faster pace, there was little to show in terms of planning or program implementation during the months running up to the next major U.S.-GVN conference, held on Guam, March 20–21, 1967.[54] Additionally, the State Department continued to resist discussions with Komer and his staff regarding the relationship between the massive U.S. investment in South Vietnam and the recruitment of more able GVN political leadership to carry out pacification. Holbrooke decried that the agency "dealt with this office reluctantly and as seldom as possible."[55]

Additionally, Leonhart's report at the end of December 1966, which Komer forwarded to the president, was not sanguine. "The lack of progress in pacification remains the crux of the Vietnam problem," Leonhart concluded. The ambassador then made a compelling argument that the duration and extent of the war, the persistence or fading away of the Viet Cong/NVA, and the likelihood of negotiations all hinged on pacification because the GVN's ability to stand on its own depended on local security. It was the weakest instrument. Leonhart also noted the divisions in opinions about the nature of the war and priorities between the civilians and military, a rift that was more noticeable and deeper than what he had found on his two previous trips to the war zone in 1966.[56]

Komer added his views a month later in a note to the president in which he maintained that "pacification was creeping forward, but not much more." He reasoned that the civilians had insufficient resources to do the job and that the military, which had the assets, gave "it only a lick and a promise. There is still a grievous lack of integrated, detailed civil/military pacification planning in Vietnam." There was also an "appalling lack of vigorous, integrated management of Vietnam affairs in Saigon" caused by Westmoreland's inadequate coordination with Lodge and Porter. If the United States was going to maximize its chances of accelerating results in 1967–68, then some radical step in management might be necessary.[57] Similarly, he griped to McNamara that it was discouraging that the U.S. mission in Saigon and MACV had still not developed the "realistic and detailed" 1967 pacification/RD plans both men felt were necessary.[58]

Komer tried to remain upbeat about overall progress in Vietnam, but he also tempered his optimism with the recognition that "pacification is by its very nature the toughest job we face in Vietnam," essentially because the local guerrillas and infrastructure were difficult to "locate and root out . . . especially when much of the countryside is friendly to them—as in the [Mekong] Delta."[59] After a ten-day visit to Vietnam in February, he reaffirmed his belief that momentum could be achieved in 1967: "Wastefully, expensively, but nonetheless indisputably, we are winning the war in the South." He recognized that it was sheer mass and power that were contributing by "grinding down the enemy." Pacification, he noted, was lagging behind, but he still believed it was moving forward. At a press conference with the president after his February visit, he publicly displayed his usual optimistic self. Komer summarized the main conclusions he had drawn from his trip, which enabled him, he said, to make his most encouraging report to date. Progress had been made in opening surface transportation facilities—highways, railroads, and coastwise shipping—as alternatives to airlift; drafting a constitution and planning national and local elections; improving the economy as a result of the slowing of inflation, the increased availability of import financing, a rise in tax collections, the prospects for an adequate 1967 rice crop, and the easing of congestion in the port of Saigon; and reorganizing the U.S. Office of Civil Operations and increasing the effectiveness of the South Vietnamese army, which had assigned progressively more of its units to pacification after training by mobile training teams. As a result, it would be difficult for the Viet Cong to maintain its strength in the South in 1967, a view Westmoreland and McNamara shared. The proof, these two maintained, was in the Viet Cong's intensified terrorist campaign against district capitals and pacification teams and in a doubling of the number of enemy defectors, a sure sign of declining morale. McNamara likewise interpreted the attacks as a sign that the U.S. and GVN effort to win control of the countryside was succeeding. It is questionable whether the president shared Komer's or the others' sanguinity; even Komer's staff believed his views needed tempering.[60]

Holbrooke, who had accompanied Komer on his sixth trip to Vietnam in February, moderated Komer's fervor with his less optimistic view that pacification was hardly on the move. At best, Holbrooke admitted, we can say, "we are finally building a base for successful pacification," though even that statement was a "risky proposition."[61] At that point, such distinctions did not matter. Even Komer admitted a "vigorous top team in Saigon" was still missing and "better civil/military coordination . . . in the critical gray area of pacification" was required.[62] But Komer had reasonable cause for optimism about progress in the other war; a CIA analysis suggested that evidence indicated that the overall U.S. effort was having a greater impact on the capabilities of the Viet Cong, including the guerrilla effort and its infrastructure, than was generally appreciated.[63]

Johnson was now ready to move forward with the McNamara-Komer option for organizing pacification support under the U.S. military with a civilian deputy running the program. He had also decided on civilian leadership changes in Vietnam since Lodge would be leaving shortly. This news suited Komer; in the intervening months he had become a vocal critic of Lodge. On returning from his February visit to Vietnam, he vigorously advocated his removal as ambassador, telling the president that better management of U.S. programs in support of pacification was crucial and that "the sooner you replace Lodge with a top manager the better."[64]

Johnson used the Guam conference with the South Vietnamese leaders on March 20–21, in part to introduce Ellsworth Bunker, the distinguished diplomat, as the new U.S. ambassador to South Vietnam, and Ambassador Eugene Locke, one of Johnson's political allies from Texas who was serving as U.S. ambassador to Pakistan, as his new deputy, replacing Porter. Komer was to be the first civilian head of pacification under Westmoreland with the personal rank of ambassador to underscore the importance of his assignment and the president's interest in pushing the pace of pacification. The announcement of Komer's appointment disappointed a number of U.S. officials at the embassy in Saigon and in the field. Some had hoped that the respected Porter would replace Lodge. Komer was unpopular among these same officials. As one veteran Saigon newspaper reporter noted, "During his many visits to South Vietnam in recent months he has displayed enormous curiosity and diligence, but his exuberance and tendency to frame glowing reports have created resentment." One official labeled Komer "a Guildenstern at the court of Lyndon I—willing to please his President at all costs." Another unidentified source added gratuitously, "Komer will find out that Saigon isn't Washington."[65]

Johnson had asked Komer in February if he would be willing to go to Vietnam. Komer had said yes. "As a professional with 25 years' service, when the President says go and do a job, I'll try to do it," Komer recollected in 1969. He continued, "It's simple professionalism."[66] Nonetheless, he was not pleased with the new assignment. "The only thing I failed to realize," he later wrote, "was that if you build a better mousetrap you're likely to be the first one asked to test it. To my surprise, I was told to go out and make it work."[67] He was displeased for another reason as well. For nearly three months, he had expected a high-level presidential appointment in Saigon. When he learned of his new job just days before the Guam conference, he disclosed to the president that the arrangement had taken him aback. He had thought he would be replacing Porter as the deputy ambassador with responsibility for the entire civilian effort. Instead, he complained, his new position was even lower in stature and significance, since he would be dealing with pacification only as a deputy to Westmoreland. Johnson also sent mixed signals. At a news conference at the end of the Guam conference, he implied that Komer would remain a White House aide but would also spend more of his time in Saigon. This made no sense to Komer or other U.S. officials. Regardless of the details, Johnson was clearly signaling that he thought the war could be ended only if military action was supported by effective political and economic activities. He expected closer collaboration between the military and civilian efforts, and he intended to hold his new team accountable for maintaining a balance between the resources dedicated to each element. Senator John C. Stennis and other members of the Preparedness Subcommittee of the Senate Armed Services Committee released a report that agreed with Johnson's determination to spur pacification. In the subcommittee's view, winning the other war was critical to realizing the overall objectives of the conflict.[68] Komer had no time for self-pity or to reflect idly on the president's and Congress' viewpoints.

Immediately following the conference, Komer flew to Saigon with Westmoreland. Over the next two days they negotiated how the new organization, consisting of OCO and the Revolutionary Development Support Directorate in MACV, which Westmoreland renamed Civil Operations and Revolutionary Development Support (CORDS), would be integrated into the existing MACV framework. Further, CORDS, as the U.S. organization for pacification, would have a single chain of command running from Saigon to the districts, the lowest advisory level. The person who headed the program at each level would be the best available leader, regardless of whether he was civilian or military. The two also discussed Komer's specific duties. He would not act "just as a coordinator and adviser," but in effect, as "the component commander in charge of the American contribution to pacification" with sole authority and answerable only to Westmoreland, who could fire him if he were unsatisfied with Komer's performance. He would also be the primary interlocutor with GVN on pacification matters. The two reached their agreement quickly, and Komer returned to Washington to write his final report and to draft the formal presidential directive putting him into business as part of MACV but with a direct reporting channel to Bunker as well, a point on which the ambassador was insistent.[69] The two men's acceptance of this organizational construct was a unique achievement, attesting to Komer's management acumen and his powers of persuasion.[70]

During Komer's visit, Army general Creighton Abrams was named as Westmoreland's new deputy. Westmoreland told Komer that he intended to use Abrams primarily for "revamping the ARVN, PF, RF, CIDG [Civilian Irregular Defense Group], etc.," in addition to acting as Westmoreland's "general alter ego and taking over in his absence." Komer would supervise pacification planning, management, and evaluation.[71] He had told Johnson earlier that pacification was a problem in field execution, and he would now be responsible for implementing his own proposal.[72] However, he had one more task to perform for Johnson.

Westmoreland had a surprise for the president. After the conference, he sent Johnson a request for 100,000–200,000 more troops and authority to take action against the infiltration routes in Laos and Cambodia, mine the harbors in North Vietnam, and intensify the bombing. The request set off a two-month-long reappraisal of the U.S. strategy in the war, with the Non-Group leading the assessment. On April 24 Katzenbach assigned the members to prepare papers on the current situation in Vietnam, the possibilities of negotiation, and the military and political ramifications of escalating the war in the South and the North; he later asked for a fourth paper on pacification, which Leonhart would write as he was taking over Komer's duties in the White House.[73]

Because Komer was leaving for his new duties in Saigon, he sent the president a memorandum about Westmoreland's request in which he questioned the requirement for more troops. In a reversal of his earlier position, he argued that although Hanoi would not likely negotiate, the National Liberation Front might. However, even that was unlikely given Hanoi's control of the organization. He also wrote that increased bombing or mining the harbors would not increase the pressure on Hanoi but would entail some risk. If anything, the focus should be on getting the South Vietnamese armed forces to take on greater responsibility and setting up a situation favorable to bringing some U.S. troops home. Further, a strengthened and more potent civilian pacification program was essential to create a viable GVN capable of fending for itself and attracting the loyalty of the South Vietnamese population.[74]

McNamara's chief "whiz kid," Alain Enthoven, assistant secretary of defense for systems analysis, agreed with Komer—additional troops would hurt pacification. In his estimation, it was a "race" between building a viable South Vietnam and Hanoi's bet that U.S. public support would be lost before this goal could be accomplished. Successful pacification depended on improved support of the Vietnamese armed forces and a more vigorous national government, not on creating disincentives for the South Vietnamese to help themselves. Success would be the result of time, patience, and economic as well as political progress, not of winning military battles.[75] Consequently, Westmoreland's request was shelved, primarily on the basis of domestic politics. Johnson judged the request politically unacceptable, for it required a reserve call-up and partial mobilization.[76]

President Johnson similarly understood that in the other war, the "battle" had only begun, as he termed it in a personal letter he wrote Komer on May 1, four days before the latter left for Vietnam. In that letter, Johnson wrote that he might be the "only man who knows the full measure of talent, loyalty and energy you have given so unselfishly to your country during six years in the White House." He continued by expressing his pride and gratitude for Komer's service and the debt he owed him for his counsel, judgment, and integrity, adding that these were "qualities of mind and character I prize and will greatly miss." The White House would be a "less buoyant place" without him, but Vietnam "can doubtless profit as much from your spirit as for your skills. I have found them equally irrepressible." Johnson stated that he could part with them only because they would now be used for the urgent purpose of the Vietnam pacification program. "Its priority is absolute," Johnson wrote. "Its success will depend in critical part on the unique knowledge and drive you bring." Johnson believed that Komer was up to the challenge he would face in Vietnam, as he had demonstrated many times before his ability to confront hard problems and beat the odds.[77] The letter took out some of the sting Komer felt at his reduced status in the new leadership team in Saigon.

––––––––––

Komer's significance in the reemphasis on pacification is important, noted the authors of the Pentagon Papers.[78] In short, he won the bureaucratic clash with USAID, the CIA, the State Department, and the U.S. embassy in Saigon over pacification when the president agreed to place the program under Westmoreland's command using a single manager concept. He indirectly ensured that there would be a new civilian leadership team to head this venture, even if he unwittingly and reluctantly became a member of it. To accomplish these ends, Komer used his aggressive personality, his disdain of bureaucracy, his business education, his firsthand observations in Vietnam, and—reaching back two decades to the historical study he wrote as a junior officer after World War II—his awareness that the U.S. military had the capacity for nation building.

He also had a deep appreciation of the war in which he was involved. As one historian notes, Komer "stood responsible for the subtle shift" in the U.S. strategy in Vietnam. "No longer could Westmoreland view counterinsurgency in strictly linear terms. Pacification and the big-unit war would occur simultaneously and on increasingly equal footing."[79] He recognized that the previous pacification plans had been fragmented into numerous, frequently competing priorities and were often incoherent. Their failure also resulted from the enemy having the initiative in the countryside and a lack of adequate resources to make the program work. The last two impediments had been overcome, but that did not ensure success.[80]

Komer understood Vietnam as a political-military struggle, which demanded a political strategy to maintain the GVN's stability and, ultimately, to foster a transition to representative government and effective institutions that would help diminish Hanoi's claim that the conflict was a "nationalist war against puppet governments dominated by a colonialist-capitalist country, i.e., first France and then the United States."[81] The political strategy also included a grasp of Maoist insurgency theory and recognition of the criticality of the Viet Cong infrastructure that sustained the guerrilla war. But for pacification to have a chance of success, Komer held that three principles had to be followed.

First, pacification "must remain a Vietnamese job," and the ARVN would have to secure the countryside. The ARVN, the weakest link, needed revamping and to accept its role in working with the RD cadres. Second, "the absolute prerequisite to the success of pacification is adequate continuous local security." Such security was the responsibility of the Vietnamese military, but it also necessitated strengthening security forces at the district and village level. Generally, it demanded a prioritization of resources, focusing primarily on the area around Saigon, the Mekong Delta, and the coastal strip, where most of the South Vietnamese people lived. Komer even cautioned against the use of statistics as a reliable measurement of success in these endeavors. Security was a relative concept, he argued. Further pacifying the entire country was not the objective. Instead, the proposition was what he called a "super Malaya," to reduce the guerrilla activity to the point that it did not interfere with the normal functioning of the country and its stability was no longer in doubt. Achieving this aim was as much a psychological victory as a political-military one.[82]

The third principle was the coordination of civil-military operations, which preferably involved planning between the United States and the GVN at every level. If that could not occur, then at least there should be joint planning and management in the field at the province level among the military, the RD cadres, and the police, especially the paramilitary Special Branch. It was imperative that two separate wars—a military war under Westmoreland and a political-economic war under the U.S. ambassador—not be fought in Vietnam.[83]

It is evident that Komer was knowledgeable about the French theoreticians and British counterinsurgency practices in Malaya. He was also conversant with Maoist guerrilla warfare theory and had met with the renowned Vietnam expert Bernard Fall as well as read his books on the French experience in the first Indochina war in order to understand the operational environment.[84] However, in taking charge of pacification in Saigon, he embraced Clausewitz's dictum: *"The first, the supreme, the most far-reaching act of judgment that the statesman and the commander have to make is to establish by that test the kind of war on which they are embarking; neither mistaking it for, nor trying to turn it into, something that is alien to its nature. This is the first of all strategic questions and the most comprehensive."*[85]

CHAPTER 7

In Country

*W*orried about ground fire, the pilot of the U.S. Air Force KC-135 jet tanker maintained a high altitude over the Central Highlands of South Vietnam.[1] Behind the cockpit, the portable seats installed in the half-empty upper deck made the aircraft a "McNamara Special," so called because of the secretary of defense's frugal measures to reduce the costs of VIP travel. The cabin, which had no inner shell, was uncomfortable, alternately hot and cold, and the relentless deafening roar of the four engines made routine conversations shouting matches. There were no windows to look out; it was more like a sensory deprivation chamber, the passengers uncertain if it were night or day.[2]

At that moment, however, Maj. Gen. Walter T. "Dutch" Kerwin, the new chief of staff for MACV, did not care about the cabin temperature or the lack of visibility to the outside world. He did not even worry that a month earlier, 100,000 people marched in the streets of New York protesting the war or that the U.S. military strength in Vietnam had reached 400,000 troops.[3] He just wanted to get off the plane.

The flight, which left from Andrews Air Force Base outside Washington, D.C., for Vietnam three days ago, had been no "hearts and flowers."[4] It was quite evident to Kerwin by the time the plane had reached Hawaii for briefings at U.S. Pacific Command that the two men with him could not have been more different. It was also chillingly apparent that the relationship between them would not be cordial. Gen. Creighton Abrams, the fabled World War II hero at the Battle of the Bulge who thought he was going to be the new commander of MACV but would soon find out differently, was "calm, resourceful, down-to-earth." The other man was Robert Komer, who Kerwin characterized as "egotistical, abrasive and volatile," but with a "tremendous brain."[5] Kerwin feared that in his new job he would spend the next several months acting as a referee separating two prizefighters. Finally and thankfully, the plane banked sharply for the runway of Tan Son Nhut Air Base. The date was May 4, 1967.

A few miles away, Daniel Ellsberg, a USAID employee, sat in the U.S. embassy listening to Komer's press conference, which was held after the plane had landed in Vietnam and broadcast on Armed Forces Radio. Komer was assertive and exuberant with the reporters. He said that he had seen pacification progress when he was special assistant to the president and that the program would ultimately achieve success. Shortly after the conference ended, Komer, his brassy voice resounding throughout the building, arrived at the embassy. "He was whirling, filling the room with energy and enthusiasm," Ellsberg would recall years later. Komer greeted Ellsberg, whom he had known when the latter was on McNamara's staff. The two moved to Komer's office, and Komer closed the door. Ellsberg asked Komer if he believed what he said at the press conference. Komer replied unguardedly, "Dan, do you think I am crazy?" Ellsberg was perplexed and asked why he had taken the job. Komer replied succinctly that if the president asks you to do something, you do it, "no matter how hopeless it is."[6]

Komer's experiences had made him one of the "connoisseurs of Third World adversity,"[7] a diviner of statistics, and always a reverent practitioner of scientific management. He would reveal these beliefs in the first few months of his tenure as deputy for pacification, its high priest, arguing that a successful counterinsurgency program was a matter of better management and motivation. It was less about "winning hearts and minds," a phrase Komer disparaged in private.[8]

By the time Komer and Abrams arrived in Saigon, Johnson still had not approved the directive that would transfer pacification responsibilities to Westmoreland and designate Komer as the general's deputy. Johnson wanted Ambassador Ellsworth Bunker, who had arrived in Saigon a month earlier, to agree to the arrangement. Further, the president did not want to create the perception that he was undermining the civilian leadership in Saigon or diminishing the ambassador's role as his envoy. His concerns were unfounded. Bunker readily assented, particularly to Komer's new role. The two men had worked together congenially in the Kennedy administration.[9]

On May 9 the president's signature on the directive, which Komer had fashioned before he left Washington, made official the new organizational arrangement devised by Komer and Westmoreland. Komer would supervise the military and civil aspects of pacification. Additionally, the directive specified that pacification would be integrated under a single manager with MACV charged this responsibility under the overall authority of the ambassador. The current functions and civilian personnel of the OCO in the U.S. mission would be transferred to MACV. Komer would implement this task as deputy for pacification with the personal rank of ambassador.[10]

Consistent with his personality, Komer did not wait for Johnson to make the appointment official. As Westmoreland acknowledged years later, "The Lord knows the President handed me a volatile character in Bob Komer," but he was also the right person for the job of pulling the disparate bureaucracies involved in pacification into an effective team.[11] Westmoreland added, "He pushed himself and his people hard. He had imaginative ideas, usually sound. Striped pants might work later, but at the start, abrasion was in order and Bob Komer worked overtime on that."[12] As evidence, in his first few days in South Vietnam, Komer made immediate trips to the field and dined with the most hard-nosed civilian officials critical of the new organizational arrangement. These men believed that the military would inundate Komer with reports, studies, and project proposals to neutralize his authority and range of motion.[13]

Montague also laid out the challenges Komer would confront as the civilian official on Westmoreland's immediate staff. He did not pull any punches. "Battles must be won now, not later," he informed his boss, arguing that Komer's advantage diminished every day that he was no longer the special assistant to the president. Montague, arguing that Westmoreland did not tell his field commanders how to organize, exhorted Komer to gain control of all pacification assets from Saigon to the provinces and to seize the authority to reorganize the pacification efforts as he saw fit. Most of all, Komer had to preserve his relationship with Bunker to give him an alternative channel of influence.[14] He had an ally in Bunker, who supported pacification as an integral element for winning the war and said so at his first Mission Council meeting in Saigon soon after arriving to take up his post: "I dislike the term 'The Other War.' To me this is all one war. Everything we do is an aspect of the total effort to achieve our objectives here."[15] The term was banished from the lexicon.

Komer understood his situation completely. Being perceived as being in control was imperative, as was acting quickly to put his stamp on the program. He told Bunker a day after arriving, "I have come out from

Washington with an 8–10 point crash program to show better results in pacification. My intention is to start pushing it as soon as I am anointed."[16] He also understood Montague's argument that he had advantages at this point because of his ties to the president and that his political capital would diminish rapidly. He moved quickly to establish the trappings of power as the only civilian leader on a military staff. He adorned the walls of his office in MACV headquarters with six pictures of him with the president.[17] The close association was like a "half-concealed dagger" that Komer would use even against Westmoreland and Abrams, if necessary.[18]

He also created a minor bureaucratic stir a few days after his arrival, when a military policeman held up his entrance to MACV headquarters because he did not know who he was or what his rank was. The incident embarrassed Komer, and when he entered his office that morning, he demanded that the black, chauffeur-driven Chrysler Imperial that Westmoreland had provided him be fitted with a plate signifying that he was equivalent to a four-star general, just like Westmoreland and Abrams. Dutch Kerwin did not want to deal with Komer's request after Montague relayed it to him, so he sent his deputy, an Air Force general, to Komer's office. The deputy explained that as a civilian he was not entitled to such a plate. This statement only fed Komer's fury, and after a tongue lashing, the deputy retreated only to return an hour later and offer a compromise solution: a special plate that resembled the one the secretary of the Army had. The suggestion mollified Komer, and the plate was affixed to his car.[19] Among MACV officers and others, the incident was portrayed as another example of Komer's imperious personality and egotism. One U.S. general listed Komer's flaws without a respite: "He was abrasive, overbearing, devious, obsequious, conceited, self-centered, touchy about his rank of ambassador and its four-star prerogatives, and devoted only to his own advancement and to the success of his mission of pacification."[20] The incident also reflected what Komer understood to be his precarious position as a civilian. As one observer explained to Ward Just, the *Washington Post* correspondent, "Once he [Komer] steps through the door at U.S. military headquarters he is on his own, the pigeon among the cats."[21]

On the morning of May 11, the tall, slim, urbane Bunker, impeccably attired in a beige suit, striped shirt, and silk tie, stood before the Saigon press corps at the U.S. embassy and announced officially that Westmoreland would have overall control of the U.S. role in pacification. Westmoreland, speaking from the same platform a few minutes later, indicated that he planned to delegate a significant part of his responsibilities as senior adviser to the Vietnamese armed forces to Abrams. It was a job that was likely to bruise Vietnamese egos and provoke charges of an American takeover. Komer would be responsible for the civilian aspects of the program, although he would also control military personnel. After Westmoreland spoke, Bunker answered the reporters' questions in a courtly manner for twenty minutes. He supplied few details; he left that up to Westmoreland and his staff.[22] As Bunker reported to the president, "I have confidence once the organization settles down in its new framework with General Westmoreland's assumption of responsibility and with Bob Komer's enthusiasm, energies, and talents applied to supervision, we shall make more rapid progress."[23] Komer was now in charge of an enterprise consisting of 3,900 personnel, two-thirds of whom were military, operating in four corps headquarters, forty-four provinces, and 222 district capitals, and with a budget of approximately $350 million, an operation that *Fortune* magazine characterized as a "massive program."[24]

Proving Bunker's assessment correct, Komer immediately set out to ensure that all personnel under his influence recognized the primacy of the ambassador's authority in South Vietnam, to include pacification support to the South Vietnamese even though the pacification programs had been placed under military command. He encouraged Bunker to emphasize this point and promote pacification objectives by ordering "action programs" for three crucial areas: transition to an elected South Vietnamese government, overhauling the South Vietnamese armed forces, and strengthening pacification, both U.S. and South Vietnamese efforts.[25] With respect to the last, Komer and Bunker agreed that the development of an action plan for RD should have priority.[26]

The U.S. civilian reaction to Bunker's announcement ranged from bitterness to resignation to optimism. "Everything depends on Komer," a civilian official declared. "If he does not make it, it means the end of civilian influence."[27] Some military staff members were less than enthusiastic about having a civilian in their midst, especially one that had the authority to assign officers and the power to examine every facet of military operations as they related to pacification. They were also chary of White House expectations that results would be quick and of a dilemma that had bedeviled Komer's predecessors: how to quantify victory. According to Just, "There has never been a plausible yardstick by which to measure the winning of the war in Vietnam."[28]

Komer also walked a tightrope between two differing perceptions of the war: the military believed the war was one of North Vietnamese aggression, and the civilians thought that it was fundamentally a civil war. These two viewpoints produced radically different measures to determine victory. The military relied on body counts, while the civilians focused on less tangible metrics, such as peasant attitudes toward the Saigon government and whether Viet Cong strength was growing or vanishing. One veteran newspaper correspondent, long suspicious of military statistics, noted, "This [distinction] becomes crucial when Komer begins to read reports from the field, reports which come through military channels and over the signature of the top American military commander in the Corps areas."[29]

Westmoreland was sympathetic to the challenges Komer confronted. To demonstrate the close relationship between Komer and him, the general designated an office next to his at MACV headquarters in downtown Saigon for Komer and invited him to attend the weekly strategy planning meetings.[30] Westmoreland considered Komer's intellect of considerable value. Nonetheless, despite these symbolic gestures, Westmoreland did not want Komer's mission to usurp his firmly held strategy of attrition. "Pacification was never the end all for me," the general would comment a decade and a half later, "and I received pressure to put emphasis on pacification at the risk of allowing the main force to have a free rein." In Westmoreland's view, the Viet Cong "were not a serious threat to the Saigon regime," just a "nuisance."[31] This bias was perceptible, and one reporter declared that Komer had little time to prove his capabilities to the U.S. military and the civilians and influence South Vietnamese government leaders.[32]

Meanwhile, Komer and Montague secluded themselves in Komer's office and began work on a concept of operations to move forward with Komer's vision of pacification for the remainder of the year and into 1968. Komer's views about how to proceed were evident in his guidance: "Pacification is a key program with more complications than operations against main force units. Yet the provision of lasting security is the key first step in any pacification effort, and this is as much military as civilian." He challenged the status quo by adding, "The great problem lies in the management of the relatively low grade resources devoted to pacification. There is a complex structure of varying units and forces in the countryside where pacification takes place."[33]

The immediate effort was to organize the field functions in pacification and nation building by merging OCO in the embassy and CORDS in MACV. Komer's Harvard Business School education became evident as he directed the consolidation, calling CORDS a "subsidiary corporation" with himself as "general manager." A steering group under his control was established to develop detailed plans for integration of civilian activities into MACV. He also furnished principles for organizing CORDS to ensure effective direction of the total civilian and military effort with a single chain of command from Saigon to the district level. These principles called for preserving OCO's organizational integrity and minimizing disruption of ongoing activities, but they also demanded operating economies, consolidation of facilities, and funding under the single manager where possible.[34] Komer held that everything possible had to be done to optimize the use of existing GVN and U.S. forces, assets, and resources to limit the need for further U.S. add-ons.[35]

A few weeks later Westmoreland approved the MACV directive formally establishing Komer's position as deputy for CORDS. The document charged Komer with supervising the formulation and execution of all plans, policies, and programs, military and civilian, that supported the South Vietnamese government's RD and related efforts. His duties also included advising the Vietnamese agencies responsible for providing local security in the rural areas and destroying the local Viet Cong infrastructure (VCI), that is, the guerrilla's command and control element. In essence, almost every nonmilitary program, except for public administration training and public health programs, which remained under USAID, eventually came under Komer's control. Even the CIA relinquished its control over the RD cadre program.[36]

The result of this consolidation, according to one knowledgeable observer, was that despite Bunker's admonition that only "one war" was being fought in Vietnam, Komer essentially established a separate and independent component within MACV with the artifice of unity of command. He credits Komer's "keen mind" and "single-minded drive" and Westmoreland's reluctance to rein Komer in lest he be blamed if the pacification program failed for this successful maneuver.[37] However, it is clear that the directive not only gave Komer substantial power and authority but also testified to the "comprehensive nature and massive scale of the effort" that he had to lead.[38] As one of Komer's staff observed, Komer was a "very hard-nosed, tough-minded, straight forward, plain-speaking, very bright guy," wholly "intolerant of bureaucracy in any form." He was not going "to be sealed off as nothing more than a little political advisor, sitting in a nice office with a rug on the floor and an American flag. He saw his responsibility as being fully operational, taking his missions from Westy [General Westmoreland] and then carrying them out."[39]

A day after his latest bureaucratic success, Komer traveled to the countryside to meet with Gen. Fred C. Weyand, commander of the I Field Force Vietnam, and his friend John Paul Vann, whom Komer made the CORDS chief for the area. Komer rehearsed his approach to pacification with this audience. He told them that an integrated U.S. civil-military staff was the goal. Management and motivation were the problems, Komer declared. He asked Weyand and Vann to motivate the entire South Vietnamese government. It was their program. The impression Komer made was mixed. Weyand had very little interest in Komer or his role. Instead, he relied heavily on Vann, whom he admired immensely, to manage the pacification program in the corps area. Lt. Col. William R. Corson, who headed the Marine Corps Combined Action Program in I Corps, was not impressed. He believed that Komer's application of management techniques to simplify and streamline staff procedures was a major gain but was amused by Komer's approach to leadership when he attended Komer's first meeting with I Corps' CORDS personnel. Corson likened the civilian's style to a "farmer hitting the mule with a wagon tongue to get their attention" but providing no guidance on "what they were to do."[40]

By the end of the first week in June, Komer had met with each of the U.S. corps commanders and let them hear firsthand his belief that the most important action was to enhance the quality and capability of the South Vietnamese territorial militia, the RF and PF.[41] Additionally, Komer had read a study by a CIA operative in Saigon, Nelson H. Brickham, which argued that an attack on the VCI should be a major effort. This view was consistent with Komer's own study and analysis during his tenure as special assistant. Komer considered this effort the most important task after implementation of CORDS and a necessary component of pacification and RD. In fact, South Vietnamese RD teams, responsible for political, economic, and social development in the countryside, were instructed to "root out the VC infrastructure." However, finding the VCI was not solely an intelligence problem and thus required the integrated management of existing military and civilian intelligence, police organizations from Saigon to the field level, the GVN leadership, and U.S. advisers. The management structure would mirror CORDS. However, just as upgrading the territorial militia was integral to creating security in the countryside, a similar effort would be needed to improve the National Police in terms of its intelligence gathering, intelligence exploitation, search and arrest, interrogation, and detention of Viet Cong to attain this objective.[42]

If anything, despite these challenges, Komer believed in himself, his abilities, and his optimistic prognostications. Although Bunker and Westmoreland warned Komer about communicating with the White House directly, he continued to do so. On June 3 Komer took advantage of a visit to Saigon by one of Johnson's closest aides, Harry McPherson, "who is staying with me and swilling my booze," to pass on his latest thoughts to LBJ. Komer asserted that the United States is "gaining momentum" and that "by the next winter it will be clear for all to see that we have gained the upper hand." He complained that the political rivalry and the squabbling between Head of State Nguyen Van Thieu and Prime Minister Nguyen Cao Ky presented a nagging problem. He also saw fit to comment that Westmoreland's request for more U.S. troops was not the answer. The United States needed to demand more of the South Vietnamese: "I am more convinced than ever that we can get a lot more for our money out of the Vietnamese, at peanut cost to us in more advisers, more equipment, more incentives, more insistent on canning incompetents and weeding out the corrupt." It was not a question of winning the war in South Vietnam; it was a question of "how fast we want to win it." Additional troops were not necessary. Komer concluded the letter with both fawning and determination to prove himself to Johnson: "When I quail at all my problems of getting pacification moving, I think of the problems *you* confront. I'd rather be pacifier than President, and you can depend on me to keep after my share of this war."[43]

But with Westmoreland, he offered a different assessment, arguing that it was important to "get our case across to McNamara." "Stalemate," he argued, was the perception outside Vietnam no matter how much MACV used such metrics as kill ratios, favorable weapons ratios, or defector rates. "Every stranger's view remains the same. . . . Vietnam appears to be a neverending war."[44]

The sniping at home threatened to undermine CORDS in its infancy. USAID administrator William Gaud, in a memo to under secretary of State Nicholas Katzenbach, sought an ally to restrict CORDS' mission. Gaud wanted USAID to continue to control public safety and other related programs, thus fragmenting U.S. programs into two areas—RD and nation building. He sought to undermine the single manager concept

Komer championed. Komer learned of Gaud's subterfuge and informed Westmoreland that Gaud was "proposing to carve up our new empire before we even win the war with it." He told Westmoreland he would take care of Gaud by having McNamara quash the proposal with Katzenbach.[45] It was a rear guard action of no consequence. Johnson's decision was inviolable, and Komer moved rapidly to build the new organization. The sniping in Vietnam did not abate either. One senior U.S. colonel, when asked if he and his peers liked having a "four-star" civilian in their chain of command, replied, "About as much as a dead rat."[46]

Nonetheless, combining the OCO and MACV staffs occurred smoothly and quickly. CORDS was integrated into the MACV staff as MACCORDS with L. Wade Lathram, a USAID official and the former director of OCO, designated as assistant chief of staff of CORDS on Westmoreland's staff. Brigadier General Knowlton, who headed MACV's Revolutionary Development Support Directorate, became Lathram's second in command. Komer also needed a respected and knowledgeable military deputy. Montague recommended Maj. Gen. George I. Forsythe, the assistant chief of staff, G-3, at U.S. Army Pacific who Komer apparently knew. Forsythe had close ties to Thieu. Montague wrote the general beseeching him to take the position, and Forsythe agreed. He assumed the position of assistant deputy for CORDS on June 20. Forsythe had little choice; Komer and Gen. Harold K. Johnson, the Army chief of staff, had agreed to this assignment in early May. The leadership of the new organization was now in place. By July 1 organization of pacification activities from Saigon to the district level had been completed.[47]

Komer directed his MACCORDS staff to undertake a comprehensive assessment of the pacification program as of the end of May. The results, while sobering, also pointed out flaws and the challenges Komer confronted. Komer and his team argued that their efforts would be the first cohesive pacification program since the South Vietnamese government's Strategic Hamlet Program (1962–63), which had been doomed because it lacked the military initiative that the United States was now providing with the buildup of its military forces. Komer's plan stressed that the South Vietnamese were dedicating more resources to RD than they had in the past and that more RD teams were in place, but the RD program had a limited effect on the loyalties of the peasant and did not help to wrest control from the Viet Cong, who were killing RD cadre at an alarming rate because of a lack of military protection.[48] In truth, the VCI remained an effective shadow government. Overall, leadership at all levels of the Vietnamese government had failed to cope with the demands of the war. Before Komer had left Washington, Holbrooke had warned him that he would have to deal with the power struggles among the ARVN generals, which could lead to even further disunity among the country's leaders.[49] Additionally, corruption dissipated the government's ability to gain the allegiance of major portions of the country. Therefore, the strengthening of rural institutions, positive progress on a constitution, and national, village, and hamlet elections should provide a lift to pacification. The current vertical direction from Saigon and control of separate programs by various ministries hampered the local populations' involvement and failed to provide a foundation for the nation-building process that needed to follow RD.

Based on this overall assessment, Komer and Montague developed an action plan called Project Takeoff, named in honor of the economic development concept Walt Rostow described in his book *The Stages of Economic Growth*. Rostow hypothesized that there were "take-off" stages in the development process, peaks when societal pressures made developing societies susceptible to Marxist control.[50] The U.S. government had to be aggressive to eradicate the problems the assessment found, and that meant involving the highest levels of government, not just the Ministry of Revolutionary Development, in Project Takeoff. Bunker noted, "As is so often the case, GVN performance remains the crucial factor." The U.S. team would press the GVN to adopt the Project Takeoff principles and develop their own plan to achieve them. However, Bunker feared the GVN would not take immediate action because of the impending presidential election. The goal was to press the GVN to comprehend that elections and movement toward representative government were a "fundamental part of pacification. Elections should support and foster other pacification efforts and vice versa."[51]

Project Takeoff, which Bunker and Westmoreland approved, singled out eight programs for special, priority attention: (1) improve pacification planning for 1968; (2) accelerate the Chieu Hoi (or Viet Cong defector) Program; (3) mount an attack on the VCI; (4) expand and improve the RVNAF's support of pacification; (5) expand and support the South Vietnamese RD teams; (6) increase the U.S. and South Vietnamese capability to handle refugees; (7) revamp the South Vietnamese police and police field forces responsible for countering the insurgents; and (8) press for land reform.[52] Komer saw Project Takeoff as a way to get the U.S. "house in order." He and Montague briefed the U.S. corps commander and the province senior advisers in each region to sell the concept and got Prime Minister Ky's ambiguous approval to move forward.[53] Finally, Komer realized that not all eight efforts could be conducted immediately, so he decided to focus on three: extend local security, improve the RD efforts, and root out the VCI.

In June Komer provided Westmoreland with his plan to attack the VCI, which, in keeping with the CIA operative's analysis, he characterized as being more than an intelligence problem. Efforts to locate the VCI had to include exploitation, that is, "careful, patient police work" was required. Komer's perspective was based on his discussions with and study of how Sir Robert Thompson used police and intelligence assets in fighting the Communist insurgency in Malaya. Most critically, organization was a problem. Numerous U.S. and GVN organizations were involved; coordination was poor, particularly at the province and district levels, and intelligence sharing was almost nonexistent. To evaluate the organization problem, Komer had asked the CIA in Washington to conduct a study on how to pursue a more effective attack on the VCI. On receipt of the CIA's report, he worked with Montague, the CORDS staff, and CIA's Saigon Station personnel to modify the principles in the study to the situation in South Vietnam. They concluded that a joint U.S.-GVN management structure, under CORDS, and intelligence sharing by MACV with the field-level units were necessary to make the plan feasible. MACV would provide the analysis and advisers, but the GVN would carry out the mission using police, specifically, the National Police Field Force, the Special Branch, and the Provincial Reconnaissance Units. Komer recommended to Westmoreland that he create a Saigon-level committee of the relevant U.S. agencies (MACV, CIA, and CORDS), under his leadership, to initiate this plan. The new program would be called Intelligence Coordination and Exploitation (ICEX).[54]

Westmoreland directed Komer to share this plan with the MACV staff. Komer immediately clashed with the departing MACV intelligence chief, Maj. Gen. Joseph McChristian, over it. On his last day in Vietnam, a few hours before departing, McChristian "became aware" of the new plans for attacking the VCI; Komer, perhaps cunningly, had outmaneuvered him.

Years after the event McChristian wrote, "To put it mildly, I was amazed and dismayed."[55] He met with Komer to protest that the memorandum had not been coordinated with him. "I have a lot of reservations about it," he remarked, "and I'm going to go to General Westmoreland right now and tell him about this and I would like you to go along with me, if you wish." Komer looked up from the document he was reading. "Have a good trip home, Mac," he said. McChristian then questioned Westmoreland, who told him, "Don't worry about it. I'll take care of it." McChristian would later remark that the incident on his last day in Vietnam felt as if he "had been kicked in the stomach."[56] Not all of the J-2 staff disagreed with Komer's approach. Col. Daniel Graham, MACV's chief of current intelligence and estimates, found Komer to be "a fairly astute intelligence officer," who recognized that where the VCI was concerned, intelligence had a political and a military dimension and that this relationship had to be taken into account.[57] However, Graham's view did not count. Komer had upset other MACV generals with his proposal. Westmoreland would have to decide.

A few days later Westmoreland called Komer; Kerwin; Maj. Gen. Will Pierson, MACV's head of operations and plans; and the new intelligence chief, Maj. Gen. Philip Davidson, into his office to thrash out whether CORDS or the MACV Intelligence Directorate should lead the campaign against the VCI.[58] Kerwin, Abrams' protégé, who resented Komer's propensity to evade his office on pacification matters, which only made his job of managing the sprawling MACV staff more difficult, assented that damaging the infrastructure made sense. However, he believed the proposed approach was wrong. Instead, Kerwin offered that the initiative be run as a regular military operation under Davidson. Davidson stressed that unity of effort was necessary on intelligence matters and that Komer's approach upended President Johnson's directive for unification of pacification under General Westmoreland.[59]

Westmoreland offered Komer the opportunity to rebut that position. Komer stated that, first, he had been studying this problem for several months and that the dissenters arrayed against him did not know anything about the subject. Second, the failure to counter the VCI to date was ample proof that assigning the task to military intelligence would fail. The J-2 staff was focused on order of battle and analysis of the Communist military units' strength and location, not on the guerrillas among the people. He objected to an existing organization becoming responsible for a mission it would deem secondary. If it were regarded as secondary, it would be neglected. Third, rooting out the VCI was a police function, and thus, the GVN had to manage it; the Americans could not do it for them.

Westmoreland turned to Kerwin and said that Komer seemed to know this issue better than anyone else did and that it ought to be done his way. The generals stood up and filed out. Davidson considered the meeting a charade. Westmoreland had decided to support Komer before convening the meeting because he had no interest in pacification, and now, if the plan failed, Komer could not blame it on his lack of support.[60] Westmoreland and Bunker formally approved ICEX on June 18.[61]

Komer fully understood that the clandestine Viet Cong political and administrative structure was essential to Viet Cong success in terms of winning the village war. Rooting out this hard-core cadre of 100,000 to 150,000 members, at its height, was one of the most critical tasks the pacification program confronted. His rationale was simple, "Get after the VC guerrillas, destroy the VC's political structure, and the NVA" would be in "a considerably weaker position, even though Hanoi" could continue to send units south.[62]

Attacking the VCI was typical of the problems in Vietnam—everyone, including the GVN, recognized the importance of counteracting the VCI and had done so for years, but there was no dedicated effort to addressing it managerially and operationally. Further, the South Vietnamese police elements would have to be rebuilt for this mission and an integrated anti-VCI program set up. The closest existing effort of this type was the District Intelligence Operations Coordinating Center (DIOCC), which the CIA and Marines had established in early 1967 in one of the districts.[63] That organizational concept could be replicated in other districts throughout the country, first on a "US-only basis," to generate the "integrated, organized attack on the VC infrastructure [that] has not been mounted countrywide." Komer depicted the plan as "analogous to a 'rifle shot' rather than a 'shotgun' approach. Instead of cordon and search operations, it will stress quick reaction operations aimed at individual cadre or at *most* small groups."[64] Further, ICEX could not be simply a program devoted to identifying and capturing Viet Cong cadre. It had to be a complete system with field courts and interrogation and detention centers. Lastly, ICEX would have to be under Komer's personal control because it was a joint military-CIA program and he could arbitrate disputes. His leadership would also ensure that the program would not be ignored.[65]

The CIA's chief of station in Saigon, John Hart, nominated Evan J. Parker Jr. to serve as Komer's director of ICEX. In this capacity, he would run a staff of 164 people. Parker, a World War II Army veteran who had served in Burma and whose CIA service had him often involved with military personnel, had numerous connections in MACV. His first task was to translate the station-drafted proposal into military language and format. The resulting MACV directive was published on July 9. Komer and Parker then set out to construct the ICEX machinery throughout the MACV hierarchy under the direct control of CORDS.[66]

A month after ICEX was approved, William Colby, chief of the CIA's Far East Division, visited the CIA's Vietnam Station and gave Komer good marks for his efforts in underscoring the importance of eliminating the VCI. He reported that since his last visit to the station, CIA officers had contributed to this effort in addition to providing order of battle information, as was their traditional function in a war zone.[67] Colby also noted improvements in RD and political intelligence. However, other major problems persisted, most notably, the South Vietnamese police apparatus was not capable of eliminating the Viet Cong's covert control of the hamlets. Colby observed that Komer's ICEX organization was too immature to have the necessary effect. Nonetheless, he concluded that the Viet Cong was experiencing problems while the South Vietnamese and U.S. demonstrated a "steady improvement in the ability . . . to fight a people's war." Such praise from Colby could not be easily dismissed. Not only was he an able intelligence officer, but he had more than eight years of Vietnam experience, including an assignment as chief of station in Saigon. As Helms remarked, "It would be hard to find a more knowledgeable observer."[68]

Colby was not alone in his assessment that progress was being made. Komer's critics conceded that he "accomplished more than they had expected during his first two months in Vietnam." Some who had considered resigning rather than serving under Komer had now become his devoted admirers. They believed that he had built an effective organization that would be the slingshot for accelerating the pacification effort. Further, Komer boosted civilian morale by giving the civilians a large role in managing pacification in the field; nearly one-half of the forty-four province advisers were U.S. civilians. Many had believed that they would not be qualified for these positions because they entailed advising

Vietnamese officials on security issues, but Komer was most interested in placing officials who could obtain results. Komer demanded, often in a raised voice, that he and his largely civilian staff be consulted before issuing orders that affected his plans, so some officers continued to be resentful of his presence and his power. One senior civilian, a longtime critic of Saigon, said that he was pleased by the change in priorities. "We're beginning to get the benefits Komer talked about—military transport and supplies and that sort of stuff plus our ideas." The changed atmosphere was palpable leading one general to quip, "he was not sure who had taken over whom in this thing." Even senators were concerned that Komer's assertiveness would lead to Americanizing pacification. Komer reassured them that this was not his intent. Instead, he knew that the real test was getting the Vietnamese military and civilian leaders to do their jobs with more eagerness and effectiveness.[69]

Bunker, an admirer of Komer's efforts and of the man, also felt it necessary after a few months to step back and survey the status of the pacification program. He recognized the criticism in some unspecified "quarters" that the progress on pacification was "slow," but he saw that this was not a function of inattention or incompetence. Instead, it was a reflection of how long pacification had been neglected and how it was only now receiving the needed priority and focus. This change required "a vast amount of organization and preparatory work." Bunker was unabashedly on Komer's side, crediting his "energy" for the successful reorganization and for developing a well-conceived plan for the remainder of the year and into the next. He also noted that Komer's reorganization of intelligence assets to attack the VCI was nearing completion and that the number of RD cadres trained and operating in the field had substantially increased. However, Bunker was no doe-eyed optimist. He informed President Johnson, "It is important that we should be realistic in facing the many complex and difficult problems that lay ahead." However, he also held that progress was occurring, but that the press was not reporting it; he took it upon himself to spread the word.[70]

Certainly, there was greater confidence, higher morale, and improved motivation among the civilians involved in pacification in South Vietnam; the press reporting was more favorable, despite Bunker's concerns; and independent assessments by outsiders, such as Colby and the increasingly skeptical McNamara—who told the president that "Komer and his pacification program have exceeded expectations"[71]—tended to be favorable overall. There was also a sense that the Viet Cong recognized the impetus of Komer's new model of pacification. Intelligence reports indicated that the Viet Cong had given priority to combating RD, Chieu Hoi, and other pacification programs.[72] Such evidence must be considered carefully; it cannot be simply dismissed. Komer, in an appearance on the television show *Face the Nation* in July, showed his understanding of the imprecision of intelligence estimating when he remarked that in Vietnam calculations of enemy strength and related topics are "subject to some margin of error."[73] Project Takeoff, however, did signal to the Viet Cong and Hanoi an increased commitment to pacification on the part of the United States and, to a lesser degree, the GVN. Such commitment had to be worrisome to Hanoi. Nonetheless, Komer fretted about the competence of the GVN, "where they are 'smart crooks, rather than dumb honest men.'" And he wondered aloud whether we were "backing the right horse"—the United States "should be supporting civilian candidates for the upcoming South Vietnamese presidential election rather than military candidates."[74]

Komer had also succeeded in convincing the military of the value CORDS could bring to waging the other war, despite editorial criticism from leading military professional magazines, such as *Armed Forces Management*, that pacification was not a military mission and it would only drain Westmoreland of manpower.[75] Thus, Westmoreland's support was crucial, and perhaps it was pro forma, but he backed Komer at numerous critical moments during CORDS' early days, signaling that Komer's and his organization's role would not be weakened. Further, Komer's organizational structure and management was also accepted by the Army and Marine general and flag officers who had to carry out the pacification program in their respective areas.[76] Nonetheless, while Westmoreland stated publicly the necessity for a unified war strategy, he purposely kept pacification separate from the big-unit, or main force, war. Komer would have preferred a unified approach, but he accepted the situation as it was and hurtled into his duties.[77] As he noted years later, "If CORDS hadn't insisted on a high degree of autonomy (a story by itself), I doubt whether we'd ever have gotten pacification off the ground."[78]

In a few months, as Bunker noted, Komer's "enthusiasm, energies and talents" had transformed pacification, giving it coherence and direction. The CIA's deputy chief of station shared this view: "Whatever his faults may be, Mr. Komer is changing all of this very rapidly."[79] Although Project

Takeoff had not "uniformly improved the pacification program, it had channeled American efforts to obtain a stronger commitment to pacification from the South Vietnamese, an area where obviously more needed to be done."[80] Komer recognized this limitation and the need to bring greater emphasis and leverage to the Vietnamese role. He and Bunker were of the same mind: an efficient and better-managed U.S. organization was not sufficient. If the South Vietnamese did not carry the main burden, the program could not succeed.

CHAPTER 8

Taking Off

*T*he questioners Komer fenced with on the mid-July episode of *Face the Nation* displayed a suspicious, almost cynical, attitude toward Komer's claims of some progress in the pacification program specifically and the war in general. This skepticism, dubbed the "credibility gap," was well founded; for two years, the press had listened to the Johnson administration's claims of progress, but had seen little evidence of improvement. Americans expected Vietnam to be like World War II or even Korea; in both previous conflicts, success or advancement to victory was measured with some certitude. Komer was well aware of the media's mistrust, and he blamed this suspicion on the military, which tended to exaggerate the enemy's capability to justify additional forces.[1] Further, Secretary of Defense McNamara had not helped Komer's case that Sunday morning. In a statement a few days earlier, the Pentagon leader had wistfully told the press that pacification was making "very slow progress." Large unit action slogged on inexorably at the same time. Counteroffensive Phase III, as MACV called it, had begun a month earlier with Operation Manhattan, a combined U.S.-Vietnamese clearing action designed to drive enemy forces away from populated areas so that small units could carry out local security activities among the population. The number of U.S troops stationed in Vietnam had ballooned to nearly 450,000 while Johnson's approval ratings, which were already below 50 percent, continued to decline.

Not only were many Americans dissatisfied with the president and the war, as the sizable and growing protests evinced, but they were also angry. The summer of 1967 was long, hot, and marked by riots in the ghettos of several U.S. cities; eerily, it was also the "Summer of Love," when thousands of young people descended on the San Francisco area to experience the hippie lifestyle of drugs, music, and idealistic rebellion. Societal tensions during this time fostered a sense of stalemate regarding the war, which not only infected the body politic but also disturbed U.S. government officials. Rostow reported to the president that Senator Ernest Hollings had told him that among important U.S. senators there was a "general feeling that we are on a treadmill in Vietnam."[2] Such remarks so unhinged the White House that Bunker had to address the issue directly in one of his weekly reports to Johnson.[3]

Komer attempted to convince Washington that there was something more than stalemate in view and that outdated figures were a factor in how the press was portraying the war.[4] In August he argued to the White House that all previous pacification efforts had been inadequately funded and insufficiently protected because the emphasis had been on the anti–main force campaign, but now the situation had changed. The United States had seized the military initiative from the NVA and the Viet Cong main force units in 1966 and 1967. Komer's ingrained fondness for statistics led him to cite that 315,000 people were now involved in pacification, compared with 198,000 at the end of 1966. Further, GVN expenditures on pacification could more than double from $170 million in 1966, excluding the cost of U.S. troops, to an estimated $400 million in 1967. Yet Komer was not blinded by the numbers. He stressed that there was no central governmental direction. Instead, the GVN's efforts represented a "vast mélange of relatively low-grade assets, reporting to a number of different Saigon ministries, largely independent, and with no sense of common purpose." The solution was simple—better management. The GVN needed to pull these assets together and move them toward a common goal, that is, improving its own management structure. Komer prognosticated that the United States and the GVN had a good chance of making overall progress, "even in fits and starts." Like a confident bookie, he offered that there was a "two to one chance of achieving substantially increased momentum over the next 12 to 18 months." He also recognized that little improvement in South Vietnamese management would occur until the feuding between the heads of the Ministry of Revolutionary Development and the ARVN ceased and they began to work together.[5]

Komer set about with his usual high-octane approach to any challenge. Montague remarked that once U.S. civilian and military advisory and support functions had been consolidated and the action plan developed, Komer focused on improving the South Vietnamese management structure, for his "reach, when he wanted it, extended to the lowly district." Komer focused his attention on the local level. In his characteristically direct manner, he had "to jack up its local officials, to buy our action plan." The "effective countryside pacification of some 10,000 hamlets, 2,000 villages, 250 districts, and 44 provinces" was a massive undertaking.[6]

Komer began his effort by improving territorial security, the forces "who bore the brunt of the Communists' attacks at the village level."[7] This meant working with MACV headquarters and its South Vietnamese counterpart, the Joint General Staff. In clear opposition to Westmoreland's strategy, Komer called for clearing and holding the countryside, the crucial first phase of pacification, without which, he claimed, nothing else could be accomplished. The idea for defending the villages came from a discussion with a departing Army colonel who told Komer that he was the first person to listen to him about the importance of boosting the capability of the RF and PF, known as the "Ruff Puffs."[8] Such an approach, which Bunker heartily endorsed, was essential to success, since the "crux of the [pacification] program" was "adequate Vietnamese motivation and involvement," but it would take time.[9] Komer realized that he did not have five to ten years to get pacification moving. By now, the time for long-term programs or the oil-spot technique of counterinsurgency, in which the counterinsurgents held a location and then spread control outward from that point, was past. In fact, no one pacification technique by itself would be decisive if the U.S. and South Vietnamese harnessed their resources to it. The simultaneous, multiple-front approach was the best, most realistic option.[10]

Komer pestered MACV and the Joint General Staff to allocate fifty-four South Vietnamese battalions temporarily to local security duties. These battalions and the RF/PF would no longer be under the South Vietnamese army division commanders' control but instead would be responsible to the province chiefs. This arrangement would bolster the relationship between local governance and security. Komer wanted the importance of the RF/PF to be highly visible. He convinced the Joint General Staff to upgrade the person in Saigon responsible for RF/PF from a colonel to a lieutenant general and to provide better equipment and leadership at the province and district levels. Twenty-three province chiefs and seventy-three district chiefs were sent packing because of ineffectiveness or corruption, problems that affected most provinces and districts in the country. Assignment of province chiefs and district chiefs would be based on class rank in training. Local administration improved by emphasizing better logistics and administrative procedures, especially in the Ministry of Revolutionary Development. Komer stressed the need to expand the RD cadre and revitalize the Chieu Hoi Program to induce the Viet Cong to rally to the South Vietnamese side.[11] Further, the effort to neutralize the clandestine Viet Cong politico-administrative apparatus finally got under way when Komer urged the South Vietnamese to strengthen their intelligence capability by upgrading the National Police, especially its field forces. These measures occurred because Bunker, Westmoreland, and Komer prodded the GVN to undertake action. For its part, the GVN made promises and articulated proposals that they had in mind but did not enact change quickly.[12] In fact, one area did not change appreciably: the South Vietnamese government still did not take the refugee problem seriously.[13] This problem had concerned Komer since his White House days and would soon haunt CORDS politically.[14]

Komer proved thin-skinned about any criticism of the pacification program and even instigated a feud with Representative John Moss, a Democrat from California and chairman of the Foreign Operations and Government Information Subcommittee of the House of Representatives' Committee on Government Operations. Moss, accompanied by Representatives Lee Hamilton from Indiana and John Monagan from Connecticut, visited Vietnam in early July. During the visit, the chairman informed Komer and his senior staff that he considered CORDS a mistake that would lead only to the United States taking over pacification from the GVN and thus requiring more troops and deepening the U.S. commitment.[15]

When Moss returned to the United States, he sent a letter to Rusk that expressed concern about the "lagging and floundering pacification program" and released three unflattering reports. Komer saw the letter as a personal affront and rebutted Moss directly with a letter saying that Moss and the subcommittee's brief stay did not provide adequate time to make such an assessment and that he was perplexed by such criticism because Moss did not articulate any reservations during his visit. Komer also decided to send a note to the ranking minority member of the subcommittee, Ogden Reid. Reid provided the note to Moss, which had an incendiary effect. In the note, Komer declared that it was hard enough doing this job without being accused of doing it poorly by a member of Congress. Moss retaliated with a letter to Komer that said Komer's letter and his note to Reid were "offensive" and "insulting"; Moss sent a copy of this letter to the White House. He sarcastically stated that Komer obviously did not understand the role of a congressional investigation committee. He then reiterated to Komer his opposition to the creation of CORDS and further wrote that many U.S. officials in Vietnam thought that the change had been unnecessary. He also underscored his belief that U.S. officials needed to press the South Vietnamese for significant social and economic reforms. While some progress in pacification had been made, the predictions of success always fell short.[16] Rutherford Poats, acting USAID administrator, found the Moss reports' recommendations to be "strong-armed actions" that he likened to shooting "an ant with an elephant gun."[17]

Walt Rostow remained Komer's champion. Rostow informed the president of the quarrel in late September and advised LBJ to "let the storm in a teacup die down."[18] It did, but this was not the last time Komer confronted a member of Congress over the promises of pacification. He fenced with members of the executive branch as well. He wrote Holbrooke, who had left the White House and returned to the State Department as a special assistant to Katzenbach, asking for his support to stop the "silly cables" from his department telling Komer and his staff how to do their job.[19]

In early October 1967 Komer submitted his first report on pacification activities, which covered August. He labeled it "an unimpressive month" largely because of the GVN's preoccupation with the presidential election campaign. There were only limited results in the attack on VCI and essentially insignificant improvements in territorial security, but the recruitment of RD cadre showed signs of improvement as did the overall progress of teams in the field. In Komer's view, the "brightest spot" was the number of Viet Cong defections under the Chieu Hoi Program, nearly double those the previous year. He claimed this success was based on Viet Cong concerns that led to attacks on Chieu Hoi installations. Other areas remained problematic. The refugee situation worsened, with the number of new refugees more than doubling. Komer estimated that there were now 450,000 displaced persons needing food, lodging, and resettlement. The refugee situation also had political ramifications, which prompted an on-the-ground investigation led by a staff member of the Senate Subcommittee on Refugees, chaired by Senator Edward Kennedy.[20]

Komer's communication with the White House continued.[21] Johnson valued Komer's advice and directed Rostow to write Komer on a strictly private basis and get his "quite urgent" views on what the United States could do to "accelerate" the war. Komer, however, feared that these back-channel discussions would hurt his relationships with Bunker and Westmoreland. Neither man liked anyone going over his head. They had warned him about communicating with the White House privately, and Komer knew he could not jeopardize his relationship with the two. Nonetheless, Komer gave his candid assessment in two letters, one to LBJ and the other to Rostow. Komer underscored to Rostow that there was no "new way" to win the war and no way to guarantee definitive results in 1968. However, he believed that the bombing of North Vietnam, especially the lines of communication, was critical to success and that more attention should be paid to justifying the use of bombing campaigns to the public. It was principally up to McNamara to be the chief advocate "because he has caused half the doubts himself." He also believed that progress was being made but was not apparent because the evidence was fragmentary—"so much a mosaic of ten thousand little pieces" that most could see only a bit at a time. This lack of an overall picture created a problem for the administration with the press, an issue that Komer convinced Bunker needed to be addressed full time by Barry Zorthian, the head of the U.S. Information Service in Saigon. Komer remained confident that pacification was well under way and that Westmoreland was backing him "to the hilt." Komer signaled his frustration with the South Vietnamese and admitted that he was pinning his hopes on the new minister of RD, Major General Nguyen Duc Thang.[22]

In Komer's four-page letter to Johnson, he provided his views on the bombing of the Ho Chi Minh Trail, divined North Vietnam's line of attack for the next several months, and identified future courses of action, including improving the South Vietnamese army and the Department of Defense's interminably slow decision-making process. He also pointed out that the war was becoming increasingly "an NVA war," that "almost half the organized enemy units are North Vietnamese regular army." While he laid out plans to frustrate Hanoi, he reserved his greatest frustration for the GVN, especially Thieu, whom he saw as passive and indecisive. Komer urged LBJ to stiffen Thieu's spine with a few well-timed private messages to push Thieu and strengthen Bunker's position. He ended by assessing Abrams, as the president had requested. Komer found Abrams and Westmoreland to be "exceptional generals," with different personalities and styles. Abrams was the more direct and less proud than Westmoreland and was dogged in his pursuit once he had made a decision. Nonetheless, he felt that Westmoreland was "the best man for this particular job" because of his close relationship to the ARVN generals, which Komer deemed critical at this moment. If LBJ had any thoughts about replacing Westmoreland with Abrams, Komer had helped clarify his decision.[23]

Despite Komer's concerns that the U.S. press magnified every minute problem or setback with sedulous reporting, his own efforts received positive publicity. Philip Goodhart, a member of the British parliament, visited Vietnam and filed reports for the *Evening Standard*, *Sunday Telegraph*, and *The Spectator*. He praised Komer as a "dynamic operator" but also questioned the "tens of thousands of man-hours" field teams had to put into compiling data for Komer to assess progress. One American official complained, "I have spent 65 per cent of my time on American staff work and only 5 per cent teaching the Vietnamese how to do things—which is what I was supposed to do." Nonetheless, Goodhart sympathized with Komer. In this war without fronts, statistics were used to show results. Goodhart remarked that since his last visit in 1965, evidence of Viet Cong terrorism, measured by the number of assassinations of hamlet chiefs and teachers, had decreased substantially. Further, the war was not a stalemate, either statistically or in the week that he spent on the ground in a province that had been under Communist control for nearly twenty years. The number of votes cast in the September election for the presidency of the Republic of Vietnam indicated that Viet Cong control of the countryside had diminished by as much as 40 percent. Yet, Goodhart was not a naive optimist. He recognized that the Viet Cong, although battered throughout South Vietnam, would continue its guerrilla fighting. The North Vietnamese leadership pinned their hopes on statistics as well; they had noticed a dwindling American resolve as evinced by a U.S. opinion poll indicating LBJ's waning popularity.[24]

Goodhart's valuation was good news, especially the journalist's recognition of the importance of statistics. CORDS had spent several months refining and perfecting a new computerized technique for measuring progress in population and control of hamlets called the Hamlet Evaluation System (HES).[25] McNamara had initiated the original effort in October 1966, when he asked the CIA to develop the evaluative tool for pacification, which it did. The CIA analysts responsible for the initial concept briefed Komer, then special assistant for pacification in the White House.

He expressed doubt about the usefulness of the system and questioned whether the methodology could yield reliable data. He believed that personnel in the field would provide an overly positive assessment of the situation in their areas of responsibility. Komer also asserted that the methodology gave too much weight to the civil development side and not enough to the military and security aspects. He maintained that if the local security situation were favorable, then the hamlet would be advancing toward being pacified. The necessary conditions for civil progress might take a long time to register. Therefore, a rating system that precluded a high overall pacification grade until civil progress was evident was unrealistic, and it would produce inaccurate and overly pessimistic results. He also expressed concern about whether the system could supply reliable readings, but like McNamara, he understood that the United States had to guard against the extant GVN system, which was considered overly optimistic. As Komer told CIA analyst George Allen, he recognized that field evaluators, the whole district advisory team in fact, could be biased and thereby tend to inflate their findings positively. Komer was not alone in his concern about the pacification indicators. Chester Cooper, a veteran CIA operative detailed to the NSC staff, and Richard Moorsteen, an economist on Komer's staff, found the system flawed in terms of both the methodology and its practical application.[26] Nonetheless, after consultations with Montague, who was on Porter's staff at the time, embassy staff decided the approach worthwhile and approved the concept in December 1966. Now, ironically, Komer was accountable for overseeing this system, which he had inherited from Porter's organization.[27]

Komer was under no illusion that the system was thoroughly reliable for the very reason he had stated more than a year earlier: it depended on accurate judgments by CORDS district personnel. While they certainly were in a good position to render such considered opinions, the system was a complex measuring device reliant on conclusions about several factors such as the strength of the local VCI, the capabilities of local VC guerrillas, and the adequacy of local security forces. It was best used as a way to identify regional problems; it was not invented to measure South Vietnamese "hearts and minds" or to derive from inexperienced and non-Vietnamese junior officers anything but concrete data about the number of schools built or wells dug.[28]

However, Komer began to use the figures to demonstrate progress. As one member of his staff later remarked, "Komer did not countenance HES inaccuracy, but people were grasping for some measure, some way to measure if pacification was succeeding or not."[29] Komer told Bunker to report to Washington, "Now that the bugs have been worked out, I will be reporting these figures to you monthly, as the best available indicator of pacification trends."[30] Washington would use the statistics for that purpose as well, to convince the American public that the war was not at a standstill. With that, Komer "ran smack into an already endemic journalistic suspicion (justified by past events) of statistics, computers and 'progress' reports" both in Saigon and in the nation's capital.[31]

Komer had boxed himself in; the entire issue of how to identify and measure what was occurring in the countryside, let alone how to measure GVN progress and performance, was one of the "trickiest and most painful" aspects of this "atypical war." Traditional methods of measuring territory gained or lost were not "meaningful" given the number of hamlets and villages involved and the highly fragmented nature of the GVN effort, divided among military, RD, and police organizations. Additionally there was the constant pressure from Washington and the press to estimate how U.S. and GVN efforts were succeeding. Subjective assessments and GVN evaluations had largely proved worthless and inaccurate, so the drive for solid, quantifiable data was understandable. The solution was HES, but "it was a crude measurement system" of several tangible security and development factors that "American advisors could reasonably expect to validate" and that could be used for comparative analysis among twelve thousand hamlets. At best, HES would be helpful as a means of identifying trends, but the user needed to recognize that the statistical data might be off by plus or minus 10 percent. Komer also felt it was the best system that could be devised given the scope of the problem and the resources available to perform the evaluations.[32] Every element of pacification, from popular attitudes to success in rooting out the VCI, was hard to measure. Surveying every province, district, village, and the 12,600 hamlets was the only way to do so, and then the data had to be aggregated to attain nationwide results—a difficult statistical effort even under optimum conditions.[33]

As another sign of Komer's recognition of the system's deficiencies, he and other senior CORDS officials and staff visited the field frequently to attain firsthand judgments from discussions with local advisers. Komer also established the Pacification Studies Group, consisting of U.S. and South Vietnamese evaluators, to perform field assessments and thereby operate as an autonomous source of information on activities in the countryside. Their reviews supplemented the monthly reports from CORDS advisers at the province and district levels.[34] Nonetheless, for all the attempts to pro-vide independent analyses, HES would become a bitter topic of argument in the coming months. Perhaps the kindest explanation made for Komer's misstep regarding HES data came from Townsend Hoopes, who served as a high-ranking political appointee in the Defense Department during the Johnson administration. But he even did not fully absolve him: "Komer, an able, ebullient, and hard-driving man, was quite aware of the danger-ous imprecision of his reporting system or indeed any system that could be devised to measure pacification. . . . But like others in Saigon, he was the victim of relentless White House pressure to show dramatic progress in the war; to some extent, he was the victim of his own compulsive optimism."[35]

––––––––––––––

Komer's efforts to force the South Vietnamese to remove or reassign cor-rupt and incompetent government leaders, military officers, and civilian officials did not end with the blowup over the refugee situation. He asked Westmoreland to intervene personally with senior GVN officials on more than one occasion. In one case, he provided Bunker and Westmoreland with a list of sixty-two province officials deemed corrupt or incompetent.[36] The weeding out of these officials became one of Komer's major efforts, but as it had been in carrying out so many of the other initiatives that Komer proposed, the GVN proved to be dilatory.

By late September 1967, with Thieu and Ky elected as president and vice president earlier in the month, Komer believed that CORDS was on a solid footing, and he now devoted considerable time to pressing Thieu and other senior GVN officials from the Ministries of Interior and Agriculture on taking charge of the pacification effort. He and Bunker were heartened when Thieu accepted a list of initiatives that the U.S. mission had sug-gested, which included reorganizing the armed forces to give new empha-sis to security, strengthening the role of the province chiefs, and enhancing the functions of the village councils and hamlet chiefs in planning devel-opment activities.[37]

The discussions with GVN officials also focused on the importance of local security, especially the RF/PF; the upgrading of leadership at the local level; the more effective coordination of civil-military aspects of pacifica-tion, particularly the importance of public works and construction proj-ects; and the plans to attack the VCI. Komer realized a solo approach was not sufficient; he needed Bunker to press Thieu on these issues as well.

Additionally, Komer asked Forsythe to meet and correspond with Brigadier General Nguyen Van Kiem, special military assistant to Thieu and one of President Thieu's closest advisers, who was an old friend of Forsythe's, as another channel for communicating Komer's views to the president. Komer believed this concerted effort to meet with Thieu and others during the fall and into the winter was profitable, especially when he learned from Forsythe, based on discussions with Kiem, that Thieu had a "personal interest in pacification."[38]

Thieu and Ky were also conscious that the new government had to begin to demonstrate visible results to the people in the near future, perhaps the next six months, to gain their support. These efforts included attacking corruption and enhancing pacification. Bunker thought the six-month period arbitrary but welcomed the recognition that concrete results were needed to solidify popular support of the regime. Attacking the VCI was identified as one of the top issues for the coming months.[39]

In late November, Bunker, Westmoreland, and Komer returned to the United States to meet with the president and hold a general review of U.S. policy and strategy in Vietnam. Komer took time to write to the editors of the *Washington Post* to explain the new emphasis on the RF/PF. Above all else, "the desire for protection and an end to fighting in the hamlets is the highest popular aspiration," Komer wrote. Providing such security attracted the "allegiance of the rural populace." Yet, he underscored that security was a first step and that improvements in living conditions were equally important and "may just have some reflection in increasing popular allegiance to the GVN."[40]

After the weeklong series of meetings with the president, Komer met with reporters. They seized on Westmoreland's prediction that a military phaseout might begin in two years. When reporters asked whether pacification could also be phased out in two years, Komer responded that pacification would take longer than military operations. One reporter queried, "Would it take generations then?" Komer emphatically replied, "Great things just don't happen." For once, Komer the optimist, as some wags called him, spoke carefully and realistically, stressing that he was encouraged by the GVN's commitment to pacification. He concluded the interview with words of caution directed as much internally as to the public: "I don't want to paint too rosy a picture. As I said, this is a slow, gradual process. It is gradually becoming apparent that more of the people are giving their positive allegiance to Saigon with each passing month."[41] The next day he appeared on NBC's *Today* show and again was restrained in his remarks about pacification, saying that dramatic gains were not the nature of such an enterprise—no surge, no decisive turning-point battles. As one reporter remarked a decade later, "few of these nuances got into the stories about what Komer said."[42]

Returning to Saigon, Komer immersed himself in 1968 pacification planning with General Thang, who was now in charge of RF/PF, and the new RD minister General Nguyen Bao Tri. The GVN also decided to revive its Central Revolutionary Development Council, chaired by Prime Minister Nguyen Van Loc and including all the relevant ministers. Komer had supported reestablishing the much needed coordination body.[43] In assisting the GVN with its 1968 planning, Komer wanted to guard against a too ambitious plan, which is how he judged Thang's 1967 plan. Many of the "young Turks" in the State Department and in the field, such as Richard Holbrooke and Frank Wisner, a foreign service officer serving as a province adviser, believed Komer was expecting too much from the GVN, pressing too hard. Komer rejected such protests. The problem had to be understood expansively. There were forty-four provinces involved in pacification; while some would receive priority attention, none could be neglected.[44] However, Komer would push for a 50 percent increase in the number of hamlets pacified over the 1967 goals.[45]

On December 1 Komer met with the press again to underscore his view that the trend among the population was toward loyalty to the new South Vietnamese government by discussing the new HES. He expressed substantial confidence in the new measurement system as he had given refinement of the HES his personal attention by prodding the CORDS Research and Development Division responsible for conducting research on pacification progress, furnishing additional funding to improve the product, and studying and reviewing the results that the system produced. He had also hired civilian firms to investigate and validate the findings; their conclusions were used to remedy perceived weaknesses in the system. Komer also knew from his experience, as did John Paul Vann and others, that in addition to a system that was broadly accurate and a snapshot of the situation at the end of each month, a personal, on-the-ground assessment by U.S. regional advisers was essential. Thus, HES did not dominate decision making in Saigon, but it was a useful management tool for making overall resource allocation decisions.[46]

Despite these efforts to improve HES, Komer admitted that measuring local security or "winning hearts and minds" was a difficult task. "Conventional military techniques do not give you a very good idea of the hamlet security picture." He continued, "Moreover, how can you measure the winning of hearts and minds?" It was impossible to apply psychological tests to some 17 million people. Instead, the goal was to measure the physical factors that impinge upon the farmers' attitudes. Komer described for the press the elaborate grading system being put in place. He admitted that the system was not perfect. The purpose was to create a more objective, accurate, and systematic assessment of the more than twelve thousand hamlets than had been possible when HES was first established in 1966. He derided those who visited a hamlet and drew conclusions about the pacification conditions countrywide from this infinitesimal sample size. Komer considered the press conference a success and took satisfaction in learning later that a journalist conducted his own analysis of local security in Long An Province and stated that his analysis corroborated the HES statistics.[47]

Others did not share Komer's view that the press conference was successful or that HES was a reliable instrument to measure pacification. Writing in the *New Republic*, William Lederer, who coauthored *The Ugly American*, a 1958 best-selling novel about U.S. power and arrogance set in a fictional Southeast Asian country, savaged the evaluation system. "Ambassador Komer, who is in charge of pacification and whose integrity is respected by all who know him, finds himself in a difficult, perhaps untenable position. First, he has accepted responsibility for a program which has been a failure since 1956. Second, the U.S. military in Saigon resented his coming—after all, he is a civilian."[48]

Lederer asserted that HES represented the underlying problems of measuring success in counterinsurgency: the data entered into the system were suspect because U.S. advisers, 90 percent of whom did not speak Vietnamese, were unable to interview the local population. Lederer suggested that the information the advisers received was tainted because it relied on interpreters who might not speak the local dialect, communication between interpreters with poor English and the advisers, and a tendency on the part of the local population to tell anyone who asked what they wanted to hear, thereby creating a "daisy chain of misinformation."[49] In response to this and other criticism, Komer remained confident, underscoring that pacification was, by nature, a slow and not dramatic process of extending security, helping people, and showing them that the GVN cared about its citizens.[50]

Komer's success convincing the GVN of the value of his ideas was more notable. He scored a major breakthrough when on December 5 the GVN presented its program for attacking VCI and it was almost identical to the U.S. plan Komer and his staff had conceived. The GVN agreed to establish a management committee structure from Saigon to the district level, with the National Police in the lead and working with the army and the RD teams, which the prime minister approved a few weeks later. The GVN named the program Phung Hoang (All-Seeing Bird), but the Americans called it by the name that closely approximated it in the English language, Phoenix.[51]

Komer had already secured additional funds for the newly named Phoenix Program from Washington and another $27 million from the Defense Department to upgrade roads and waterways to spur the economic aspect of pacification by opening the "farm to market" routes. Additionally, General Thang had embraced the notion of bringing on additional advisers to work with the RF/PF and was developing plans to expand the PF training program, but the expansion would require U.S. assistance with building the facilities to make the training program viable and funding the increased salaries Thang wanted to pay. Bunker was euphoric about these developments and planned to push the GVN leadership on other areas that were not yet advancing, including Komer's concerns about the continuing high rate of RD cadre attrition. Komer attributed this decline to the fact that membership in the RD cadre was voluntary so a person could quit anytime he or she desired.[52]

Komer traveled to Washington at the end of the month and presented President Johnson with a picture of the pacification program as gaining momentum. He did not ask the president for anything. This bothered Johnson, so he asked Komer if he needed anything. "No, sir," Komer replied. Johnson persisted, but Komer refused to budge. Finally, Johnson blurted, "Then what are you back here for? You're the only fellow who's been in this office in six months who wasn't asking for something." Komer buckled. He explained to the president that one of the reasons he was in Washington was because he had contracted a disease called tropical sprue and that he might be "carried out on his shield." Komer wanted to begin training a successor. Johnson asked him who he wanted, and Komer asked for Rostow. Johnson replied that Rostow was "too important for that." So Komer asked for William Colby from the CIA. Johnson picked up the telephone, called Rostow, and told him to contact Helms and "tell him to give Komer some guy named Cohen." Rostow got the name right. By the time Komer returned to his office, Helms had called him several times. When they finally connected, Komer was "treated to some of the more impressive invective" of his career.[53] Yet, Helms' dressing-down did not dissuade Komer from his goal to train the next deputy for CORDS.

As 1967 ended, Komer reflected on what progress had been made in the past six months. In a letter to John Paul Vann, Komer wrote, "Despite our many frustrations, CORDS nets out for my money as quite a success. Together, we formed a new organization, hammered out a sensible work program for it, consolidated and focused our resources on the chief priorities, formulated realistic concepts for the pacification offensive and helped the GVN develop sound plans for 1968. I know all of this is just a running start." At this point, he believed, "the problem is not our U.S. team, but how to energize the GVN. . . . They are the ones who must make pacification go."[54]

With the establishment of CORDS, it appeared for the first time that the U.S. support of pacification was no longer fragmented among the U.S. agencies, which had only served to weaken previous efforts. He had made numerous high-level contacts in several of the GVN ministries to press for economic and agrarian reforms. He had also made some progress in gaining Thieu's trust, a step made easier because of Forsythe's close relationship with Brigadier General Nguyen Van Kiem, special military assistant to Thieu. The first sign of a closer relationship appeared when Thieu requested copies of the HES reports so he could use them as a crosscheck with what his ministers were telling him. Still, for months Komer wrangled with Thieu over the criticality of territorial defense, including an upgrade in local leadership at the province and district chief levels as well as more effective coordination of the civil-military aspects of pacification, especially public works projects.[55] However, just before Christmas, Komer succeeded in convincing Ky to agree to strengthen the RF/PF and to tie them into the RD team activities.[56] The agreement was an important step in attaining Komer's territorial security objectives.

Bunker held Komer in high regard for his work over the past six months and commented to the president that motivating the GVN to organize for attacking the VCI had been Komer's personal project. He deserved "full credit" for this advance. The ambassador was also delighted with the progress that Komer was making with the GVN on 1968 pacification planning, characterizing it as more systematic and ensuring it received the level of attention it needed, especially financially. Nonetheless, Komer and Bunker remained concerned with the refugee problem and Senator Edward Kennedy's impending visit to examine the situation firsthand. The senator would "be able to find plenty wrong with GVN's handling" of this issue, but they thought that the U.S. mission and the GVN could claim solid improvements in refugee care over the last six months. They would inform Kennedy of these improvements but also acknowledge that more needed to be achieved.[57]

Bunker was not the only one pleased with the progress made. On December 23, after attending a memorial service for the Australian prime minister Harold Holt in Melbourne the day before, Johnson made a brief stopover in Vietnam. Meeting him in Cam Rahn Bay, the president awarded Komer, along with Bunker and Locke, the Presidential Medal of Freedom, the highest civilian award for an exceptional meritorious contribution to security or national interests. The citation recognized Komer's record of government service in "posts with a high degree of sensitivity, involving often the most confidential relationship with his superiors and with the office of the President" and praised him for "the steady progress being made in the crucial area of pacification."[58] The accolades would be fleeting.

In the final months of 1967, U.S. officials in Saigon began to believe that they had reached a catalytic moment that would unleash sufficient energy to propel the war toward a victory for the United States, South Vietnam, and its allies. Perhaps this euphoria was misplaced or merely wishful thinking. Komer believed there was an unstated feeling that the war had to be over before the 1968 election.[59] Komer, Rostow, and Johnson unquestionably appreciated the validity of a remark that North Vietnamese premier Pham Van Dong had made to the late Bernard Fall, an expert on Vietnam: "Americans do not like long, inconclusive wars and this will be a long, inconclusive war."[60] The irony was that nearly everyone in Saigon at the end of 1967 was convinced "real, serious progress" was being made in the war, but no one could measure it; no one could identify when the turning point would be reached.[61]

The optimism should not be discounted as phantasmagorical as there were indications that the United States was making progress on destroying all components of the enemy's interrelated military and political systems. This conclusion was particularly true for the "big unit" war and to a lesser degree for pacification in the countryside, but even here, U.S. and ARVN military action had weakened the Viet Cong to a point where an effective and immediate GVN paramilitary and political offensive might have been able to turn the tide.[62] Charles A. Joiner, a professor at Temple University, in an independent assessment, agreed that the Viet Cong was damaged and now more reliant on North Vietnamese supplies and on NVA units for its main forces operations in the South. Nonetheless, the VCI remained a "principal source of strength" and the Viet Cong a "formidable competitor."[63]

Even such a voluble critic as David Halberstam, who visited Vietnam in November to research an article for *Harper's* magazine and who remained pessimistic about the chances of victory, observed that such an end might be attainable.[64] Halberstam wrote, "You simply grind out a terribly punishing war, year after year, using that immense American firepower, crushing the enemy and a good deal of the population, until finally there has been so much death and destruction that the enemy will stumble out of the forest, as stunned and numb as the rest of the Vietnamese people."[65] The balance of forces and the resultant offensive military strategy adopted during 1967 against Communist main force units and the commitment of about 50 percent of the ARVN forces to pacification in the clearing-securing role created a more favorable climate for pacification.[66] As one study later concluded, "Thus, 1967 marked the first year that conditions for pacification were favorable, that is, major Communist military interference could be blunted, and a climate of political stability permitted concentration on the pacification effort."[67] There was also sufficient evidence that the Viet Cong felt increasingly threatened by the success of the pacification program, as there were enlarged efforts to disrupt it through attacks, assassinations, and kidnapping. RD cadre had a "30% better chance of being killed than the military forces."[68]

Certainly, for Komer, the eight months had been largely a success derived from his own boldness and skill as a bureaucratic infighter as well as support from Westmoreland and Bunker, who often overrode their military and embassy staffs to ensure that CORDS remained viable in its early stage of development. When he arrived in Saigon, Komer had two categories of actions in mind. The first category included unilateral actions that the

United States could take without active GVN participation. He had largely succeeded in implementing these, one of the most critical being revamping the U.S. efforts to attack the VCI.[69] Komer had also made believers out of those who thought he would fail. He proved he was up to the task, that he could make pacification a priority among U.S. organizational elements and in the GVN. The American bureaucratic reorganization for support of the GVN pacification was a success; even his critics conceded this point, stating that the bureaucracy was better organized than it had been any time in the past and that there was a sense of direction that could be attributed at least in part to Komer.[70]

Granted, his relationships with some of the senior MACV staff were far from genial as a result. Abrams had become progressively more a rival. The two engaged in fierce duels, both rhetorically and organizationally, the enmity intensifying as Komer's growing autonomy infuriated Abrams.[71] Kerwin, who fomented disagreements over details and concept of operations regarding CORDS, was also an opponent, miffed by Komer's end runs because they created more managerial difficulties for him in his role as chief of staff. Further, Komer had built a sizable fiefdom that fostered jealousy among many of the senior MACV staff. CORDS constituted one of the largest staff sections in the military headquarters, which created demands for personnel, funding, facilities, and even computer resources, needed to prepare its many reports.[72] However, Bunker and Westmoreland viewed these issues as minor nuisances, requiring careful handling at times, but certainly not creating self-defeating turmoil. The principal claim they could invoke was that the pacification program was set up for success.

The second, more demanding category of action remained ahead: actions requiring GVN participation after U.S. advice and pressure.[73] In essence, this objective required CORDS to work in the districts and provinces of South Vietnam, instituting a political-administrative system to undertake the "much more complicated problems of nation building and the creation of viable government."[74] These were the essential elements of Westmoreland's Phase III counteroffensive and crucial in the effort to establish for those in Washington "the honest sense we all have that we are making real, serious progress."[75] The truth was evident to all, officials, academics, and journalists alike: this endeavor rested principally on the GVN. Komer and CORDS could only act like "beaters" in a hunting expedition, flushing the prey for the hunter to kill.

CHAPTER 9

The Year of the Monkey

*N*ew Year's Day 1968 was not a time for resting from the previous night's festivities. Senator Edward Kennedy, in his capacity as chairman of the Senate Subcommittee on Refugees, arrived in Saigon to see firsthand the treatment of South Vietnamese who had been displaced by combat. It was his first trip to Vietnam since 1965. Kennedy had held a series of hearings on refugee problems in 1967, hauling senior State Department and USAID officials before the subcommittee to testify. Based on reports from his staff and other government agencies, he argued that the other war was being lost because the massive displacement of the rural population to cities was creating what the anthropologist Gerald Hickey called a "rootless urban proletariat."[1] Kennedy also claimed that the GVN was insensitive to the plight of its own people, which only bred resentment and undercut its legitimacy.[2]

During the twelve days that Kennedy was in Vietnam, he visited twenty-five refugee camps and spoke with hundreds of people. When he left, the senator gave no indication that he was displeased with how CORDS and the GVN were handling the treatment of refugees. Then, on January 25, Kennedy gave a blistering speech to the World Affairs Council of Boston in which he summarized his observations. He admitted that the Viet Cong was capable of great cruelty, but the war also required the South Vietnamese to demonstrate their determination, and in his assessment, they did not have the political will, the "heart," to win. He accused the GVN of insensitivity toward its own people, particularly the peasants, and of forcing the United States to assume responsibility for the war and the risks that the government should be taking.[3]

When Komer received a copy of the speech, he was livid. He called it "demagoguery," a speech filled with hearsay and exaggeration. It was a one-sided view. It looked at only "the dark side," cited only the derogatory, and ignored all the constructive efforts that had been undertaken. It failed to recognize that both allied and Viet Cong military operations generated refugees. In response to the Kennedy hearings months earlier, Komer had directed that the number of refugee advisers in the field be doubled. He had also pressured the South Vietnamese government to emphasize refugee affairs in the 1968 national plan, increase funding for refugee programs to resettle or return refugees, and remove three of the five refugee chiefs for ineptitude. Furthermore, refugee flows were trending downward in 1967 from the peak the previous year.[4] Perhaps Komer, believing he deserved better from the brother of the president he had once served faithfully, also felt betrayed.

Komer's frustration boiled over later that month when he and Maj. Gen. George Forsythe met with Maj. Gen. William DePuy, who had arrived in Saigon to assess the situation for the chairman of the Joint Chiefs of Staff, Gen. Earle Wheeler. DePuy found Komer and Forsythe distressed about the overall capacity of the Vietnamese government—the ministries were not well organized, and they had not begun any of the new programs that Thieu had articulated in his inaugural address as president. Komer had already expressed these complaints to Bunker. Additionally, the South Vietnamese armed forces continued to be an impediment to progress. Their restructuring, which MACV had worked out, was at a standstill, even though Thieu had directed the reorganization on January 2. The ARVN corps and division commanders, disregarding the directive from Saigon, continued to exert "warlord" control over pacification efforts in their regions. Even more worrisome were the impediments to RF/PF enhancements. Corrupt province chiefs were still in place, and province chief designees had not been sent to the training program at Vung Tau. Instead, they were scheduled for an inferior training course in Saigon, but that program had not been initiated.[5]

Their tale of woe continued. The new vice chief of the Joint General Staff had no authority over provincial affairs.[6] His predecessor, General Thang, had demanded increased authority and the removal of two corps commanders who ignored Saigon's directives. Thang told Thieu that it was nonsensical to conduct pacification planning for 1968 as long as these two commanders remained. Out of frustration, Thang resigned and now sat in his villa "cooling his heels." The CIA station viewed his resignation as a "serious threat to the GVN pacification effort" as Thang was one of the few senior military officers who provided leadership. Bunker, Westmoreland, and Komer recognized that sidetracking Thang could become a cause célèbre. The U.S. press, which had declared a four-month moratorium on criticizing the new government, would accuse Thieu of backsliding. Thang beseeched the Americans not to pressure Thieu to have him reinstated. If Thieu acquiesced, Thang knew he would be a figurehead.[7]

In his report to Wheeler, DePuy emphasized the lack of movement and Thieu's reluctance to act even on basic organizational and personnel decisions. South Vietnamese and U.S. leaders, DePuy reported, were preoccupied with the likelihood of a major NVA offensive in the northern provinces, probably Khe Sanh, even though that could be handled with current forces. In the end, motivating the inert GVN to act was a more difficult problem. DePuy ended his report with a chilling reminder of what was at stake: "Of all the things regarding SVN [South Vietnam] that should be worrying Washington now, it is my opinion that this subject should be number one."[8]

Komer and Forsythe, however, did not give up easily, despite their annoyance and the scope of the effort they had to pursue. Komer informed CORDS personnel in the field to start applying pressure, "leverage" as he called it, to improve the performance or secure the removal of incompetent or corrupt GVN officials. Leverage would be applied as a last resort and as a series of expressions of increased concern to GVN officials in the province, a method he likened to tightening screws. If such measures at the lower level did not improve performance, then MACV would begin withholding U.S. resources, funds, commodities, and tactical support.[9]

Forsythe also went on the offensive. He met with Thieu a few days after the discussion with DePuy. At that time the Vietnamese president outlined his approach to the reorganization, stating that eventually the corps and division commanders would be removed from the political arena and concentrate on their military responsibilities. In Forsythe's view, Thieu exaggerated the threat of a coup, which he used as an excuse for moving on reorganization slowly in order to gradually reduce his military constituency's power. Forsythe did not doubt Thieu would proceed slowly and cautiously for a variety of reasons. However, this approach had deleterious effects. RD cadre and province RD chiefs suffered poor morale, the junior officers of the army grew impatient about nothing being done to eradicate corruption in the armed forces, and the government ministers felt powerless to act on new programs and uncertain of Thieu's support should they act independently.[10]

Komer and Forsythe also met with Thang and his designated successor, General Nguyen Van La, to discuss next steps. Thang acknowledged that the most important pacification objectives for the year were twofold. First, focus on a means to improve the RF/PF in terms of morale, personnel, and the contribution they could make to RD. Second, make training programs for province and district officials more effective.[11] Komer agreed with this assessment. A few days earlier he had outlined guidelines, approved by Westmoreland, for the 1968 pacification effort in a memorandum he sent to the senior CORDS advisers in the corps tactical zones. The memorandum emphasized five areas: (1) improving the RF/PF for territorial security, (2) continuing the attack on the VCI, (3) helping the GVN to provide better refugee care, (4) preventing regression in the already secured hamlets, and (5) nurturing the economic revival of South Vietnam. Nonetheless, he remained dissatisfied with the level of progress that had been made since his arrival in May. Granted, CORDS controlled more funding, personnel, and equipment than OCO had, but the number of newly secured hamlets increased by only 268, not the 1,103 Komer had set as a goal. Komer carped about the ARVN's lack of initiative, contending that territorial security was not expanding under his clear-and-hold strategy despite U.S. military successes against the enemy.[12] Additionally, the attack on the VCI, an effort that accomplished little, was in jeopardy. Thieu wanted the head of the National Police, General Nguyen Ngoc Loan, removed from his post because he was a "Ky man." Komer complained in response that Thieu was more interested in personal loyalty than in retaining effective personnel, and Loan was effective in attacking the VCI.[13]

Other pacification programs were showing similarly meager results. Komer had gone to Vietnam with high hopes of stimulating Viet Cong and NVA defections, and the White House had made defections one of Bunker's principal objectives, but the latest statistics were discouraging. When the Chieu Hoi figures, which Komer and the White House portrayed as a significant indicator of how well the war was going, were publicly released on January 13, they showed only 951 Viet Cong defections to the GVN side in December 1967. It was the lowest number for the year and indicated another month of decline since the March 1967 high of 4,918 defectors. Komer had predicted 43,000 Viet Cong and North Vietnamese would defect in 1967; the actual figure was 27,178. It was an embarrassment, and the downward trend fueled demands from the House Appropriations Committee and the Senate Foreign Relations Committee for monthly statistical reports on the war. Representative Don Riegle, a Michigan Republican, stated that he was troubled by the decline in defections and the rise of U.S. casualties; both raised "questions about the true progress of the war." The figures "are the sort of critical trends we just have to get answers to. Congress has to bore in on them and find out why we're not doing better against the guerrillas."[14]

Nonetheless, Komer remained distinctly upbeat, although he knew he had to address the poor results. Sir Robert Thompson added to his problems when *Newsweek* asked the man it "credited with masterminding the successful British pacification effort in Malaysia" to comment on whether the United States would win the war. Thompson responded that victory was possible if the United States reduced its bombing of North Vietnam and refocused the effort to interdict the infiltration of forces from the North, while also carrying out a "political offensive" that concentrated on rebuilding South Vietnam and, in particular, "eradicated or at least lessened the VCI within South Vietnam.[15] Thompson's view allegedly upset Komer, as the latter believed Thompson unjustly criticized the veracity of the reports stemming from Saigon.[16]

On January 24 Komer gave a press conference in Saigon reviewing pacification efforts in 1967 and outlining his plans for 1968. He reiterated to the press that pacification was by its nature slow and less dramatic because of its complexity and the large number of interlocking programs. The 1967 pacification plan was an improvement over the previous year and was more realistic than its predecessor was. The program was better organized, and more assets, funding, and personnel were dedicated to it. However, it was not, he admitted, as productive as had been hoped, although the HES, a less than perfect measuring device, indicated positive trends in some areas. "I am not going to kid you," Komer conceded. "This [positive trend] did not all come about because we gained more hamlets. The increase is partly a movement of the population to the cities where there are better jobs and more security." His personal observations from trips to the field and other indicators, such as the movement of agricultural products along major highways and waterways, were further evidence of economic revival in the countryside. In typical Komer fashion, he offered the facts as he knew them and remained confident that 1968 would demonstrate even more progress. He did not sugarcoat the future but outlined the challenges that remained—GVN inefficiency, corruption, RD cadre attrition, and poor local leadership performance: "So while I don't see miracles in the offing (I still don't see them, boundless optimist tho [*sic*] I am), I don't think you can call pacification any longer 'stalled' or 'a failure' or 'faltering.' At the least, I think we are up from a crawl to a walk. Next year may be we'll get up to a trot."[17] Nonetheless, some reporters resented his efforts at the press conference to use the media for what they believed were "propaganda purposes."[18]

As January neared its end, Komer's attempts to arouse the GVN could be measured only by the number of meaningless meetings with government officials. The end of the month would bring the Vietnamese holiday known as Tet, the lunar new year. It was a time of celebration, and historically a period when the Viet Cong declared a cease-fire. This year would be no different. In midmonth, the Viet Cong released a communiqué announcing its plan for a seven-day cease-fire beginning on January 27. The communiqué indicated that South Vietnamese would be allowed to return to their home villages in Viet Cong–held areas, but they must travel alone and without weapons. The United States and South Vietnamese responded by announcing its plans for a two-day cease-fire. U.S. officials urged the South Vietnamese to release North Vietnamese prisoners on the eve of Tet to coax Hanoi to reciprocate by releasing captive U.S. airmen.[19]

The seven-day cease-fire declared by the Viet Cong went into effect as promised. MACV announced that U.S. forces would honor a thirty-six-hour cease-fire declared by the Saigon government to begin on January 29. Meanwhile, U.S. forces remained on alert not only because previous truces had been spoiled by violations, with each side accusing the other of bad will, but because there was sporadic but growing intelligence that a Communist offensive was being planned. Three weeks earlier the Joint U.S. Public Affairs Office had commented on a document captured by a soldier of the U.S. 101st Airborne Division. The document mentioned that the time for a "general offensive and a general uprising" was approaching, but no specific date was given. However, the document revealed specific methods of attack, mentioning that the key objectives would be cities and towns and the liberation of Saigon. Other reports, including that of a North Vietnamese officer who surrendered near Khe Sanh and an enemy document that the U.S. 4th Infantry Division captured, corroborated this document.[20]

U.S. forces gave these indicators credibility, but the GVN, which authorized leave for 50 percent of its forces, did not. Sporadic fighting at Khe Sahn on January 28 pointed to the potential of attacks. U.S. Air Force, Navy, and Marine aircraft maintained pressure on Communist forces, flying more than four hundred sorties, including three B-52 strikes, in a twenty-four-hour period. There were other minor attacks throughout South Vietnam, including Viet Cong infiltration of the U.S. airfield at An Khe, during which two U.S. airmen were killed. U.S. officers expected the enemy to launch a major offensive soon after Tet, although the Marine commander at Khe Sahn expected the attack at any time.[21]

Saigon, however, took on a festive air on Monday, January 29. For the next three days, businesses and most government offices closed, the midnight curfew was lifted, and revelers crowded the city streets, jamming traffic and becoming easy prey for pickpockets and robbers. They were days of frivolity and solemnity, a time to eat and drink, a time for prayer, for entertaining family and friends, and for settling accounts as the Year of the Goat gave way to the Year of the Monkey at midnight, with the sounds of thousands of firecrackers to frighten bad spirits away.[22]

By midnight on Tuesday, January 30, Wade Lathram, one of Komer's principal staff members, had already experienced the euphoria of Tet and the good feelings among the GVN leadership that had seeped into MACV headquarters. He stood on the roof of his Saigon apartment building with the other residents watching the fireworks and enjoyed the celebration. When it was over, he went to his room and fell asleep. At 2:30 a.m., he was awakened by the sound of firing and explosions. Then the chatter on his radio started. At first, he thought that Vice President Nyugen Cao Ky was staging a coup, but after he listened for a few minutes, he realized that the presidential palace and the U.S. embassy were under attack.[23] Asleep in his eight-room house a few blocks from the embassy, Komer awoke to the gunfire as well but assumed it was the sound of fireworks. A few minutes later, his housemates, Major General Forsythe and Colonel Montague, appeared in his room with pistols in hand and informed him that the embassy was under attack. They were concerned that their residence was next. Komer asked about actions he should take, but they answered there was nothing for him to do, "so he went back to sleep."[24] The three men had little appreciation for what was actually occurring.

The Viet Cong had attacked Saigon, thirty-eight of the forty-four provincial capitals, and the U.S. air base at Danang. Viet Cong sappers blew a hole in the concrete wall of the U.S. embassy and occupied the compound but were finally overwhelmed and killed. Other Viet Cong guerrillas attacked the buildings of the South Vietnamese Joint Chiefs of Staff, Vietnamese navy headquarters, the Philippine embassy, and Ton Son Nhut air base. At Independence Palace, where Thieu had his offices, there were shell bursts, and one of the buildings caught fire. Helicopters and AC-47 gunships took off. Flares floated in the darkness, and tracer rounds zipped through the night. The fighting persisted beyond sunrise and into daylight. Reports indicated that several provincial capitals had been successfully invaded by Viet Cong units. A U.S. military spokesman stressed that the allies were in control of all the cities attacked except for one. General Westmoreland stated that the attacks demonstrated that the truce was a "hoax and fraud."[25] In a statement broadcast over Hanoi Radio, President Ho Chi Minh of North Vietnam declared he was "very happy with the victories" of the Viet Cong. He accused the allied forces of breaking the truce and claimed that Viet Cong forces held Hue, Nha Trang, and Quang Tri. He described the Viet Cong attacks as an "answer to a speech by President Johnson two weeks ago saying the Americans were winning the war."[26] The public relations battle began.

Fighting outside Saigon continued for a fourth day. Westmoreland called it a "go-for-broke proposition," "a maximum effort." He believed that the enemy was capable of continuing its campaign for several more days but remained confident that further attacks could be blunted. He added that the climactic "main effort" would come in the two northernmost provinces and involve a commitment of thirty thousand or more North Vietnamese soldiers. Although official reporting was incomplete and late, the U.S. embassy released casualty figures, giving enemy losses as 4,959 killed and 1,862 detained and allied losses as 555 dead and 1,698 wounded.[27]

Within a few days, the allied forces overcame the Viet Cong attacks. Hue remained the exception; fighting in this provincial capital lasted three weeks and left the city in ruin. CORDS personnel estimated that 60–80 percent of the city had been damaged, leaving 80,000 people out of a population of 150,000 homeless. The Viet Cong attack had given way not to an urban uprising but to a massacre of innocents: 2,800 South Vietnamese and foreigners were killed; local authorities found their bodies in mass graves on the periphery of the city after the battle ceased.[28] The situation in other cities was less horrific but had severe effects. The CORDS staff estimated that based upon incomplete reports, 289,000 people were internally displaced, more than 10,000 homes destroyed, 759 civilians killed, and more than 8,000 wounded. A week later, using additional reports, the figures were revised to reflect 13,000 civilians dead, 27,000 wounded, and more than 600,000 refugees. Property damage was thought to be approximately $173.5 million.[29]

The attacks had done considerable damage to Komer's reputation. For the last few months, Komer, the president, and his chief advisers had genuinely believed that the United States and the GVN were winning. Komer had claimed major gains in security. Halberstam had heard about such predictions upon his arrival in Saigon in November 1967 and asked Barry Zorthian, the Joint U.S. Public Affairs Office chief, "What's all this crap Komer is putting out about the war being over in six months?"[30] As Komer would later remark, "The difference between November [1967]—hey, we're finally winning—and the next thing you know the U.S. embassy in Saigon us under attack—well, that robbed me of all my credibility and that of everybody else, especially the president."[31]

Komer had little time to sulk. Initial reports indicated that in addition to a severe refugee problem, the South Vietnamese government's footing in the countryside had been weakened. Nearly one-tenth of the RF/PF outposts, or about five hundred out of five thousand, had been overrun or abandoned as the government moved these forces from the rural areas to defend cities and towns. The losses were shocking: sixty thousand RF/PF soldiers killed, missing, or believed to have deserted. RD cadre teams, the ARVN battalions assigned to protect them, and the National Police and National Police Field Forces were deployed to the cities and towns, causing territorial security to plummet. The nascent Phoenix Program came to a near halt with the analysts at the existing intelligence centers devoting their efforts not to the VCI but to furnishing current intelligence to allied forces.[32]

Don Oberdorfer, reporting for Knight-Ridder newspapers and convinced that Tet had set back pacification, visited several provinces, but he could not determine whether the obstacle was permanent or not. As he sat in one U.S. pacification adviser's office, he noticed that the map on the wall was riddled with bullet holes from the battle in the province headquarters. But he also saw the large number of local Viet Cong who had been killed.[33]

Tet exposed the Viet Cong leaders who had discarded their cover in anticipation of a military victory and resulted in heavy losses for Viet Cong guerrillas, sappers, and local force battalions. U.S. figures for casualties during the offensive were estimated at 32,000 killed and 58,000 captured. Oberdorfer calculated that approximately 40 percent of the VCI were killed or captured by allied counterattacks. Most of the casualties were experienced middle- or low-level leaders who not only maintained the insurgents as cohesive small units but also were knowledgeable about the local political and military situation. The Politburo in Hanoi decided to let the Viet Cong insurgents bear the burden of the assaults and kept Viet Cong main force units in reserve or for support.[34] Nonetheless, it was a striking defeat for Hanoi, which the Central Office of South Vietnam, the Viet Cong headquarters, confirmed on February 1. Its report cited how it failed to seize many of the primary objectives, hold occupied areas, and motivate the people to rise up against the GVN.[35]

Komer perceived Tet as a "desperate gamble" by the Viet Cong and a direct result of a growing U.S. military presence as well as a surging pacification program. Although the attacks caused dislocation and disruption, these were momentary setbacks. The attacks cost the Viet Cong enormously. "They had snuffed out the best of the southern cadre by sending them into the cities. . . . After Tet, it really became an NVA war," said Komer.[36] He was the first in the MACV headquarters to realize that these losses had "changed the whole picture in the countryside."[37]

Although Komer wanted to take advantage of the Viet Cong losses by reviving the pacification effort immediately, he was forced to wait. On the morning of February 2, Bunker chaired a Mission Council meeting to examine what urgent actions were needed, especially by the GVN but also by the United States, to surmount the psychological advantage gained by the Viet Cong through their attacks on the urban areas. The council members agreed that the most pressing need was visible and effective GVN leadership to restore confidence and to foster recovery from the attacks. The Americans would have to help, and although Komer thought this was a job for AID, Bunker and Westmoreland thought otherwise. They told Komer that he was the only person who could "make this thing go, and CORDS the only organization with the drive to boot."[38] He and his staff now had a new supporting role: pacification was to turn into a relief effort, with CORDS assisting the GVN with its recovery program. Bunker would talk to Thieu about forming a joint task force, headed by Prime Minister Nguyen Van Loc on the GVN side and Komer.[39]

Later in the day, Bunker and Westmoreland met with Thieu to discuss the immediate needs of the government and the Vietnamese people. Thieu stated that he would maintain martial law and the curfew until the security threat came under control. Bunker replied that the United States was prepared to help by any means. The ambassador stated that the immediate objective was to return to the pre-Tet situation in which the government and populace could work and security was established, with the police and other security forces openly visible. He urged Thieu to continue the effort to root out the VCI in Saigon and other cities and told him that mobilizing the population for all these ends was critical. Bunker concluded by proposing for the president's consideration formation of a joint task force, which could plan and execute the measures needed to return the situation to normal as soon as possible. The emphasis would be on security first so that the roads and airports would be open to commerce and the country's economic life restored. In addition there would be a vigorous and creative psychological operations campaign to blunt Communist propaganda. Westmoreland added his views about the necessity of restoring health care and sanitation services, refugee care, and the rebuilding of schools and houses. He then suggested that Loc and Komer head the task force and report to the president but should delegate supervision to Vice President Ky. The task force would be composed of personnel from the relevant GVN ministries as well as CORDS. Thieu agreed in principle and asked the two to return the next day and brief their organizational and related recommendations. The next meeting settled the decision; Komer was designated as Ky's adviser for Project Recovery, the name given to the GVN's relief efforts.[40] Bunker reported in his weekly cable to President Johnson that Komer had established a command post in the presidential palace with a "small group of bottleneck-breakers and problem solvers" who were "working there to pull together civil-military operations on both GVN and American sides."[41] Both Bunker and Komer saw the Tet emergency as a means of forcing Thieu to undertake a sweeping overhaul of the GVN bureaucracy and, particularly, its leadership.[42]

The American press corps in Saigon, however, saw the recovery effort as a setback for pacification. On February 4 Ward Just, writing in the *Washington Post* declared, "Pacification is dead." Komer wrote the journalist a note saying that it "was the liveliest corpse, quoting Mark Twain."[43] He then went to work with his usual gusto.

Komer looked for expedient measures to quicken the recovery effort, and CORDS devised the ten/ten/five program. Every refugee head of family received ten bags of cement, ten sheets of roofing, and five thousand piasters. They could use the material and the money to build housing. CORDS also pushed the GVN to establish a multibillion-piaster special recovery fund administered by the prime minister. The purpose was to short-circuit the normal bureaucratic processes to ensure that funds reached those in need. MACV provided logistical support, primarily transportation, and ferried GVN officials throughout the country to assess the situation. CORDS took the lead for planning and program development, while the GVN was responsible for execution. Komer attended Thieu's cabinet meetings, during which he sat at the table with the president. Operation Recovery was having an unanticipated benefit: strengthening relations between CORDS and the GVN.

The GVN recognized the need for a closer working relationship with the United States on pacification to restore public confidence. The South Vietnamese believed that the capture of the ancient royal city of Hue and the massacre of its civilians presaged what would occur if the North Vietnamese won the war, and this bloodbath turned public opinion in favor of the regime. Thieu now recognized that Komer's insistence that the rural population be able to defend itself was sensible and necessary. The GVN was able to overcome its fears that weapons provided to the people would end up in enemy hands. Tet made clear the once faint perception that South Vietnam was in a struggle in which everyone was a stakeholder. Consequently, Thieu signed the new General Mobilization Law, which made all Vietnamese men, ages 18 to 38, liable for military service. Further, the GVN armed villagers and organized them into the People's Self-Defense Forces (PSDF), one of William Colby's initiatives. Colby argued that by arming all the able-bodied villagers, male and female, Saigon sent a message of trust and confidence in the people's ability to counter the Communists.[44] Mobilization did have, however, some negative repercussions for pacification. It increased the number of RF/PF, but the GVN was also drafting technicians, especially engineers and agricultural specialists, which Komer needed for pacification. Komer asked the CORDS provincial senior advisers to provide him with an evaluation of the impact. When they pointed out the problems that this was creating in the field, Komer "raised hell in the Recovery Committee." After one meeting, one of Thieu's aides cornered Komer: "The President asked me to tell you that he would be immensely grateful if you would stop bugging him on drafting all the wrong people in full meetings of the cabinet. He now has it loud and clear; you have sent him fifteen memos on the subject, and have raised it orally eight times. You are embarrassing him in front of the cabinet. He will do something about it, but please do not raise it again in the cabinet."[45] Komer got his way. The GVN devised a system whereby these pacification workers would leave their jobs for nine weeks, receive military training, and then return to the field.

———————

Tet also forced President Johnson and his senior advisers to reexamine their strategy, not only in view of the attacks, but also in consideration of eroding American public opinion. Johnson met with the Joint Chiefs of Staff on February 9 and with McNamara, Rusk, Rostow, and his personal adviser, Clark Clifford, a day later to discuss a cable from Westmoreland on the situation. The major points of discussion at the meetings concerned whether more U.S. military forces were required and the state of the South Vietnamese military capability, but Rostow also raised the viability of pacification in the countryside. He noted that most of the RD cadre had moved to the cities and stressed that the RD cadre and ARVN units needed to move quickly to the countryside to take over territory that had previously been held by the GVN. His concerns were drowned out by continued debate over U.S. forces, the strategy, and logistical requirements. Finally, the president asked General Wheeler directly, "Are you worried about the refugees?" Wheeler responded by pointing out that Komer "has turned his entire effort into refugee care. Our people are working with the ARVN, sharing food with the Vietnamese and doing all they can." This answer satisfied Johnson.[46] In fact, Komer had already been out traveling in the countryside, assessing the security situation, refugee flows, and physical damage to villages and the provincial capitals, and reporting his findings to Westmoreland.[47]

By mid-February many of the GVN pacification teams had returned to the countryside. The American public had little interest in such events particularly after the country's most revered newsman, Walter Cronkite, presented his assessment of the war in Vietnam at the end of a CBS News special on February 27. "It seems now," he intoned, "more certain than ever that the bloody experience of Vietnam is to end in a stalemate. . . . To say that we are closer to victory today is to believe, in the face of the evidence, the optimists who have been wrong in the past. To suggest that we are on the edge of defeat is to yield to unreasonable pessimism. To say that we are mired in a bloody stalemate seems the only realistic, yet unsatisfactory, conclusion."[48]

On February 20 Vice President Hubert Humphrey, while visiting with the Executive Council of the American Federation of Labor–Congress of Industrial Organizations (AFL-CIO) in Bal Harbour, Florida, conceded to reporters that pacification efforts had stopped. Acknowledging that the offensive had "wreaked great havoc" in terms of life and property, he quickly reminded the press that the Viet Cong and North Vietnam's military objectives had been frustrated by an effective ARVN response. He claimed as well that the Tet offensive "may have left the Saigon government stronger than before."[49] However, Vice President Nguyen Cao Ky and Major General Nguyen Duc Thang undermined Humphrey's optimistic remarks the next day when they resigned from the Central Recovery Committee. The U.S. press reported this development as a major setback for the Johnson administration since Ky and Thang had been held up by U.S. officials as examples of Saigon power brokers working together to overcome the devastation of Tet.[50]

Komer recognized the damage that Tet had done to the psyche of the American public. He was not so tone deaf as not to perceive the impact that Tet had and began to wonder for the first time "if we might lose." He also fretted about how these recent events had undermined Bunker and Westmoreland's credibility. In the previous November, Komer recalled, both men had returned to Washington to tout success, reporting confidently to Johnson, "Boss, finally all this stuff you have given us is beginning to pay off, and we look forward to 1968 as a big year of success for us." Now Washington did not believe them.[51]

As Komer remarked about the situation years later, "Bus Wheeler with his three dwarfs, [Phil] Habib, [George] Carver, and [Gen. William] DePuy, come out about the twelfth of February. The [Joint] Chiefs have decided, because they are too panicked, that we're losing."[52] Komer understood that with the Pueblo incident (the seizure of a U.S. Navy ship by the North Koreans in late January 1968) and the possibility of another Berlin crisis, there were no strategic reserves. The Joint Chiefs planned to meet with the president and urge him to call up the reserves because they feared a second front in Korea. Wheeler asked Westmoreland how many more men he needed if the reserves were mobilized. In April 1967 Westmoreland had requested 200,000 additional troops, but Washington had denied the request. He had since updated the request and found the revised document on his desk. As Komer told the story, handing the document to Wheeler, Westmoreland told him that if the request was approved, it would "speed up the pace of victory. . . . They are on the run now. By God, if you'll give me the resources I'll chase them back into Cambodia, Laos and North Vietnam." In Komer's view, Westmoreland's remarks emboldened him to let Wheeler glimpse his plan to follow the enemy into the sanctuaries. "If you're going to call up the reserves," he told Wheeler, "and the other theater commanders are bidding, I too am going to put in a bid: two hundred thousand more men in two tranches: a hundred thousand in '68 and a hundred thousand in '69. I'll win your war for you in three or four years."[53]

By the time Wheeler returned to the United States, the issue was moot. The administration had decided against heroics concerning the Pueblo, and the Berlin crisis had proved ephemeral. Komer was infuriated with Wheeler for not explaining that Westmoreland's request was predicated on two conditions: calling up the reserves and authorizing troops to attack the sanctuaries. Wheeler never mentioned Westmoreland's conditions or plans to the president. Thus, Westmoreland looked foolish—the commander had requested additional troops to secure victory when Washington was convinced that the United States and the GVN had suffered an enormous defeat. Komer was also enraged by what he believed was Wheeler's disloyalty. He claimed that Wheeler had sanctioned the "three dwarfs" to tell the president, "Those guys in Saigon are smoking opium. We think the situation is much worse than they do. We have just been out there and we disagree with Komer's optimism, with Westmoreland's optimism, with Bunker's optimism, and Thieu's optimism." It was no longer a question of winning but of staving off defeat. Westmoreland's request was leaked to the press with no mention of the conditions. Komer seethed, feeling that the U.S. leaders in South Vietnam had been betrayed: "The goddamn Chiefs of Staff. Wheeler's the evil genius of the Vietnam war in my judgment."[54] Komer's anger was testament to his loyalty to the MACV commander, but it also reflected his belief, like Westmoreland's, that the Tet offensive was a harrowing setback for the Viet Cong and the North Vietnamese and that the U.S. military should have taken advantage of the situation.[55] Their insight proved to be correct. As Andrew Birtle notes, "The enemy reacted to the severe losses he suffered in 1968 by withdrawing many of his main forces to the relative safety of the hinterlands and cross-border sanctuaries where they nursed their wounds and waited for America's withdrawal to create more favorable circumstance."[56]

Westmoreland's response to the issue was more measured than Komer's, despite his reputation being further frayed.[57] He was admittedly shocked when the *New York Times* reported that his troop request had ignited a "divisive internal debate within high levels of the Johnson Administration." He too likely felt betrayed by Wheeler, as the request for additional troops had been prompted by the earlier discussion between the two generals, based on a reappraisal of U.S. policy, and made "in the context of a new strategy or of collapse of the South Vietnamese Government and armed forces." Ultimately, with the denial of the request, Westmoreland was disappointed but understood the political pressure Johnson confronted. He would "continue to prosecute the war in terms of the old parameters."[58] Komer too would soldier on, but for a man considered to have reliable political antennae, he had seriously misjudged the mood in Washington and the political will of the American people.

Perhaps somewhat chastened by this outcome, on February 24 Komer spoke with reporters to discuss the impact of the Tet offensive on pacification. One reporter believed the ambassador's remarks were "perhaps the most candid confession of any senior U.S. official in Vietnam."[59] A few weeks earlier Komer had worried about the "defensive-mindedness" of the ARVN commanders who were remaining close to the cities and towns. He informed the reporters that only fifteen of the fifty-one ARVN battalions assigned to support pacification before Tet were back in the countryside. He offered then that it was too early to determine the effect of Tet, that a detailed assessment was ongoing, but that it would be mid-March before field reports would be available so a full assessment could be made. However, in essence, he told them, "a partial vacuum [had] developed in the countryside."[60] The burden of recovery, he stressed, was on the South Vietnamese government—he was using the press to prod Thieu. Identifying him not by name but as a high-ranking U.S. official, the *New York Times* quoted Komer: "The real question now is who will fill the vacuum in the countryside. It depends how fast the South Vietnamese government moves in and how aggressive and how fast the enemy will be."[61] Komer was more pleased with the GVN's speed and decisiveness regarding recovery.[62]

In the interim, Bunker was performing damage control, trying to allay White House concerns in his weekly cable to the president dated February 29. He reported that the recovery and relief program was moving forward with no apparent loss of energy now that Ky had turned over direction of the South Vietnamese effort to Prime Minister Loc. Bunker attributed the momentum to three factors. First, Thieu had intervened personally, which displayed both a wide understanding of the issues and decisiveness but also a keen personal interest in being seen as a leader. Second, Minister Doan Ba Cang, who had replaced Thang, proved to be a "more hardnosed and efficient coordinator" than his predecessor. Lastly, he praised Komer, Forsythe, and the CORDS staff for their effective coordination. Consequently, Saigon was returning to normal, with food prices declining 15 percent below pre-Tet levels, public utilities functioning, and rubble being cleared away. Bunker could see similar progress in the provinces, although at a slower pace. He admitted that pacification had been set back, but contrary to press reports, it was not dead. "While it is imperative that we move fast, we have by no means lost the race," Bunker wrote. He assured the president that the GVN and United States would take the offensive in the countryside to ensure that the Viet Cong did not use this period to step up recruitment, replenish food stocks, and erode the previous GVN pacification gains and to restore the slumping morale of the South Vietnamese population.[63]

Bunker's cable was backed up by an analysis Komer had conducted weeks earlier. The CORDS staff concluded that there were both problems and opportunities post-Tet. Since the urban areas were the primary targets of the attackers, most of the pacification areas were unmolested. Only a few provinces, less than ten, reported extensive damage to hamlets pacified the year before. The chief concern was the overall state of security in the countryside and particularly along the major highways. In some cases, territorial forces were moved to protect province and district towns, and in others, they assumed defensive positions but retained assigned missions. The RD cadre was also withdrawn from as many as half of the pre-Tet hamlets to provide security and labor for recovery operations. More troubling was that as many as 50 percent of the provincial leaders had not returned to duty. Further, the return to normalcy was not occurring rapidly. Continued restrictions on the movement of people were plaguing commerce. Nonetheless, pacification suffered serious setbacks in only one-fourth of the provinces and assets were not vitally affected. To recover, the staff recommended a two-phase effort coinciding with the next two months, March and April. In March, the focus would be on demonstrating the GVN presence to the people and opening the highways and other major lines of communication. The April phase would concentrate on deploying the forces as intended in the 1968 pacification plan.[64] However, it was also clear that the 1968 plan would have to be modified because Tet had interrupted its execution and diverted CORDS assets to urban recovery.[65]

Komer returned to Washington at the end of February, supposedly for consultations on post-Tet pacification efforts. but as Bunker indicated in a back-channel message, in fact he needed rest. Komer was exhausted and discouraged. Although Bunker pleaded with Rostow not to let Komer become enmeshed in Washington meetings on Vietnam, Komer conferred with several officials, and they remarked that he was not his normally ebullient self.

LBJ wanted to see Komer, and on the evening of March 7, Komer sat with the president in the Oval Office and confirmed that Tet had sidetracked the pacification program.[66] Intimates of the president leaked to columnists Rowland Evans and Robert Novak that Johnson's interest in pacification was now in decline. "In long Johnsonesque monologues," he had taken to "emphasizing the shooting war and de-emphasizing pacification" since the January offensive. The days when the president would discuss the progress of pacification, citing Komer's statistics, were no more.[67]

President Thieu at least listened, but his attention did not mean action. Hoping a discussion would persuade the GVN to move faster, Bunker took Komer to report privately to Thieu on his Washington trip when the latter returned to Saigon. Bunker led off the meeting by telling Thieu that Komer would provide him a candid appraisal of the current situation and GVN performance. Bunker added that this was not an official call based on instructions from Washington, but an honest discussion of Komer's assessment of Washington concerns. Komer did not sweeten his views. He hammered heavily on the deep discouragement of the U.S. press, public, and a sizable portion of Congress by the success of the Viet Cong offensive and the GVN's slow response in ridding itself of corrupt and incompetent leaders, recovering the countryside, attacking the enemy, and rebuilding the cities. Komer stressed that these factors had intensified antiwar sentiment and hardened attitudes against the Johnson administration. Komer also emphasized that President Johnson and his top advisers remained resolute and unflustered. Nonetheless, how the GVN acted in the next few months was critical; the GVN had to demonstrate that it could conduct a full-scale counteroffensive to eliminate the threat to the cities and reclaim control of the countryside.

Komer summed up by saying that it would be difficult for the United States to justify additional support to the GVN or even to maintain its current level of support if the GVN did not take far-reaching steps to show that it was countering the enemy threat and taking advantage of the damage done to the VCI. He ended by apologizing for giving such a bleak view, but he owed the president a candid evaluation.

In response, Thieu at first offered excuses about how difficult it was to persuade the GVN to act together, but then he asked guilelessly, "Should I have a change of government?" When Bunker asked what he meant, Thieu said he wanted to know whether he should dismiss Loc or any other ministers. Bunker replied that he realized the difficulty of forcing Loc out, but he gave no indication that Thieu should replace the prime minister. Komer was equally noncommittal suggesting only that Thieu must take charge, as Loc was indecisive. He then added that the president should give Loc a few months to sweep out the corruption; if he could not, then he should be replaced. Thieu smiled but did not respond. After two hours of conversation, the meeting was over.[68]

The pacification program suffered a setback because of the Tet offensive, but as was true of so many aspects of the war, it was difficult to measure the magnitude. Still, it was clear that a race for the countryside was now in progress. The salutary effect of the offensive was that a large segment of the VCI had made itself visible, which would make it somewhat easier to root out. As Komer and Bunker maintained, the essential, immediate tasks were to push supplies to the provinces, settle the internally displaced in camps, and push the security forces back into specific local areas to reestablish security. Knowledgeable observers concluded that there was now a "greater feeling of unity and more willingness to contribute to the common cause than has ever been witnessed before in this country."[69] However, as both men understood, such nationalist fervor was fleeting and stimulating the GVN to act on it was always problematic given its political fragmentation and bureaucratic battlegrounds.

Thieu had still been organizing and consolidating his government when Tet became the first major crisis of his tenure. The creation of the Central Recovery Committee, which Bunker and Westmoreland urged him to form, and Komer and Forsythe's leadership behind the scenes energized the GVN response. However, Thieu's realization that he had to lead visibly probably made the difference in the response to the crisis.[70]

The shock of Tet, however, could neither be wished away nor compensated for by leadership made more evident or superb emergency response. The press now considered Komer and the administration delusional about the future of pacification and, because of limited access to the countryside, resorted to conjecture. Walter Cronkite, the doyen of television and radio anchors, asserted without evidence that pacification had been "set back by years, certainly by months." London-based Sir Robert Thompson, writing in the *Washington Post*, claimed that nation building and pacification were "now in ruins." In a contention characteristic of reporters who "oversimplified the complex official statistics," another reporter, based in the United States, openly mocked the HES figures, calling them a matter of statistical deception.[71]

For the next two months, Komer defended his reputation as a spokesperson for CORDS. In fact, he had predicted shortly after Tet that the HES figures would indicate a decline in "relative security" for the coming month. However, his remark went unheeded by the press, and now his credibility was in doubt. Komer never claimed to be able to secure areas permanently, although he can be faulted for not stressing this distinction during his January 24 press conference.[72] Nonetheless, even Komer would admit that such terms as "standstill" and "paralyzed" were apt descriptions of pacification in the month following the Tet offensive. He was even more forthright when a *Newsweek* reporter asked him how long it would take to get the pacification program back into action: "I haven't a clue and I don't think anyone else does either."[73] That observation summed up the situation completely.

CHAPTER 10

The Old Fox Gets Fired

The slender and shy William Colby, who arrived in Saigon in early March, had done some thinking about his new role as assistant chief of staff for CORDS on the long flight over the Pacific Ocean to Vietnam. He knew he had better be prepared to offer Komer some ideas about how to quicken the pace of pacification and obtain concrete accomplishments in the field. As chief of the CIA's Far East Division, he had felt the "full force" of Komer's personality and expectations three years earlier, when Komer, in his role as Johnson's special assistant for the other war, insisted Colby brief him on the CIA's programs in South Vietnam. Colby experienced "all the negative adjectives" that had been employed to describe Komer's personality, but he would later write, "I also thought he was about the best thing that had happened in the Vietnam war to date." Komer understood the criticality of the war at the village level. He saw the problems panoramically, not from the parochial viewpoint of the agencies involved, and coerced the various agencies into accepting an "overall 'central pacification' strategy" that provided unity of command without subordinating pacification to the military emphasis on the search and destroy mission, as had happened to earlier initiatives. Moreover, "he was fearless and tireless in browbeating the bureaucracy, military and civilian, to do what was needed."[1]

Colby believed that in light of the Tet offensive, the next important steps were to enhance community self-defense and integrate the various CIA programs throughout South Vietnam into a national approach. He believed he would have Komer's support, but he also recognized that more organizational shifting was not sufficient. There had to be tangible results, and they had to be achieved quickly given the poisonous effect of the Tet offensive on the American public's perception of the war. To accomplish these goals, he decided to spend his weekends in the field after a full week of work at MACV headquarters. He would spend Saturday evenings with province and district advisory teams and then Sundays mornings examining local operations before heading back to Saigon later in the day.[2]

One of the first visits he made was to see John Paul Vann, who ran the CORDS program in the III Corps Tactical Zone. This area consisted of the twelve provinces north and west of Saigon, which together were considered the most important part of South Vietnam because of their proximity to the national capital. Vann and Colby had met only once before at CIA headquarters, and Vann had been critical of the RD cadre teams that the CIA had been organizing. Vann was worried that Colby would hold this against him. After Colby's arrival, Vann had him meet with one of the village chiefs and his men, whom Colby found brandishing rude swords made from automobile springs. The message was not lost on Colby. The village chiefs and their militias needed weapons to fight off the Viet Cong insurgents, who were armed with AK-47s. But that was not the only signal Colby received. He and Vann came to an understanding that it was essential for the war to be fought by building communities and gradually pushing the Communists away from the population.[3]

Vann had made this clear to Komer as well, but Colby and Vann realized that Komer was distracted by the recovery effort. As Colby witnessed after he arrived in Saigon, "the country was in a state of ravaged turmoil and chaos." Substantial sections of the key cities and provincial capitals remained burned out and in rubble, hundreds of thousands of people were still displaced, and in several areas, transportation, markets, and other basic services were nonexistent.[4]

Nonetheless, in March Vann proposed a new approach to pacification to Komer. Vann argued that "the first basic requirement, security," was still unmet. "You cannot expose the population to the inroads of the enemy every night and expect them to willingly cooperate with the government or overtly reject the Viet Cong."[5] The focus must be on village security rather than the hamlet, and an RF company needed to be assigned to each village on a continuing basis with a PF platoon posted permanently in each hamlet.[6] Colby recognized that Komer had already established the groundwork for this approach when the previous year he had moved responsibility for U.S. support of the RF/PF under CORDS. Komer understood that these forces were withstanding the worst fighting against the Communists and deserved better support and equipment.[7]

The movement of GVN personnel back into the countryside had begun with the return of nearly all the RD cadre to the hamlets. Thieu had also issued orders that the RD teams were to return to their normal duties of sociopolitical development, rather than managing refugee camps or guarding cities and towns.[8] Additionally, the pacification situation was now clearer after surveys conducted by U.S. advisers in the provinces, assisted by experienced evaluators, many of whom spoke Vietnamese, and visits from Komer and his top staff. The major conclusion was that there was not as much damage to pacification as had initially been feared or claimed in press reports. The problem was not the loss of assets but the slow recovery of ARVN and U.S. advisers from the shock of the Tet offensive. Soldiers and advisers were returning to rural areas that had been lost to the Viet Cong only gradually, despite Komer's aggressive prodding and support on the issue from Westmoreland. Komer directed that the IV Corps Tactical Zone, in the Mekong Delta, be the focus of immediate pacification attention because of the poor situation in that region and because it was the top priority in the 1968 pacification plan. At the same time, as Komer and Bunker impressed upon Thieu when they met with him in mid-March, adjustment of the planned priorities was required to reassert the GVN presence in the countryside as quickly as possible and to gain an advantage in the next three to six months. Thieu agreed in principle and then proceeded to lay out his ideas for launching a pacification counteroffensive. This assured Komer and Bunker that Thieu was committed to moving more quickly and asserting his control of the program, and with the initial emergency period over, pacification could be reemphasized.[9] Then Lyndon Johnson made a commitment of his own.

On March 31 President Johnson was scheduled to address the American people on television at 9:00 p.m. eastern standard time, which in Saigon coincided with the meeting of the U.S. Mission Council. Bunker, Westmoreland, Komer, Barry Zorthian, and George Jacobson, the mission coordinator, gathered in the chancery's third floor conference room to listen to the speech. They tuned into Armed Forces Radio, and Johnson's voice filled the room. Several of the officials had been briefed on the speech, and the prepared remarks had been transmitted to the embassy hours earlier. The men listened silently, as the president followed the prepared text precisely. As the president came to the end of his speech, one of the officials stood to turn off the radio, but unexpectedly, the president continued to speak. He said that there was hardship, "trials and tests ahead"; that the strength of the nation lay in the unity of its people; and that he would not allow the presidency to become embroiled in the partisan divides developing this election year. He would not devote an hour or a day of his time to partisan causes or any obligations other than "the awesome duties of this office—the Presidency. . . . Accordingly, I shall not seek, and I will not accept, the nomination of my party for another term as your President."[10]

When Johnson finished speaking, there was silence in the conference room. As reporter Don Oberdorfer wrote, "The men just sat there looking at one another, measuring each other's surprise and wondering about the future of the war the President had led and the future of those whose careers had been tied to his."[11]

Within a few days, Komer regained his balance. Success in pacification depended solely on Thieu, and now the leader knew that the South Vietnamese had to "shoulder the burdens of the war," as Bunker phrased it.[12] Komer reminded the ambassador that the United States still had not capitalized on the enemy's defeat at Tet and the greater determination of the GVN. "Our bargaining position is a lot stronger than Washington seems to think," he said. He added that this favorable situation would erode if the relationship between Saigon and Washington soured. "If we can't convince Washington, we'll be in a descending spiral out here," he concluded.[13] A day later Bunker conveyed the message to LBJ and his advisers at a meeting at Camp David, but it had little effect. The discussion drifted to other topics.

Nonetheless, Komer saw some other areas where U.S. leverage might work. The Tet recovery effort had forced the GVN to work more collaboratively across agencies through the Central Recovery Committee. In a letter to Thieu, Komer suggested that the committee be used as a model for pacification. The Central Revolutionary Development Council was ineffective; the efforts of the eight ministries involved were still fragmented. The program needed a single body to bring the various activities that would be under Thieu's leadership together. However, once again, the government did not move forward with urgency, and two weeks later Komer griped to Thieu about the lack of follow-through after policy was set and direction given to the ministries.[14]

Komer took more satisfaction in field reports from the HES that showed the pacification program was recovering. He was also buoyed by the growing success of the Phoenix Program, which indicated that a number of important Viet Cong members had been identified and killed, captured, or persuaded to defect.[15] In a televised news conference on April 19, Komer declared that the Communist attacks had done less damage than he had originally believed. He admitted that the psychological effects lingered, primarily in the Mekong Delta, where half of South Vietnam's population lived. But his optimism was apparent as he rattled off statistic after statistic. The recovery had been slow since February, but the data from U.S. advisers indicated that the number of secure hamlets was up to 61 percent at the end of March after dropping to 59.8 percent at the end of February. The return of ARVN forces to the countryside was one of the reasons for this small gain as was the larger presence of National Police forces. Yet, Komer hedged his bet: "I grant that we may not be as far along at the end of 1968, if the war continues until then, as we had planned to be." Pacification is "just not going to be susceptible to dramatic movement like the siege or relief of Khesanh."[16] He was right. A month later the data took a turn for the worse.

Komer had a second chance to be a congressional lightning rod for the Johnson administration when in mid-May he made public a report that portrayed the "painfully slow but apparently steady recovery of the pacification momentum" since March. Two weeks later the Senate Foreign Relations Committee damaged this optimism when it released its own report using Pentagon statistics and concluding hamlet security and enemy defections had reached new lows. Further, South Vietnamese desertions climbed to a record high in March. The percentage of secure hamlets was now at its lowest point in two years.[17] Remarks that Komer made in late March about the setback that pacification suffered after Tet surfaced to trouble him.

Thieu, however, perceived the issue differently and requested that Komer meet with him to discuss the way ahead. Komer pointed out pacification was lagging because of inadequate administrative machinery to carry it out. He proposed that the Central Revolutionary Development Council be revived to provide top-level impetus and monitor implementation. Thieu assured Komer and other U.S. officials that he was working on the leadership issue.[18] A week later Thieu announced the resignation of the Loc cabinet and his decision to ask Tran Van Huong to serve as prime minister. Huong had a reputation for honesty and toughness as well as stubbornness, but Thieu did not see his potential inflexibility as an obstacle to a good working relationship. Huong accepted the invitation immediately and announced his new cabinet a week later; Bunker considered this action a sign of movement toward civilian government.

Komer asked for a meeting with Huong, and it occurred on May 31. He took Clay McManaway, CORDS chief of plans and programs, with him because he wanted the civilian to continue as CORDS liaison to the prime minister's office.[19] Komer recognized the significance of the date upon meeting Huong and told the new minister what a happy coincidence it was that their first meeting was occurring on "Demi-Tet," the fifth day of the fifth month of the lunar calendar. It was, Komer remarked, an auspicious day for beginning a new relationship. He then turned to the substance of the meeting, and the conversation ranged over a variety of topics. Komer put the first marker on the table by stressing the importance of the GVN's Ministry of Revolutionary Development and the need for it to be maintained in the new government. Huong immediately agreed and told Komer that he considered the ministry's role to be so critical that he would retain the RD portfolio himself in addition to serving as prime minister. The prime minister then stated that his pacification goals were twofold: first, securing the people and, then, involving them in the programs, especially health and education. Komer agreed but said that equally important was an increase in the peasant's income through increased agricultural production and price policies that favored the farmer over the consumer. Huong was surprised by Komer's remark and enthusiastically agreed. He informed Komer that he was the son of a peasant and had worked at manual labor. He became animated, declared himself a man of the people, and reminded Komer that he had once been a member of the Viet Minh and had seen his compatriots commit atrocities, acts that prompted him to switch sides. Thus, he knew firsthand that protecting the peasants from Viet Cong terror and giving them confidence in the government were paramount. Komer knew his cue. He agreed and then pushed for improved leadership at the province level; this was code for weeding out corruption. Huong asked that the Americans provide their expertise and added, "We must be certain of the facts and all related factors before moving against anyone." For the next several minutes, they discussed two other topics, proper distribution of American aid to those in need and the importance of the Chieu Hoi Program. Huong enjoyed his conversation with Komer and walked him to the door. The feeling was mutual. Komer was encouraged by the prime minister's grasp of the situation. He is an impressive man, he thought as he walked with McManaway to his car. Huong had displayed wisdom, strength, and confidence.[20] This perception proved valid when the prime minister, true to his word, retained the RD portfolio.[21]

Although the Viet Cong launched a mini-Tet offensive that same month, the field reports from all the provinces indicated that pacification programs were hardly affected by the uptick in violence. Activity continued but the pace remained slow, and the reports highlighted just how much the Viet Cong controlled the countryside, with serious regression in a number of hamlets that were once relatively secure. As Bunker noted, "satisfactory progress" was "hard to come by," partly because it was inherently a slow-moving enterprise, but also because the GVN was not giving pacification high-level attention. The Phoenix Program also continued to show modest results. Komer's frustrations were evident to Bunker, who told President Johnson he sympathized with the CORDS chief.[22]

———————

In June, Robert Shaplen, a veteran reporter on Vietnam, wrote an article for the *New Yorker* about the Phoenix Program based on an interview with Komer. Shaplen stressed the improvements made by centralizing intelligence collection and analysis at the provincial and district levels. Komer told Shaplen that there had been five thousand arrests of alleged members of the VCI. The confident Komer forecast that by the end of the year, twelve thousand arrests would be made. Yet, Komer also outlined the program's flaws, such as the unhealthy competition among the South Vietnamese intelligence and counterintelligence services and the lackadaisical attitude of some South Vietnamese officials to act quickly before a suspect could get away. Shaplen highlighted the seemingly endless ability of the Viet Cong to replace its losses and the corruption that permeated the National Police.[23] This last point came from Komer's belief that the enemy was stepping up its efforts to organize and control the countryside and to harass the cities. Komer's confidence in the GVN's commitment to the Phoenix Program stemmed from his meeting with Minister of the Interior Tran Thien Khiem, who, as the official responsible for the National Police, indicated his full support for the Phoenix Program and informed Komer he was working on the necessary decree for Thieu's approval.[24] Over the next few weeks, Khiem asked Komer to meet with him several times to discuss components of the Phoenix Program, and he took some actions that signaled his intent to move decisively on VCI matters.[25]

Finally, on July 1 President Thieu signed Presidential Decree No. 280-A/ TT/SL, a result of Komer's briefing to Thieu on the status of pacification the previous month, in which he outlined several deficiencies despite the commitment in 1968 of 585,000 GVN personnel and a U.S. contribution of 114 billion piasters (approximately $970 million) to pacification.[26] The new directive established the Phoenix Program as the means of directing, controlling, and coordinating the GVN's efforts against the Viet Cong. The publication of the document, written with the help of Komer and Colby, legalized the Phung Hoang Program; set goals for how many VCI should be killed, captured, or granted amnesty under the Chieu Hoi Program; and decentralized intelligence collection and exploitation from the Saigon and corps levels to the provincial and district levels where operations occurred. It represented not only an advance in attacking the VCI but culminated the CORDS staff's efforts to push the GVN in this area.[27] A few days later Komer approved a CORDS directive that set out the U.S. role in Phoenix—advisory and not operational. U.S. support was to be in the form of a "joint civil/military action program . . . to complement and support the Vietnamese Phung Hoang (PH) program for intelligence coordination and exploitation for elimination of the Viet Cong Infrastructure." The emphasis was on police operations and no longer, as ICEX had promoted, on the CIA-backed provincial reconnaissance units.[28]

The Phoenix Program was not the only area of Komer's interest. He kept prodding the prime minister and other senior officials, such as Huynh Van Dao, minister of state in the Prime Minister's Office, on a number of issues, from pay raises for the PF to the need for a mobilization deferment policy for key civil servants, police, and RD cadre members. Komer argued that the lack of a deferment policy undermined rural civil administration and pacification efforts because people who were integral to these efforts were being inducted into the military and their skills lost. Further, these groups were already contributing to the war effort in a manner similar to the RVNAF. Komer estimated that 53 percent of the RD cadres would be drafted; the Ministry of Health, Social Welfare, and Refugees would be particularly hard hit. He also threatened to withdraw U.S. financial support to the RD cadres and National Police. After all, he observed, there is "no point in spending money to support programs which will then be destroyed by general mobilization." But his effort was of little avail because four months later he would still be complaining about the mobilization order's effect on district and provincial administration and the loss of administrators and technicians.[29]

Komer also continued to press for improvements in the RF/PF capabilities by writing frequently to Lieutenant General Nguyen Van La, deputy chief of the Joint General Staff, to offer ideas for improvements, pass on allegations of corruption and bribery in the RF/PF, urge him to evaluate the reasons for high desertion rates, and complain about the shortage of trained officers and noncommissioned officers, which stemmed from the army's reluctance to fill training quotas.[30] Komer was always prodding, pushing, making recommendations, pointing out deficiencies, and having his staff monitor progress, but he also recognized the criticality of U.S.-GVN integration and of teaching the GVN, making it clear that pacification was a GVN program. For all his efforts, Komer believed that the results were not forthcoming.

In mid-July, Clark Clifford, now secretary of defense, accompanied by Assistant Secretary of Defense Paul Warnke, visited Vietnam to obtain an impression of the situation for the president and to meet with Thieu. Clifford, a man grounded in political realities made more effective by his confident mien and deep voice, was a forceful proponent of having the ARVN and other South Vietnamese forces take over more of the war. He spoke with Abrams and the corps commanders but was not particularly impressed with the military's upbeat assessments. He was more concerned about intelligence, which indicated that the enemy was preparing for large-scale attacks in July or August. Clifford was, however, impressed with Thieu's commitment to pacification and listened to the president and Komer when they stressed to him the criticality of reducing the number of tasks required of GVN/RVNAF pacification personnel so that territorial security could be emphasized. Only days earlier Komer had argued to Bunker and Abrams that the pacification effort needed additional time. It would take another three to four months before "we will be in a position either to prove that our whole Vietnam enterprise has at long last borne fruit or, at the worst, to begin disengaging gracefully behind a GVN/RVNAF which is at least strong enough to have a fighting chance of holding up its end."[31] This perspective was not heartening to Clifford or Warnke. Colby believed that no one in South Vietnam had dispelled the view that the visitors had held when they arrived—the United States was deep in a quagmire and the sooner it got out, the better.[32]

That message may have been perceived by Thieu for after meeting with President Johnson in Honolulu in mid-July, he returned to Saigon insisting that his top-level ministers understand the criticality of pacification.

He also decided that the effort would be managed through the Central Revolutionary Development Council with him chairing it, a development Komer had urged months earlier. Additionally, Khiem began pushing RD activities in the field and pressing the attack on the VCI.[33]

These developments heartened Komer, but he confronted challenges within the U.S. ranks. He believed that Abrams, commander of MACV since Westmoreland had returned to the United States to be the Army Chief of Staff, and the new MACV chief of staff, Maj. Gen. William Rosson, were marginalizing him. In fact, Abrams, according to an aide, "blamed Komer for much of the surprise of Tet" because the latter had been too optimistic in his press statements about the increased security in the countryside and improved intelligence capability. Additionally, the aide recounted, "Abrams was deeply suspicious of Komer and believed he provided rosy estimates of progress to please his political masters in Washington."[34]

The relationship between Abrams and Komer irreparably ruptured in July. Abrams and Rosson criticized Komer's management in the presence of the CORDS staff. At first Komer let it go but then decided otherwise the next day. Wounded by Abrams' public criticism, he wrote the general privately telling him that although he could accept criticism, the way that this incident was handled "cuts close to the bone." Abrams was decidedly interested in having CORDS run like a military organization and believed that Komer was interfering in corps commanders' and provincial operations. Komer countered that while he admired the military system, it was not appropriate for pacification, which relied heavily on civilian efforts in a variety of organizations as well as adaptability. Further, he had never interfered in corps operations or provincial administration, but he did have a responsibility to inquire as to problems and progress related to the CORDS mission. In criticizing Komer publicly, Abrams had succeeded in giving the staff the impression that the two were seriously at odds. Komer believed that he could "even sense a decline in staff responsiveness." In short, Abrams had undermined Komer's authority. Thus, Komer gave Abrams an ultimatum. If he did not like the way he managed, then "you ought to change me." He would not cause a problem. He would "bow out gracefully."[35] Abrams blinked first. Komer remained in charge of CORDS.

Throughout August, Komer pressed Thieu for greater GVN attention to pacification. Sitting in Mission Council meetings every Monday morning at the U.S. embassy was the uncomplicated part of the job. The remainder of his week, he spent persuading, cajoling, and or even pressuring GVN cabinet ministers. Eventually, Komer convinced Thieu not only to organize pacification seminars on the activities being pursued in each of the corps areas but also to emphasize the need to integrate the efforts of the RD cadres, police, and military more effectively.[36] Komer pressed Thieu to unify pacification efforts, not just RD, but again it was a matter of how quickly Thieu would move. At the end of August, Komer had his answer. During the pacification seminars in two corps tactical zones, Prime Minister Huong announced that pacification was a national program and that the Central Revolutionary Development Council would become a more active body by seeking to coordinate the pacification efforts of all eight ministries and not just the Revolutionary Development Ministry. Thieu concluded the seminars by urging greater attention and effort on pacification measures.[37] Komer was ready to take advantage of this change of view.

Komer recognized that with Johnson's decision not to run for reelection and with the growing dissent in the United States, the administration was living on borrowed time in Vietnam, to say nothing of the additional difficulty he encountered given his fractious relationship with Abrams. Earlier in August Komer along with Colby, McManaway, and Montague had decided to create a detailed action program that would be a successor to Project Takeoff. Komer's idea was a short-term surge effort for three months before Tet 1969, which marked the start of the 1969 pacification year. The central goal of the plan was to increase the number of relatively secure hamlets by a thousand. This would be accomplished by assigning a PF platoon to every hamlet, organizing an elected hamlet government, setting up a hamlet self-defense unit, and carrying out one self-help project. The group added other general goals to the plan, including increasing the PSDF to 1 million personnel (200,000 of them armed) and VCI defectors to twelve hundred per month. In short, they believed the prospects for pacification were "favorable barring a sharp drop in GVN morale or new attacks of the Tet magnitude."[38]

When Komer proposed the plan to the MACCORDS staff, staff members protested that 1968 was a dead year, and they wanted to work on the 1969 program. Komer rebuked them: "To hell with that; we may not even be here in 1969 if we don't get the show on the road." He took the deliberate but calculated risk of expanding pacification. Still, his staff was not convinced and argued that he would be repeating the mistakes of the Strategic Hamlet Program or the overly ambitious RD program of 1967. Komer and Montague reasoned that the main drive of the 1968 plan would be to get the ARVN out in the countryside and take advantage of enemy exhaustion after the Tet and May offensives.[39] Komer would not give in, and ultimately, his arguments for taking the risk prevailed.

He and McManaway viewed the pacification offensive as an interim measure on the way to the more important objective of breaking South Vietnamese obstinacy and inaction and as a step toward an extension of security in the rural areas. After eliminating VC influence in areas Komer deemed strategically important with the limited resources available, the United States and GVN could instigate the final "consolidation" phase of solidly installing the GVN presence in the countryside in 1969. These steps were designed to ensure the political control and legitimacy of the government in Saigon.[40]

Before Komer could get the initiative under way, the Viet Cong launched mortar attacks and ground assaults in all four corps areas. The damage was slight, and the enemy's losses were high; the enemy's third military offensive had failed, and consequently, it was switching to a political strategy.[41] The results convinced Komer that the time to act was now. At Komer's direction, and perhaps given his acrimonious relationship with Abrams, Colby briefed their new approach at the MACV Commanders Conference in September and outlined that it would consist of four simultaneous "campaigns": (1) a "spoiling" one in which conventional military forces pushed enemy main forces away from the villages and attacked their bases; (2) a "preemption" campaign to bring territorial forces and government personnel into areas under menace from the enemy; (3) a "pacification" campaign to strengthen important population centers and their lines of communication against enemy interference; and (4) a "political" campaign to institute democratic legitimacy through elections from the village level up to larger political entities to produce popular support against the Communist threat. The objective, Colby concluded, was to launch these initiatives "to turn the war around by the anniversary of the Tet offensive in February 1969." Abrams thanked Colby for the briefing. He then approved the concept and told Komer to formulate a detailed plan. Komer and his staff worked furiously for a few weeks to develop specific goals to be achieved.[42] If some of the provincial advisers deemed their assigned objectives to be unrealistic, "Komer listened and was even ready to reduce goals in response to a good argument, but he was forceful with anyone who he sensed merely wanted to do business as usual."[43] With the plan complete, Abrams and Komer went to Bunker. Bunker agreed with the concept and told them that he would set up a meeting with Thieu so that Komer could explain the objectives to the president.[44]

In mid-September Bunker, Komer, and Abrams met with Thieu and a half dozen senior Vietnamese officials in the president's private conference room. Komer laid out his proposition. Thieu's reaction was not enthusiastic. He too saw 1968 as a lost year and thought that the allies should concentrate on the 1969 program. He turned to General Cao Van Vien and said, "General Vien, do you think this is militarily feasible?" Vien gave a cautious, bureaucratic reply: "I defer to General Abrams because he is more familiar with this; this is a new plan that I have not yet been briefed on." Abrams endorsed the program but put Vien in an untenable position: "Well, General Vien will know more about the feasibility, because it mostly involves Vietnamese assets, but I think it is emphatically worth a try." Vien was not about to be boxed in: "I'm inclined to agree with General Abrams, but I must first consult with the four corps commanders on the military feasibility of the plan."[45] The idea was going nowhere, and the meeting ended.

Komer decided immediately to end run General Vien. He sent a personal message to the U.S. corps commanders asking them to speak to their Vietnamese counterparts and endorse the plan. He then called the CORDS deputy, who had already been briefed on the plan, in each of the corps tactical zones, and told them to do the same. It was a winning tactic. The Vietnamese corps commanders informed Saigon that the plan was feasible, and Vien reported the same to Thieu. Komer wanted to get the plan under way by October 1.

By late September Thieu and Prime Minister Tran Van Huong realized that the survival of their country rested on winning the countryside. The various Viet Cong and North Vietnamese offensives since January, Johnson's refusal to commit more troops, the political uncertainty of the November U.S. elections, and the incalculable outcome of the Paris peace talks, which had begun in May, left them sober and with few options but to bolster pacification. The Viet Cong goaded them as well. They stepped up terrorism, established "people's committees" in the villages, and boosted their Alliance of National Democratic Peace Forces to appeal to neutralists and leftists. Huong said publicly that the "cities can prosper only when the countryside is secure," but neither he nor Komer had any illusions that new rhetoric or slogans could convince semiliterate rice farmers to throw in their lot with the government. Nonetheless, "it is time," Komer told his senior advisers, "to put first things first."[46]

Thieu began his outreach to province chiefs and military commanders in early September by exhorting them in his weekly tours of the rural areas, where at least 60 percent of the population lived. Priorities were reestablished—shore up rural security, wipe out the Viet Cong underground, remove corrupt and ineffective officials, equip the people with weapons, revitalize village government and the rural economy, and improve the plight of refugees and Viet Cong defectors who rallied to the government. The United States and GVN agreed to concentrate this effort in a hundred key districts where 75 percent of the people lived, which were clustered around major roads, cities, and the most productive land for rice growing.[47]

Komer and his "old hand" critics agreed that the time was propitious. The Thieu regime was stable and had become respectable through its slow steps toward reform and the appointment of more capable men. The war had become "semiconventional" since Tet, with the North Vietnamese regulars having to assume a larger role and proceeding to take on the U.S. military's massive firepower in a number of attacks. Despite the detractors' views, Hanoi's attempt to disrupt pacification efforts had succeeded in only a few localities and areas where security had never been certain anyway.[48] The trend in rural security and security for the total population was mostly upward.[49] Komer felt relieved and vindicated, and Abrams shared that view. "We won't strike out a third time," Komer told his staff, counting Tet and the May offensive as the first two strikes.

Komer was not concerned about the slowness of the "nation building." In the wake of Tet, old notions that had survived beyond the establishment of CORDS began to die—"hearts and minds" could not be won by pajama-clad RD cadres preaching "reform from below" or by the State Department's faith that elections or radical land reform would create rural resistance to the Viet Cong. Komer and his team held security as the principal concern. The new measure of success was the number of local officials sleeping in their villages at night, unmolested, and not the number of schools built or irrigation projects initiated. The RF/PF, better armed and larger in number since the general mobilization, was the bedrock of security in rural areas. A fourteen point RF/PF improvement plan was devised. MACV committed to increase the number of its five-man mobile advisory teams, which lived with and trained the local forces, to 217 by year's end. It also established mobile advisory logistics teams to ensure that these local forces were resupplied quickly and paid on time. Komer kept his eye firmly on the trends and directed his advisers to provide monthly data for

an evaluation system for territorial forces. Yet, he remained realistic; correct-
ing the RF/PF deficiencies would be a long, slow process.

Komer was right. Preliminary HES data released in mid-August indicated that most of the hundred key pacification districts (out of 252 districts in Vietnam) were slowly recovering from the effects of the January
and May offensives and only a half dozen were affected by the August fighting. Komer was straightforward in his assessment to the press: "These setbacks will probably be enough to offset the progress elsewhere to make
August show little gain, statistically, over July on a nationwide basis." There
were some positive signs, but they were few. Overall, the Viet Cong proved
that they could contest the pacification program with their attacks, including the assassination of RD cadre.[50] In some respects, the targeting of the
RD workers was confirmation that economic and political development
was gaining.

For Komer and Abrams, the question was whether diverting more men
and equipment to pacification would speed up the effort. The ominous
warning from U.S. leaders was that it could be another six months before
the data would show results at the local level and perhaps a year before the
Thieu government could demonstrate whether it could get pacification
moving in earnest. At a luncheon with Saigon business leaders in September,
Komer insisted that the overall trend in pacification was encouraging but
that there was "still a long way to go." He noted particularly that systematic Viet Cong terror and assassination remained and that a large portion of
the refugees still lacked adequate care.[51] Quickening the pace of pacification
to a more favorable level became the priority. Montague, who had examined HES data, agreed that the situation was favorable; he reported that the
June figures indicated that hamlet security and GVN influence were at the
"highwater [sic] mark."[52]

Komer outlined the principles of his pacification "counteroffensive"
to Abrams. He believed that "the idea of an all-out pacification coun-
ter-offensive is a natural. We are apparently largely pre-empting Hanoi's
'third-phase' offensive, which lays the enemy open for a counter-stroke."
His finely tuned political antennae had not been lost either. He continued,
"Moreover, the political need for increased momentum makes it imperative that we seize the opportunity. We may have until a new administration takes over next January to prove that this war is no longer stalemated.
If we can, we may have bought the time to achieve a favorable settlement.
If we don't, we may be up the creek without a paddle." Komer argued that

the only way to make a counteroffensive work would be to convince Thieu and Huong to agree to a systematic plan with specific goals and deadlines. Otherwise, he warned, "we will end up like the VC/NVA—long on words but short on performance."[53]

Komer continued to take an upbeat stance on pacification. In a report to Bunker in mid-October, he argued that Tet, mini-Tet, and the abortive third-phase offensive had hurt the Viet Cong and Hanoi. The general mobilization had also helped by increasing the size of the RVNAF and the paramilitary forces. Further, the equipment, training, and performance were "on the upgrade," and the Thieu-Huong regime had "found its feet." The GVN had a major anticorruption campaign under way, was purging ineffective provisional and district leadership, and was engineering an effective recovery program after Tet and mini-Tet.[54] Komer's optimism was understandable as two weeks earlier he had met with Thieu, who had agreed to move forward on a new counteroffensive and do so quickly.[55] However, Theodore Shackley, the new CIA chief of station, sent to CIA headquarters a report his analysis branch had written that questioned the veracity of the U.S. and GVN figures and the progress of pacification. When Komer learned of the report, he was enraged, but nothing came of the assessment.[56]

By the end of September, there was also growing optimism about the Phoenix Program, which Khiem had energetically pushed to the extent of increasing the number of district intelligence and operations centers. Figures indicated that perhaps as many as ten thousand Viet Cong leaders had been killed, captured, or persuaded to defect. The evidence, according to one study, suggested that the program handed the Viet Cong severe losses in those areas where the GVN adopted it fully. Although it had taken considerable time to coax the GVN to organize the program and effectively operate it, it seemed to have the potential to make "an increasingly vital contribution to pacification."[57]

Komer tempered his optimism by deciding that after nearly a year and a half in Vietnam, it was time for him to leave, to begin charting his future. He had prepared for this some months back when he asked the president to appoint Colby, someone he trusted, someone who could take his place if he were killed or incapacitated, as his deputy.

In mid-September, Komer had written McGeorge Bundy asking for his counsel.[58] Komer also told Rusk that he had kept his end of the bargain, been LBJ's faithful servant, and been a "good Democrat."[59] While he believed that pacification was successful, it was a "shoestring operation."

He hated to leave and not see his work through to the end, he told USIA Director Leonard Marks, but his sour relationship with Abrams was disheartening.[60] Moreover, Johnson's term was running out, and there was no guarantee that Vice President Hubert Humphrey, the Democratic nominee, would win the 1968 presidential election. Time was also running out for his ambitions. He wrote Harry McPherson, special assistant to the president, a letter, noting that in the waning days of the administration, others, some of whom had not made the contributions he had, were receiving appointments as ambassadors. He asked McPherson to put in a word for him in the hope that "being out of sight won't leave me out of mind" for potential positions, foreign or domestic.[61] McPherson dutifully passed on Komer's concerns to Johnson, who decided Komer deserved another assignment. Rostow called Bunker and informed him that the president wanted to appoint Komer to an ambassadorship. Bunker replied that he had no objections, and after the call, he informed Komer of the president's intentions. At first, Komer felt guilty about leaving, but then he added that while he appreciated the opportunity it was too late in the administration to attain Senate confirmation. Bunker urged him to take the position and worry about confirmation later; Komer followed this advice.[62] The seasoned diplomat told Komer that a change in party did not necessarily mean that he would lose the position; he himself served in several ambassadorial assignments for Democratic and Republican presidents.[63]

On October 28 LBJ designated Komer as U.S. ambassador to Turkey using a recess appointment, which would be subject to Senate confirmation in January 1969. Nonetheless, the rumor circulating among military officials and particularly Abrams supporters was that Komer had been fired; even if he had not, Gen. Fred Weyand's view had merit: "Abrams got rid of Komer," either directly or indirectly.[64] The White House also announced that Colby would succeed Komer as deputy for CORDS, and Komer pleaded with Bunker to ensure Colby received ambassadorial rank as "both the military and the Vietnamese are unduly protocol conscious."[65]

The news of the changes in leadership made little difference to Thieu. The president planned to step up pacification and secure under government control the more than a thousand hamlets now rated as contested. Komer wrote George Carver, "Thieu himself has taken hold of pacification. . . . My own sense is that we have finally achieved self-sustaining pacification momentum—even though plenty of headaches still lie ahead."[66]

On November 1 Thieu launched the Accelerated Pacification Campaign, a name Komer coined, which would last until January 31, 1969. The objectives to be achieved during this three-month period included upgrading at least a thousand contested hamlets to relatively secure ratings on the HES scale, neutralizing at least three thousand VCI cadre, inducing five thousand defectors under the Chieu Hoi Program, expediting the organization of one million self-defenders and arming at least 200,000, and conducting an information campaign to demonstrate to the people that the GVN had seized the initiative and was moving rapidly to end the war.[67] Then Saigon shut down for the weekend.

The only U.S. official in Saigon that weekend was Komer, who on the morning of Sunday, November 3, gave a final press conference. Komer was his blunt self, mocking Viet Cong claims that it controlled 80 percent of South Vietnam. Like a good debater, he cited enemy problems and allied progress since Tet. By the end of the year, he declaimed, thanks to Thieu's new pacification drive, close to 70 percent of South Vietnam's population would be under "relatively secure" government control.[68]

Komer made his farewell to Thieu on November 5. He continued to be buoyant about the future: "I made much of my conviction that we were steadily winning the war." He also criticized the psychological operations and information agencies of both governments: "When the enemy was losing, he claimed he was winning. When we were winning, we acted as if we would lose." Thus, he strenuously urged the president to broadcast an announcement about the accelerated pacification campaign and to describe its objectives and tasks. "What was needed," said Komer, "is a strong, clear call by the top leadership of the GVN to consolidate the victory we were well on the way to winning." It was his last piece of advice. The president thanked him for the help he gave to the GVN and then presented him with a fabulous piece of lacquer and an inscribed picture of himself. The audience ended and so did Komer's official responsibilities as an adviser.[69]

On November 8 Colby picked up Komer at his villa in Saigon and drove him to Tan Son Nhut for an airplane to Hong Kong, where he would board a connecting flight home.[70] Thirty-two months after LBJ summoned him to the Oval Office and designated him special assistant for peaceful reconstruction in Vietnam, Komer was no longer in charge of the other war. Nonetheless, right up to the end he was, as he said in his departing speech, a "reasoned optimist" who continued to "see growing hope for an end to this war—perhaps sooner than many yet dare to think." Hanoi also took note of his departure. It was a single sentence but a tribute nonetheless, linking him to a mythical animal in Asian mythology: "The cunning old fox got fired."[71]

Komer's nearly three-year role in the Vietnam War ended on the tarmac of Tan Son Nhut Air Base that November morning. Komer had "made his name in Vietnam," but it was a "blip" in terms of his government service, one historian has noted.[72] He "proved to be at best a transitional figure in the pacification program for Vietnam," another has written.[73] His detractors in Vietnam, as was the case throughout his career, often made his personality their principal complaint. There is no doubt, that he was a polarizing figure. As Colby, the "Army brat," self-admittedly deferential to military authority, observed, negative adjectives clung to Komer—abrasive, arrogant, egotistical, self-serving. Even the less derogatory terms to describe him, as used by officials and reporters, "ebullient" and "perennially optimistic,"[74] were not necessarily intended as admiration but were often synonyms for naiveté and hewing to the official line. His private reports, Gabriel Kolko mentions, "accurately assessed the political, economic, and organizational constraints operating to keep his programs from succeeding."[75] Additionally, while it is factual that Komer's tenure in Vietnam was brief—eighteen months—this was not extraordinarily abbreviated for most U.S. officials. In fact, he was unlikely to remain much longer than he did predominantly because of his poor relationship with Abrams and because he understood Washington politics. Komer's power was ebbing by late 1968. If Vice President Humphrey were elected president, Komer might have stayed longer, but Humphrey was not his patron. A Republican victory at the polls would assuredly lead to his removal as CORDS chief since he was a Johnson appointee, and the probability of reward for his service diminished substantially.

Certainly he was a transitional figure, between the demise of OCO and the maturity of CORDS under Colby, but as John Prados stated, Komer did "the heavy lifting" before Abrams and Colby assumed full responsibility.[76] Further, Komer's organizational skills, leadership, and understanding of the criticality of the GVN's responsibility for pacification formed the basis on which his successor managed the program effectively after Komer departed. As one Saigon-based reporter wrote, he "was respected by his field people as an energetic, adroit manager (a rarity in Vietnam). He was admired for his encouragement of 'in-house' critics and innovators, for his willingness to 'stand-up to the generals,' and his eagerness to help solve the problems of a far-off district advisor or take issues to the Vietnamese."[77] Frank G. Wisner, a young foreign service officer who served in Vietnam on the CORDS staff and as one of Komer's senior province advisers, and who later held several high-level posts in the Departments of State and Defense, credited Komer with introducing reforms in the pacification effort that promoted a more flexible response to U.S. and GVN requirements.[78]

Army brigadier general Douglas Kinnard claimed, "Notwithstanding [these] aspects of his personality, Robert Komer was one of the most competent and effective high-level American officials to serve in Vietnam."[79] Even Sir Robert Thompson conceded after the Tet offensive, during a visit Komer engineered to offer the counterinsurgency expert a firsthand view of pacification under CORDS, that the emerging pacification strategy was feasible and suitable. In his report for RAND, he applauded the establishment of CORDS and the Phoenix Program's focus on coordinating intelligence and operations at the province and district levels. Although he found problems in both efforts, he believed that once those were rectified, the planning process and the coordination measure would be crucial to success.[80]

"All war is an exercise in management," the former foreign service officer and *Time* foreign correspondent Walter Guzzardi Jr. wrote.[81] In eighteen months under Komer, CORDS provided not only horizontal integration of the civil and military components of pacification, but also ensured vertical integration through the establishment of lines of control and communication from the embassy in Saigon to the districts in the countryside. It also shook up the South Vietnamese bureaucracy and, consequently, increased the effectiveness of the government by increasing authority and responsibility for the provincial governments and loosening up the rigid bureaucratic channels in the capital.[82] As one authority has noted, "Nonetheless, after 1967 the pacification program made significant strides in gaining population support for the Government of Vietnam when resources and leadership began to flow into it."[83]

In short, as Maj. Gen. Philip Davidson, the MACV chief of intelligence, who had his quarrels with the CORDS chief, admitted, Komer "achieved something no one before him had been able to do—he made pacification work." Davidson attributes his success not only to "ability and energy, but to that greatest of all benefactors, good luck."[84] Luck or chance or fortune is an element of warfare long recognized as a verity of the battle-field; it is mentioned numerous times by Thucydides in his history of the Peloponnesian War and enshrined in Clausewitz's remarkable trinity as the "play of chance and probability." It is alleged that Napoleon was once asked by a subordinate what qualities he wanted in his generals and he replied that they be lucky. Davidson also notes that timing is critical to military success, and Komer's timing was exceptional. It was the Tet offensive and Thieu's consolidation of power as head of state that finally catalyzed the GVN's embrace of its pacification responsibilities with any sense of urgency. However, "luck is [also] the residue of design,"[85] and Komer designed an integrated U.S.-GVN pacification program that functioned and was ready to be implemented fully. Referring to Komer's response to the Tet offensive and the devastation of the VCI, Davidson declares, "But it was Komer who was the first to see and exploit this stroke of fortune. He reinstated and expanded the pacification program into the countryside and spurred the South Vietnamese government into (for them) heroic efforts in expanding and stabilizing their control over the people."[86] As Komer observed, development of a "pacification consciousness" in U.S. and South Vietnamese military and civilian leaders requires time and pressure; he could have added "bull-headed persistence," as one historian has noted, which served Komer well. Nonetheless, Komer was still dissatisfied with the status of pacification when he left South Vietnam.[87]

Komer realized that the Vietnam War was a "tale of two cities"— Saigon and Washington, D.C.—and that leadership of CORDS and pacification had not only a conceptual but also a rhetorical component. He was the most accessible U.S. official in Saigon, but few journalists bothered to discuss with him in private the issues and challenges surrounding pacification and none developed any expertise. Komer used the press purposely to keep pacification present in the minds of the Washington bureaucracy and thereby make that bureaucracy more responsive to his requests for personnel and funding. As a veteran of Washington policy and budget clashes, he knew CORDS, unlike the other organizations in Saigon, had no bureaucratic supporters in Washington. Thus, he had to demonstrate, through the press, that CORDS was an enterprise worth the investment.[88] The Accelerated Pacification Campaign was Komer's last attempt to prove the value of CORDS, his legacy. The campaign represented, in Colby's words, "the first integrated civil-military program to move into the country, establish security, attack the Vietcong apparatus and begin the process of national mobilization under a comprehensive and integrated plan."[89] When the campaign concluded in January 1969, most observers considered it to be "generally successful" and that was probably sufficient for Komer.[90]

PART THREE

REVIVAL *and* DEPARTURE

CHAPTER 11

A New Transatlantic Bargain

*T*he thousands of Newcastle residents lining the streets and jostling each other in the city square had not come to see the prime minister of Great Britain that day in early May 1977 but the man who accompanied him in the motorcade, the president of the United States. On the steps of city hall, the lord mayor met the distinguished entourage and honored the president by making him a freeman of the city, entitled to graze cattle in the city's parks. Jimmy Carter thanked the dignitary and then delighted the throng by shouting, "Awa' the lads," the rallying cheer used by the fans of the city's soccer team, the Newcastle United. The crowd let out a shout of approval. He knew how to work a crowd. Prime Minister James Callaghan, recognizing his supporting role, later said to reporters, "He's a knockout. Why compete?"[1] Carter, chief executive and tourist, acquitted himself well right from the beginning of his first overseas visit as president, and he did the same a few days later at the NATO summit.

The new president and his foreign policy advisers considered the summit a successful meeting. Carter, in his opening remarks to the other leaders, issued a call for increased defense spending by the NATO members, thereby setting the character and tempo for the meeting and restoring vital American leadership in the alliance, after the turbulent U.S. entanglement in Vietnam.[2] Yet, it was not his national security adviser, Zbigniew Brzezinski, or his secretary of state, Cyrus Vance, who had defined Carter's plan in which to exert U.S. leadership. Instead, it was a new adviser to his secretary of defense, Harold Brown—Robert Komer, who had returned to government after an eight-year hiatus.

Komer had an opportunity to reexamine NATO as U.S. ambassador to Turkey in the waning days of the Johnson administration. Some said Johnson rewarded Komer for his ardent and loyal service. This view appeared credible when Dean Rusk awarded Komer the State Department's Distinguished Honor Award for his "outstanding contributions to United States military and civil objectives in Vietnam."[3] Others claimed it was compensation for his ouster from the CORDS job at a point when the personal antagonism between Gen. Creighton Abrams and Komer had reached a crescendo. Even Komer, a proud and self-confident man, admitted that he had left Vietnam with his "tail between his legs."[4]

Regardless of the reason, the Ankara assignment was a "fascinating prospect" to Komer. It was also a gamble, because if the Democrats lost the presidential election in November, then he would likely "get the boot" as a Johnson appointee.[5]

On December 3, 1968, Komer presented his credentials to the Turkish government, but he had already become famous for the riots and anti-American campaign his presence generated among Turkish leftists. Several hundred protestors tried to block his plane's arrival at the Ankara airport when he landed on Thanksgiving Day. The protests did not end there. A month later students overturned and burned his official limousine during a visit to a Turkish university. The leftist press, calling him a "monster" and a leading exemplar of the "ugly American," vilified him as a CIA agent and accused him of atrocities and torture in Vietnam. The nationalist press was equally disparaging. Komer recognized that his selection was damaging U.S.-Turkish relations and embarrassing the government of Premier Sulayman Demirel, so he made efforts to deny these charges at the recommendation of the foreign minister and to reduce the sizable and visible U.S. military presence, which was viewed as an erosion of Turkish sovereignty by the nationalists.[6]

Meanwhile, his gamble had not paid off, and the negative publicity likely did not help. He had naively expected the new administration under President Richard Nixon to retain him because of his acquaintanceship with Nixon's new national security adviser, Henry Kissinger. William Bundy wrote Kissinger recommending that Nixon retain Komer, and some officials within the Department of State urged Kissinger to speak with Nixon about confirming Komer.[7] However, four days after Nixon's inauguration, the administration withdrew the names of all Johnson nominees the Senate had not confirmed, including Komer. Komer submitted his resignation a few weeks later, as all ambassadors were required to do upon instructions from the secretary of state, but he also indicated his willingness to stay in Ankara and serve the new administration loyally.

On April 4 Komer lost his "dream job" when the White House announced that William Handley, a career diplomat, would replace him.[8] Komer left Ankara in May, stating at a final press conference that he was optimistic that bilateral talks between Turkey and the United States would stop the erosion in the two countries' relationship.[9] However, his views no longer mattered; the press report was simply filler for an inconsequential section of the *Washington Post*. Many Turks believed his resignation only encouraged the "extreme left, which is trying to undermine" Turkey's ties to the United States and NATO.[10] Komer returned to the United States and accepted employment as a senior staff member with RAND Corporation.

Over the next three years, Komer returned to the issue of Vietnam. He remained a passionate cheerleader for pacification, writing two articles in *Army* magazine in 1970 explaining what the Johnson administration had been attempting to achieve in Vietnam through the pacification program, justifying its efforts, and remaining remarkably upbeat that the United States and South Vietnam were winning the war.[11] In June 1970, as RAND's program manager for defense studies, he visited Vietnam for two weeks, traveling around the countryside to assess the pacification situation. When he returned to the United States, he wrote a report on his impressions that U.S. officials in Washington and Saigon had requested. Ever the optimist, he was astounded by the overall level of security in the countryside, which led him to observe that the United States and the GVN had attained the military advantage, secured extensive jurisdiction over a substantial portion of the population, and even made dramatic economic gains, particularly in agricultural production, as well as overall physical infrastructure improvements.[12]

However, Komer's glasses were not completely rose colored. He cautioned that the political struggle, the destruction of the VCI, and the strengthening of the GVN's position before Hanoi altered its strategy of protracted war or endeavored to accomplish its objectives through negotiations remained problematic. The Viet Cong, he concluded, remained a powerful opponent of the Saigon regime. He was even less sanguine about the Phoenix Program, which he now deemed unsuccessful.[13] He wrote a separate contemptuous report, titled "The Phung Hoang Fiasco," in which he remarked that in only one province was there a Phung Hoang effort "worthy of the name." With respect to the other nineteen provinces he visited, he recounted a number of technical and administrative problems, a lack of GVN commitment and solid leadership, and second-rate U.S. advisers. He also reported John Paul Vann's conviction that the statistics were falsified and sent Colby a copy of the report. The CORDS chief, who, as one critic claimed, would "achieve infamy" as the organization's "principal apologist," sent a letter to Komer three months later rebutting the criticisms. Komer returned fire and sent a copy of both letters to Henry Kissinger.[14]

A year later, in July 1971, Komer again engaged in the public debate by writing to the chairman of the House Committee on Government Operations' Subcommittee on Foreign Operations and Government Information, which was holding hearings on U.S. assistance programs in Vietnam. He decried the slanted portrayal of U.S. involvement in South Vietnam. He termed the conflict a "catastrophic war" but at the same time denounced the tactics of its critics, who had created "a new mythology to buttress charges of ecocide, genocide, and war crimes." He was "distressed to see everything we Americans tried to do in Vietnam put in the worst possible light." Admitting his parochialism, he asserted that the "GVN pacification effort we Americans helped support and shape in 1967–1971 will ultimately be judged on balance as one of the few generally constructive aspects of the Vietnam tragedy."[15] The hearings, which examined the Phoenix Program, had a devastating effect on Colby's reputation, as he was accused of running a program dedicated to assassination and other extralegal activities. As one scholar has commented, "Ultimately, the record should show that Phoenix was not an assassination program per se," but its quotas and its flaunting of accepted norms of behavior in war legitimated mayhem on the part of the GVN and its American advisers.[16] Komer's association with Phoenix would not have the same effect on his later career. This may simply be because the information the Nixon administration declassified regarding Phoenix "neutralizations" reported statistics since 1968, after Komer's tenure as deputy for CORDS, but quotas were certainly one of his preferred management techniques.[17] An alternative view is that the Phoenix Program was not sufficiently mature until after 1968, when the GVN finally established operational intelligence centers at the local level and American advisers began staffing them. Therefore, the abuses began after that date.[18]

At this time, Komer also began studying pacification systematically, as the Department of Defense was still funding counterinsurgency research at

RAND. In particular, RAND analysts studied how governments organized politically and militarily to defeat insurgencies. Komer was one of several "notable RAND authors" to tackle the subject.[19]

Reflecting on his Vietnam experience and convinced that there were inherent constraints on innovation and adaptation built into bureaucracies, Komer began to consider the influence of bureaucratic impediments on successful counterinsurgency. As a member of RAND's Political Science Division, he attended the annual meeting of the American Political Science Association in September 1970 and presented his initial thinking in a paper titled "Impact of Pacification on Insurgency in South Vietnam." Not only was this paper an explanation of the pacification program that he had helped establish in 1967, which he called the "new model" pacification program, but he argued that it was an effective means of addressing the key problems associated with a rural-based insurgency.[20] The paper subsequently appeared in the *Journal of International Affairs* and was reprinted in a book on the Western response to revolutionary warfare.[21] For the latter publication, Komer felt compelled to add an epilogue to the essay in which he admonished critics of the Vietnam War for their lack of unemotional analysis and ad hominem attacks or intimations. Specifically, he felt compelled to answer the complaint that he was "deserving of trial" as a war criminal, a charge that one of the other authors in the book levied against him for his leadership in the war. Komer retorted that he was "unaware of any *qualified* [emphasis in the original] observers" who had made that charge and could only deduce that the pacification program had been "lumped with all the rest that the U.S. did or supposedly did in Vietnam as a subject of blanket condemnation."[22]

The paper was followed two years later by his first major assessment, *The Malayan Emergency in Retrospect: Organization of a Successful Counterinsurgency Effort*, a case study of the successful counterinsurgency the British and Malayan governments conducted against Communist insurgents in Malaya from 1948 to 1960, particularly the policy and strategy used. The study concluded with a comparative analysis of the Malayan experience with the counterinsurgency effort in Vietnam, which underscored the numerous differences between the two situations.[23] After its publication in February 1972, Komer wrote a second analysis, one that he had been reflecting on since he had returned from Turkey.

Komer described this study, *Bureaucracy Does Its Thing: Institutional Constraints on U.S.-GVN Performance in Vietnam,* completed in August

1972, as a retrospective look at his Vietnam experience, but it was more. The report was a sharp and insightful reflection on how bureaucratic factors led to the American failure to adapt to the type of war the United States was fighting in Vietnam. Specifically, Komer argued that bureaucracies have long-standing repertoires and deep-seated cultures that work against innovation, which is critical in fighting insurgencies. These factors also weigh against being able to effectively coordinate the military and civil components needed to be successful.[24]

As U.S. involvement in the Vietnam War wound down, so did the Defense Department's funding of RAND studies on counterinsurgency, and by 1972 the think tank's research focused on conventional force deterrence in Western Europe and strategic nuclear forces.[25] Komer realized that he had to turn his energy elsewhere and seized upon NATO and its strategy for a conventional response to the Warsaw Pact threat.

Beginning in 1973, Komer and his team of RAND analysts wrote three classified studies about NATO in support of Nixon's, and later President Gerald Ford's, secretary of defense, James Schlesinger, and his successor, Donald Rumsfeld, who undertook the difficult task of strengthening the alliance to meet the threat of the Soviet Union's military gains. The first RAND study assessed how best to adjust NATO's defense posture in the event of a mutual and balance force reduction agreement between NATO and the Warsaw Pact, an arms control effort for conventional forces. The second considered "rationalization" of NATO's defense posture, that is, the acknowledgment that military and economic advantage would accrue from the promotion of commonality, or at least compatibility, in doctrine, organization, procedures, and equipment. The final study, *Alliance Defence in the Eighties* (AD-80), published in 1976, urged NATO to design a program that would provide an integrating framework for the alliance's conventional requirements to tackle the expanding capacity of the Warsaw Pact to initiate a massive attack with little warning. Komer believed that while NATO was a success as an alliance, it had botched its early potential as an institution designed to capitalize on defense cooperation among its members.[26]

However, Komer's unclassified 1973 essay, "NATO's Self-Inflicted Wound," was the seminal document on this topic. In this short think piece, Komer demolished the conventional thinking about the U.S.-European strategy and presaged the work he would undertake as a senior Department of Defense official in the Carter administration. He argued that NATO's military posture was inconsistent with the member states' policy. There was nothing amiss with NATO's policy of flexible response and a forward strategy designed to deter or block a westward Soviet attack. What was wrong was the strategy's charade of attempting a vigorous conventional military response before going nuclear, when NATO's collective capabilities were nothing more than a speed bump in the Soviet's advance.[27]

The conventional approach was tolerable during the period of American nuclear supremacy, when the Europeans lived under the protection of the U.S. nuclear umbrella, which deterred Soviet adventurism. The allies also did not want to contemplate a destructive replay of World War II by strengthening NATO's conventional shield. Consequently, the NATO allies had not invested in conventional capability. Now NATO confronted a dilemma because nuclear parity made conventional deterrence critically important, a necessary precursor to nuclear escalation. Nevertheless, an American president would think long and hard before pushing a nuclear button and opening the United States to devastation.[28]

Komer offered a solution. The avenues to a viable conventional defense were simple: make better use of reserve forces; reallocate funding for naval forces to field adequate ground and air forces and then restructure them to gain more combat power; and posture U.S. forces for much quicker ground and air reinforcement of NATO.[29]

In 1975 Komer led a major unclassified study of NATO's defense posture, which made a number of recommendations to rationalize NATO's defense posture in a period of constrained resources by concentrating on a few priorities and exploring a variety of options regarding land, air, and sea forces, particularly to stop a Warsaw Pact "blitzkrieg" attack. This study was followed a year later by a paper that criticized the U.S. military failure to consider the force structure requirements for coalition warfare. Komer argued that the United States needed to prepare for this requirement, especially with respect to a NATO scenario; he again emphasized the importance of stopping the initial blitzkrieg onslaught.[30]

Komer also devoted time to addressing defense issues within a broader and more public context. In the summer of 1976 he debated Soviet-U.S. military balance with Congressman Les Aspin, a Democrat from Wisconsin and prominent member of the House Armed Services Committee, in the pages of *Foreign Policy*. Aspin argued that the threat to the United States from the growth in the Soviet military budget was deceiving as a measure of superiority and that not all the budgetary increases signaled threats to U.S. interests, although some were alarming. Komer disputed Aspin's conclusions, accusing him of using "largely meaningless" analytical comparisons that must have been done "on the back of an envelope." By any gauge, he argued, the Soviet Union was not only outspending the United States but also possessed numerically superior forces, a fact that the United States could not disregard particularly with respect to NATO.

Komer was also helping a democratic presidential candidate to shape his message on defense. Calling himself a "conservative democrat," Komer contributed three position papers on NATO to Jimmy Carter's campaign: the first when Carter was a candidate, a second when he became the Democratic nominee, and lastly after he won the election and the foreign policy transition team called Komer to ask for his advice on NATO.[31]

On January 5, 1977, members of Carter's incoming administration held an informal NSC meeting. Vice President–elect Walter Mondale chaired this meeting of the key members of the new foreign policy team: Vance; Harold Brown; Andrew Young, who would be the U.S. ambassador to the UN; Charles Schultze, designated to head the Council of Economic Advisers; Ted Sorensen, whom Carter had nominated for director of central intelligence; and Brzezinski. The group concluded its business by commissioning a number of studies, including one on European policy that was to be finished by March.[32]

A week later President-elect Carter met with congressional leaders at the Smithsonian Institution in Washington, D.C., as part of his promise for "open diplomacy," as opposed to the "secret" procedures of the Nixon administration. Before the meeting, Brzezinski remarked to Carter that it might be useful to create a briefing book that laid out the four-year foreign policy objectives of his administration. Carter wholeheartedly endorsed the proposal and announced it at the meeting, informing the assembly that Brzezinski and his staff would take the lead on the project. The goals would be based on a memorandum Brzezinski and two colleagues had written during the transition period. The tenth and final objective incorporated improving NATO's military strength and readiness as a feature.[33] Among defense priorities, Western Europe came first, which demanded new initiatives in NATO and the enhancement of conventional U.S. and allied forces to counter the growing military advantage of the Warsaw Pact.[34] Harold Brown, confirmed as secretary of defense on January 21, 1977, had the sizable task of meeting the demands of Carter, Vance, and Brzezinski, but he could not devote his entire attention to them. He needed help.

––––––––––––

The telephone in Komer's RAND Corporation office rang shortly after Carter's inauguration. Komer answered and heard Harold Brown's voice in reply, asking for assistance: "Bob, I want you to help me figure out what to do about NATO." Komer was about to tell him to read his RAND studies and the position papers he had written, all of which were prescriptive, when Brown added the words that Komer could not resist—"and help me push it through the bureaucracy." "Now there was a chore worth doing," Komer thought. He agreed, but on one condition, he told Brown. "I will only do this working for you directly." The secretary agreed.[35]

Komer joined Brown at the Pentagon almost immediately but stayed on the RAND payroll because he was not certain how long it was going to take to build a new NATO strategy. Between February and the beginning of April, Komer and a team of RAND and Defense Department analysts wrote what he called the "Komer Report." It was a detailed, operationally oriented study that proposed how NATO could meet the growing Soviet power and turn around the organization's loss of strategic superiority based primarily on the earlier RAND studies, but it was also informed by two NATO analyses sponsored by Gen. Alexander Haig, Supreme Allied Commander, Europe, and Adm. Isaac Kidd, the Supreme Allied Commander, Atlantic. Komer sold the concept within the Pentagon to the Joint Chiefs of Staff, the military services, and pertinent officials in the Office of the Secretary of Defense and in the State Department. He then held discussions with a few European and NATO officials, including NATO secretary general Joseph Luns and General Haig, to attain their tacit approval before its formal introduction to NATO. The report, which validated NATO's fundamental purpose and strategy, but questioned its ability to carry out that strategy, became the blueprint for the Carter administration's NATO initiatives.[36]

Komer also wrote an article, "Ten Suggestions for Rationalizing NATO," which appeared in *Survival*, the journal of the British International Institute for Strategic Studies. The short piece, again based on the RAND studies, introduced his ideas on how the alliance should go about rebuilding a credible collective defense posture. In Komer's view, "There is really no such thing as a NATO defence posture, only a collection of heterogeneous national postures, which differ far more in their equipment, organization, and procedures than do their Warsaw Pact counterparts."[37]

In late April President Carter decided to call the London NATO summit on the advice of Harold Brown and Henry Owen, a senior NSC staff member at the White House. The Defense Department preempted any action by the NSC staff; the completed Komer Report allowed the department to dominate the agenda. However, Komer's initiative was not accepted without reservation. Members of the NSC staff had agreed that the objective of the summit was to reassure the allies of the U.S. commitment to NATO and its strategy. Komer's defense improvement program was viewed as an important initiative in that regard, but its emphasis on conventional defense was questioned as the primary thrust of U.S. policy. "It was likely to smell *in toto* to the Allies as a half-change in strategy. . . . We must be careful lest our initiatives swamp our initial purpose of reassuring," an NSC staff member wrote to Brzezinski.[38] Regardless, Brzezinski forwarded Komer's "Program for Revamping NATO's Defense Posture" to Carter, along with Brown's transmittal memorandum reminding the president that he had previewed these initiatives in February.[39]

Komer's plan won out. The Carter administration was transforming U.S. policy. Of the change, Komer wrote, "From being the greatest unilateralists in NATO, we have become the high priests of multilateralism."[40] This thrust was consistent with the administration's dedication to multipolar diplomacy and signaled its intention to address the long-standing Western European complaint that the United States did not satisfactorily consider the requirements or difficulties of its allies in making determinations involving all member states and the alliance as a whole.[41]

At the May summit, Carter announced the three major initiatives that Komer had designed. The first called for near-term critical, defense improvements, which signaled that NATO intended to meet the Warsaw Pact's growing conventional capability head on. Second, NATO would improve cooperation in research, development, production, and procurement of armaments. Third, and most critical, the members would design a longer-term defense program to strengthen the alliance on a systematic basis. These proposals constituted Carter's first foreign policy initiative.[42]

Almost immediately after the London summit came the NATO defense ministers' meeting, at which Brown had to amplify the substance of the proposal. Brown proposed nine priority areas that Komer believed defined the elements of a long-term defense plan that all the member states had to adopt. The allies added a tenth area concerning reserve mobilization. Komer also understood that the political viability of his plan required a discussion of long-range theater nuclear forces to make it acceptable to the Europeans. To ameliorate that concern, Komer reluctantly added the strengthening of NATO's theater nuclear posture to the plan, particularly given the decline of U.S. strategic superiority and the Soviet's introduction of the SS-20 ballistic missile. Nonetheless, he was concerned that NATO would become fixated on this topic and neglect the primary thrust of the plan, which was to enhance conventional defense. Regardless of his concerns, the allies agreed to the plan and created ten high-level groups to address each of the priority issues that ranged from force readiness and reinforcement to improved logistics and air defense.[43]

Brown was flush with success but knew that implementation of the plan required Komer's resolve, particularly since some NSC staff members believed that the Komer Report required further analysis.[44] On the flight back to the United States, Brown remarked that their collaboration had already proved fruitful and suggested that Komer work for him full-time on NATO issues. Komer wanted a senior appointment, but Brown demurred. He held out only the promise of a presidential appointment. Ultimately, Brown created a unique role for Komer: special adviser to the secretary of defense for NATO affairs. Brown knew that once he unleashed Komer, there would be no holding back. He cautioned Komer to remember he was a staff officer, not a manager: "Therefore on anything you think needs to be done you ask me and if I agree with you I will decree it. . . . An advisor is not a manager."[45] Such a title did not fool anyone in the Department of Defense. Komer had access and power in addition to being, as Richard Kugler has noted, "a recognized NATO expert," who "brought to the Pentagon a sense of strategy and programs." He was one of the secretary of defense's advisers who "provided the intellectual and bureaucratic horsepower needed to breathe life into Brown's activist approach to NATO."[46]

Settled in the Pentagon, essentially becoming "Mr. NATO," Komer knew that he needed a senior military officer to act as his interlocutor with the military departments because a civilian could not convince the military services to reveal their positions or to cooperate. He selected Lt. Gen. Kenneth B. Cooper, an Army engineer who had just left his assignment as vice commander in chief of U.S. Army Europe. He added a few "young hot-shots" from the services, and this group became his staff.[47]

Komer well understood the nature of his work as he began it in May 1977. He had to convince two audiences of his validity and the feasibility of his ideas for the long-term development of NATO's conventional capabilities: the Defense Department's military bureaucracies and the NATO members, especially their militaries. Komer began work on his program to overhaul NATO, now called the Long-Term Defense Program (LTDP), with both audiences, attempting to convince them to abstain from focusing on the near-term and begin concentrating on out-year considerations, running from 1979 to 1984.[48] He was under no illusions. The rationale underlying the LTDP was "our perception that we needed some kind of an agreed programme whereby we could get the Allies to come along with us in the rearmament we saw as necessary in NATO."[49] In this endeavor, he had support, not only from Harold Brown but also from Brzezinski and the NSC staff.

However, something more was required to move the bureaucracy, and on August 24 Carter signed Presidential Directive (PD)-18, "U.S. National Strategy," which gave specific direction on U.S.-Soviet relations. It called for the U.S. government, together with allies and friends, to counterbalance Soviet military power and influence in important regions, including Europe, through a blend of military forces, political activities, and economic programs. The president stressed that the United States and its allies would maintain a military balance with the Soviet Union and its allies at least at the current favorable level. More pointedly, the United States would fulfill its commitment to NATO allies to raise the level of defense spending by approximately 3 percent per year in real terms as the allies had committed to do.[50] Komer had what he needed, a presidential mandate that not only supported the LTDP but also forced the U.S. armed forces to think in terms of coalition warfare, to view NATO as a genuine alliance of nations.

Komer knew that moving the military bureaucracies toward his vision of an improved NATO would require overcoming the concerns of the military services. Some high-level Army officers supported him; not surprisingly among them was General Haig. Haig, when interviewed in October 1977, saw NATO's improvement toward preparing its forces to execute the NATO strategy of forward defense, putting a heavy concentration of forces along the NATO front to deter an invasion and combat one if launched, as "highly promising."[51]

Harold Brown envisioned a plan that would give NATO a conventional military capability to prevent a rapid Soviet victory with conventional forces by providing a line of defense for thirty days near the German border. Otherwise NATO would have no alternative but to rely on a nuclear response, a risky option. Therefore, NATO had to increase its level of supplies in Europe to thirty days, improve the interoperability of its command and control systems and the readiness of its forces, and expand its reinforcement capabilities. It did not need to make major changes in the number of forces.[52]

Komer pushed the Army to purchase weapons and equipment that were interoperable with the other alliance members' militaries. The concept of NATO military forces being able to communicate with one another or use the same ammunition was not new, but Komer made it a substantial piece of his plan. He also called for rationalization and standardization of NATO procedures. These three concepts—rationalization, standardization, and interoperability—became known as RSI. The Department of Defense would not spend money on new systems as much as it would more efficiently allocate existing resources for NATO.[53]

Congress too had an opinion about how to remedy NATO's conventional force shortcomings. It had taken an interest in NATO's conventional posture since President Harry S. Truman first put American forces in Europe after World War II. In the intervening decades, Congress had often called for troop reductions in Europe and carped about the allies' reluctance to assume their equitable share of the cost of the alliance. In January 1977, just days after the inauguration, Senator Sam Nunn, a Democrat from Georgia, and Senator Dewey Bartlett, a Republican from Oklahoma, had caused a stir when, as the chair and ranking member of the Armed Services Committee, they released a report titled "NATO and the New Soviet Threat." "It is the central thesis of this report," the authors wrote, "that the Soviet Union and its Eastern European allies are rapidly moving toward a decisive conventional military superiority over NATO." The report decried NATO's current capability to meet the Warsaw Pact threat: "The viability of current NATO force posture in Europe and perhaps even NATO's strategy of flexible response and forward defense is questionable. There now exists a disparity between the Alliance's declared strategy and the ability of NATO forces to implement this strategy."[54]

Although Nunn and Bartlett briefed Carter and Vice President Walter Mondale on their findings before releasing them publicly, there was no question about their motives in one scholar's mind. Nunn in particular was presenting NATO's military effectiveness as a topic for public debate and serving as the means by which U.S. military officers who provided him information could articulate their concerns.[55] The gauntlet had been thrown down at the new administration's feet.

Harold Brown answered the Nunn-Bartlett report directly when he testified before the Senate Armed Services Committee's Subcommittee on Manpower and Personnel, which Nunn chaired, regarding NATO posture and initiatives. Because of the NATO summit, the subsequent meeting of the NATO defense ministers, and Komer's work on the LTDP, Brown was able to articulate the steps the Carter administration had already taken in terms of both short- and long-term initiatives. Although Brown was the principal witness, Komer and Lt. Gen. Edward C. Meyer, the Army's deputy chief of staff for operations and plans, accompanied Brown and answered the more specific military and policy questions asked. Nunn appreciated the forthright and comprehensive answers he received from these two men and credited Komer with having a solid understanding of NATO issues. He added for the record, "I have a great deal of respect for you and General Meyer."[56] Nunn's respect for Komer derived from his essay "NATO's Self-Inflicted Wound," which served as the basis for a 1974 bill the senator introduced to increase NATO, and particularly U.S., combat power in Europe to protect against a Soviet attack.[57]

Two months later, on October 3, 1977, Komer, accompanied by Meyer and Lt. Gen. William L. Creech, assistant vice chief of staff, U.S. Air Force, testified as the principal witness before the House of Representatives' Committee on International Relations, Subcommittee on Europe and the Middle East, chaired by the respected Indiana Democrat, Representative Lee Hamilton. Although this committee had no jurisdiction over the Department of Defense, Komer used the opportunity to explain the administration's plan to strengthen NATO. Unquestionably, he had become its point man for NATO issues. He gave a dazzling performance, displaying his encyclopedic knowledge of the subject throughout the hearing and relying on Meyer and Creech only when he needed them to reinforce a point he made.

Komer was respectful but direct in his opening remarks: "The first point I want to underline is that this administration has made strong NATO deterrent capabilities in close cooperation with our allies one of its highest priorities." He stressed that the Carter administration was not changing

NATO's underlying strategy of strategic deterrence and flexible response. Instead, he highlighted that the administration was taking the unprecedented step to design a long-term cooperative defense program, a program that tied capabilities to resources. "The trend is upward," he declared, but there was a caveat: "It is going to take a lot of time to reach fruition, given all the obstacles that have long been involved," a five- to ten-year effort in his estimation. Nonetheless, short-term improvements in three high-priority areas—antiarmor, increased war reserve stocks of munitions, and greater readiness and quicker reinforcement—would be implemented in 1978. The evidence of the U.S. commitment to the long-term defense plan was the administration's fiscal year 1978 budget.[58]

For nearly two hours, Komer answered the subcommittee members' questions. As a witness, Komer was subject to any question a member wished to pose, and he dueled with members over a considerable span of topics, ranging from the Strategic Arms Limitation Talks and the ill-fated neutron bomb to costs and warning times. Komer demonstrated his skillfulness with every challenge. He told the subcommittee members that the administration's focus on NATO was to create "a seamless web of deterrence," and he went on to remind them that "we as a continental island have a strategy of projecting our forces overseas. We would like to defend the United States as far away from our shores as possible." Further, he said that operating effectively in coalition warfare, perhaps the alliance's greatest deficiency, was critical to the defense of Europe.[59] Komer had passed his first congressional test, but it would not be his last. He would appear as a witness on NATO issues three more times in early 1978 in his role as special adviser.

Komer did not have time to ponder his successful congressional appearance. He had more work to do to advance the president's agenda within the Department of Defense and with the Atlantic alliance.

For decades, the U.S. planning model for a war in Europe assumed that the Europeans and forward U.S. forces would have to sustain themselves for a period of thirty to sixty days, while the United States mobilized slowly and then transported massive numbers of forces overseas. This approach was feasible for the two world wars, but Komer knew it was no longer practicable because the NATO–Warsaw Pact conventional force balance had been altered by the 1970s. The allies would be easily overrun, and the war would escalate to the use of nuclear weapons long before U.S. forces arrived in Europe. Additionally, Komer knew that the allies could not sustain a conventional war for longer than thirty days, probably less, since they had never agreed to sizable logistical stockpiles, particularly for munitions. If they ran out of ammunition before U.S. forces arrived, then it made no sense to send reinforcements. Komer argued that the United States had to accelerate the process of deploying ground and air forces to NATO. Using surface transportation was not the answer because the Soviet's submarine fleet and air forces would interdict the reinforcing forces.[60]

Komer further argued that U.S. contingency planning for a NATO scenario was flawed. The planning assumption was that mobilization would occur on the same day as the Warsaw Pact attacked. In other words, civilian policymakers could not be relied upon to allow the militaries to prepare until it was almost too late; there would be no strategic warning. This view contrasted with the intelligence community's assessment that a substantial period of warning existed, at least four days and maybe double or triple that amount. As a former intelligence analyst, Komer agreed with that perspective. He believed that the United States should double its ground forces in Europe within a week. He understood that the Air Force, being a more mobile service in both its active and reserve structure, would have little difficulty meeting the demand to move quickly. The problem was that there were not enough airfields in Europe available to absorb these forces. Komer resuscitated a concept that Air Force general David C. Jones devised called the collocated operating base (COB) whereby U.S. Air Force units could bed down on allied airfields if the allies would build sufficient facilities to receive them.[61]

The situation for the U.S. Army was more difficult to solve. How do you get five division equivalents (approximately 95,000 soldiers) to Europe in ten days? Komer devised a creative solution—preposition the equipment. It would be a "come as you are" war. Komer and his staff suggested the idea of a five- to seven-division prepositioning program to Lieutenant General Meyer. The cost analysts in the Office of the Secretary of Defense determined that this was the most cost-effective method, and the Army leadership agreed to it if Congress funded the concept.[62]

Komer also had to solve the problem of deploying vast numbers of troops to Europe and supporting them simultaneously. Presently, there was not sufficient airlift, and sufficient support staff could not be accommodated in the theater of operations. To address this deficiency, Komer conceived of and proposed the "transatlantic bargain" as part of the LTDP. The agreement consisted of the U.S. promise that it would greatly speed up ground and air reinforcement if the allies would provide transportation for these forces, manage their reception, and support them logistically for thirty to sixty days. Komer devised several methods to ensure allied support on the ground, including host nation support agreements with the allies, increased spending on infrastructure, COBs for aircraft, and use of European airliners and merchant vessels to transport U.S. forces. The Europeans agreed, but Komer was not fooled by this facile acceptance. The allies realized that it would cost them little, and although they did not vocalize it, they doubted whether the U.S. forces would arrive in time to prevent the Soviets from overrunning them. It was a realistic, perhaps cynical view but thoroughly practical as well since the United States would be paying the largest share whereas the Europeans' costs would be spread over several nations.[63]

Within the walls of the Pentagon, Brown and Komer fashioned the fiscal year 1979 defense budget request, submitted to Congress in January, to reflect the 3 percent commitment the Carter administration had made in 1977. The request also reflected the Carter administration's reordering of its priorities toward NATO's deterrent posture, the dominant scenario for which the United States had sized, equipped, and configured the bulk of its peacetime conventional forces. Brown had sought a higher budget, but the Office of Management and Budget pressed for a lower amount and received the president's approval.[64] The request was billed as "the NATO budget," although it met the one and a half wars strategic concept (that is, it sufficiently funded a major conflict involving NATO and a lesser conflict, principally one on the Korean peninsula). One newspaper reported, "Service leaders, acutely aware that NATO is the name of the game, are putting Vietnam out of their minds concentrating on widening their roles in Europe." Komer was portrayed as the mastermind of this rethinking.[65]

As Komer conceptualized the LTDP, he faced with the underlying sensitivity of NATO agreements, which are based on consensus. Komer had argued for stockpiles in Europe large enough to support forces beyond thirty days. Komer sensed that the existing NATO strategy was ambiguous enough that he might be able to increase the supply levels to sixty days. He broached the subject with the allies in Brussels, but a British official argued that Komer was trying to change the NATO strategy. Komer wanted to know how far he could go on changing the strategy. It was a question of interpretation. The Europeans understood the strategy to be a brief conventional pause lasting no longer than thirty days. The United States understood it differently: the conventional war could be indefinite.

This difference in interpretation was purposely left ambiguous because clarifying it could have led to a significant division in NATO. Komer recognized the seriousness of the issue and backed off. He asked instead, "Does an additional seven days imply a change in strategy?" The official replied "no." Komer then proposed going from thirty days of stocks to thirty-seven on his own authority at that moment. He knew he could go no further without imperiling the LTDP and other NATO initiatives the United States wanted. As Komer later remarked about pressing this point, the Europeans would have thought, "My God, the Americans are trying to shift to a conventional defense of Europe and withdraw the nuclear umbrella."[66] In short, Komer would have undermined the concept of nuclear deterrence, which would have grave consequences for U.S.-NATO relations.

It took a year of wrangling with various NATO working groups to attain working-level agreement on LTDP. The plan was officially accepted at the May 1978 NATO summit as the alliance's defense program. To sell the plan, the administration bypassed the NATO organizational mechanism and pressured national governments directly, a tactic Komer defended: "We're talking about radical changes, and bureaucracies naturally resist them. Mr. Carter and Mr. Brown have got religion about NATO, and we're driving this home to the allies." It was a demanding program, called one of "the most ambitious defense programs since the establishment" of NATO in 1949. All members pledged to accept the goal of 3 percent real growth (including inflation) in their defense budgets. The Americans picked the growth figure but were not successful in having the member states commit to that figure. Nonetheless, Komer, whom reporters called a "prime architect" of the plan, believed that endorsement by the heads of states was the most critical part of the initiative because funding the LTDP required this amount at a minimum.[67]

The Carter administration considered the alliance's approval of the LTDP a success as well, and the U.S. press lionized Komer for his persuasive skills inside the Pentagon and within the alliance. A *Wall Street Journal* editorial declared, "The Carter administration's best move in national security policy has been its effort to upgrade the North Atlantic Treaty Organization." For his efforts, Harold Brown awarded Komer the Distinguished Public Service Award, the highest civilian award that the secretary can confer, describing him as a person of "intelligence and imagination," a "statesman of vision and a leader in turning words into accomplishments." President Carter sent Komer an inscribed photograph of himself with a commendation for his "hard work."[68]

Although in 1979 the Allies agreed to sustain defense expenditures to 1985 and to improve capabilities, within years the results were inadequate. This was not surprising, as imposing such a program on a collection of sovereign states is difficult, but economic restraints also affected the results. Nonetheless, the General Accounting Office, the audit arm of the Congress, judged the LTDP as being "the most significant planning document to come out of NATO in a long time."[69] A few years later one scholar summed up the LTDP as successful, writing that "alliance members collectively considered alliance requirements for the next fifteen years in a number of key areas was itself an achievement."[70] Another remarked that Komer was the engine that drove the LTDP and that Carter's reelection defeat and Komer's subsequent exit from government "removed the driving force behind the LTDP at the operational level."[71] Komer's role as LTDP's prime mover would continue to be a source of pride for him, but new duties and an event thousands of miles from Europe would force his attention elsewhere.

CHAPTER 12

Pentagon Policymaker

*S*tanley Resor, the incumbent undersecretary of defense for policy, resigned in March 1979 so that he could return to his law practice. Although he was responsible for supervising the Pentagon's overall strategic policy, his eight-month tenure was marked by frequent clashes with the Pentagon bureaucracy and serious problems gaining the cooperation of the department's assorted components. Secretary of Defense Harold Brown had a substantial stake in finding a solid replacement; he created the position a year earlier because he believed that there was too little consideration of policy issues below his level.[1]

Over the summer Brown interviewed a number of replacement candidates, all of whom refused the job. Lloyd Cutler, White House counsel, whom Brown was pressuring to take the job, told Brown that an ideal under secretary for policy was already working in the Pentagon; all he has to do was appoint him. Cutler recommended Komer.[2]

The appointment was not as easy as Cutler had envisioned it. Komer had sought a high-level position in the administration shortly after Carter's election, but when nothing was offered, he fretted that his association with the Vietnam War was a millstone and made him unacceptable to the Mondale wing of the Democratic Party. Another reason was also pertinent; he was part of the old guard. His appointment, at least in 1977, would have symbolized to some of Carter's advisers a capitulation to the recognized Washington power elite.[3] Additionally, Komer's appointment to the under secretary position required Senate confirmation, and although Democrats controlled that body, his nomination could meet opposition in that chamber.

Nonetheless, Brown agreed that Komer was well qualified, had proved he could handle the Pentagon bureaucracy with aplomb, and had made a substantial contribution to the administration's policy goals with respect to NATO. In early August Brown asked Carter to nominate his aide to the vacant position on the strength of Komer's NATO efforts. The request was immediately controversial and set off a debate among White House officials worried that Komer's identification with the Vietnam War would injure the administration, but Brown vigorously supported his nomination. After more than a month of bureaucratic bickering, Carter agreed with Brown's request and announced Komer's nomination on September 27, 1979.[4]

The appointment delighted Komer. Not only was it recognition for his efforts concerning NATO, but it would give him a more powerful platform on which to push NATO issues and to become involved in other issues on which he had strong opinions, such as those concerning the Middle East. His confirmation hearing on October 17 did not detract from the pleasure he felt. It turned out to be a perfunctory event. Mississippi Senator John C. Stennis, the Senate Armed Services Committee chairman, asked him why he wanted to serve in this capacity, and Senator John Tower, the ranking Republican from Texas, commented that he was very familiar with Komer's background and added that he was pleased to see him before the committee. The only other senator present was the Republican senator from Virginia, John Warner, who had no questions and stated he would support his confirmation given his distinguished record of public service. His time in the witness chair lasted less than five minutes. The Senate confirmed him on October 19.[5]

––––––––––

For the first few weeks after beginning his new duties, Komer continued to manage the NATO initiatives and intended to keep it that way. He doubted whether anyone else was equal to the task or had the requisite level of expertise that he had gained over the past several years. He also reorganized his staff because he felt that the incumbent assistant secretary of defense for international security affairs could not devote his attention adequately to political-military affairs between the U.S. defense establishment and other nations as well as to a variety of functional issues. Subsequently, he appointed Walter Slocombe, who worked for the assistant secretary, to a new position, deputy under secretary, and gave him responsibility for arms control and policy planning, among other duties. Komer's confidence in Slocombe meant that the latter had substantial autonomy. Lastly, Komer devoted himself to house-keeping issues. He believed that one of his responsibilities was to improve the Defense Department's strategy making and ensure that operational plans developed by U.S. commanders throughout the globe were consistent with the secretary's policy direction.[6] However, two events were to turn his and the administration's immediate attention elsewhere.

The first event occurred in Iran on November 4, 1979, when radical anti-American demonstrators took over the U.S. embassy compound in Tehran in support of the Islamic revolution and held fifty-two occupants hostage. The incident provoked a heated debate in Washington as to why the United States failed to anticipate this outcome. Some blamed the State Department and the U.S. ambassador to Iran for suppressing the pessimistic and farsighted cables of the ambassador's subordinates. Other critics censured Brzezinski's theory of bolstering "regional influentials." They argued that its basic assumption was discredited and flawed by an overly naive equation that military power plus oil wealth equaled political stability. Brzezinski had failed to consider how corruption, mismanagement, and religious opposition could undermine the shah's legitimacy among his own people.[7] Moreover, on November 24, after asking the Joint Chiefs for potential military options to free the hostages, the president learned that the United States was powerless to act because it lacked sufficient capabilities in the region to do so. On December 4, at a NSC meeting, Carter directed Brown to make a rapid deployment force operational immediately. He also told the Departments of State and Defense to develop plans for attaining access to air and naval bases in the region. Brzezinski recommended three sites: Somalia, Oman, and Kenya.[8]

Carter had directed the formation of the rapid deployment force in August 1977 through Presidential Directive 18, which gave special emphasis to the Middle East. The directive declared that in a crisis the projection of U.S. forces into the region must be considered as high a priority as that of reinforcing South Korea.[9] A net assessment the administration conducted in the first few months of its tenure identified the Persian Gulf, particularly Iran, as the area of the world most susceptible to Soviet pressure and the most likely place for a conflict requiring the deployment of U.S. forces. Therefore, the U.S. military needed to be able to respond rapidly to crises in that region of the world.[10] A related Defense Department study included several recommendations for how these forces might be used in non-NATO contingencies. The underlying concept of operations was to build existing forces flexible enough to be capable of acting independently of allied operating bases. The Persian Gulf was one of the areas where this concept would be used.[11]

The Defense Department, however, had not acted on the president's direction except for some perfunctory planning. Instead, it continued its focus on NATO, which it considered its principal initiative. Defense budgets, which had suffered a 38 percent decline since 1968, also made it unaffordable. The Department of State had acted similarly, refusing to engage regional states diplomatically in discussions about the potential necessity for the deployment of a contingency force to the region. Continuing the current policy wherein the U.S. presence was not highly visible was considered the best approach because of U.S. support of Israel. Radical Arabs could use a more overtly pro-U.S. policy to disrupt and possibly destabilize moderate Arab regimes.[12] As one senior State Department official who had substantial experience in the Arab world acknowledged, the decision not to engage diplomatically was the result of years of conditioning in the belief that an increased military presence was unnecessarily inflammatory.[13]

Carter's recollection of the net assessment's warning and the rapid disintegration of the pro-American regime made him obsessive about the vulnerability of Western interests in the Persian Gulf. Additionally, U.S. intelligence made him and his principal advisers progressively more aware of the Soviet Union's focus on increasing its force projection capabilities, which included planning and exercises dedicated to a Soviet invasion to capture and control Middle East oil fields.[14]

The second critical event followed on December 25, when the Soviet Union invaded Afghanistan. The operation, according to Brzezinski, represented "not a local but a strategic challenge."[15] Soviet premier Leonid Brezhnev told Carter that events internal to Afghanistan required the Union of Soviet Socialist Republics (USSR) to save the unstable pro-Soviet government there. Carter and his principal advisers discounted the possibility that the Soviets feared the Islamic fundamentalists in their backyard sowing discontent among Muslims in the USSR. Instead, they perceived the Soviet Union's use of force to increase its domination beyond its borders for the first time since the late 1940s as portending ominous designs in the Persian Gulf, potentially including an invasion of a militarily weakened Iran.[16]

Carter was initially stunned and felt personally betrayed and disappointed by the Soviet invasion because of his efforts to win ratification of the second Strategic Arms Limitation Treaty (SALT II). He recovered and seemed to one of his close aides to toughen, to become more forceful and ready to act.[17] The first sign of his determination came on December 30, when he told journalists that the United States now confronted in the Persian Gulf a wider strategic challenge that would necessitate a broad response.[18]

Brzezinski followed Carter's lead a few weeks later, by remarking in an interview that "three central strategic zones" existed where the United States had vital interests: Western Europe, the Far East, and a newly emerged area, the Middle East. Further, he saw these zones as interdependent: a threat to the security of one was a threat to the other two. Almost simultaneously, he sent a memorandum to Carter laying out the long-term objectives needed to cope with the consequences of the Soviet action in Afghanistan, reiterating the regional strategic framework he had advanced before, and underscoring that an increased defense budget would be required for a sustained effort.[19] A year earlier, when he had first suggested the new security framework, he had also recommended that the president declare his plans publicly in a major speech. Carter had demurred then.[20] Now the time was ripe, and the president's upcoming State of the Union address would be the venue.

In his State of the Union message on January 23, 1980, the president articulated the new U.S. policy on the Middle East and Southwest Asia, using language that Brzezinski furnished to Carter's speechwriter:[21] "Let our position be absolutely clear. Any attempt by any outside force to gain control of the Persian Gulf region will be regarded as an assault on the vital interests of the United States of America, and such an assault will be repelled by any means necessary, including military force."[22]

Détente was dead. Brzezinski now enjoyed Carter's complete support and approval. No longer was the president fluctuating between the national security adviser and Cyrus Vance, his secretary of state, to maintain harmony; the fluctuation, after all, had only produced incoherent U.S. foreign policy. Brzezinski was the bureaucratic victor: the Soviet invasion justified his long-held views that challenging the Soviets was the best stance. Confrontation, not the State Department's preferred posture of balanced cooperation and competition, dispelled the perception of American weakness, which he believed had only emboldened the Soviets to aggressive action in Ethiopia and now Afghanistan. The latest crises also allowed his long-held interest in an American-led security framework and presence in the Persian Gulf region to be realized. But the "Carter Doctrine," as the press soon named it, required more than rhetorical flourishes.[23]

To provide a basis for direction in the embryonic Persian Gulf security framework, Brig. Gen. William Odom, a member of Brzezinski's staff, delineated a number of activities, categorized as military, diplomatic, economic, and intelligence issues, which required immediate implementation.[24] The first visible indication of the new military approach was the president's fiscal year 1981 budget request, which included a substantial increase in defense spending, approximately $35 billion more than the previous year's request to Congress.[25] As Secretary Brown informed Congress in late January 1980, "The President and I believe the prospect for renewed turbulence in the Middle East, the Caribbean, and elsewhere, and the possibility of new demands on our non-nuclear posture, require additional precautionary actions. As a consequence, we will accelerate our efforts to improve the capability of our Rapid Deployment Forces (RDF)."[26] Such a tangible budget increase in addition to the declaratory policy dictated that the halfhearted planning for an RDF that had been ongoing for months now needed to be an immediate priority for the Defense Department.[27]

Komer, testifying in his new capacity in February, was even more specific at a Senate hearing on the subject. In the Persian Gulf, the emphasis would be on deterring Soviet incursions first and then defending the region. Given that strategy, the immediate requirement was the ability to project forces overseas rapidly and effectively. The RDF, in his view, would have to rely on speedy movement of personnel and equipment to the region using the concept he had promoted for rapid NATO reinforcement, prepositioning of matériel. To this end, the Defense Department budget request, he informed the members, was approximately $300 million, $220 million for the floating bases (maritime prepositioning ships to store heavy equipment and supplies) and $81 million for developing suitably large transport planes, the Air Force's C-X program.[28]

With the 1980 presidential election only months away, the decision to proceed with the RDF was good politics as Carter was badly sagging in the polls. The defense budget increase and the president's forceful declaration could possibly bolster his support among some constituencies, silence his critics, and give him an advantage over his Republican adversary. However, the commitment was not complete; there were still reservations at the Defense Department, where some officials complained about declining readiness of the forces and the lack of funding to replace older, increasingly less reliable weapons.[29]

William Odom was irritated that the Pentagon's action on the military aspects of the emerging Persian Gulf security framework was solely budgetary given events and clear presidential direction. When widespread action did not materialize immediately, he considered Komer, whom Brown selected to lead the effort, to be a purposeful impediment.[30] Brzezinski did not share that view of Komer, nor did Komer's staff, who credited him with being an "activist" under secretary, the "czar" of the planning process, "making things happen" and improving coordination and communication among the various Pentagon offices involved in the project.[31] While Komer agreed that President Carter had a valid requirement for a Middle East strategy and the Department of Defense had been unresponsive for months, there were legitimate concerns about the size of the force, its use, and capability, to say nothing of a strategy, which required thoughtful analysis and deliberation.[32]

One distraction had already materialized: the Army and the Marine Corps started vying for command of the new force as soon as Carter decreed its immediate creation in December. Both services nominated strong candidates, so Brown asked Komer for his opinion as to who should be selected. Komer replied that either one would be outstanding, but he believed the Defense Department could attain its objectives sooner if a Marine was picked first and then an Army officer. Consequently, Marine major general P. X. Kelley, promoted to lieutenant general, was designated the first commander in December 1979, and the headquarters was established formally at McDill Air Force Base in Tampa, Florida, on March 1, 1980. The RDF, renamed the Rapid Deployment Joint Task Force (RDJTF), would have a headquarters of a few hundred personnel only. Under this concept, there would be no new combat units but a "reservoir of forces" drawn from the four services, which were largely based in the United States, and configured in a variety of force packages tailored to meet various crises. Although originally the RDJTF was not dedicated to a specific region, the Persian Gulf area was recognized as the most area it would be used first. Brown did not make this definite until August 1980, after the Joint Chiefs approved a revised charter for the task force. As to command and control, the RDJTF was under the operational control of the commander of U.S. Readiness Command, led by a four-star Army general.[33]

Meanwhile, Komer asked Gen. David C. Jones, chairman of the Joint Chiefs of Staff, for a paper on Middle East military strategy since it was the Joint Chiefs' responsibility to formulate such plans. Brzezinski was already pestering the Pentagon for the document. Jones told Komer that the document could not be written because the service chiefs could not agree on how the subject should be approached. The Navy wanted to defend the Persian Gulf oil from the Arabian Sea, which to Komer was a ludicrous notion. What good would it be for the Soviets to control the oil fields while the United States controlled the oil routes? The Air Force preferred air interdiction of Soviet forces moving along the land routes through Azerbaijan to prevent them from reaching the oil fields. This strategy was rational, but as Komer pointed out to the Air Force leaders, it meant that 90 percent of the tactical aircraft would have to be based in Turkey. As a former U.S. ambassador to that nation, Komer knew that such a large and visible presence of American forces would be unacceptable to the Turks, and he confirmed his outlook in discussions with the Turkish defense minister.[34]

Meanwhile, Defense Department analysts and planners had deepened their assessment of the Soviet Union's ability to project forces into the region now that two essential parts of the so-called Northern Tier barriers (Iran and Afghanistan), which separated the USSR from the Persian Gulf, had eroded. The concern was that the Soviets had a distinct advantage because of proximity, but closer examination revealed that the Soviet forces faced enormous operational limitations in securing the Gulf's oil fields; they would have to contend with long-distance airborne assaults, vulnerable lines of supply, and limited air cover. Such restrictions allowed U.S. forces time to deploy, conduct air interdiction of Soviet resupply and reinforcements, and secure critical terrain. Thus, defense of the gulf was feasible, but deterrence, the major element of U.S. policy, was even more practical because U.S. forces could slow and make difficult Soviet attainment of operational objectives.[35]

Komer shared this perspective and dismissed an outright Soviet invasion of the Persian Gulf as an unlikely contingency. He considered the administration's opening response to the Afghanistan invasion as somewhat histrionic. In his view, any Soviet intervention in the region's oil fields would come in phases, not as a complete takeover. Not all the Soviet army divisions were ready for immediate deployment into the region either. They also suffered from mobilization and deployment problems, particularly airlift, and had to travel difficult terrain, with many choke points, and substantial distances before they could reach the Iranian oil fields.[36] However, Komer had to be careful not to promise that a U.S. force in the Persian Gulf region could "whip the Russians."[37]

Given the Joint Chiefs' lack of agreement on a military strategy and Komer's firm views on the threat, General Jones suggested that Komer and his staff develop the strategy. If Jones found it acceptable, he would tell Brown that he did, and if Brown approved it, then the document could be forwarded to the White House. Komer agreed and soon had a thirteen-page paper that laid out military options in the Persian Gulf, primarily in response to a Soviet incursion, but also in the case of other contingencies. His paper proposed the rapid deployment of forces and an active defense in the Zagros mountain passes of Iran. It was a high-risk concept, but if successful, it would either deter the Soviets or hold them off long enough to deploy a more robust force and defend well forward of the vital oil fields in the Persian Gulf. Jones liked the paper, and he and Brown suggested a few changes before the secretary sent it to the White House. Brzezinski and his staff were pleased with it as well, and it was distributed to the other relevant agencies. At a subsequent NSC meeting, the document was approved as the basic outline of a new Middle East strategy.[38] In essence, the Carter Doctrine, as Komer envisioned it, changed the very foundation of the U.S. defense strategy: the security of Europe, that is, NATO, and the reinforcement of South Korea. The new strategy he offered consisted of preparing to fight a major theater war in Europe as well as two simultaneous smaller contingencies or "half wars," Korea and the Persian Gulf.[39]

In March Secretary Brown publicly revealed the major tenets of the new strategy, and although he stressed that it consisted of "non-military components," it was clear that the emphasis was on conventional deterrence of Soviet aggression. The military components consisted of increased peacetime presence in the Persian Gulf; prepositioning of equipment; enhanced mobility using air and sealift capabilities; access and transit rights; and frequent deployment and exercises in the area.[40] After the fall of the shah in January 1979, the United States sought out locations where U.S. forces could have access to the Middle East, but as Odom wrote, the administration did not want to make itself "dependent upon the survival of a single regime in order to protect [our] access."[41] By August the Departments of State and Defense concluded arrangements for access with Oman, Somalia, and Kenya, the three countries Brzezinski had recommended.

———

Komer now spent a substantial portion of his time developing specific program initiatives to give substance to the strategy. The Army and Air Force were recalcitrant to shift funding from NATO to the Persian Gulf. The Marine Corps was not eager either, but it now had the mission of leading the RDJTF. The primary prepositioning site would be the British-owned island of Diego Garcia in the Indian Ocean.

Komer was well familiar with the island. In 1963 he realized that U.S. interests in the region were changing because the British had begun pulling out of the strategic arc from the Suez to Singapore. The United States had no presence in that region, only at its margins: Turkey, South Korea, Japan, and Guam. Therefore, the U.S. ability to project forces into the Middle East and South Asia was minimal and highly dependent on aircraft carriers. When U.S.-India relations fizzled during the Kennedy administration, Komer explored the idea of basing U.S. forces in the region. He learned that the British had once offered the Roosevelt administration use of Singapore in 1940, but the Americans turned it down. Komer had also dismissed the use of Singapore because buying land for military bases there would be too expensive, to say nothing of the political obstacles that might arise. Allied bases were available, but he assumed they were too vulnerable. An adversary would strike them first, for example, in Iran, unless they were protected. Nonetheless, he continued to analyze this approach and eventually determined that leasing a land station from the British might prove feasible. The British responded favorably to this idea and after several months offered an island off the Mozambique channel, Aldabra, which the United States found acceptable. However, the offer was withdrawn when the British government suspected difficulties in Parliament. The British then offered Diego Garcia, 2,300 miles from the Persian Gulf. Komer saw advantages to this location, but it would be 1971 before the United States and Great Britain concluded an agreement making the island available to U.S. forces.[42]

Since the early 1970s, the Defense Department had made improvements to the island, principally by adding a communications station, support buildings and hangars, a runway with taxiways and aprons, and a ship channel and turning basin. The department would now have to build up Diego Garcia's air and naval facilities, at an estimated cost of nearly $1 billion. The RDJTF would also have equipment onboard maritime prepositioning ships (MPS) berthed at Diego Garcia.[43] The Marines, however, were concerned that if the funding were applied to these vessels, then it would be taken from the budget for amphibious ships, which it needed to perform its core mission. Thus, the attitude among the services was that if the president and the secretary of defense wanted such a force, then the funding should be in addition to current levels. The secretary would also have to direct the services to fund this new mission, so Komer asked Brown to provide specific direction regarding RDJTF priorities and ensured that strategic planning was not disconnected from the programs needed to execute the strategy.[44] Komer also allayed the Marines' fears by assuring them that funding for the MPS would be additive as would be the supplies aboard the ships needed to support Marine brigades.[45]

Working with Russell Murray, the assistant secretary of defense for program analysis and evaluation, Komer had the secretary approve additional guidance that set both the direction and goals for RDJTF-related programs in the department's future financial plans beginning with the fiscal year 1982 budget. Murray's staff was also able to identify most of these programs as discrete items. The result was a paper that permitted useful high-level debates about options.[46]

Komer then directed his staff to examine the armed services' financial plans using this information and determine whether they were complying with Brown's direction that placed emphasis on the Persian Gulf. If a staff member found that the services were not funding these requirements, then he or she was to inform Komer. In turn, Komer and Brown would find the offsets needed to fund the requirements. The means now existed to ensure that a strategy-funding mismatch did not exist for the task force and that RDJTF initiatives were protected in the budgeting process.[47]

Komer recognized that basing in the Indian Ocean and projecting forces into the Middle East created a crucial problem in time compression. Ideally, the United States wanted to project its forces overseas before a conflict began so that it could deter it. Rapid deployment was essential, but Komer questioned the meaning of the word "rapid." To deploy three divisions to the Persian Gulf would be an enormous undertaking, especially in terms of logistical support. The distance between the United States and the Persian Gulf region was 12,500 nautical miles by sea and 8,000 nautical miles by air. The emphasis had to be on projecting combat capability. Supporting these forces for an extended period with food, ammunition, and other supplies could not be done simultaneously. Komer's solution to this problem again came from his NATO experience. The supply and support would have to come from the local governments. This assumed that the task force would be operating in a "permissive environment," relying to some degree on local ports and airfields.[48]

In mid-1980 Brown, at Komer's recommendation, announced that the Defense Department would rely on its allies and friends worldwide to meet American initial fuel and lubricant requirements from their stockpiles. Komer thought that the Defense Department should approach governments in the Persian Gulf region and make it known that if they wanted U.S. security, then they would have to construct hardened storage and distribution facilities and to stock them with the needed products.[49]

Komer reasoned that the logic of this approach could be extended to other supplies. He knew that the second most important commodity that U.S. forces would need in the Persian Gulf was water. Consequently, the gulf states built large desalting plants to support military requirements. Additionally, the governments in the region would provide the infrastructure necessary to sustain U.S. forces logistically, such as ports and repair installations. For example, the Saudis were acquiring Hawk missiles, manufactured by Raytheon Corporation, and a maintenance facility operated by contract employees hired by Raytheon. If U.S. Army troops deployed to the region, their Hawk missiles could be repaired at that facility. Komer urged the Saudis to overbuild the facility so that it was capable of processing and reworking more missiles. He thought that the Saudis would be willing to finance that upgrade provided the facility remained a Saudi Arabian installation.[50]

In August the press reported that overall the military buildup to protect the Persian Gulf was advancing faster than commonly realized and with little debate among lawmakers. U.S. aircraft carriers and a Marine amphibious force had been diverted to the Arabian Sea, seven ships loaded with tanks and ammunition were already positioned at Diego Garcia, and U.S. Air Force early warning airplanes were operating out of Egypt and Saudi Arabia. Secretary Brown stated that the United States would have to spend $20 to $25 billion over the next five years to build a more credible RDJTF. Komer, in a moment of typical bravado, chortled, "You can have policy and strategy out the kazoo. But without money it's only rhetoric." Nonetheless, these developments and expected costs were stunning, particularly since the Carter Doctrine and the strategy was controversial, to say nothing about "the civilian at the Pentagon charged with making this all happen," Robert Komer, "the most influential civilian within the Pentagon since former defense secretary Robert McNamara," according to an article in the *Washington Post.*[51]

Detractors complained that the RDJTF, while largely a "tripwire" force, politically destabilized the region. Other skeptics ridiculed the task force, contending that after several months, it was essentially a toothless fraud. The units designated for the task force were currently lined up for the defense of Western Europe and Korea in various war plans. This was tantamount to a shell game. Additionally, rapid deployment necessitated substantial airlift and sealift to deploy forces to the region in time to blunt a Soviet invasion; this problem was exacerbated by the Army's penchant for procuring tanks that were too heavy to transport on cargo airplanes and by the Navy and Air Force's failure to place emphasis on lift capability.[52]

Komer acknowledged that these deficiencies would require additional funding and dealt with them in the fiscal year 1982 Defense Department budget request along with the planned out-year budgets, recognizing that it may be years before these operational shortcomings were rectified. Nonetheless, as an indicator of the Carter administration's commitment, over the five-year defense program, the funding request would be nearly $10 billion, more than $6 billion for airlift capabilities and $3 billion for the additional prepositioning ships.[53]

Another flaw Komer saw was that the administration had not adequately addressed its military assistance requirements in the Persian Gulf, yet regional cooperation and capabilities were critical. He complained to the White House, with Brown and the Joint Chiefs' support, but the Office of Management and Budget opposed any additive funding for security assistance, as did the State Department. Komer then pressed for a presidential decision on the subject given its criticality to the Persian Gulf initiatives. David Aaron, the deputy national security adviser, set November 7 as the date for a joint State-Defense paper outlining various options.[54] Komer realized that he was racing against time and he had his doubts that Carter would be reelected.

On November 4 time ran out: Carter lost his reelection bid. Three days later Brzezinski chaired a meeting on the development of the Persian Gulf security framework. He began the discussion by stating that the president had committed the United States to a policy that would "ensure the security of the region over the next decade." He continued by adding that the policy was vital and "may be the most important legacy of the Carter administration." However, the president needed to understand that "successful implementation is going to be expensive." Defense Secretary Brown added that Congress had to understand the criticality of advancing security assistance programs as a means of developing solid relations with countries in the region and building up their combat capabilities. At this point the discussion became animated, and lines were drawn between the Defense Department and the Office of Management and Budget, represented by John White, who argued against funding that was additive to the current proposed budget. Komer "counterattacked by strongly implying that without the high visibility explicit in the additive option, 'we will continue to be choked by bureaucratic miasma.'" Despite Brzezinski's best efforts, the discussion became circular and "bureaucratic miasma" set in—an ad hoc working group chaired by Odom would study the issue quickly and produce a paper within a day or two. Carter had been defeated at the polls, but the Office of Management and Budget continued to act as if the administration had won reelection. Brzezinski's plea that "before we start looking for new jobs, we owe it to the nation to bequeath the best possible security framework to the new Administration" went unheeded.[55]

Less than a month later, at an NSC meeting, the president insisted on a directive codifying the Persian Gulf security framework.[56] This final national security issue, acted on in the waning days of Carter's presidency, ultimately enshrined the administration's policy while also serving as one of its legacies. The Persian Gulf had been Brzezinski's preoccupation at first; he had been the catalyst for the policy change. But a catalyst cannot sustain a reaction, a point Brzezinski acknowledged in his memoir. "Harold Brown and Robert Komer," he wrote after returning to private life, "took the initiative in fashioning a comprehensive document outlining a long-range military plan for the Persian Gulf. . . . This document was a bold and forward-looking statement, and both Brown and Komer deserve a great deal of credit for leaving it on our successors' agenda."[57]

CHAPTER 13

The Sin of Unilateralism

*K*omer did not exit the Pentagon quietly. On February 14, 1981, his final day in office, he delivered a farewell attack, rebuking the military services for narrow-minded thinking and parochialism. All the services, he complained, were "trying to have their cake and eat it too" by requesting billions of dollars to acquire doubtful new weapons instead of "putting the forces they already have in fighting shape." He singled out the Navy in particular, dismissing as propaganda its claim that it had lost its edge against the Soviet fleet. Komer maintained that U.S. Navy military leaders had discounted the contribution of allied navies in war and understated the vulnerability of the Soviet. Such claims "drove him up the wall. Like this business that the Navy must have 600 ships. The problem is capability, not numbers." If the Navy needed more ships for the Indian Ocean quickly, he remarked, the sensible step would be to have the Air Force cover Soviet ships in the Mediterranean and the U.S. Sixth Fleet deploy to the Indian Ocean. Komer conceded that the one mission in the Mediterranean that land-based air forces might not be politically available for would be an Arab-Israeli conflict, but the signing of the Egypt-Israel peace treaty had reduced the threat of such an event. He then proceeded to blast the other services and finally ended his lecture when he ran out of invective. Tomorrow, he would be a private citizen responsible for haranguing students as a visiting fellow at George Mason University and an adjunct faculty member at George Washington University.[1]

For the next several months Komer clenched his teeth as he read in the newspapers about the Reagan administration's proposed defense policies and programs, but he did not react. He spent his days teaching courses on national security policy at the two institutions. In the fall of 1981, however, his undeclared truce ended when he put together a series of lectures, titled "Security Challenges of the 1980's," as part of George Mason University's ongoing effort to educate the student body, faculty, and surrounding community on the important issues of the day. Komer introduced the series and the subject, and then the audience heard talks by former secretaries of defense Harold Brown and James Schlesinger, the former secretary of the Navy Robert Murray, and the former director of central intelligence and Komer's CORDS colleague, William Colby. The lecture series concluded with Komer addressing what he had come to believe was the most pressing security issue of the decade: "The Imperative of a Coalition Approach."[2]

In opening his lecture, Komer stated that he was addressing this topic primarily because coalitions were one of the least understood yet most important aspects of U.S. national security posture. The second reason for the speech, however, returned him to the concerns that he raised in his final press interview as under secretary of defense for policy: the Reagan administration's actions were undermining U.S. alliances, particularly NATO, which the United States could ill afford at this time. While Komer supported the president's increase in defense spending, he disagreed strenuously with how the administration portrayed the Soviet threat. The characterization was misleading because it assumed that U.S. military forces were inferior and, more importantly, that they would fight the Soviets on their own. The United States could count on its NATO allies in a conflict with the Warsaw Pact whether that conflict took place in Europe, the Persian Gulf, or Northeast Asia; the allies helped protect U.S. vital interests globally. Mutual defense, despite its drawbacks, including the weakness inherent in an alliance of sovereign states, had been the guiding principle of postwar U.S. foreign policy, and it had served the nation well. Improvements in capabilities and cost sharing were needed, as the United States overwhelmingly made the largest contribution in terms of funds and forces. But it was ludicrous to suggest that while the United States would actually fight its adversaries through alliances, it should allow its peacetime posture to be one in which it planned and budgeted as if it were a solitary actor. This mind-set, Komer reminded the audience, was what the chairman of the Joint Chiefs of Staff, Gen. David Jones, called the "sin of unilateralism."[3]

Instead, the alliance needed to be strengthened and made more efficient, particularly in a period with a lagging economy with high inflation. He had hoped that the Reagan administration would continue some of the

Carter initiatives, but instead, it had chosen a "go it alone" strategy that was not only wasteful but also risky, particularly as the Soviet military buildup continued and threatened to undermine deterrence. "Hence," Komer concluded, "we owe it to our allies as well as to our own American electorate to clarify our nuclear purposes, to explain how our awesome capabilities are really to deter nuclear war and that in a situation of stalemate we must cope conventionally too with a Soviet Union whose capabilities are fast becoming greater than our own." The allies could no longer have it both ways; while they enjoyed the nuclear umbrella of the United States, they needed to build a credible conventional capability to meet the requirements below the nuclear threshold in order to make nuclear war less probable.[4]

Komer's lecturing did not end with the George Mason University appearance. In October 1981 he spoke at the Miller Center of Public Affairs at the University of Virginia. This time his lecture was no less polemical or partisan. He used it to rehearse his arguments for the dispute that was to come. Although the Miller Center asked him to address the topic "The President, the National Security Council and the Secretary of Defense," he focused his attention on the issue of strategy, a topic, he argued, that was largely neglected in U.S. defense circles, both within and outside government.[5]

After providing the audience with the historical context for U.S. strategy from the beginning of the twentieth century to the present day, Komer returned to the familiar theme of alliances in an era of nuclear stalemate. He voiced his growing concern that the United States seemed to be "slipping backwards" into a maritime strategy and that the Reagan administration's program proposals evinced a definite bias in terms of strategy implementation. He said, "When I look at the programs of the current administration, the allocation of funds between the services and see that almost three-fifths of the biggest single allocation to conventional forces, which is the Navy, goes for three more big carrier task forces—in addition to the twelve they've already got—that to me, suggests we are moving in the direction of a maritime strategy."

A reliance on carriers signaled that the administration's new strategy was to attack the Soviet Union's periphery with conventional bombs since carrier aircraft had a limited range and "puny striking power." Such an attack would be of minimal value because the Soviet Union was a land power. Additionally, carriers could not get too close to their targets, principally Soviet navy bases, because they were vulnerable. Carriers were also not necessary to sea control, which was one of the long-standing roles of the U.S. Navy and of particular importance in a NATO conflict. Lastly, Komer repeated his view that a maritime strategy was "essentially isolationist, go-it-alone," and not conducive to building stronger relations with U.S. allies, which were indispensable in matching the Warsaw Pact military capability. The alternative, as he had stated previously, was the coalition approach and building a capability to defend Persian Gulf oil; a maritime strategy could not do this.[6]

Two months later, in December 1981, the Pentagon announced that the United States would seek maritime superiority over the Soviet Union. The *Washington Post* heralded the change on its front page as the harbinger of "basic changes in the deployment of U.S. military forces" around the world, including a reduction of force in Europe. Reagan administration defense officials blamed the Carter administration for neglecting the sea forces, which Komer, when interviewed, vigorously disputed, adding that maritime superiority had flaws. "The real issue," he said, was "whether we should sink so much of our constrained defense resources into offensive force projection by aircraft carrier task forces to make it impossible to meet our North Atlantic Treaty Organization and Persian Gulf commitments." Further, defeating the Soviets would not come from "nibbling at" their flanks with carrier strikes, and seeking another $50–100 billion for "big nuclear-powered battle groups" was a "wasteful diversion from higher priority needs." In a thinly veiled reference to Secretary of the Navy John F. Lehman Jr., Komer stated, "The trouble with the new civilian strategists is that they don't understand strategy. Nor do they grasp how dependent the United States has become on our many rich allies, or they wouldn't propose a force structure so sure to undermine our alliances."[7] Two opponents had been identified, and the battle would begin with the fiscal year 1982 defense budget request.

Secretary of the Navy Lehman's quest for the so-called six-hundred-ship Navy and its foundation as the Reagan administration's maritime strategy began when he urged Congress, three weeks after Ronald Reagan's inauguration as the fortieth president of the United States, for its permission to double its shipbuilding program in fiscal year 1982. According to Lehman, the authorization would be the first step toward restoring U.S. maritime superiority over the Soviet Union. It was also a signal that the Reagan administration would continue to use its campaign tactic of attacking the Carter presidency's neglect of U.S. national security as a means of securing higher military spending. Komer found this claim wanting as well as upsetting.

Lehman was not alone in his urging the Senate to restore U.S. naval superiority. Adm. Thomas P. Hayward, the chief of naval operations, was like-minded. A year earlier, during the Carter administration, Haywood had testified that the United States enjoyed a thin margin over the Soviet Union that would remain until 1985. Now, under a new administration, he claimed that the margin had disappeared and added further insult by sniping that the Carter administration's final budget proposal was "wholly inadequate."[8] Hayward also described the Carter administration's defense budget request, a record high peacetime request, as an "implicit acquiescence to maritime inferiority." "For the first time in anyone's recollection, the U.S. Navy is unable fully to meet its peacetime commitments," Haywood remarked. It "would have to vacate 'essential' areas of the world to respond to an emergency."[9] This remark was an affront to Komer, who had been the administration's chief defense strategist. Yet, he remained silent as the administration proposed extensive increases to the fiscal year 1982 defense budget.

Three months later, in April 1981, at a luncheon meeting with *New York Times* editors and reporters, Lehman, fueling his reputation as a hard-liner, reiterated his intent to build a naval capability superior to that of the Soviets. He asserted that such a maritime strategy could "make the cost of aggression so high" that the Soviet Union would gain nothing if it attacked the NATO allies and conquered Western Europe to the English channel. Lehman contended that such a move would make the Soviet Union the "world island," a reference to the work of British geopolitical theorist Harold Mackinder, while the United States held the rest of the world. Revealing for the first time an outline of the new naval strategy, Lehman stated that his intent was to make the U.S. Navy strong enough to bottle up the Soviet fleet by denying it exits from the Barents Sea, north of the Soviet Union; the Baltic and Black Seas to the west and south; and the Sea of Okhotsk and the Sea of Japan to the east. "There is little that the Soviets can do to prevent us from closing off their fleets," he told the group. A naval confrontation with the Soviets would be global. "There is no such thing as a localized conventional war at sea between the Soviet Union and the United States. Attaining maritime superiority eliminated Soviet advantages, he claimed; for it would prevent the Soviets from closing the Persian Gulf and picking off the northern and southern flanks of NATO.[10]

The policy shift to seek maritime superiority became a matter of public record by the end of 1981, when it was leaked to the press that the debate that had raged within the Pentagon for months was taking shape in the draft classified planning guidance to the military services and Defense Department components for fiscal years 1983 through 1987. The proposed guidance maintained that the Soviet threat had shifted from central Europe to other regions, including the Persian Gulf, and given this development, more emphasis was needed on protecting sea-lanes and increased naval force structure. Moreover, the guidance directed the military services to structure their forces to achieve maritime superiority.[11]

Lehman, the leading advocate of the policy change, argued that if it meant a reduction of U.S. forces in Europe, then the NATO allies could make up the difference. After all, the United States would be protecting the sea lines of communication over which oil and other critical materials travel to the benefit of the entire alliance. He had won Secretary of Defense Caspar Weinberger over.[12]

In an interview, Lehman confirmed that he had pressed for forces that were more mobile because "we have a whole new geopolitical situation. What's new is a consensus within the administration that the Soviet threat is global. It's not just central Europe." Army general Donn Starry, the commander of U.S. Readiness Command, opposed the thrust toward naval superiority and warned his civilian superiors that this change would be tantamount to sacrificing military control in Europe and South Korea.[13]

Sympathetic to Starry's argument, Komer agreed to an interview with the *Washington Post.* He always made good copy because of his candor, and this case was no exception. He began by vigorously disputing the Reagan administration approach as a canard motivated by partisanship. "The real issue," he reiterated, is "whether we should sink so much of our constrained defense resources into offensive force projection by aircraft carrier task forces to make it impossible to meet our North Atlantic Treaty Organization and Persian Gulf commitments."[14]

Komer was not finished. "To give up on Western Europe and Persian Gulf oil" to pursue Lehman's form of maritime superiority "could lead to strategic disaster. It would be playing right into Soviet hands." The "chief flaw," he asserted once again, "is that you can't really cope with a great Eurasian heart power like the U.S.S.R. by nibbling at its flanks with carrier strikes. Therefore, seeking another $50 billion to $100 billion in more big nuclear-powered battle groups, which are primarily for this nibble and not for sea control, would be a wasteful diversion from higher priority needs."[15] The press saw blood in the water, and they could not have asked for two more colorful antagonists than Komer and Lehman, men with similar personalities—brash, stubborn, and verbally combative.

―――――――

On February 7, 1982, Komer began a frontal assault on the Reagan maritime strategy when the *Washington Post* published his essay, "The High Cost of Ruling the Seas." A cartoon of a menacing Russian bear prying open with his teeth an American submarine in a bottle accompanied the piece. The opening words of the essay were ominous. Komer avowed yet again that the primary reliance on maritime superiority was "dangerously skewing" how scarce defense resources would be allocated, compromising U.S. ability to defend its vital interests in Western Europe and the Persian Gulf. The culprits were Lehman and Assistant Secretary of Defense for International Security Affairs Francis J. "Bing" West Jr., a former Marine officer and RAND Corporation analyst. Komer argued that these two and their disciples held that Europe could not be defended successfully any longer because U.S. nuclear superiority had vanished and the NATO allies would not pull their weight in maintaining ready conventional forces. Therefore, emphasis should be on sweeping the Soviet navy and merchant fleet from the seas and attacking it in its bases with carrier strikes. Komer called this argument "superficially convincing," with implications "more serious than even the billions of dollars involved."[16]

The real issue, he continued, was not whether the United States should retain maritime superiority. That was an imperative. "The question is how to do it, and how much we can afford to spend on it," he wrote. What was demanded, Komer contended, was a balanced strategy that fulfilled U.S. commitments in Europe, South Korea, and the Persian Gulf. Komer then attacked the cost of building carrier battle groups, arguing that they were not designed for controlling vital sea-lanes but would be used to project forces against the Soviet Union. He doubted the efficacy this tenet would have on a country with a huge heartland, given the paltry offensive power that carriers could muster and the unlikely survivability of the carriers once in position to launch their aircraft. Further, this strategy suggested the United States could conduct countervailing operations without its allies. This was a preposterous notion. "Could we close the Baltic without Scandinavian cooperation? Close the Dardanelles without Turkish acquiescence?"[17]

In sum, the Pentagon's new naval thinking smacked of a "go it alone" philosophy. Komer granted that the United States and the NATO allies had not invested enough or wisely, in the present NATO strategy, but the Reagan administration's approach was "a poorer bargain." "For the cost of one more carrier battle group," he wrote, "the United States could fund most of the required NATO and Persian Gulf equipment, and for a second one, it would provide the sealift and airlift needed urgently to project forces." He urged Congress to scrutinize the true costs for advocating a maritime strategy.[18]

While the White House and Pentagon remained strangely silent in the face of this assault, Komer rallied on. Five days later, he featured prominently in a *Washington Post* article on the Reagan administration's defense budget, as part of group called "Democrats for Defense." Komer's picture was to the right of the text, and he looked every inch the defense intellectual: mustachioed, bald, wearing aviator glasses, a tie, and a button-down collar shirt too small for his neck, the ubiquitous briar pipe clenched between his teeth. The group had held a news conference during which Komer and his colleagues signaled general support of the Reagan administration's increase in military spending, although they did not agree with its focus. The Democrats for Defense emphasized the readiness of existing troops and additional funding for airlift to move forces to trouble spots.[19]

Komer harshly criticized Secretary of Defense Weinberger's first report to Congress on defense policy. He persisted with his message that the report's lack of emphasis on NATO and its massive investment in maritime superiority "looks more like a unilateral, go-it-alone approach." However, Komer's message was not simply meant to provide an alternative to the Reagan administration's budget request. It sought to bolster Democratic congressional leaders by emphasizing that the party could not be viewed as weak on national security. John G. Kester, a former special assistant to Secretary of Defense Harold Brown, cautioned that the "Democratic Party must not fall into the trap of thinking that defense is not a legitimate need." Representative Les Aspin added his voice to Komer's when he stated that the administration did not know what it was talking about, that Weinberger's plan lacked a "philosophical underpinning," detailed threat analysis, and well-defined requirements to meet those threats.[20]

––––––––––

In the summer of 1982 Komer threw gasoline on the fire with a twenty-one-page article in the journal *Foreign Affairs* titled "Maritime Strategy vs. Coalition Defense." To make his argument more provocative, he simplified the issues in contention. A maritime supremacy strategy "tacitly acknowl-edges Soviet predominance on the Eurasian landmass and stresses U.S. exploitation of the medium which we can most readily dominate—the sea." Coalition defense advocates, in contrast, recognize that the United States must produce a convincing conventional defense of three high-priority areas—Western Europe, Northeast Asia, and the oil-rich Persian Gulf littoral—primarily through increased coalition burden sharing and a more efficient collective effort. Komer claimed that the Reagan adminis-tration was "trying to ride both horses," a futile and expensive proposition since economic limitations would force the administration to choose. The Pentagon's price tag alone would necessitate a choice of strategy. Full fund-ing of the administration's strategy would cost $750 billion more than the already projected $1.6 trillion. Figures of that magnitude would require U.S. defense budgets to be stretched out and would compel the administra-tion and the Congress to confront tough choices between strategic missions and the various capabilities required to execute them. Cost would over time drive the choice of a strategy.[21]

In fact, Komer argued, the administration and the Senate authoriza-tion bill were backing the United States into a maritime strategy by fund-ing two carriers while deferring procurement of the Army's AH-64 attack helicopter, which was needed to counter Warsaw Pact armor in Europe or a Soviet armor thrust into the Persian Gulf region. This was not the way to determine strategy. The competing resource allocations must be premised on understanding the strategic consequences. A maritime strategy beggared already inadequate NATO and Persian Gulf commitments, undermined alliances, and failed to protect vital interests in three regions. Komer added that coalition defense strategy was not flawless either, as the coalition may not want to shoulder the increased defense spending needed to generate the conventional capability that would deter the Soviets. Nonetheless, he opted for the latter. After all, there were no other options. "America would find it difficult to live and prosper in a world in which we dominated the seas but our chief competitor dominated the economic resources of the Eurasian landmass," he wrote.[22]

The debate continued when Adm. Stansfield Turner and Capt. George Thibault added their voices in a *Foreign Affairs* article titled "Preparing for the Unexpected: The Need for a New Military Strategy." Turner, the for-mer director of central intelligence and Naval War College president, and Thibault argued that the Navy needed to focus on its traditional sea control mission and agreed that Komer's concern about building a navy around a few carriers at the expense of the other services' requirements was valid. Nonetheless, they criticized Komer as making a strong argument for maintaining the status quo.[23]

Responding with a letter to the editor in *Foreign Affairs*' winter issue, Komer replied that the Turner and Thibault recommendation regarding sea control was "sensible," and "I believe that their suggestions for the kind of navy we should build would go too far to provide the indispensable maritime superiority component of any sound coalition defense." However, their approach was a variation of the maritime supremacy model. Komer argued that Turner had succumbed to the "likelihood fallacy," a strategy based more on potential threats than on attention to interests. Komer lectured that the logical objective of any strategy is to protect vital interests; he was quoting Lord Palmerston, the British political leader, who said, "There are no permanent allies, only permanent interests." Nonetheless, Komer preferred Turner and Thibault's navy, but it still smacked of the "same old unilateralist naval parochialism."[24]

Lehman could not dismiss Komer as just another armchair strategist or disregard his klaxon call that had set off further debate just when Congress was going to appropriate funds for his vision of the Navy. He also could not ignore a four-star admiral's views. He sent a letter to the editor as well, claiming that Komer and Turner were misinterpreting the Reagan defense program, first by suggesting that it weakened the NATO alliance and second by arguing that the Navy was building the wrong ship for the wrong naval mission. Stating that both authors relied on "defective rhetorical devices," he accused Komer of both setting up a false choice between coalition defense and maritime strategy and at the same time admitting that control of the seas is a necessity for a successful coalition defense. As to Turner and his colleague, their attack on *Nimitz*-type carriers was flawed because it misused lessons from the Falklands War; plus they admitted that small carriers would not necessarily be cheaper. Both men were branded as Carter administration lackeys who had used the discredited technique of satisfying "budget cutters and the defense reductionists" with sleight-of-hand maneuvers that resulted in a navy relegated to convoy duty and an unworkable strategy of passive defense.[25]

Komer replied, unloading on Lehman while remaining thick skinned about the secretary's political polemics. "Secretary Lehman clearly wins the prize for rhetoric," he began. Komer called the expenditure of $50 billion on three carriers as contributing to an unbalanced defense strategy. Moreover, these ships were fit only for sideshows like the Falklands. Turner's feelings seemed to have been bruised. In his reply to Lehman's letter, he pointed out first that the secretary's attacks on Komer and himself had turned the debate into a partisan struggle: "Carterites versus Reaganites." Sadly, such partisan polemics only cheapened the discussion. He concluded that Lehman's strategy of taking the fight to the Soviets' home bases and airfields was more a public relations device, rousing and patriotic; he had "yet to find one Admiral who believes that the U.S. Navy would even attempt it."[26]

Assaulted in the pages of *Foreign Affairs*, Lehman used public forums to plead his case. The opinions of critics such as Komer, Turner, and MIT professor William Kaufmann, a longtime consultant to the Pentagon who had written the annual report to Congress for almost every secretary of defense in the 1960s and 1970s, did not count. "Sorry," Lehman chortled in what the *National Journal* called his December 1982 "gotcha speech," "it's too late to stop it . . . we've got the 600-ship Navy."[27]

Nonetheless, the maritime strategy opponents began to have an influence on Capitol Hill. By early spring 1983 the Democrat-controlled House of Representatives and the Senate Budget Committee voted to cut the Reagan defense buildup by almost half. Congress was reconsidering the cost of the new military strategy, especially congressional critics who marveled at the Pentagon's budget tricks—"low balling cost estimates," essentially making down payments on expensive weapon systems that would keep them alive and constituents employed. Further, the members fretted over a "readiness gap" because heavily front-loaded procurement had left scant resources for maintenance and operations.[28]

Congress members were not the only people having second thoughts. There was dissent in the Pentagon. In a May 1983 interview, Adm. James D. Watkins, the chief of naval operations, distanced himself from Lehman on the question of whether Navy carriers and other warships would sail into the jaws of Soviet defenses in the Kola Peninsula during war. Watkins praised Lehman but said that the secretary was in the "'administrative chain' of command, not the operational one that decides where each ship goes in an emergency." Watkins added that U.S. aircraft carriers would protect vital sea-lanes, not go "charging off" into areas where the Soviets could use their land-based aircraft to attack U.S. ships.[29] The internal bickering had begun.

How the Navy should spend its budget became a source of squabbling between the gruff, self-confident former captain of industry, Deputy

Secretary Paul Thayer, whom Weinberger charged with shaping the defense budget, and Lehman. The dispute was over Thayer's decision to cut $8 billion from Navy shipbuilding funds over the next five years and $10 billion from naval aircraft programs in the fiscal year 1985 budget request and to transfer some of the funds to the Army and claim the remainder as savings. In a company town, with so much at stake, it was only a matter of time before reports of the clash between Thayer and Lehman trickled out of the Defense Resources Board's inner sanctum on the third floor of the Pentagon, where deliberations regarding strategy, force structure, and budgets occurred.[30] The meetings themselves were "verbal slugfests." Thayer became so exasperated with Lehman at one point that he told the Navy secretary to "shut up," to which Lehman reportedly replied, "Mercy."[31]

Thayer questioned Lehman for using lower inflation projection and fuel costs in his budget assumptions than the rest of the Pentagon did. He wondered why Lehman believed shipbuilding costs could be held down. Richard DeLauer, the under secretary of defense for research and development, publicly ridiculed Lehman's plan to send aircraft carriers into Soviet waters, arguing that it only made them more vulnerable to Backfire bombers and cruise missiles. Army general John W. Vesey Jr., chairman of the Joint Chiefs of Staff, told Thayer that slighting the Army was undermining the need to invest in a more flexible and mobile ground force. Lehman scurried to the White House to speak with the president's national security adviser, William P. Clark, in whom he found a sympathetic ear. Lehman still had a trump card—Ronald Reagan, who was on the record as stating that a six-hundred-ship Navy, with fifteen aircraft-carrier battle groups as a nucleus, was a necessity.[32] It was now a matter of who had the most powerful allies.

The feuding spilled openly into a nasty quarrel in the halls of Congress, with Lehman claiming that he was "getting sick and tired of spending 98 percent of my time up on the Hill undoing the damage that senior defense officials are doing to the president's budget." "What I am trying to do," he stated in a telephone interview with the *Washington Post*, "is simply counter the guerrilla warfare by these defense officials who don't seem to understand what the president's program is all about." He accused senior defense officials of undercutting the naval aircraft program by persuading the Senate Appropriations Committee's defense subcommittee to delete $16 million in funding for the Navy's A-6 aircraft modification program. The quarrel became politically unhealthy; one member of Congress called Lehman's persistent lobbying and disdainful behavior "outright insubordination." A defense industry expert characterized Lehman as having "drawn his saber."[33]

The only person who could persuade him to return it to its sheath was Weinberger, and Thayer made that appeal. It was the proverbial gunfighter's showdown as far as Thayer was concerned; he even remarked, "This place isn't big enough for both of us." Weinberger agreed that budget disagreements should not be fought in public and privately asked Lehman to show restraint in his public statements. The secretary also asked the Defense Department press spokesman to tell reporters that he expected all defense officials to present their views within the department's budget machinery.[34]

Weinberger had his way. The battle raged on, but the clamor was stifled by the thick concrete walls of the Pentagon. The secretary of defense sought to appease all the claimants by fashioning a preliminary fiscal year 1985 budget of $322.5 billion. A month later the magnitude of this increase became apparent when Congress appropriated a quarter-trillion-dollar budget for fiscal year 1984, $11 billion short of the administration's request. Nonetheless, the spending bill was the single largest in U.S. history, more than the entire federal government's budget in 1973. Although Congress approved almost every major weapon system the Reagan administration wanted, the appropriation was nearly $70 billion less than the projected 1985 defense budget. Lehman, however, won another skirmish in the budget battle when Congress restored $15 million for development of an advanced version of the A-6 attack aircraft.[35]

President Reagan and Weinberger still supported the six-hundred-ship Navy, and that's what mattered. Weinberger agreed entirely with Lehman that the Navy suffered from a "decade of neglect" in its appropriations, which had led to insufficient numbers of ships and capabilities to counter the swiftly expanding Soviet navy.[36] Lehman received funding approval in the fiscal year 1985 Department of Defense budget request to build the new *Arleigh Burke* class of destroyers that had been a source of contention between the Navy and Thayer and DeLauer. In essence, Weinberger fashioned a truce by making every armed service a winner in the budget wars, thereby delaying the vicious rows that occurred during the summer.[37] While the New Year may have brought good tidings to John Lehman, questions about the efficacy of the maritime strategy surfaced again, this time with more stridency.

In the winter of 1983 the journal *International Security* published an article by Jeffrey Record, a defense expert at the Institute for Foreign Policy

Analysis in Washington, D.C., titled "Jousting with Unreality: Reagan's Military Strategy." Not only did the title of the article lack subtlety; the opening sentence also stated boldly that the Reagan defense strategy, as articulated by Weinberger and Lehman, was a "standing invitation to potential strategic disaster." Record cited Komer as a source and commended him for what he had "trenchantly observed": the maritime strategy contained a hidden problem, which was that the administration's ambitious plans exceeded the nation's strategic grasp. The Reagan administration was ignoring some essential lessons of military history while holding delusions about future conflict. The maritime strategy espoused by Lehman was unrealistic and militarily unsound. It too readily dismissed the Soviet submarine and land-based air forces' ability to destroy the U.S. surface fleet as it aggressively approached the Russian homeland—Record called it "a venture into the jaws of defeat."[38]

Komer now reentered the fray in early 1984. He had been refining his arguments, and they had been published as a chapter in the monograph *Rethinking Defense and Conventional Forces*, along with essays by Senator John Glenn and Professor Barry Carter of the Georgetown University Law Center. Komer wrote that a better Soviet strategic capability meant that nuclear deterrence of a conventional attack was obsolete. Instead, a coherent coalition strategy based on a credible conventional deterrent was needed. Such an approach would stabilize explosive areas of the world and prevent attacks on U.S. vital interests in Western Europe, Japan, and the Persian Gulf. He continued criticizing the six-hundred-ship Navy as being too costly, providing marginal strategic advantage, and crippling the modernization that other parts of the Navy required, and he warned that the future cost of the carrier-heavy Navy would ultimately result in a "readiness crunch."[39]

Komer's last point was perceptive. In March 1984 the *Washington Post* reported that after three years of the Reagan military buildup and an investment of $362 billion, fewer Army and Air Force units were combat ready. Only the number of combat-ready Navy units had increased, more than doubling, but surprisingly, the mission readiness of Navy aircraft had slipped 3 percent. The report was particularly timely as Congress was starting to review the administration's fiscal year 1985 budget request of $305 billion, an 18 percent increase over the previous year's funding level, procurement funding in the request exceeded funds for operations and maintenance by 10 percent.

For the next two months there was calm until Komer whipped the Reagan administration again in a May 1984 *Los Angeles Times* op-ed in which he characterized a carrier-heavy navy as a waste-heavy force, a costly mistake foisted on the taxpayer by Lehman's wrongheaded objectives. He cited the enormous costs already spent, $82 billion, and noted that another $77 billion was to be spent over the next five years in order to purchase three more nuclear-powered carrier battle groups. Big carrier battle groups, he announced, were not useful for the sensible mission of protecting the sea lines of communication. Smaller carriers would do for that mission. Aircraft carriers would have to be relatively close to Soviet territory for their air-craft to reach the assigned land targets. This proximity would be disastrous because it would make the carriers vulnerable to Soviet attack.

Further, the carrier battle groups could not prevent the Red Army from marching through Western Europe, seizing Middle East oil fields, or intimidating our allies and friends in Northeast Asia—"all without a single Soviet solider ever setting foot in salt water." That is because, he continued, Russia was a great land power and not dependent on control of the seas. The Reagan administration's expensive maritime strategy threatened U.S. capacity to assist its allies in these three vital regions. Komer again shifted his attention to Lehman, noting that the secretary had recently bragged of already having his six-hundred-ship Navy under contract. Such arrogance, Komer believed, not only caused the United States to drift toward a prime dependence on a maritime strategy, but also reflected the Reagan adminis-tration's policy of "global unilateralism." "We seem to go out of our way to create differences with our allies," Komer wrote. "Regarding them as weak and unreliable, the Administration sees added advantage in reorienting our conventional military toward relying on supremacy at sea rather than retaining the more balanced posture of the past."[40]

Now it was Admiral Watkins' time to battle with Komer. In a letter to the *Los Angeles Times*, he responded to Komer's earlier commentary. His opening paragraph was quarrelsome: Komer's argument that there are two competing strategies, maritime versus continental strategies, "is phony." He accused Komer of creating an artificial dichotomy when the former Pentagon official knew well that the stated U.S. strategy was deterrence of conflict and, should that fail, then assurance of a forward defense far from U.S. territory and the waging of global war through coalition operations with the allies.

Behind the smoke screen of Komer's "throwaway lines" was a more fundamental question: How should U.S. naval forces be employed to achieve this national strategy? The answer was simple. They should be used to deny the Soviet navy the ability to cut off "our allies from any hope of U.S. support." This demanded forward maritime operations to protect NATO. Otherwise, the United States would be creating a "Maginot-Line naval strategy" to defend the sea lines of communication to Europe but little else. NATO was more than the defense of West Germany; it included the defense of Denmark, Greece, Turkey, and Norway, he argued. Thus, the maritime strategy was not a "go it alone" strategy but one that recognized the needed contributions of the other armed services and allies.[41]

Not everyone in the U.S. Navy swallowed Watkins' arguments, and the dissent was particularly galling when it came from a member of his own staff. In a prize-winning essay titled "Escalation and Naval Strategy," which appeared in the August issue of the U.S. Naval Institute *Proceedings*, Capt. Linton F. Brooks, a member of the chief of naval operations' staff, lengthened the debate that had now been going on within and outside the Navy for more than three years. Although Brooks moderated his disapproval of the strategy by agreeing that U.S. naval assets needed to be prepared to operate near the Soviet Union and that the United States should not cede any area of the world to the Soviets, he still undercut the declared policy. He did so by resuscitating the argument that the forward strategy could encourage an escalation of conventional conflict between NATO and the Warsaw Pact into a nuclear one. The Soviet strategy, he stated, called for preemption should the government perceive that the nation was threatened by approaching U.S. naval aircraft capable of nuclear strikes. If that perception were acted upon, then the U.S. maritime strategy would "fail catastrophically" because the carriers, an "irreplaceable strategic reserve," would be unlikely to survive attack. Better to use them in peripheral missions than leave them useless at the bottom of the ocean.[42]

Komer was not through either. Shortly after Brooks' article was published, Komer's *Maritime Defense or Coalition Defense?* was published. The book was an expansion of his earlier arguments that went beyond the strategic issues into a broader discussion of defense reform. His points were threefold. First, the United States needed to reconsider its strategy. One step in this process should be reforming the role of the Joint Chiefs of Staff to ensure a more balanced, joint strategy. The Reagan administration had plainly shown that with the current system, strategy could devolve into "an amalgam of parochial service views." Second, priorities must be refocused toward conventional capability in Europe, and defense resources needed to be used more effectively and efficiently. The third point was derived from the second. Burden sharing needed to be equitable among the NATO allies, meaning the alliance should be less dependent on the United States.

Peter Nailor, an instructor at Britain's Royal Navy College, praised the book in the Royal Institute of International Affairs' journal and complimented Komer for serving his country well for thirty years, much of it at the core of American political and military affairs. He noted that although Komer's arguments were not new, they were carefully considered, the product of wide reading and "a belief in the power of reason." Komer, Nailor wrote, should be praised for his energy and his persistence, but he doubted that Komer's exhortations would result in the change he adumbrated because reform would require an attention to performance that is uncommon on the foreign and military policy agenda. Many of these changes, Nailor concluded, were, "by themselves, relatively small, the orchestration of the whole is much greater than the sum of the parts."[43]

Steven Miller, who taught defense studies at MIT and was the editor of a forthcoming book on military strategy and World War I, wrote a review that appeared in the renowned Sunday *New York Times* book review section. Miller applauded Komer for raising "broad questions of strategy" that were often neglected in the discussion of American defense policy. He found the book a stimulating polemic on the character of strategy and the merits of the alternatives featured in the title. The book was enlivened by Komer's contention that the Reagan administration's defense strategy was the product not of design, but of default. Many might disagree with Komer, Miller wrote, but Komer had provided a service, one requiring a discerning analysis of strategic choices. What was shocking, Miller continued, was that if Komer was correct, then "the Reagan Administration will have spent billions of dollars moving American defense policy in the wrong direction."[44]

One administration official who sought to render Komer's views meaningless, especially in the upcoming battle over the defense budget, was Dov Zakheim, a senior Reagan political appointee in the Defense Department who would later serve as that department's comptroller during George W. Bush's presidency. His review of Komer's book was published in the winter 1984–1985 issue of *Political Science Quarterly*, and it was hardly an objective assessment. He began by characterizing Komer's views as the product of a realization that his work as a Carter administration official would not by implemented fully by his Republican successors. He also argued that Komer's points were outdated because the Reagan administration had achieved many of them. However, by the end of the review, Zakheim had softened his tone, stating that while Komer's views were partisan, they were not polemical. Instead, they were a sincere but mistaken attempt by a high-minded civil servant to tackle supposed defects in existing policy.[45]

On Capitol Hill, Republican and Democratic legislators alike militated against President Reagan's defense budget request, which was feeding a ballooning deficit, but Weinberger and Lehman remained optimistic. Despite the tough talk about eliminating funds for major weapon systems and high-pitched shrieks about the secretary's intransigence over another sizable increase in defense spending, Weinberger and Lehman believed that it was more likely that Congress would chip away at hundreds of accounts to reduce the request. Referring to two ships built in Pascagoula, Mississippi, Lehman asked sardonically, "You think the Mississippi delegation is going to let us zero-out the LHD [amphibious ship] or an Aegis [cruiser]? No. We would just get fewer. Every little dog will get his little bit, and you'll just end up with higher prices." Other members of Congress were fighting to home-port ships in their state.[46]

Meanwhile, Komer's utterances became shriller. In a front-page article that appeared in the February 3, 1985, issue of the *Washington Post*, Komer chewed out the secretary of defense: "Weinberger reigns, but he does not rule. He has devoted the bulk of his attention to getting money out of a reluctant Congress—and relatively little attention to what the money ought to be spent on. . . . He's been, not a bad manager, but a non-manager."[47]

Komer was not alone in his ferocity. Some on Capitol Hill were determined to make deep cuts in military spending. Whereas Weinberger, known as "Cap the Knife" from his budget director days in the Nixon administration, wielded a stiletto on the defense budget request, the Congress came at the document with a cleaver. Senator Mark Hatfield, a Republican from Oregon and chairman of the Senate Appropriations Committee, called Weinberger "a draft dodger in the war on the federal deficit." His Republican colleague, Senator Charles Grassley of Iowa, remarked that the secretary "ought to recognize that the business-as-usual stuff can no longer work." House Majority Leader James Wright, a Texas Democrat, ridiculed as nonsense Weinberger's claim that those who sought cuts in military spending wanted to "weaken the security of the country." Weinberger even had critics to his rear. White House chief of staff Donald Regan suggested that the defense budget was not "untouchable." Weinberger responded to the disapproval with a wave of television appearances, congressional wooing sessions, and press interviews.[48]

On February 7 Komer and his fellow Democrats for Defense held a press conference of their own, issuing their fourth annual report on the defense budget to draw attention to their critique. Komer, along with one of his former deputies, Walter Slocombe, and retired general Kenneth B. Cooper, were the most vocal members of the group, and they faulted the administration's priorities in a number of areas. In particular, Komer rebuked the Navy for its inattention to funding fast-moving transport ships. "We've got more forces in the United States," he remarked, "than we can deploy overseas in a hurry. I'd like to buy more transportation and fewer things that shoot."[49]

Weinberger was now "wrestling with a zeppelin."[50] The convergence of Komer's catalyzing criticism and newfound congressional backbone on the deficit was having an effect. Added to these factors were recent audits by the Department of Defense inspector general that indicated the military services were spending millions of dollars on weapons that had not yet proven affordable or necessary.[51] Komer's claim that Weinberger was more adept at fund-raising than he was at managing the department seemed to have some truth.

Komer fired his final volley in the autumn of 1985 with an essay in the journal *International Security*. The piece, titled "What Decade of Neglect?" was his final defense of the Carter administration's record. In it, he vigorously argued against Weinberger's claim that the Defense Department the Reagan administration inherited was the result of the Carter administration's inattention to national security requirements.[52] With that final pronouncement, Komer essentially left the debate.

As one of the architects of the maritime strategy, retired Navy captain Peter Swartz averred that Komer's criticism of the maritime strategy had two benefits. First, it sharpened the Navy's thinking. It forced naval officers to develop policy and strategy in a single document that every officer would be familiar with and understand. In short, it gave substance and vigor to naval thinking in contrast to the lack of strategic thinking that occurred in the 1970s. Second, Komer opened up the debate on the six-hundred-ship Navy and Lehman's proposals, a healthy initiative in a democracy.[53]

CHAPTER 14

The Wisdom of Hindsight:
Vietnam Reassessed

*V*ietnam haunted Robert Komer. He had not suffered an infernal descent into combat trauma like many veterans of the war, nor was he harried by protestors and accused of war crimes like some former Johnson administration officials. Instead, Robert Komer, a man of the intellect, was haunted by a nagging question: "Why, whatever our purposes, did our massive intervention accomplish so little for so long—until finally the U.S. turned its back on Vietnam?"[1]

It would be a decade and a half after Komer left Vietnam before he again devoted substantial attention to the conflict. The sociologist Richard Sennett, complaining about McGeorge Bundy's appointment as a professor in New York University's History Department in 1980, illustrated one reason that Komer and others involved in the war shied away from writing about it. Sennett declared Bundy's appointment disturbing because "Americans were trying as hard as they can to forget Vietnam."[2] As *New York Times* reporter Fox Butterfield noted in a February 1983 article titled "The New Vietnam Scholarship," a small group of journalists, scholars, and military experts had quietly begun to examine the war anew as the tenth anniversary of the Paris Peace Accords approached. The purpose of this rekindled interest was not to prove whether the war was a "noble cause," as Ronald Reagan pronounced, but to understand what happened and why and, in doing so, to challenge some of the treasured beliefs of both the Right and Left.[3] It is into this scholarly fray that Komer again waded, and he seemed to have a particular opponent in mind—Col. Harry Summers, an instructor at the U.S. Army War College at Carlisle, Pennsylvania, who had reexamined the military aspect of the war in his 1983 book, *On Strategy: A Critical Analysis of the Vietnam War.*

What particular animosity Summers created within Komer is certainly not immediately evident from Summers' book as he scarcely mentions Komer and, when he does, it is to quote from *Bureaucracy Does Its Thing* to buttress one of his arguments. Yet, Summers' overall argument was likely the germ of Komer's dissatisfaction.

Komer reviewed *On Strategy* for the British academic journal *Survival.* It is a savage assessment, beginning with these words: "Colonel Summers' widely quoted critique of U.S. strategy in the Vietnam War is having a modest vogue in the United States. This is partly because it is so unusual to have a serving U.S. officer writing about strategy, and one who has studied Clausewitz at that. It is also because he offers a professional soldier's apologia for why the US performed so badly in Vietnam. This said, I cannot think of much else to recommend the book. Despite the Clausewitzian logic in which he clothes his argument, it is poor history, poor strategy, and poor Clausewitz to boot."[4] Besides the fact that Summers dedicated the book to Komer's nemesis, retired general Walter T. Kerwin, which must have rankled, it is Summers' analysis of U.S. performance that infuriated him.

Komer attacked what he believed were four flaws in Summers' work. The first was Summers' failure to understand the nature of limited warfare and the inevitable constraints it required, particularly in the nuclear age when the United States felt compelled to pursue a strategy that would accomplish its political goals while minimizing the odds of wider conflict that required costs and risks out of proportion to the limited aim involved. Clausewitz, Komer snorted, would not have ignored this point. Such an oversight also demonstrated, in Komer's view, Summers' lack of historical appreciation. Summers must have forgotten that during the Korean War Gen. Douglas MacArthur's impetuous advance to the Yalu River sparked a Chinese Communist intervention that resulted in a longer conflict and additional casualties and that forced the Americans and their allies to settle for a return to the status quo ante.[5]

In Vietnam, the United States had to take into account the Soviet Union and China as factors, and thus, it followed the same limited political objective that it ultimately adopted in Korea and that Summers had endorsed—to preserve the integrity of South Vietnam while steering clear of a wider war. This objective explained the political constraints on operations against North Vietnam, such as the careful restrictions on air strikes, mining, and ground operations outside of South Vietnam. Komer agreed that this approach limited U.S. ability to "bring Hanoi to its knees, but it had little to do with a lack of appreciation for sound military theory or preferred strategy." Komer reminded Summers that such an approach has "everything to do with what Clausewitz called the political objective of war."

Second, Komer flayed Summers for not understanding the nature of the Vietnam War and accused him of sharing the narrow outlook of the many military participants in the war who insisted that Vietnam was not a "civil war" or "revolutionary war" but principally a conventional conflict. "It is a pity," Komer noted, that Summers "offers so few facts to back up his thesis." Komer then cited the Army's 1965 PROVN study as making exactly the opposite point that Summers argued. Komer granted that while the war ironically ended in 1975, when the North Vietnamese regular army invaded South Vietnam and defeated the South Vietnamese regulars, from 1955 to mid-1966 the war was primarily an insurgency-type conflict to which U.S. military advice and support was so ill-suited that it damaged South Vietnam's ability to respond to the threat adequately.

Komer's third point related to the previous one: Summers was guilty of "standing reality on its head" with his argument that the U.S. Army pursued a defective strategy in South Vietnam and squandered its military superiority by attacking the guerrillas rather than the enemy's regular forces, especially the NVA. Summers maintained the United States should have left the ARVN to the counterinsurgency effort and concentrated its efforts on thwarting North Vietnamese aggression. Komer offered a different view as a senior participant in Vietnam decision making from 1966 to 1968 who worked assiduously for greater emphasis on counterinsurgency but to no avail. The United States and South Vietnamese militaries were so obsessed with the "main force" war that they spent most of the time trying to locate and destroy the enemy's organized forces to the detriment of counterinsurgency.

Fourth and finally, Summers, Komer decried, developed no alternative strategy to pursue. Instead, he merely endorsed Gen. Bruce Palmer's 1977 suggestion that the United States should have cut off the North Vietnamese infiltration routes through Laos. Komer conceded that this approach looked better in hindsight than what the United States did, but he questioned whether it would have changed the ultimate result. He mused that in all likelihood, North Vietnam, knowing that it was the better contender, would have just continued to wait the United States out. That is the most pertinent point of all. In the final analysis, Komer asserted, the South Vietnamese regime was a weak vessel, beset with factionalism and corruption, rescued by the United States and propped up until its crushing defeat after the Americans withdrew. "And the United States pulled out because the home front turned off on a war that lasted so long, cost so much and became so divisive." Yes, Komer concluded, "there are lessons to be drawn from Vietnam, but they are not the ones that Colonel Summers draws."

Komer's pillorying of Summers' book was not the splenetic venting of a biased participant or the result of jealousy because of the attention Summers' book received in the press. Komer believed sincerely that Summers' thesis was incorrect and overly simplistic and that he misrepresented or misunderstood the actual nature of the conflict. The preeminent American military historian Russell Weigley, as well as other scholars and some serving military officers, shared this view.[6]

Komer's disagreement became part of the ongoing debate among three rival schools of thought regarding fundamental issues involved in the Vietnam conflict, particularly its strategic dimension. For these two men as for many others, the principal question was, why did the United States fail to achieve its objectives in Vietnam? One of the camps was "the hawks," comprising such well-known military officers as Gen. William C. Westmoreland and Adm. U. S. Grant Sharp as well as Dave Richard Palmer, who had served in Vietnam and was the author of *Summons of the Trumpet: U.S.-Vietnam in Perspective*. They argued that the United States had failed to use its military power to its best advantage in Vietnam. Failure to attain the nation's aims was the fault of the civilian leadership, particularly President Johnson and Secretary McNamara, who formulated and imposed upon the military the ill-conceived and restrictive strategy of gradual response, which stymied the military from performing its designated mission. The hawks had implicit faith in the ability of military power to achieve the stated American policy objectives; hence their focus was almost exclusively on the military instrument, and they scarcely concerned themselves with such problems as the political situation in Vietnam and pacification.[7]

A second school of thought, the "limited war advocates," argued that the likelihood of achieving was U.S. strategic objectives in Vietnam was nil given three critical factors: the political conditions in Vietnam itself, U.S. historical experience, and the inability of the political leaders to discern clearly whether U.S. interests in Vietnam were truly vital. The distinguished academics Robert E. Osgood, the author of *Limited War Revisited*, and Stanley Hoffmann were the foremost representatives for this position, although it had its antecedents in the earlier views of a number of liberal doves and some conservative intellectuals, such as the realist Hans Morgenthau.[8] In short, the decision to intervene in Vietnam was, at the very least, misguided and, at the worst, bordered on delusion. A clear-headed strategic appraisal would have revealed that Vietnam constituted a no-win situation in terms of both interests and support of our ally, for South Vietnam was, in Osgood's view, "a fractured society with no experience in self-government and no unifying traditions or sense of nationality, governed by urban elites remote from the village and peasantry, dependent on an incompetent civil service and an untrustworthy army."[9]

While the hawks dismissed the importance of counterinsurgency in obtaining U.S. strategic objectives, the limited war advocates held that counterinsurgency techniques would not have made a difference in the outcome. The United States was not prepared by historical experience or by temperament to wage a protracted engagement against an enemy dedicated to waging a revolutionary war. In the limited war advocates' view, there was nothing to suggest the American public was committed to such a venture, including the financial and human costs that the nation would bear between 1965 and the withdrawal of its forces in 1973.[10]

Scholars have relegated Komer to the third school of thought, the "counterinsurgency school," along with British expert Sir Robert Thompson; U.S. Air Force brigadier general Edward Lansdale, who advised the Philippines government during its Communist insurgency in the 1950s and became a leading voice in fashioning U.S. policy and strategy in Vietnam; and Komer's CORDS colleague John Paul Vann. Guenter Lewy, political scientist and author of *America in Vietnam*, served as the counterinsurgency school's champion within scholarly ranks. Although Lewy was considered an articulate postwar supporter of the counterinsurgency position, Komer's *Bureaucracy at War* must be considered superior because of its unique and innovative analysis of politico-military performance from both strategic and operational perspectives. Lewy, in contrast, examined the war's morality and the competence of the effort. In fact, Lewy borrowed from Komer the line of reasoning that the strategic fiasco of Vietnam resulted from the military's inflexibility and devotion to tradition, conventional thinking, and an organizational culture that had little relevance to Vietnam.[11]

Bureaucracy at War, published in 1986, became Komer's final written word on Vietnam. Although it is an updated version of his earlier RAND study in which he concentrated primarily on the neglected issue of U.S. and South Vietnamese performance rather than policy, he rationalized its worth: "This updating actually strengthens my original case, because in a real sense South Vietnam's 1975 collapse offered a final demonstration of its inability, and that of its U.S. ally, to win a revolutionary war the way we fought it."[12]

Komer readily admitted his parochialism regarding the conflict in general, and pacification in particular, given his role as a participant in the refinement of the GVN pacification effort both in the White House and in Vietnam. He acknowledged that it was difficult to be objective about one's own performance. However, this experience also taught him firsthand the operational and bureaucratic difficulties of translating policy into successful performance, thereby contributing insights as well. Any book that sought to understand how the United States and its ally lost a war must be dispassionately critical and, he contended, perceive how institutional constraints, not just flaws of leadership, hindered performance and, ultimately, the attainment of victory.[13]

Komer began his argument by stating that although the U.S. contribution to the war was cumulatively enormous, it yielded meager results with disproportionate costs and tragic side effects. The reasons for this, he argued, were numerous, complex, and interrelated. They certainly included the distinctive and alien conflict environment, repeated misjudgment of the enemy, the enemy's ability to frustrate U.S. objectives tactically and to escalate in kind at every stage, the American inheritance of the French colonial mantle, and perhaps, most critically, the incremental nature of the American response. Advisers and troops on the ground were tasked only with what U.S. policymakers deemed minimally essential at every stage. Yet, these reasons, and the miscalculations they represented, were not sufficient to explain the poor performance of the United States and its South Vietnamese ally. The irony was that while the United States recognized how different the Vietnam conflict was from any major war in previous U.S. experience and how difficult it would be to succeed, it continued to act in a manner contrary to the vast amount of information and knowledge it had. It certainly was not for a lack of "money, machines or men" or a failure of leadership, although the leadership did fail at various times and at various levels.[14] Thus, the nagging question remained: Why did the United States perform so poorly?

The reasons, Komer claimed, "lie in the realm of various built-in constraints which greatly inhibited the translation of perception into policy, policy into program, and program into performance."[15] The greatest single constraint to U.S. ability to achieve its aims in Vietnam was the comparative weakness of the Saigon regime. Komer called this problem "the flawed nature of our chosen instrument." William Colby disagreed with this analysis and articulated as much in the book's foreword, but Komer remained resolute on this point. He believed that the United States had supported weak regimes from its 1965 intervention until its withdrawal in 1973 and that this flaw was a major factor in Saigon's 1975 collapse. In this respect, Komer agreed with the limited war advocates: the GVN was incapable or unwilling to respond to the challenges it confronted. U.S. inability or reluctance to force the GVN into facing them only exacerbated the situation.[16]

Almost equally important was the broad array of political, financial, and resource constraints—usually resulting from deliberate policy determinations—which set limits from the beginning on how the United States decided to deal with the Vietnam situation. Here Komer took issue with the hawks by arguing that the soundness of the policy of gradualism was not the issue. The important point was that this policy approach led to a cautious and deliberate incrementalism, and the incremental approach concealed a more damaging factor: gradualism allowed institutional constraints to surface. These well-known constraints of organizational behavior included using the instruments available but not assessing whether they were relevant, living with what one could get, and failing to adapt responses to what is required by the situation. Komer cautioned that this point should not be overemphasized because it was one of many factors. However, these constraints "helped render the U.S./GVN response to an unconventional insurgency/guerrilla war unduly conventional, expensive and slow to adapt." This was the missing perspective in the analysis of the Vietnam conflict, argued Komer, and it was the principal thrust of his book. The behavior of large, hierarchically organized institutions suited particular situations, namely, routine roles and missions. It was not suited for atypical situations the organizations were not designed for or equipped to cope with.[17]

In Komer's view, each bureaucracy involved in the Vietnam conflict, U.S. or GVN, played out its standard organizational repertoire. From this basis, three axioms follow. First, a bureaucratic organization will use its existing capabilities and act consistently with its internal goals, performance standards, and measurement and incentive systems—even when these conflict with the assigned mission. Second, the larger and most dynamic of the institutions, in this case, the U.S. and GVN militaries, will tend to dominate the others and to force them aside. Third, institutional constraints shaped how the U.S. government dealt with the war in a largely compartmentalized fashion, paying little heed to unified management, which diluted managerial focus and impeded adaptation to the circumstances on the ground.[18]

Komer pointed out that there had been attempts at adaptive response in the areas of technological innovation and one example of large-scale institutional innovation—CORDS and the "new model" pacification initiated in 1967. Here he declared that the managerial key had been the creation of CORDS. Once this essential organizational step, which enhanced the U.S. advisory and supporting role, had occurred, then attention could be focused on the GVN's pacification structure and territorial security, which was the foundational for all other pacification activities. However, Komer admitted that despite these efforts, the pacification program had numerous shortcomings and weaknesses and had been "at best only a qualified success." Yet, it had salutary effects in that it promoted collaboration between the allies and was able to address many of the atypical problems of a people's war in South Vietnam; it was the only one of all the U.S.-supported efforts tailored specifically to this end. Considering that pacification efforts cost only a fraction of the amount consumed with the "big unit" war, it was also cost-effective.[19]

Komer concluded his monograph with two questions. Was there a viable alternative strategy? Moreover, what lessons could be learned? In response to the first question, Komer dismissed the view that the United States should never have expected the outcome to be anything other than what occurred, a catastrophe. Although there were environmental, political, institutional, and policy constraints, it is not logical to assume that approaches other than those adopted would not have resulted in a different outcome. Komer argued that a feasible, suitable, and acceptable alternative strategy would have been what he called the "counterinsurgency strategy," which had its antecedents in the U.S. experience in the Philippines against the Huks, the military arm of the Philippines Communist Party, and the British experience in Malaya in the 1950s.[20]

The counterinsurgency strategy, although often ill defined and varying in content and emphasis, had been advocated by a number of U.S. civilian and military officials, especially Assistant Secretary of State Roger Hilsman, an old OSS hand, as early as 1964. Hilsman, along with other proponents of this approach, argued that overmilitarizing the war had been a mistake and that political aims had to have primacy over military ones. Attention and resources should have been applied to creating workable, accountable, and responsive local government in the rural areas and numerous sociopolitical and economic development programs. The Vietnamese would have had to put their hand to the tiller in order for this strategy to succeed. In fact, Komer demonstrated through a review of the Pentagon Papers that counterinsurgency was a major element in policy thinking in both Washington and Saigon from 1955 on, but that it was never articulated in definitive form nor was it presented to policymakers as an alternative to the conventional approach in an either-or fashion. The first full-scale attempt at a "primarily counterinsurgency-oriented strategy" occurred with the CORDS program in 1967; before that discussion of counterinsurgency was merely "brave talk." The reason for this neglect was simple in Komer's mind; counterinsurgency was not part of the institutional repertoire of the major GVN and U.S. agencies involved. It had a band of supporters, but they were individual voices and not a major organizational entity promoting this form of strategy. Furthermore, even if such a strategy had been accepted, the organizational capabilities for executing it did not exist. Neither the United States nor the South Vietnamese built the institutional capacity for counterinsurgency on a large scale until 1967, and even then, it was a corollary to the conventional response, which the United States and GVN emphasized in the 1963–65 period.[21] However, would a pacification alternative have worked?

In answering this question, Komer recognized that he was working with a historical "if." Regardless, he offered an opinion based on the role that the pacification program played in the turnaround of the war between 1968, after Tet, and 1971. On this point, he is on firm ground, and in fact, many scholars, counterinsurgency practitioners, and military experts would later agree with him. Still, he realized that the pacification example "was hardly a pure test of a counterinsurgency-oriented strategy as a preferred alternative." In other words, the counterinsurgency effort was not the only factor involved in that improvement. The conventional war contributed tremendously to the security environment that allowed the pacification program to thrive in that period. In Komer's view, 1964 was the critical date on which to determine the probability of success. After 1964, the NVA's infiltration of the South grew and a pacification-oriented, clear-and-hold strategy was no longer practicable. Thus, counterinsurgency would have had its best chance for success before 1964–65, before the insurgency escalated into a quasi-conventional war. Although much of his argument remains an historical "if," Komer held on tenaciously to the idea that pacification did not fail, and indeed by the time the United States withdrew its troops, it had finally become a qualified success. The irony is that the conflict ended in the way the Americans thought it would begin, with North Vietnamese attacks using conventional forces.[22]

Komer recognized the Vietnam conflict as a "fortified compound war," in which Maoist strategy, as modified by North Vietnam, was employed. This form of warfare uses the simultaneous combination of a conventional or main force and a guerrilla or irregular force against a superior major power. The minor power, in this case North Vietnam, is able to continue to wage successful combat operations because the main force has the protection of safe havens and a major-power ally.[23]

Finally, Komer addressed the lessons to be learned from the manner in which the United States intervened in Vietnam. Given his previous analysis, Komer argued that Vietnam "cried out for innovation and adaptation." However, he was sensitive to the dangers inherent in taking past experience as an explicit model for the future: the lessons of the past might not be applicable in different circumstances. Tacit acceptance of analogies could lead to gross misperceptions about how best to deal with different contingencies. Given these caveats, he sought to frame useful lessons in terms that were sufficiently generalized to be broadly applicable, yet specific enough to be operationally useful. Four lessons met these criteria.[24]

The first was the need to understand that "atypical problems demand specifically tailored solutions," not the playing out of existing institutional repertoires. Second, the policymaker must consider fully the capacity of the institutions involved to act as intended. Third, adaptive response requires not only well-designed policy but also adequate mechanism to ensure that the policy is implemented effectively and to force adaptation when needed. Lastly, when the United States is largely fighting a war by surrogate, effective methods for attaining optimum performance of the proxy is vital.

Komer contended that these lessons were generally achievable only by forcing adaptation and that six additional issues needed attention. The first was identifying and choosing "flexible and imaginative leaders at all levels" and not relying on the usual institutional criteria to determine qualified candidates for various positions. The established personnel and selection systems were not necessarily useful in supplying the type of leader needed in an atypical environment. The military had to recognize that a superb commander might not be the right person when an adaptive program manager or adviser for a foreign government and its forces was required. Civilian agencies had to recognize that the demands on executives in peacetime were not comparable to those during wartime, which required different talents.

Second, training and incentive systems needed to place value on flexibility and adaptability instead of conventional solutions. "Doing it by the book" was not always appropriate. Leaders might have to write the book as they went along. Third, it might be necessary to create autonomous ad hoc organizations if existing organizations could not adapt quickly, when specially tailored programs did not exist, or where such programs crossed agency lines. However, these ad hoc organizations needed to receive funding, personnel, resources, and support to perform the task. This approach could mean breaking the bureaucratic crockery rather than trying to meet the need through use of an existing organizational structure.

Fourth, multidimensional conflicts that require politico-economic as well as military responses could best be addressed by unified management at all levels. As Komer wrote, "Interagency coordination and pulling all strands together only at the White House level may suffice for policy formulation." However, in the field, this mechanism was insufficient to induce integrated effort, responsiveness to priorities, and satisfactory follow-through to "prevent individual agencies from marching to their own bureaucratic tunes." When the president had determined that the U.S. effort necessitated the implementation of activities across normal agency responsibilities, it was advisable to establish a special ad hoc apparatus at the Washington level to manage it. There were several credible options, including an agency acting as executive agent, an ad hoc task force, or a special organization within the White House. Regardless of the option selected, there had to be a clear grant of presidential authority and solid presidential backing to offset the bureaucratic bickering that would inevitably occur. Equally important was unified management at the field level. The "country team" approach was not optimal because the agencies represented in the embassy were not under the control of the U.S. ambassador. In most cases, it would be better for the ambassador to be a proconsul with absolute authority over all policy implementation efforts and agencies. This approach raised the issue of the separation of civilian and military responsibilities. However, the top post in the field could be either civilian or military depending on the situation and the caliber of the leadership available.

Fifth, an effective unified manager needed to have his own staff wherein unified planning, operations, and evaluation could occur; and finally, there had to be increased emphasis and value placed on thorough evaluation and analysis of performance. These factors and achieving adequate performance from allies or client states were crucial, and ensuring that client states could execute operations effectively was the responsibility of the United States.[25]

Komer concluded that these lessons "seem restatements of the obvious," and they were certainly not the only reasons behind the poor performance of the United States and its ally, but given that they were "more honored in the breach than the observance," they were worth underscoring once again. Unfortunately, scholars and U.S. government officials would just as soon forget Vietnam than profit by learning from its costly operational efforts.[26]

The reaction to Komer's analyses of the Vietnam conflict was mixed and scarce. Eliot Cohen, writing about the original 1972 RAND study for an article in the journal *International Security*, declared that while an intellectual understanding of the demands and problems associated with "small wars" was a critical step, it would not inevitably result in implementation of the policies required to conduct this form of warfare successfully. He considered Komer's study of the Vietnam era bureaucracy to be "eloquent" on this point.[27]

In a review of *Bureaucracy at War* for *Parameters*, the U.S. Army War College's journal, Richard Hunt, who would become the leading historian of Vietnam pacification, argued that while the book was an updated version of the 1972 study, it deserved the same high level of attention that Summers' *On Strategy* and Gen. Bruce Palmer's *The 25-Year War: America's Military Role in Vietnam* had received. In a more nuanced assessment, Hunt observed that Komer "compellingly develops a broad and provocative thesis." Nonetheless, he believed Komer gave short shrift to the enemy's adaptability and persistent control of the initiative. Additionally, he found Komer's contention that CORDS was the shining example of successful organizational adaptation hollow, and given the substantial shortcomings of the South Vietnamese, solving American bureaucratic dysfunction might have been irrelevant to the outcome of the war. Lastly, although Hunt understood that a detailed analysis of what CORDS accomplished might have left Komer open to charges of self-aggrandizement and parochialism, it would have reinforced his argument significantly.[28] Thus, Hunt remained skeptical of Komer's arguments.

However, Andrew Pierre's review in *Foreign Affairs* stated that Komer had measured American performance in Vietnam "cogently and pungently" and that his assessments about "institutional constraints and weaknesses in the management of war were germane far beyond Vietnam." Nonetheless, the reviewer also captured the final verdict on Komer's work: "This book deserves more attention than it is likely to receive. American performance in Vietnam is not a popular subject."[29] Komer characterized the nearly imperceptible response to the book as a major disappointment.

—————

Throughout the 1980s, as the new scholarship flourished, Komer's stress on the importance of organization, accountability, and measurement of performance in *Bureaucracy at War* and during his leadership of CORDS was criticized as tantamount to declaring that the Vietnam War was a management problem and not a sociopolitical one.[30] There is a kernel of validity in this comment. Komer's study of counterinsurgency practice as applied to Vietnam reinforced his belief that counterinsurgency required the introduction of a fundamental management principle, unity of command, and the weaving together of civil and military elements. Inarguably, he was a member of the managerial class, for which his education at Harvard Business School had prepared him, and this culture, derived from industrial engineering with its emphasis on pragmatic problem solving and the application of analysis and expertise to concrete experience, had an influence on how he approached problems. In this mode, problem solving required the optimum manipulation of resources to attain organizational effectiveness and efficiency.[31]

Komer clearly recognized the political, social, and economic components of fighting the war, especially in a "people's war." He indicated publicly that unified management or unity of command would not have won the war alone, any more than airpower would have. Komer held that without unity of command, the United States and South Vietnam were "actually fighting several *separate* [emphasis in the original] wars rather than one war."[32] Moreover, the assessment overlooks a key insight of Komer's, one that occurred years before he conducted a systematic analysis of the Vietnam conflict: that organization and management, especially organizational performance, were essential to the execution of U.S. policy and strategy. Komer understood strategy as the relationship between U.S. policy objectives and the means or application of resources needed to secure those aims. He elevated organization to a major strategic concept without which the strategy could not be implemented successfully. As part of that organizational construct, he accepted the long-held notion that military resources must be integrated with sociopolitical and economic development elements.

Scholars and practitioners writing in this period credited Komer with devising and implementing a needed organizational framework. Richard Shultz asserted that Komer and the establishment of CORDS were essential to the development of the political-military strategy that the Nixon administration would conduct under the name "Vietnamization" from 1969 to 1972. As Shultz noted, the change in strategy was signified by important changes in U.S. leadership in South Vietnam. Specifically, Komer contributed to an expansion "of the scope and pace of pacification" that was critical to the Vietnamization strategy. Shultz essentially agreed with counterinsurgency expert Douglas Blaufarb that the programmatic elements of the strategy were appropriate for the type of conflict being waged; a viable counterinsurgency strategy was created. However, once such a strategy was embarked upon, its success was in the hands of the South Vietnamese government, which was beset with problems it could not overcome to execute the strategy successfully.[33]

Herbert Schandler has suggested that Komer recognized the import of the civil programs in Vietnam, the administration of which had been fragmented as well as inefficiently planned and executed. CORDS represented, in his view, "an innovative and unique organization" that integrated U.S. civilian and military support and provided a single channel of advice and assistance to the South Vietnamese.[34] Donald Vought, a U.S. military officer, contended, "Before Komer began to hack at the Gordian knot of bureaucratic tunnel vision, there was no coherent policy or central control agency for pacification efforts."[35] He was not alone among U.S. military officers in that assessment. Gen. Bruce Palmer recognized that the foundation Komer set down for pacification, including disrupting the VCI and upgrading and expanding the RF/PF's capability, made possible the evolution of a successful pacification program in 1970–71.[36]

William Colby, who certainly had a more biased view, but who had gained insight perhaps because of his parochialism, agreed with his military counterparts when he wrote that Komer in CORDS produced an innovative organizational approach to fighting a "different kind of war." Further, Colby judged Komer to be one of four men who in 1967 "would finally find a strategy to fight the war and invent the organization to carry it out." Colby also underscored another important element in the establishment of CORDS, the effect that the organization had on the South Vietnamese president Thieu. The organization not only provided Thieu an independent reporting channel but also was attentive to territorial security.[37]

Brigadier General Tan Dinh Tho, formerly of the South Vietnamese army, observed that CORDS enhanced the overall pacification effort because it provided cohesive U.S. support for the GVN for the first time. Further, the charismatic effect of two positive, hard-driving leaders, Major General Nguyen Thang and Komer, gave new momentum to pacification. Nonetheless, Tho argued that it was highly questionable that the pacification effort ever won the "hearts and minds" of the rural population. Ultimately, pacification was a GVN responsibility, and the program faced considerable problems in hamlet security and development while having to contend with successful Viet Cong tactics that disrupted nation-building efforts and U.S. policies that neglected the other war until 1967.[38]

Nonetheless, contemporary counterinsurgency theorists and practitioners understand the far-reaching implications of Komer's counterinsurgency thinking, judgments that transcend the Vietnam War. In September 2007 Australian counterinsurgency expert David Kilcullen, speaking at the Gray Research Center, Marine Corps Base, Quantico, Virginia, remarked that the first requirement for understanding an insurgency is to have an appreciation of the environment in which it is occurring and how its character can alter given changes in the situation. Further, simply understanding the environment and controlling the people, terrain, and information are insufficient. Military and political leaders need to comprehend that a "framework, doctrine, systems, processes and structure are required to enact this understanding." Komer, in Kilcullen's view, understood this point, for these aspects are the institutional constraints that he first identified in 1972 and that continue to be valid decades later as inhibitors to implementing counterinsurgency "best practices."[39]

CONCLUSION

*K*omer never became an elder statesman. He served as a consultant to the National Intelligence Council from 1982 to 1986, at the request of its chairman, Henry S. Rowen, and to the RAND Corporation, where he was not interested in playing a major role, in the 1980s and 1990s.[1] "That I should end up writing RAND reports after I had been a presidential assistant and Under Secretary of Defense was too much for me," he wrote. He had enough money and no further interest in the "bookwriting [*sic*] business."[2] The final pages of his unpublished memoirs have a wistful, almost dispirited tone; in them, he seems deprived, cheated of the joys public service had given him for thirty years. He died of a stroke on April 9, 2000, in Arlington, Virginia, and was buried in Arlington National Cemetery. His simple marble headstone is similar to the thousands of others in that hallowed ground: his name, rank (lieutenant colonel, U.S. Army), wartime service, and the dates of his birth and death.

Over the years Komer's name became almost exclusively linked to the folly of the Vietnam War, despite the fact that this conflict represented only a small portion of his nearly three decades of government service. The linkage served to damage a broader understanding of the essential role he played as a Cold War strategist.

Komer's principal function throughout his lengthy government career in this era entailed recognizing that the strategist's foremost obligation is to protect the fundamental interests of the nation. That is a humbling and vital imperative. As Fred Charles Iklé, who served as undersecretary of defense for policy in President Ronald Reagan's administration, remarked,

"Given the magnitude of the stakes involved, strategy is not a vocation for stunted minds."[3]

Strategic practice requires creativity, imagination, and even prescience.[4] Studies of innovators find that they are jealous champions. However, in order to thrive, innovators must be protected because others view them as "obnoxious, impatient, egotistic, and perhaps a bit irrational in organizational terms."[5] Professor Theodore Levitt of Harvard Business School has noted that the important point is not the contribution of ideas; there are plenty of creative people in organizations. There is, however, a dearth of innovators: pragmatists who convert ideas into action, who develop a plan and get it implemented, often through bullheadedness.[6]

Komer was the "perceptive pragmatist," a leader who integrates action and reflection, productivity and people. A person who understands that one cannot "succeed solely as a hands-on problem solver or as a hands-off philosopher."[7] Thus, Komer integrated action and reflection within the constraints of time demands that the organization placed on him. Practical wisdom is indispensable to statecraft. The pragmatic tradition is endemic in the exercise of U.S. foreign policy and American strategic thinking.[8] As Cecil Crabb asserts, "American foreign policy is operationally pragmatic."[9]

Komer also exhibited two other characteristics of a pragmatic statesmen, which Hans Morgenthau observed: "a sense of limits—limits of knowledge, of judgment, of successful action—and a commitment to a grand design, born of a sense of purpose that neutralizes the doubts arising from the awareness of limits." Additionally, ideas are not enough for "in the political world, ideas meet with facts, which make mincemeat of the wrong ideas and throw the pieces into the ashcan of history."[10]

As a strategist, Komer was trying to prevent "reactive leadership"— letting events, usually crises, dictate actions. This form of leadership does not act unless compelled to do so.[11] The alternative is to develop and implant a vision that has clarity, consensus, and commitment. In this context, the strategist cannot be a soloist. He or she must create a vision that brings people together and gives them a sense of common purpose. A vision alone does not guarantee a successful action. However, there are factors that cultivate visionary leaders and help their vision prevail. They include credibility with others, being near or at the top of the organizational structure, the relevance of the ideas, and the ability to persuade others to collaborate.[12] Komer considered these factors as he dealt with the change in South Asian policy. He was not alone in envisioning a new policy, but he had a clear picture or image of the possible, which he shared with others, such as Galbraith, Talbot, and Bowles, and won the commitment of other champions, such as Kennedy and Rusk.

Rationality also has an important association with pragmatism. Practical, calculated approaches to problems were ingrained in Komer through his education and experience. He used these approaches in the White House as he grappled with the complex art of foreign policymaking, which he defined as "the rational calculation of your [government's] interests and of the factors that affect your [government's] ability to achieve these interests and then, on the basis of this, the construction of a policy to that end." He did not dismiss the irrational as a factor that must be considered, but preached instead that "unless you can disassociate the practical hard facts with which you must deal, or the attitudes with which you must deal, from the emotional biases and prejudices of one kind or another," then you cannot fashion a sensible policy approach.[13] Rationality was elevated to a virtue. As John Collins observed, "Objective strategists substitute reason for emotion as they systematically pick other men's brains, including those at polarized extremes. . . . The mission is to sift through the evidence, retain what seems useful, and discard the nonsense."[14]

As noted earlier, when Johnson entered office, Komer's role changed principally from innovator to agent because Johnson's management style was substantially different from that of his predecessor. Although Johnson foisted the agent role on Komer, the president had confidence in Komer's knowledge of foreign affairs, that is, his technical skills, but he also perceived a talent that Komer probably did not recognize within himself, as someone who could engage effectively in diplomacy. The term "diplomacy" is not used here in the conventional sense but as Peter Vaill uses the term, as the process of adaptation, "where there is an ongoing interaction of interest and proposals."[15] What Johnson discerned in Komer was not only a dedication to U.S. national interests and shared values, but also the energy and the courage to uphold those interests and the capacity to work across boundaries.[16] Komer had a strong sense of fairness, of ensuring equal treatment. At the same time, he had to attend to the strategic "harmonizing of relationships across boundaries," which are by their nature self-reinforcing and which often force parties to be out of touch with each other, so much so that they cannot see each other's point of view.[17]

Being an agent of the president was uncomfortable for Komer—too messy and contingent. He could not rely solely on his analytical skills or his strategic vision. Instead, he had to locate other competencies within himself, such as persuasion, negotiation, and most of all, forbearance, and trust them. Unbeknownst to him, these were the very aptitudes he would need in South Vietnam for his dealings with a foreign government that was often a source of frustration to its American allies.

Komer also integrated his innate energies and ambitions with the president's needs and opportunities. Philip Selznick observed that "the task of leadership is not only to make policy but to build into the organization's social structure. . . . It means shaping the 'character' of the organization, sensitizing it to ways of thinking and responding, so that increased reliability and the elaboration of policy will be achieved according to its spirit as well as its letter." Selznick calls this the "institutional embodiment of purpose."[18] It is not a one-way phenomenon. In becoming the special assistant for pacification, Komer was identified with the notion of the pacification czar; a two-way embodiment was complete.

The definition and clarification of purposes, that is, objectives, is a fundamental step in strategic leadership. Purposes are not given. They do not exist independently of members' perceptions and values.[19] Leaders must act by trusting their perceptions and values even in the face of their doubts and second thoughts and in a world in which other forces act and thus make situations and circumstances unstable and unpredictable.

For the two years Komer served under Gen. William Westmoreland as deputy for CORDS, Komer provided vision and inspiration and made use of his superlative organizational skills to enable this organization to undertake its pacification mission. CORDS was a unique and innovative organizational response—combining counterinsurgency with economic, social, and political development, across agency and government lines—in a theater of war.

The U.S. Army's renewed interest in counterinsurgency because of conflicts in Iraq and Afghanistan has led it and other U.S. government agencies to recognize Komer's contribution to counterinsurgency operations.[20] Thus, CORDS may prove Komer's most enduring legacy, although he is often not given the full credit he deserves as the architect of this concept for integrating civilian and military support to the South Vietnamese government. However, CORDS as an organizational concept cannot be separated from the person who conceived it as a "useful model to consider for other COIN [counterinsurgency] operations."[21] His 1972 RAND study, *Bureaucracy*

Does Its Thing, was required preparatory counterinsurgency reading for personnel assigned to Multinational Force–Iraq's (MNF-I) strategy office.[22]

However, recognition of Komer's role extends beyond counterinsurgency. Richard K. Betts stressed that the central questions in Komer's *Bureaucracy Does Its Thing* are applicable in other cases and, in particular, in Iraq. As Betts established, historical analogies can be misleading and potentially dangerous when drawing policy lessons. However, he noted, it is equally perilous to "ignore what instructive similarities" exist in this "classic postmortem of American mistakes in the Vietnam War."[23]

Betts was not alone in restoring the importance of Komer's ideas. Robert Gates, the former secretary of defense, also underscored the significance of Komer's contribution regarding organizational behavior in a speech at the National Defense University in 2008. Gates emphasized the continued relevance of Komer's analysis of the national security apparatus, both the civilian and military components, during the Vietnam War. Gates' point was not to "re-litigate that war or suggest that the institutional military hasn't made enormous strides in recent years," but to emphasize how large, hierarchical institutions tend not to adapt after problems are recognized and solutions proposed. These tendencies must always be guarded against or overcome.[24]

During his tenure in the Carter administration, Komer combined the roles of practitioner and leader, fashioning the military instrument of the Carter Doctrine, devising the strategy for this purpose, defining its objectives, prioritizing those objectives, and seeking the resources to implement them. Regarding Persian Gulf security during the Carter administration, the NSC staff was responsible for the overall foreign policy strategy, but there was equally a need for each of the component parts to have a strategy. A strategic vision does not "automatically just cascade down the hierarchy; at each level it needs to be revivified by leaders who have thought deeply about what the strategy means for them and their people."[25] Since the Carter Doctrine was predicated on use of the military instrument, Komer's strategic vision was key but reliant on others outside the Defense Department to support it, namely, State Department leadership and U.S. diplomats in the region. This presents one of the most difficult hurdles of strategy because not all will necessarily commit to the strategic vision. This is where personal relations are critical. Good relations are forged by working one-on-one with a counterpart and ensuring that the strategy meets other individuals' concerns. When it does not, the strategist must adjust it to meet those concerns. Thus, Komer's working relationship with the under secretary of state for political affairs was critical, as was attending to the views of diplomats in the region.

Robert Komer brought together the intellectual and emotional qualities needed in the Cold War strategic environment. He manifested the attributes the historian Richard Immerman considers of critical importance for strategists: inquisitiveness and an eagerness to learn both in order to acquire knowledge and to develop one's mind, the ability to communicate ideas coherently, to think critically, and to tolerate ambiguity.[26] Immerman adds that in addition to these attributes that produce "a muscular mind," there is the importance of intellectual courage— "a willingness to make a decision in the face of conflicting evidence . . . and to do so even if it means reversing an initial judgment."[27] This form of thinking, broadly and conceptually, is the foundation of strategic thinking, the essence of strategic mastery. This is not to suggest that Komer was flawless. He was not an even-tempered person, but he was certainly cognizant of his less endearing traits. Most importantly, he did not hold grudges but was generous and gracious even with those who opposed his ideas or disliked him personally. However, his difficult personality is an indicator of another of Komer's attributes—passion.[28] Mastery of an art requires dedication, demands persistent discipline, and compels emotional investment.

The making of strategy is ultimately an art. The master of the strategic art integrates knowledge and originality and abandons orthodoxy in the face of convention to perceive differently, to think creatively, to seek innovation, and to remain open to new ideas. Making strategy requires asking fundamental and sometimes difficult questions about the political objectives being sought, the cost of pursuing such ends, the limits of national power, the nation's political will and the acceptability of the ends to be achieved and the means applied, and the very nature of whether the intended strategy "overlooks points of difference and exaggerates points of likeness between the past and the future."[29]

Taking such a stance and asking such questions require boldness and courage, for in seeking artistry, because of the risks and the degree of difficulty involved, there is a substantial likelihood of experiencing failure.[30] The Cold War era represented such a challenging strategic environment, one in which Robert Komer practiced the strategic art.

NOTES

INTRODUCTION

1. Robert Komer, Larry Berman, and Moya Ann Ball, "Lyndon Johnson's War" (panel discussion, moderated by Douglas Brinkley), in *Vietnam 1954–1965 Conference,* sponsored by the U.S. Naval Institute and McCormick Tribune Foundation (Elkridge, MD: A.V.E.R. Associates, 1996), CD 1, conference recording 05.

2. Ibid.

3. Ibid.

4. McGeorge Bundy, foreword to *Maritime Security or Coalition Defense?* by Robert W. Komer (Cambridge, MA: Abt Books, 1984), x.

5. Andrew McFadzean, "Interviews with Robert Bowie: The Use of Oral Testimony in Writing the Biography of Professor Robert Richardson Bowie, Washington Policy Planner and Harvard University Professor," *Oral History Review* 26, no. 2 (Summer/Fall 1999): 30.

6. Paul Kennedy, "History from the Middle: The Case of the Second World War," *Journal of Military History* 74, no. 1 (January 2010): 38.

7. Tim Weiner, "Robert Komer, 78, Figure in Vietnam, Dies," *New York Times,* April 12, 2000; Robert W. Komer, *Blowtorch,* unpublished manuscript (6th draft), n.d., i. Made available to the author by Dr. James A. Thomson, president and CEO, RAND Corporation, Santa Monica, CA. See also "The Guam Gambit," *National Review,* April 4, 1967, 334; and Stewart Alsop, "Vietnam: The President's Next Big Decision," *Saturday Evening Post,* March 25, 1967, 26.

8. See as an example, David Halberstam, *The Best and the Brightest* (New York: Random House, 1972), 632, 648.

9. John Prados, *The Blood Road: The Ho Chi Minh Trail and the Vietnam War* (New York: Wiley, 1998), 375. Prados argues that Walt Rostow, President Lyndon Johnson's national security adviser, was an exception. See also David Milne, *America's Rasputin: Walt Rostow and the Vietnam War* (New York: Hill and Wang, 2008), 11.

10. Michael Dobbs, "Cool Crisis Management? It's a Myth. Ask JFK," *Washington Post,* June 22, 2008.

11. John R. Galvin, "What's the Matter with Being a Strategist?" *Parameters* 19 (March 1989): 83–84.

12. Carnes Lord, *The Presidency and the Management of National Security* (New York: Free Press, 1988), 88; Meena Bose, *Shaping and Signaling Presidential Policy: The National Security Decision Making of Eisenhower and Kennedy* (College Station: Texas A&M University Press, 1998), 54; Erwin C. Hargrove, *Jimmy Carter as President: Leadership and the Politics of the Public Good* (Baton Rouge: Louisiana State University Press, 1988), 153.

13. Colin S. Gray, *Strategic Studies: A Critical Assessment,* Contributions in Political Science, Number 70 (Westport, CT: Greenwood Press, 1982), 79.

14. Louise Fitzsimmons, *The Kennedy Doctrine* (New York: Random House, 1972), 10.

15. Bernard Brodie, "General André Beaufré on Strategy: A Review of Two Books," RAND Paper P-3157 (Santa Monica, CA: RAND Corporation, June 1965), 2–3.

16. Colin Gray, "The Strategist as Hero," *Joint Force Quarterly,* no. 63 (3rd Quarter 2011): 37.

17. Richard A. Chilcoat, *Strategic Art: The New Discipline for 21st Century Leaders* (Carlisle, PA: Strategic Studies Institute, U.S. Army War College, 1995), 2, 3, 6.

18. Ibid., 7–8; Harry R. Yarger, *Strategy and the National Security Professional* (Westport, CT: Praeger Security International, 2008), 14.

CHAPTER 1. A MAN OF PROPER AMBITION

1. Joseph Burkholder Smith, *Portrait of a Cold Warrior* (New York: G. P. Putnam's Sons, 1976), 78–79.

2. Ray S. Cline, *The CIA under Reagan, Bush, and Casey* (Washington, DC: Acropolis Books, 1981), 145.

3. Smith, *Portrait of a Cold Warrior,* 78–79.

4. Ibid.

5. Federal Bureau of Investigation, Security Clearance Investigation Files, re: Robert W. Komer, obtained by the author under the Freedom of Information Act, request no. 1066206–000. Hereafter cited as "FBI File."

6. City of Clayton, Missouri, "History," http://www.claytonmo.gov/Resident/History.htm.

7. Ark Garment Company (Lockwoven Co.), company profile, Manta, http://www.manta.com/c/mmc1q89/ark-grament-co.

8. T. S. Eliot, letter to Marquis Childs, quoted in *St. Louis Post Dispatch,* October 15, 1930.

9. Washington University in St. Louis, "Facts, History, and Traditions," http://www.wustl.edu/about/facts.

10. James G. Hershberg, *James B. Conant: Harvard to Hiroshima and the Making of the Nuclear Age* (New York: Alfred A. Knopf, 1993), 77.

11. Morton Keller and Phyllis Keller, *Making Harvard Modern: The Rise of America's University* (New York: Oxford University Press, 2001), 13–14.

12. Hershberg, *James B. Conant,* 80–81.

13. FBI File; and Robert W. Komer, CIA Official Personnel File, obtained by the author under the Freedom of Information Act, request no. 1066206–000. Hereafter cited as "CIA Personnel File."

14. Mary Dearborn, *Mailer: A Biography* (Boston: Houghton Mifflin, 2001), 23.

15. Komer, *Blowtorch,* chap. II, 1. Douglas Komer made this version of Komer's unpublished memoir available to the author. References to the memoir are designated in the following manner: chapter number using roman numerals and then the page number. Each chapter was numbered anew in subsequent revisions.

16. Robert W. Komer, "Civilian Strategists in the Great War: Lloyd George and Churchill and the Conduct of the War" (AB honors thesis, Harvard University, 1942), Harvard Archives, Cambridge, MA. Komer's thesis is uneven in its pagination because he eliminated sixty pages from the text to meet the length limitation.

17. Ibid.

18. Ibid.

19. Harvard Class of 1942, *Twenty-Fifth Anniversary Report* (Cambridge, MA: Harvard College, 1967), xiii.

20. FBI File; Komer, *Blowtorch,* chap. II, 2; Keller and Keller, *Making Harvard Modern,* 119.

21. Harvard Class of 1942, *Twenty-Fifth Anniversary Report,* 709. See also Robert W. Komer, interview by Joe P. Franz, January 30, 1979, Oral History Interview I, Lyndon Baines Johnson Library (LBJL), Austin, TX, 1.

22. Komer, *Blowtorch,* chap. II, 2.

23. Keller and Keller, *Making Harvard Modern,* 119–20; FBI File.

24. Komer, *Blowtorch,* chap. II, 2; FBI File.

25. Komer, *Blowtorch,* chap. II, 2.

26. Ibid.; Stetson Conn, *Historical Work in the United States Army 1862–1954* (Washington, DC: U.S. Army Center of Military History, 1980), 87–88.

27. I. C. B. Dear, ed., *The Oxford Companion to World War II* (Oxford, UK: Oxford University Press, 1995), 45.

28. Ibid., 45–46.

29. Ibid., 46.

30. Carlo D'Este, *World War II in the Mediterranean, 1942–1945* (Chapel Hill, NC: Algonquin Books, 1990), 139.

31. Ibid., 149, 150.
32. Ibid., 150.
33. Carl von Clausewitz, quoted in Lloyd Clark, *Anzio: Italy and the Battle for Rome—1944* (New York: Atlantic Monthly Press, 2006), xvi.
34. Dear, *Oxford Companion to World War II,* 46.
35. Walter Slocombe, e-mail message to author, May 5, 2011.
36. Dear, *Oxford Companion to World War II,* 46.
37. Komer, *Blowtorch,* chap. II, 3–4; U.S. Army Center of Military History, *Anzio Beachhead, 22 January–25 May 1944* (1949; repr., Washington, DC: U.S. Army Center of Military History, 1990).
38. Komer, *Blowtorch,* chap. II, 6–10; FBI File.
39. Robert W. Komer, "The Establishment of Allied Control in Italy," *Military Affairs* 13, no. 1 (Spring 1949): 20–28.
40. Komer, *Blowtorch,* chap. II, 11; Robert W. Komer, foreword to *Civil Affairs and Military Government in the Mediterranean Theater* (Washington, DC: Office of the Chief of Military History, n.d.), iii.
41. Robert W. Komer, Application for Federal Employment; and Judson Lightsey, letter to Robert W. Komer, March 12, 1947, both in CIA Personnel File; Harvard Class of 1942, *Twenty-Fifth Anniversary Report,* 709.
42. John Ranelagh, *The Agency: The Rise and Decline of the CIA* (New York: Simon & Schuster, 1986), 102–3; William Colby and Peter Forbath, *Honorable Men: My Life in the CIA* (New York: Simon & Schuster, 1978), 68; Nathan Miller, *Spying for America: The Hidden History of U.S. Intelligence* (New York: Paragon House, 1989), 308.
43. Komer, Application for Federal Employment; and Lightsey, letter to Komer, March 12, 1947.
44. Robert W. Komer, letters to James R. May, April 14, 1947, and May 16, 1947; Andrew R. Van Esso, letter to Robert W. Komer, July 15, 1947, all in CIA Personnel File.
45. Appointment telegram, October 1, 1947; and Robert W. Komer, telegram to CIA, October 3, 1947, both in CIA Personnel File.
46. Komer, *Blowtorch,* chap. III, 2.
47. Ranelagh, *Agency,* 729.
48. Harold P. Ford, "A Tribute to Sherman Kent," in *Sherman Kent and the Board of National Estimates,* ed. Donald P. Steury (Washington, DC: Center for the Study of Intelligence, Central Intelligence Agency, 1994), 4–5; Trevor Barnes, "The Secret Cold War: The CIA and American Foreign Policy in Europe, 1946–1956, Part II," *Historical Journal* 25, no. 3 (September 1982): 649.
49. John Patrick Quirk, David Atlee Phillips, Ray Cline, and Walter Pforzheimer, *The Central Intelligence Agency, A Photographic History*

(Guilford, CT: Foreign Intelligence Press, 1986), 101–3; Miller, *Spying for America,* 321; Harold P. Ford, *Estimative Intelligence* (Lanham, MD: University Press of America, 1993), 61–63; Sherman Kent, "The Law and Custom of the National Intelligence Estimate," in *Sherman Kent and the Board of National Estimates,* 46–47; Arthur B. Darling, *The Central Intelligence Agency: An Instrument of Government to 1950* (University Park: Pennsylvania State University Press, 1990), 419; Jack Davis, "The Kent-Kendall Debate of 1949," *Studies in Intelligence* 35, no. 2 (Summer 1991): 38; Godfrey Hodgson, "Yale—A Great Nursery of Spooks," *New York Times,* August 16, 1987.

50. Kent, "National Intelligence Estimate," 521.

51. Robin W. Winks, *Cloak and Gown* (New York: William Morrow, 1987), 72.

52. Ibid., 73; Miller, *Spying for America,* 243; Jack Davis, "Sherman Kent and the Profession of Intelligence Analysis," *Sherman Kent Center for Intelligence Analysis: Occasional Papers* 1, no. 5 (November 2002): 3–4; Sherman Kent, "The First Year of the Office of National Estimates: The Directorship of William L. Langer," in *Sherman Kent and the Board of National Estimates,* 143–44.

53. David F. Rudgers, *Creating the Secret State: The Origins of the Central Intelligence Agency, 1943–1945* (Lawrence: University Press of Kansas, 2000), 12–13.

54. Robin W. Winks, *Cloak and Gown* (New York: William Morrow, 1987), 81; Miller, *Spying for America,* 243; Cline, *CIA under Reagan,* 133; William L. Langer, *In and Out of the Ivory Tower* (New York: Neale Watson Academic Publications, 1977), 218–19, 220.

55. Komer, *Blowtorch,* chap. III, 2; Ralph E. Weber, *Spymasters: Ten CIA Officers in Their Own Words* (Wilmington, DE: SE Books, 1999), 180; Russell Jack Smith, *The Unknown CIA: My Three Decades with the Agency* (Washington, DC: Pergamon-Brassey's International Defense Publishers, 1989), 53.

56. Kent, "National Intelligence Estimate," 58; Weber, *Spymasters,* 180; Cline, *CIA under Reagan,* 142.

57. Anne Karalekas, *History of the Central Intelligence Agency* (Laguna Hills, CA: Aegean Park Press, 1977), 18.

58. Miller, *Spying for America,* 323; Winks, *Cloak and Gown,* 73.

59. Ranelagh, *Agency,* 196.

60. Smith, *Unknown CIA,* 158.

61. Davis, "Sherman Kent," 2–3; Donald P. Steury, introduction to *Sherman Kent and the Board of National Estimates,* x.

62. Davis, "Sherman Kent," 2–5; Ford, "Tribute to Sherman Kent," 3; Harold M. Greenberg, "Intelligence of the Past; Intelligence for the Future," in

Strategic Intelligence, vol. 1, *Understanding the Hidden Side of Government,* ed. Loch K. Johnson (Westport, CT: Praeger Security International, 2007), 170.

63. Steury, introduction, x–xi, xiii, xvi, xix; Sherman Kent, *Strategic Intelligence for American World Policy* (Princeton, NJ: Princeton University Press, 1949), xii, 3–4, 8, 39.

64. Kent, *Strategic Intelligence,* 40–41, 49, 56, 58–59.

65. Ibid., 60.

66. Ibid., 64.

67. Omar Bradley, letter to Charles Cabell, April 12, 1954, CIA Personnel File.

68. Komer, *Blowtorch,* chap. III, 3–6; CIA Personnel File.

69. Smith, *Unknown CIA,* 121.

70. Ibid., 57.

71. Komer, *Blowtorch,* chap. III, 3; Orders for Active Duty for Training, March 25, 1955; E. T. Wooldridge, letter to Robert W. Komer, March 26, 1956, both in CIA Personnel File.

72. Komer, *Blowtorch,* chap. III, 7.

73. National War College, *Academic Year 1956–1957 Course* (Washington, DC: Fort Lesley J. McNair, 1956).

74. Komer, *Blowtorch,* chap. III, 7–10; E. T. Wooldridge, letter to Allen Dulles, June 24, 1957, CIA Personnel File.

75. Komer, *Blowtorch,* chap. III, 10; CIA Personnel File.

76. Komer, *Blowtorch,* chap. III, 11; Lord, *Presidency and the Management of National Security,* 70.

77. Robert Cutler, "The Development of the National Security Council," *Foreign Affairs* 34, no. 3 (April 1956): 443–44.

78. Robert W. Komer, interview by Dennis J. O'Brian, December 22, 1969, Fifth Oral History Interview, John F. Kennedy Library (JFKL), Boston, MA, 3, 14.

79. Robert W. Komer, interview by Elizabeth Farmer, October 31, 1964, Fourth Oral History Interview, JFKL, 18–19.

80. CIA Personnel File.

81. Komer, *Blowtorch,* chap. III, 11; CIA Personnel File; Komer, Fifth Oral History Interview, JFKL, 40.

82. CIA Personnel File.

83. Ibid., 14.

84. Robert W. Komer, memorandum to McGeorge Bundy, January 13, 1961, Box 321, National Security Files/Meetings and Memoranda/Staff Memoranda/Komer, JFKL.

85. Ibid.

86. Ibid.

87. Komer, Fourth Oral History Interview, JFKL, 19; Komer, Fifth Oral History Interview, JFKL, 4; Komer, *Blowtorch,* chap. III, 14.

88. Burton Hersh, *The Old Boys: The American Elite and the Origins of the CIA* (New York: Charles Scribner's Sons, 1992); Winks, *Cloak and Gown,* 38–39, 446; Rhodri Jeffreys-Jones, "The Socio-Educational Composition of the CIA Elite: A Statistical Note," *Journal of American Studies* 19, no. 3 (1985): 421–24.

89. Harvard Class of 1942, *Twenty-Fifth Anniversary Report,* 708–9.

90. Jeremi Suri, "Henry Kissinger, the American Dream, and the Jewish Immigrant Experience in the Cold War," *Diplomatic History* 31, no. 2 (November 2008): 722.

91. Harvard Class of 1942, *Twenty-Fifth Anniversary Report,* 709.

92. McGeorge Bundy once described Komer as "a man of great energy and proper ambition." See Bundy, "Bob Komer's Future," memorandum to Lyndon B. Johnson, March 15, 1965, item #0240120030, Virtual Vietnam Archive, Texas Tech University, http://www.vietnam.ttu.edu/virtualarchive/items.php?item=0240120030.

CHAPTER 2. PRAGMATIC NEW FRONTIERSMAN

1. David Milne situates this meeting two weeks before Kennedy's inauguration. He cites a memorandum from Komer to Bundy. See Milne, *America's Rasputin,* 87. However, Komer states that the meeting occurred after the inauguration. See Komer, Fourth Oral History Interview, JFKL, 18–19. See also David Wise, "Scholars of the Nuclear Age," in *The Kennedy Circle,* ed. Lester Tanzer (Washington, DC: Robert B. Luce, 1961), 37.

2. Komer, Fourth Oral History Interview, JFKL, 18–19; Komer, Fifth Oral History Interview, JFKL, 2.

3. Komer, Fourth Oral History Interview, JFKL, 18–19; Komer, Fifth Oral History Interview, JFKL, 14.

4. Kai Bird, *The Color of Truth: McGeorge Bundy and William Bundy, Brothers in Arms: A Biography* (New York: Simon & Schuster, 1998), 186–87; Komer, Fourth Oral History Interview, JFKL, 8–9; Komer, *Blowtorch,* chap. IV, 1; Ivo H. Daalder and I. M. Destler, *In the Shadow of the Oval Office: Profiles of the National Security Advisers and the Presidents They Served—From JFK to George W. Bush* (New York: Simon & Schuster, 2009), 18; Robert W. Komer, memorandum to McGeorge Bundy, January 13, 1961, Box 321, National Security Files/Meetings and Memoranda/Staff Memoranda/Robert Komer (M&M/SM/Komer), JFKL. An annotation appears near Komer's signature block from William Bundy to his brother: "This is the man I mentioned."

5. Komer, CIA Personnel File; Komer, *Blowtorch,* chap. IV, 1; Gerald S. Strober and Deborah H. Strober, *"Let Us Begin Anew": An Oral History of the Kennedy Presidency* (New York: HarperCollins, 1993), 154.

6. Milne, *America's Rasputin,* 81; Walt W. Rostow, *The Diffusion of Power: An Essay in Recent History* (New York: Macmillan, 1972), 168.

7. Komer, Fifth Oral History Interview, JFKL, 1–2, 6.

8. Ibid., 45–47.

9. Helen Fuller, *Year of Trial: Kennedy's Crucial Decisions* (New York: Harcourt, Brace & World, 1962), 45, 63.

10. Ibid.; Hugh Sidey, *John F. Kennedy, President* (New York: Atheneum, 1964),19.

11. John J. Mearsheimer, Review of *Promise and Power: The Life and Times of Robert McNamara,* by Deborah Shapley, *Bulletin of Atomic Scientists* 49, no. 6 (July/August 1993).

12. McGeorge Bundy, quoted in I. M. Destler, "National Security Management: What Presidents Have Wrought," *Political Science Quarterly* 95, no. 4 (Winter 1980–81): 578. See also I. M. Destler, "National Security II: The Rise of the Assistant (1961–1981)," in *The Illusion of Presidential Government,* ed. Hugh Heclo and Lester M. Salamon (Boulder, CO: Westview Press, 1981), 267.

13. John F. Kennedy, *The Strategy of Peace,* ed. Allen Nevins (New York: Popular Library, 1960), quoted in Fuller, *Year of Trial,* 192.

14. Charles E. Walcott and Karen M. Hult, *Governing the White House: From Hoover through LBJ* (Lawrence: University Press of Kansas, 1995), 161.

15. Arthur Schlesinger Jr., "Effective National Security Advising: A Most Dubious Precedent," *Political Science Quarterly* 113, no. 3 (Fall 2000): 347; Arthur Schlesinger Jr., "A Biographer's Perspective," in *The Kennedy Presidency,* ed. Kenneth W. Thompson (Lanham, MD: University Press of America, 1985), 22; Ivo Daalder and I. M. Destler, "In the Shadow of the Oval Office: The Next National Security Adviser," *Foreign Affairs* 88, no. 1 (January/February 2009): 114; Bose, *Shaping and Signaling Presidential Policy,* 54.

16. Fitzsimmons, *Kennedy Doctrine,* 16–17.

17. James Reston, *Sketches in the Sand* (New York: Knopf, 1967), 477, quoted in Fitzsimmons, *Kennedy Doctrine,* 17.

18. Harris Wofford, *Of Kennedys and Kings: Making Sense of the Sixties* (Pittsburgh, PA: University of Pittsburgh Press, 1992), 355–56.

19. U. Alexis Johnson, Oral History, JFKL, quoted in Fitzsimmons, *Kennedy Doctrine,* 17.

20. Harlan Cleveland, quoted in Wofford, *Of Kennedys and Kings,* 356.

21. David Milne, "A Hawk among Hawks," *Vietnam,* August 2007, 59; David Halberstam, "The Very Expensive Education of McGeorge Bundy,"

Harper's, July 1969, 28; Bruce Miroff, *Pragmatic Illusions: The Presidential Politics of John F. Kennedy* (New York: David McKay, 1976), 5; Bruce Kuklick, *Blind Oracles: Intellectuals and War from Kennan to Kissinger* (Princeton, NJ: Princeton University Press, 2006), 1–2.

22. Charles Maechling Jr., "Camelot, Robert Kennedy, and Counterinsurgency—A Memoir," *The Virginia Quarterly Review* 75, no. 3 (Summer 1999): 439.

23. Rostow, *Diffusion of Power,* 494.

24. Stephen Peter Rosen, "Vietnam and the American Theory of Limited War," *International Security* 7, no. 2 (Autumn 1982): 99. For a contrary view, see David Milne, "Hawk among Hawks," 56.

25. Hans J. Morgenthau, *Truth and Power: Essays of a Decade, 1960–70* (New York: Praeger Publishers, 1970), 141–44.

26. Komer, "Notes for Tuesday Planning Luncheon," memorandum to McGeorge Bundy, March 6, 1961, Box 321, M&M/SM/Komer, JFKL. For a different interpretation, see Bose, *Shaping and Signaling,* 55–56. However, in this case, Komer is discussing the need for the new administration to review ("crash reviews") current policy as part of an assessment of the Eisenhower administration's basic national security policy. He also believes such reviews are "desirable as a useful underpinning."

27. David Milne, "America's Intellectual Diplomacy," *International Affairs* 86, no. 1 (2010): 65; Kenneth W. Thompson, "Kennedy's Foreign Policy: Activism versus Pragmatism," in *John F. Kennedy: The Promise Revisited,* ed. Paul Harper and Joann P. Kreig (New York: Greenwood Press, 1988), 25–33; John C. Donovan, *The Cold Warriors: A Policy-Making Elite* (Lexington, MA: D. C. Heath, 1974), 175; Theodore C. Sorensen, "Kennedy: Retrospect and Prospect," in *The Kennedy Presidency,* ed. Kenneth W. Thompson (Lanham, MD: University Press of America, 1985), 296.

28. Godfrey Hodgson, "The Establishment," *Foreign Policy,* no. 10 (Spring 1973): 10–11; Anthony Hartley, "John Kennedy's Foreign Policy," *Foreign Policy,* no. 4 (Fall 1971): 78, 83; Rostow, *Diffusion of Power,* 605, 607–8; Kuklick, *Blind Oracles,* 146–47.

29. Walt W. Rostow, quoted in Richard J. Barnet, *Roots of War* (New York: Atheneum, 1972), 19.

30. David Milne, "Obama's Foreign Policy Picks," *Los Angeles Times,* November 7, 2008.

31. Max Millikan and Walt W. Rostow, "Notes on Foreign Economic Policy," May 21, 1954, in *Universities and Empire: Money and Politics in the Social Sciences during the Cold War,* ed. Christopher Simpson (New York: New Press, 1998), 41, quoted in Nick Cullather, "Modernization Theory," in *Explaining the History of American Foreign Relations,* 2nd ed., ed. Michael

J. Hogan and Thomas G. Paterson (New York: Cambridge University Press, 2004), 217.

32. Cullather, "Modernization Theory," 217.

33. Dennis Merrill, "Walt Whitman Rostow," in *Encyclopedia of U.S. Foreign Relations,* ed. Bruce W. Jentleson and Thomas G. Paterson (New York: Oxford University Press, 1997), 4:34.

34. Walt W. Rostow, "The Great Transition: Tasks of the First and Second Post-War Generation" (speech, University of Leeds, England, 1967), quoted in Barnet, *Roots of War,* 75.

35. Robert W. Komer, quoted in Gabriel Kolko, *Confronting the Third World: United States Foreign Policy, 1945–1980* (New York: Pantheon Books, 1988), 134. See also Robert W. Komer, memorandum to John F. Kennedy, October 13, 1962, *Foreign Relations of the United States* (*FRUS*), *1961–1963,* vol. 21, *Africa* (Washington, DC: USGPO), 102–4, as an example in which Komer discusses the use of aid to further relations with Algeria under Ahmed Ben Bella, only a few weeks after the U.S. government formally recognized the government of the Republic of Algeria. Komer's advocacy ultimately resulted in Kennedy signing National Security Action Memorandum No. 221, U.S. Policy toward Algeria, which Komer drafted.

36. Arthur Schlesinger Jr., "Some Lessons from the Cold War," in *The End of the Cold War: Its Meaning and Implications,* ed. Michael J. Hogan (New York: Cambridge University Press, 1992), 60–61.

37. Andrew Preston, *The War Council: McGeorge Bundy, the NSC, and Vietnam* (Cambridge, MA: Harvard University Press, 2006), 12–14, 23–25. See also Robert D. Dean, *Imperial Brotherhood: Gender and the Making of Cold War Foreign Policy* (Amherst: University of Massachusetts Press, 2001), 10–13.

38. Kuklick, *Blind Oracles,* 135–36; H. W. Brands Jr., *Cold Warriors: Eisenhower's Generation and American Foreign Policy* (New York: Columbia University Press, 1988), 4.

39. McGeorge Bundy, quoted in William MacKaye, "Bundy in the White House," *Saturday Evening Post,* March 10, 1962, 84.

40. Barnet, *Roots of War,* 60–61.

41. See, for example, Bird, *Color of Truth,* 306–7. The Viet Cong attack on a small U.S. military post at Pleiku, Republic of Vietnam, during Bundy's 1965 visit elicited a deeply emotional response, according to eyewitnesses, and confirmed Bundy's belief that a reprisal against North Vietnam was justifiable. U.S. Army general William C. Westmoreland, who commanded U.S. Military Assistance Command, Vietnam (MACV), believed that Bundy suffered from "field marshal psychosis" when he recommended retaliation in response to the attack.

42. Preston, *War Council,* 26.

43. Stanley Hoffman, quoted in Bird, *Color of Truth,* 150.

44. Preston, *War Council,* 25–35.

45. George F. Kennan, *American Diplomacy, 1900–1950* (New York: Mentor Books, 1951), 82–89.

46. Komer, *Maritime Security or Coalition Defense?* xi.

47. Eugen Weber, "Nationalism, Socialism, and National Socialism," in *My France: Politics, Culture, Myth* (Cambridge, MA: Belknap Press of the Harvard University Press, 1991), 262.

48. Jon Meacham, "How Will He Govern? Watch the First Day," *Washington Post,* January 18, 2008.

49. Denise M. Bostdorff and Steven R. Goldzwig, "Idealism and Pragmatism in American Foreign Policy Rhetoric: The Case of John F. Kennedy and Vietnam," *Presidential Studies Quarterly* 24, no. 3 (Summer 1994): 515–30; Cecil V. Crabb Jr., *The American Approach to Foreign Policy: A Pragmatic Perspective* (Lanham, MD: University Press of America, 1985), xv.

50. Douglas Brinkley, "Dean Gooderham Acheson," in *Encyclopedia of U.S. Foreign Relations,* 1:3.

51. David S. McLellan, "The 'Operational Code' Approach to the Study of Political Leaders: Dean Acheson's Philosophical and Instrumental Beliefs," *Canadian Journal of Political Science* 4, no. 1 (March 1971): 60. See also Werner Levi, "Ideology, Interests, and Foreign Policy," *International Studies Quarterly* 14, no. 1 (March 1970): 8.

52. Andrew McFadzean, "The Bigger Picture: Biography and/or History? Robert Bowie," *Australasian Journal of American Studies* 22, no. 2 (December 2002): 53.

53. Ibid.

54. Robert W. Komer, "Factors Bearing on U.S. Policies and Plans for the Middle East" (lecture, National War College, Washington, DC, May 18, 1964). Document was declassified by the Department of Defense at the author's request.

55. Henry Kissinger, *Diplomacy* (New York: Simon & Schuster, 1994), 103–4, 125; Henry Kissinger, "Reflections on a Partnership: British and American Attitudes to Postwar Foreign Policy," *International Affairs* 58, no. 4 (Autumn 1982): 572, 584.

56. Hidemi Suganami, "Narrative Explanation and International Relations: Back to Basics," *Millennium—Journal of International Studies* 37, no. 2 (2008): 349; Richard Ned Lebow, *The Tragic Vision of Politics: Ethics, Interests, and Orders* (New York: Cambridge University Press, 2003), 361.

57. Suganami, "Narrative Explanation," 349; Lebow, *Tragic Vision of Politics,* 361.

58. Walter Lippmann, "The Rivalry of Nations," *Atlantic Monthly,* February 1958; Cecil V. Crabb Jr., *Policy-Makers and Critics: Conflicting Theories of American Foreign Policy,* 2nd ed. (New York: Praeger, 1986), 113.

59. Greenberg, "Intelligence of the Past," 173.

60. My thanks to Dr. Janeen Klinger for this point.

61. Jonathan Wright, "George Frost Kennan and the Study of American Foreign Policy: Some Critical Comments," *Western Political Quarterly* 20, no. 1 (March 1967): 157.

62. Edward Mead Earle, "American Military Policy and National Security," *Political Science Quarterly* 53, no. 1 (March 1938): 6.

63. Komer, "Factors Bearing on U.S. Policies and Plans for the Middle East."

64. Donald E. Nuechterlein, *America Recommitted: United States National Interests in a Restructured World* (Lexington: University Press of Kentucky, 1991), 1, 17–18, 55–63; Donald Nuechterlein, "National Interests and Foreign Policy Formulation" (lecture, Naval Air Executive Seminar on National Security, University of Virginia, Charlottesville, VA, November 7, 2000), http://donaldnuechterlein.com/2000/major.html.

65. John F. Kennedy, Inaugural Address, January 20, 1961, http://www.jfk library.org/Research/Ready-Reference/JFK-Quotations/Inaugural-Address. aspx.

66. John Lewis Gaddis, *Strategies of Containment: A Critical Appraisal of Postwar American National Security Policy* (New York: Oxford University Press, 1982), 203, 205.

67. Lebow, *Tragic Vision of Politics,* 318.

68. Naomi Bailin Wish, "Foreign Policy Makers and Their National Role Conceptions," *International Studies Quarterly* 24, no. 4 (December 1980): 546, 548–49.

69. Levi, "Ideology, Interests, and Foreign Policy," 5.

70. Crabb, *Policy-Makers and Critics,* 113–14; Bernard Brodie, *War and Politics* (New York: Macmillan, 1973), 342–44; Nuechterlein, "National Interests and Foreign Policy Formulation"; Donald E. Nuechterlein, *United States Interests in a Changing World* (Lexington: University Press of Kentucky, 1973), 110–11; Donald E. Nuechterlein, "U.S. National Interests and Policies in the Middle East" (lecture, Military Officers' Association of America, Charlottesville, VA, March 24, 2011), http://donaldnuechterlein .com/2011/2011.03.lecture.html; Levi, "Ideology, Interests, and Foreign Policy," 2.

71. Henry Fairlie, *The Kennedy Promise: The Politics of Expectation* (Garden City, NY: Doubleday, 1973), 289; Donovan, *Cold Warriors,* 14, 19, 184–85, 220–24; Thomas G. Paterson, "Introduction: John F. Kennedy's Quest for Victory and Global Crisis," in *Kennedy's Quest for Victory: American*

Foreign Policy, 1961–1963 (New York: Oxford University Press, 1989), 7–8. See also Michael R. Beschloss, "A Tale of Two Presidents," *Wilson Quarterly* 88, no. 1 (Winter 2000): 67, regarding Kennedy's proclivity for crisis management instead of grand design.

72. Komer, "Factors Bearing on U.S. Policies and Plans for the Middle East."

73. Ibid.

74. Komer, "Timing of Basic Policy Review," memorandum to McGeorge Bundy, April 11, 1961, Box 321, M&M/SM/Komer, JFKL. The February 28, 1961, memorandum calling for such a review was attached to this memorandum.

75. "Key National Security Problems," February 10, 1961 (introduction by Robert Johnson with attached list developed by Komer), Box 303, Policy Planning/General, JFKL; Komer, "Where Do We Go from Here?" memorandum to McGeorge Bundy, Box 321, M&M/SM/Komer, JFKL.

76. Miroff, *Pragmatic Illusions,* 37; Kennedy, *Strategy of Peace,* 65.

77. Notes from Planning Group meeting, March 14, 1961, Box 321, M&M/SM/Komer, JFKL.

78. Robert W. Komer, "Weathering the Storm," memorandum to McGeorge Bundy and Walt Rostow, March 28, 1961; Notes from Planning Group meeting, March 28, 1961, both in Box 321, M&M/SM/Komer, JFKL.

79. Robert W. Komer, "Getting the Worst of Both Worlds," memorandum to McGeorge Bundy and Walt Rostow, April 21, 1961, Box 321, M&M/SM/Komer, JFKL.

80. Kennedy, *Strategy of Peace,* 66–68.

81. Robert Komer, interview by Elizabeth Farmer, September 3, 1964, Third Oral History Interview, JFKL, 5–8; Paul F. Gardner, *Shared Hopes, Separate Fears: Fifty Years of U.S.-Indonesian Relations* (Boulder, CO: Westview Press, 1997), 87–88, 91; Arthur M. Schlesinger Jr., *A Thousand Days: John F. Kennedy in the White House* (Boston: Houghton Mifflin, 1965), 533.

82. Robert W. Komer, "Why Trusteeship Won't Work," February 17, 1961, Box 423A, National Security Files/Robert W. Komer (NSF/Komer), JFKL; Komer, Third Oral History Interview, 5–8; Schlesinger, *Thousand Days,* 533; Timo Kivimaki, *US-Indonesian Hegemonic Bargaining: Strength of Weakness* (Aldershot, UK: Ashgate Publishing, 2003), 134.

83. Robert W. Komer, "Need for Movement on West Irian," memorandum to Walt W. Rostow, November 30, 1961, Box 423A, NSF/Komer, JFKL.

84. Robert W. Komer, memorandum to McGeorge Bundy [and Walt W. Rostow], March 27, 1961, *FRUS, 1961–1963,* vol. 23, *Southeast Asia* (Washington, DC: USGPO, 1994), 333.

85. Komer, "Why Trusteeship Won't Work"; Komer, Third Oral History Interview, 5–8.

86. Gardner, *Shared Hopes,* 172–73.

87. Robert W. Komer, memorandum to Walt W. Rostow, April 5, 1961, Box 423A, NSF/Komer, JFKL.

88. Komer, "Need for Movement on West Irian."

89. Robert W. Komer, memorandum to John F. Kennedy, September 11, 1961, Box 423A, NSF/Komer, JFKL.

90. Howard Palfrey Jones, *Indonesia: The Possible Dream* (New York: Harcourt Brace Jovanovich, 1971), 200–201; Gardner, *Shared Hopes,* 174.

91. Komer, "Why Trusteeship Won't Work"; Robert W. Komer, "First Principles on West Irian," memorandum to Walt W. Rostow, April 19, 1961, Box 423A, NSF/Komer, JFKL; Robert W. Komer, memorandum to John F. Kennedy, September 11, 1961, Box 423A, NSF/Komer, JFKL; Robert W. Komer, memorandum to McGeorge Bundy, December 29, 1961, Box 423A, NSF/Komer, JFKL; Robert W. Komer, memorandum to Carl Kaysen, February 2, 1962, *FRUS, 1961–1963,* 23:512–13.

92. John Prados, *Keepers of the Keys: A History of the National Security Council from Truman to Bush* (New York: William Morrow, 1991), 119.

93. Robert W. Komer, quoted in Howard B. Schaffer, *Ellsworth Bunker: Global Troubleshooter, Vietnam Hawk* (Chapel Hill: University of North Carolina Press, 2003), 97.

94. Prados, *Keepers of the Keys,* 119; Schaffer, *Ellsworth Bunker,* 94–98, 101–2, 103; Jones, *Indonesia,* 210; Gardner, *Shared Hopes,* 178. See also David Webster, "Regimes in Motion: The Kennedy Administration and Indonesia's New Frontier, 1960–1962," *Diplomatic History* 33, no. 1 (January 2009): 95–123.

95. Robert W. Komer, memorandum to John F. Kennedy, February 28, 1962, Box 423A, NSF/Komer, JFKL; Schlesinger, *Thousand Days,* 534; Robert W. Komer, "Next Steps on WNG [West New Guinea]," memorandum to McGeorge Bundy, March 3, 1962, Box 423A, NSF/Komer, JFKL; Robert W. Komer, "Where Next on WNG?" memorandum to McGeorge Bundy, March 28, 1962, Box 423A, NSF/Komer, JFKL; Robert W. Komer, memorandum to McGeorge Bundy, May 12, 1962, Box 423A, NSF/Komer, JFKL; Robert W. Komer, memorandum to McGeorge Bundy, July 26, 1962, Box 423A, NSF/Komer, JFKL; Robert W. Komer, memorandum to John F. Kennedy, September 11, 1962, Box 423A, NSF/Komer, JFKL; Schaffer, *Ellsworth Bunker,* 101–3; Jones, *Indonesia,* 210; Gardner, *Shared Hopes,* 178,

96. Schaffer, *Ellsworth Bunker,* 96.

97. Jones, *Indonesia,* 294.

98. Walt W. Rostow, *View from the Seventh Floor* (New York: Harper & Row, 1964), 8–9, 21, 152.

99. Robert W. Komer, memorandum to McGeorge Bundy and Carl Kaysen, December 20, 1961, Box 424, NSF/Komer/Iran, JFKL.

100. "Current Intelligence Weekly Review," January 26, 1961, *FRUS, 1961–1963,* vol. 5, *Soviet Union* (Washington, DC: USGPO, 1998), 39–46; Milne, *America's Rasputin,* 75; Maechling, "Camelot, Robert Kennedy, and Counterinsurgency," 438.

101. Douglas S. Blaufarb, *The Counterinsurgency Era: U.S. Doctrine and Performance* (New York: Free Press, 1977), 52–54; Schlesinger, *Thousand Days,* 340.

102. Schlesinger, *Thousand Days,* 274.

103. Barnet, *Roots of War,* 75; James C. Thomson Jr., "How Could Vietnam Happen? An Autopsy," *Atlantic Monthly,* April 1968, 48.

104. Kuklick, *Blind Oracles,* 149–50.

105. Robert W. Komer, "Forestalling a Crisis in South Vietnam," memorandum to Walt W. Rostow, February 1, 1961, Box 447, NSF/Komer, JFKL.

106. Robert W. Komer, memorandum to Walt W. Rostow, June 14, 1961, Box 414, NSF/Komer/Guerrilla Warfare, JFKL; David Milne, "'Our Equivalent of Guerrilla Warfare': Walt Rostow and the Bombing of North Vietnam, 1961–1968," *Journal of Military History* 71, no. 1 (January 2007): 177; Walt W. Rostow, "Guerrilla Warfare in Underdeveloped Areas," in *The Viet-Nam Reader,* ed. Marcus G. Raskin and Bernard Fall (New York: Vintage Books, 1967), 108–16.

107. Robert W. Komer, memorandum to Walt W. Rostow, July 18, 1961, Box 414, NSF/Komer, JFKL; Rober W. Komer, "Are We Pushing Hard Enough in South Vietnam," memorandum to Walt W. Rostow, July 20, 1961, Box 447, NSF/Komer, JFKL.

108. Maxwell D. Taylor, *Swords and Plowshares* (New York: W. W. Norton, 1972), 197, 200.

109. Robert W. Komer, memorandum to Walt W. Rostow, May 4, 1961, Box 413, NSF/Komer, JFKL; Robert W. Komer, "The Guerrilla Warfare Problem," memorandum to Maxwell D. Taylor, Box 414, NSF/Komer, JFKL.

110. Ibid.

111. Robert W. Komer, "Next Steps in Counter-Guerrilla Exercise," memorandum to Walt W. Rostow, August 11, 1961, Box 414, NSF/Komer, JFKL.

112. Robert W. Komer, "Counter-Guerrilla Task Force Recommendations," memorandum to Walt W. Rostow, December 5, 1961, Box 414, NSF/Komer, JFKL; Counter-Guerrilla Task Force, "Elements of U.S. Strategy to Deal with 'Wars of National Liberation,'" December 8, 1961, Box 414, NSF/Komer, JFKL; Blaufarb, *Counterinsurgency Era,* 67.

113. Taylor, *Swords and Plowshares,* 201.

114. "Establishment of the Special Group (Counter-Insurgency)," National Security Action Memorandum No. 124, January 18, 1962, http://www.jfk library.org/Asset-Viewer/qJbe3E_H7kmxvtbyzSb8pw.aspx.

115. Robert W. Komer, "Cut Backs in Police Programs Overseas," memorandum to McGeorge Bundy and Maxwell D. Taylor, January 31, 1962, Box 413, NSF/Komer, JFKL; Robert W. Komer, memorandum to McGeorge Bundy, February 7, 1962, Box 413, NSF/Komer, JFKL.

116. "Support of Local Police Forces for Internal Security and Counter-Insurgency Purposes," National Security Action Memorandum No. 132, February 19, 1962, http://www.jfklibrary.org/Asset-Viewer/DxdAHc3Pb U6yjrGG3FFjZA.aspx; Komer, Third Oral History Interview, 11.

117. "Office of Public Safety Established in USAID," AID General Notice, November 1, 1962, Box 413, NSF/Komer, JFKL.

118. Robert Amory Jr., interview by Joseph E. O'Connor, February 17, 1966, Second Oral History Interview, JFKL, 25.

119. CIA Personnel File; Harvard Class of 1942, *Twenty-Fifth Anniversary Report,* 709; "Obituary: Geraldine Peplin Komer," *Washington Post,* February 21, 1996.

120. Komer, Oral History Interview I, LBJL, 16.

121. Arthur Schlesinger Jr., private communication to the author, April 1, 2005; Schlesinger, *Thousand Days,* 877, 879.

122. Phillips Talbot, interview by Dennis J. O'Brien, August 13, 1970, Second Oral History Interview, JFKL, 10–11.

123. Lucian Pugliaresi and Diane T. Berliner, "Policy Analysis at the Department of State: The Policy Planning Staff," *Journal of Policy Analysis and Management* 8, no. 3 (Summer 1989): 387.

124. Robert W. Komer, "Thoughts on Staff Organization," memorandum to Walt W. Rostow, May 1, 1961, Box 438, NSF/Komer/National Security Council Staff, JFKL. See also Preston, *War Council,* 46–47. For an assessment of Kennedy's collegial advisory system, its features, and its costs, see Alexander L. George, *Presidential Decisionmaking in Foreign Policy: The Effective Use of Information and Advice* (Boulder, CO: Westview Press, 1980), 157–58, 165.

125. Preston, *War Council,* 43.

126. Robert W. Komer, First Oral History Interview, June 18, 1964, JFKL, 4.

127. Robert W. Komer, quoted in Gaddis, *Strategies of Containment,* 241.

128. Robert Benjamin Rakove, "A Genuine Departure: Kennedy, Johnson, and the Nonaligned World" (PhD diss., University of Virginia, 2008), 73–75; Abraham Ben-Zvi, *Lyndon B. Johnson and the Politics of Arms Sales to Israel: In the Shadow of the Hawk* (Portland, OR: Frank Cass, 2004), 8; Robert W. Komer, memorandum to John F. Kennedy, January 19, 1963, *FRUS,*

1961–1963, vol. 8, *National Security Policy* (Washington, DC: USGPO, 1996), 456–57.

129. Robert W. Komer, "Hands Off the 'Neutral Conference,'" memorandum to McGeorge Bundy and Walt W. Rostow, June 21, 1961; Robert W. Komer, memorandum to Walt W. Rostow, June 30, 1961, both in Box 321, M&M/SM/Komer, JFKL.

130. Robert W. Komer, memorandum to McGeorge Bundy, January 16, 1963, *FRUS, 1961–1963*, 23:657.

131. Robert W. Komer, memorandum to McGeorge Bundy and Walt W. Rostow, March 10, 1961, Box 321, M&M/SM/Komer, JFKL. See also "Record of the 508th Meeting of the National Security Council," January 23, 1963, *FRUS, 1961–1963*, 8:460, for Kennedy's support of Komer's strategy based on a policy of engaging with the "neutralists."

CHAPTER 3. KOMER'S WAR

1. Youssef Aboul-Enein, "The Egyptian-Yemen War (1962–1967): Egyptian Perspectives on Guerrilla Warfare," *Infantry*, January/February 2004, 20; "Imam Ahmad of Yemen Is Dead; Son, Who Seeks Reforms, Rules," *New York Times*, September 20, 1962.

2. "Imam Ahmad of Yemen Is Dead."

3. Aboul-Enein, "Egyptian-Yemen War," 3; Robert Stookey, *Yemen: The Politics of the Yemen Arab Republic* (Boulder, CO: Westview Press, 1978), 226–27.

4. "Imam Ahmad of Yemen Is Dead."

5. Ibid.

6. "Imam of Yemen Reported Slain in Coup after a Week on Throne," *New York Times*, September 28, 1962; Stookey, *Yemen*, 229; Wilfred Thesiger, *The Last Nomad* (New York: E. P. Dutton, 1980), 270.

7. Joseph Churba, "Arabia Felix," *Air University Review* 20, no. 5 (July/August 1969), http://www.airpower.maxwell.af.mil/airchronicles/aureview/1969/jul-aug/churba.html.

8. Robert Komer, interview by Elizabeth Farmer, July 16, 1964, Second Oral History Interview, JFKL, 1.

9. Ethan Nadelmann, "Setting the Stage: American Policy toward the Middle East, 1961–1966," *International Journal of Middle East Studies* 14, no. 4 (November 1982): 437; April R. Summitt, *John F. Kennedy and U.S.-Middle East Relations: A History of American Foreign Policy in the 1960s* (Lewiston, NY: Edward Mellen Press, 2008), 28, 62.

10. Summitt, *Kennedy and U.S. Middle East Relations*, 62n151.

11. Komer, "Factors Bearing on U.S. Policies and Plans for the Middle East."

12. Seymour M. Hersh, *The Samson Option: Israel's Nuclear Arsenal and American Foreign Policy* (New York: Random House, 1991), 99.

13. See Mordechai Gazit's remarks in Strober and Strober, *"Let Us Begin Anew,"* 229.

14. Komer, "Factors Bearing on U.S. Policies and Plans for the Middle East." See also Komer, Fifth Oral History Interview, JFKL; and "Memorandum for the Record," November 21, 1963, *FRUS, 1961–1963,* vol. 18, *Near East, 1962–1963* (Washington, DC: USGPO, 1995), 797–801.

15. Komer, "Factors Bearing on U.S. Policies and Plans for the Middle East." See also Robert W. Komer, memorandum to John F. Kennedy, January 19, 1963, *FRUS, 1961–1963,* vol. 8, *National Security Policy* (Washington, DC: USGPO, 1996), 456–57; and W. Taylor Fain, *American Ascendance and British Retreat in the Persian Gulf Region* (New York: Palgrave Macmillan, 2008), 113.

16. Ben-Zvi, *Lyndon B. Johnson,* 6–7.

17. For a comprehensive discussion of the tests for strategy, see J. Boone Bartholomees Jr., "A Survey of the Theory of Strategy," in *The U.S. Army War College Guide to National Security Issues,* vol. 1, *Theory of War and Strategy,* 5th ed., ed. J. Boone Bartholomees Jr. (Carlisle, PA: Strategic Studies Institute, U.S. Army War College, 2012), 16–17.

18. Komer, "Factors Bearing on U.S. Policies and Plans for the Middle East." See also Komer, Fifth Oral History Interview, JFKL; and "Memorandum for the Record, November 21, 1963, *FRUS, 1961–1963,* 18:797–801.

19. Komer, "Factors Bearing on U.S. Policies and Plans for the Middle East."

20. Robert W. Komer, memorandum to Walt W. Rostow, June 30, 1961, *FRUS, 1961–1963,* vol. 17, *Near East, 1961–1962* (Washington, DC: USGPO, 1994), 173.

21. Robert W. Komer, quoted in Fain, *American Ascendance,* 113.

22. Robert W. Komer, note to McGeorge Bundy, December 8, 1961, Box 445, NSF/Komer/UAR, JFKL.

23. Robert W. Komer, "A Shift in Policy toward Nasser," memorandum to John F. Kennedy, December 8, 1961, Box 445, NSF/Komer/UAR, JFKL.

24. Ibid.

25. Ibid.

26. Robert W. Komer, "Aid to the UAR," memorandum to John F. Kennedy, February 15, 1962, Box 445, NSF/Komer/UAR, JFKL.

27. Robert W. Komer, "What Would US Get Out of Approach to Nasser?" memorandum to John F. Kennedy, January 23, 1962, Box 445, NSF/Komer/UAR, JFKL.

28. Robert W. Komer, "Presidential Meeting on Nasser Problem," memorandum to McGeorge Bundy, January 29, 1962, Box 445, NSF/Komer/UAR, JFKL.

29. Komer, "Aid to the UAR."

30. Robert W. Komer, memorandum to John F. Kennedy, February 20, 1962; Robert W. Komer, memorandum to McGeorge Bundy, February 20, 1962, both in Box 445, NSF/Komer/UAR, JFKL.

31. Robert W. Komer, "Next Steps in UAR Policy," memorandum to McGeorge Bundy, April 7, 1962, Box 445, NSF/Komer/UAR, JFKL.

32. Robert W. Komer, memorandum to John F. Kennedy, May 28, 1962, Box 445, NSF/Komer/UAR, JFKL.

33. Robert W. Komer, memorandum to McGeorge Bundy, July 12, 1962, Box 445, NSF/Komer/UAR, JFKL.

34. Warren Bass, *Support Any Friend: Kennedy's Middle East and the Making of the U.S.-Israel Alliance* (New York: Oxford University Press, 2003), 161.

35. Schlesinger, *Thousand Days,* 566.

36. Komer, *Blowtorch,* chap. I, 4. See also Douglas Little, "The New Frontier on the Nile: JFK, Nasser, and Arab Nationalism," *Journal of American History* 75, no. 2 (September 1988): 510.

37. Sandra Mackay, *The Saudis* (Boston: Houghton Mifflin, 1987), 298.

38. Anthony Nutting, *Nasser* (New York: E. P. Dutton, 1972), 321–22; Aboul-Enein, "Egyptian-Yemen War," 21; Fawaz A. Gerges, "The Kennedy Administration and the Egyptian-Saudi Conflict in Yemen: Co-opting Arab Nationalism," *Middle East Journal* 49, no. 2 (Spring 1995): 298–99.

39. Stookey, *Yemen,* 231; Aboul-Enein, "Egyptian-Yemen War," 21.

40. Mackay, *Saudis,* 299; Aboul-Enein, "Egyptian-Yemen War," 20–21, 23; Tim Mackintosh-Smith, *Yemen: The Unknown Arabia* (Woodstock, NY: Overlook Press, 2000), 109.

41. Robert W. Komer, memorandum to John F. Kennedy, October 18, 1962, Box 447, NSF/Komer/Yemen, JFKL.

42. Harold Macmillan, *At the End of the Day, 1961–1963* (New York: Harper & Row, 1973), 268.

43. Nigel Fisher, *Harold Macmillan* (New York: St. Martin's Press, 1982), 285; Macmillan, *At the End of the Day,* 263–64.

44. Robert McNamara, "Britain, Nasser and the Outbreak of the Six Day War," *Journal of Contemporary History* 35, no. 4 (October 2000): 619.

45. Komer, *Blowtorch,* chap. I, 2–3; Komer, Second Oral History Interview, JFKL, 13. See also Edward Weintel and Charles Bartlett, *Facing the Brink: An Intimate Study of Crisis Diplomacy* (New York: Charles Scribner's Sons, 1967), 44.

46. Robert W. Komer, memorandum to John F. Kennedy, October 5, 1962, Box 447, NSF/Komer/Yemen, JFKL.

47. Komer, Second Oral History Interview, JFKL, 14; Robert W. Komer, memorandum to John F. Kennedy, October 4, 1962, *FRUS, 1961–1963,*

18:158–59; "President's Talk with Crown Prince Faysal," memorandum of conversation, *FRUS, 1961–1963,* 18:162–67.

48. Macmillan, *At the End of the Day,* 267–68.

49. Aboul-Enein, "Egyptian-Yemen War," 23.

50. Robert W. Komer, memorandum to Phillips Talbot, October 12, 1962, *FRUS, 1961–1963,* 18:177–78.

51. Paper by the Officer in Charge of Arabian Peninsula Affairs (Seelye), October 17, 1962, *FRUS, 1961–1963,* 18:182–83; Robert W. Komer, memorandum to John F. Kennedy, October 18, 1962, Box 447, NSF/ Komer/Yemen, JFKL.

52. Komer, Second Oral History Interview, JFKL, 16; Department of State, telegram to the Embassy in Saudi Arabia, *FRUS, 1961–1963,* 18:198–99.

53. Robert W. Komer, memorandum to John F. Kennedy, November 5, 1962, Box 447, NSF/Komer/Yemen, JFKL.

54. Robert W. Komer, memorandum to McGeorge Bundy, November 12, 1962; Talking Points for Macmillan Call, November 14, 1962, both in Box 447, NSF/Komer/Yemen, JFKL.

55. Alistair Horne, *Harold Macmillan,* vol. 2, *1957–1966* (New York: Viking, 1986), 420.

56. Komer, *Blowtorch,* chap. I, 4.

57. Ibid., 4–6.

58. Ibid., 6–7; Komer, Second Oral History Interview, JFKL, 17.

59. Robert W. Komer, memorandum to John F. Kennedy, November 21, 1962, Box 447, NSF/Komer/Yemen, JFKL.

60. Robert W. Komer, memorandum to John F. Kennedy, November 28, 1962; Robert W. Komer, memorandum to John F. Kennedy, December 3, 1962; Robert W. Komer, memorandum to McGeorge Bundy, December 18, 1962, all in Box 447, NSF/Komer/Yemen, JFKL.

61. Dana Adams Schmidt, "U.S. Yemen Policy Stirring Middle East," *New York Times,* December 24, 1962.

62. Talbot, Second Oral History Interview, JFKL, 39–41; Christopher J. McMullen, *Resolution of the Yemen Crisis, 1963: A Case Study in Mediation* (Washington, DC: Institute for the Study of Diplomacy, Georgetown University, 1980), 3.

63. Robert W. Komer, memorandum to McGeorge Bundy, December 31, 1962, Box 447, NSF/Komer/Yemen, JFKL.

64. Weintal and Bartlett, *Facing the Brink,* 42–43.

65. Dana Adams Schmidt, *Yemen: The Unknown War* (New York: Holt, Rinehart, and Winston, 1968), 193.

66. "Presidential Meeting on Yemen," memorandum for record, February 25, 1963, Box 447, NSF/Komer/Yemen, JFKL; "Decisions Taken at President's

Meeting on Yemen Crisis, 25 February 1963," National Security Action Memorandum No. 227, February 27, 1963, 366–67.

67. Macmillan, *At the End of the Day,* 275–76; Department of State, telegram to the Embassy in the United Kingdom, February 12, 1963, *FRUS, 1961–1963,* 18:346–47.

68. Editorial Note, *FRUS, 1961–1963,* 18:392–93.

69. McMullen, *Resolution of the Yemen Crisis,* 10.

70. Weintal and Bartlett, *Facing the Brink,* 45; Schmidt, "U.S. Yemen Policy Stirring Middle East," 3; McMullen, *Resolution of the Yemen Crisis,* 13.

71. John F. Kennedy, letter to Faisal ibn Abd-al-Aziz Al Saud, March 2, 1963, Box 447, NSF/Komer/Yemen, JFKL.

72. Robert W. Komer, memorandum to John F. Kennedy, March 11, 1963, Box 447, NSF/Komer/Yemen, JFKL.

73. "President's Meeting on Yemen," memorandum for the record, March 11, 1963, NSF/Komer/Yemen, JFKL.

74. Komer, Third Oral History Interview, 1–2.

75. Ibid., 2.

76. Weintal and Bartlett, *Facing the Brink,* 51.

77. Robert W. Komer, memorandum to McGeorge Bundy, May 1, 1963, Box 448, NSF/Komer/Yemen, JFKL.

78. McMullen, *Resolution of the Yemen Crisis,* 47; Robert W. Komer, memorandum to John F. Kennedy, June 7, 1963, Box 448, NSF/Komer/Yemen, JFKL.

79. Macmillan, *At the End of the Day,* 277; Weintal and Bartlett, *Facing the Brink,* 51; Saeed M. Badeeb, *The Saudi-Egyptian Conflict over North Yemen, 1962–1970* (Boulder, CO: Westview Press, 1986), 79.

80. Memorandum for the record, July 3, 1963, Box 443, NSF/Komer/Saudi Arabia, JFKL.

81. Robert W. Komer, memorandum to John F. Kennedy, July 12, 1963, *FRUS, 1961–1963,* 18:641–42.

82. Department of State, telegram to the Embassy in the United Arab Republic, July 23, 1963, *FRUS, 1961–1963,* 17:656–58.

83. Robert W. Komer, memorandum to John F. Kennedy, August 9, 1963, *FRUS, 1961–1963,* 18:670; Robert W. Komer, memorandum to John F. Kennedy, August 16, 1963, *FRUS, 1961–1963,* 18:680; Department of State, telegram to the Embassy in the United Arab Republic, *FRUS, 1961–1963,* 18:682–84; Department of State, telegram to the Embassy in Saudi Arabia, August 26, 1963, *FRUS, 1961–1963,* 18:688–91.

84. Robert W. Komer, "The Next Round in Yemen," note to McGeorge Bundy with attached paper, September 20, 1963, Box 448, NSF/Komer/Yemen, JFKL.

85. Robert W. Komer, memorandum to John F. Kennedy, October 7, 1963, Box 448, NSF/Komer/Yemen, JFKL.

86. "Yemen Disengagement," National Security Action Memorandum No. 262, October 10, 1963, *FRUS, 1961–1963,* 18:729–30.

87. Robert W. Komer, memorandum to McGeorge Bundy, October 19, 1963, *FRUS, 1961–1963,* 18:747–48.

88. Department of State, telegram to the Embassy in Saudi Arabia, October 19, 1963, *FRUS, 1961–1963,* 18:750–51.

89. Ibid., 752–53.

90. United Nations, "Yemen-UNYOM: Background," http://www.un.org/Depts/dpko/dpko/co_mission/unyombackgr.html.

91. Schlesinger, *Thousand Days,* 566–67.

92. Komer, *Blowtorch,* chap. I, 12; Komer, Third Oral History Interview, JFKL, 5; Department of State Executive Secretary, "The Next Stage in the US-UAR Relationship," memorandum to McGeorge Bundy, September 6, 1963, *FRUS, 1961–1963,* 18:695–97; Dean Rusk and Phillips Talbot, memorandum of telephone conversation, November 13, 1963, *FRUS, 1961–1963,* 18:776.

93. Gerges, "Kennedy Administration," 310–11; Douglas Little, "From Even-Handed to Empty-Handed: Seeking Order in the Middle East," in *Kennedy's Quest for Victory: American Foreign Policy, 1961–1963,* ed. Thomas G. Paterson (New York: Oxford University Press, 1989), 169, 177.

94. Gerges, "Kennedy Administration," 310–11; Summitt, *Kennedy and U.S. Middle East Relations,* 221–22; Little, "New Frontier on the Nile," 525, 526.

95. Talbot, Second Oral History Interview, JFKL, 10–11.

CHAPTER 4. "OUR INDIA ENTERPRISE"

1. John Kenneth Galbraith, *Ambassador's Journal: A Personal Account of the Kennedy Years* (Boston: Houghton Mifflin, 1969), 378–86.

2. Peter Jackson, "Massive Chinese Attack Routs Border Indians," *Washington Post,* October 21, 1962; Michael T. Malloy, "Red Chinese Drive Back Indian Units," *Washington Post,* October 22, 1962; Henry S. Bradsher, "Nehru Calls for All-Out Resistance," *Washington Post,* October 23, 1962; Michael T. Malloy, "India Calls a National Emergency," *Washington Post,* October 27, 1962; and Shashi Tharoor, *Nehru: The Invention of India* (New York: Arcade Publishing, 2003), 211.

3. "U.S. Registers Shock over Chinese Assault," *New York Times,* October 22, 1962.

4. Theodore C. Sorensen, *Kennedy* (New York: Harper & Row, 1965), 665.

5. Robert W. Komer, quoted in M. Srinivas Chary, *The Eagle and the Peacock: U.S. Foreign Policy toward India since Independence* (Westport, CT: Greenwood Press, 1995), 120.

6. Richard Parker, *John Kenneth Galbraith: His Life, His Politics, His Economics* (New York: Farrar, Straus, and Giroux, 2005), 351.

7. Dennis Kux, *India and the United States: Estranged Democracies* (Washington, DC: National Defense University Press, 1993), 195, 224n120.

8. Ibid., 183.

9. Komer, Third Oral History Interview, JFKL, 13; Komer, *Blowtorch,* chap. VI, 1–2; Komer, Oral History Interview I, LBJL, 7–8.

10. Komer, *Blowtorch,* chap. VI, 2; Talbot, Second Oral History Interview, JFKL, 2–4; Galbraith, *Ambassador's Journal,* 158.

11. Galbraith, *Ambassador's Journal,* 158–59, 501. See Kux, *Estranged Democracies,* 224n120.

12. Robert W. Komer, memorandum to McGeorge Bundy, January 6, 1962, *FRUS, 1961–1963,* vol. 19, *South Asia* (Washington, DC: USGPO, 1996), 179–81.

13. Robert W. Komer, "South Asia Issues Decided at Meeting with President, January 11, 1962," memorandum to McGeorge Bundy, January 12, 1962, *FRUS, 1961–1963,* 19:190–91; "Courtesy Call on the President by Ambassador Nehru," memorandum of conversation, February 28, 1962, *FRUS, 1961–1963,* 19:213–15.

14. Department of State, telegram to the Embassy in India, January 31, 1962, *FRUS, 1961–1963,* 19:211–12; Komer, "South Asia Issues Decided at Meeting with President"; Walter K. Anderson, "U.S.-Indian Relations, 1961–1963: Good Intentions and Uncertain Results," in *The Hope and the Reality: U.S.-Indian Relations from Roosevelt to Reagan,* ed. Harold A. Gould and Sumit Ganguly (Boulder, CO: Westview Press, 1992), 70.

15. M. J. Akbar, *Nehru: The Making of India* (New York: Viking, 1988), 559; Macmillan, *At the End of the Day,* 227–28; Galbraith, *Ambassador's Journal,* 372–82; Tharoor, *Nehru,* 211.

16. Neville Maxwell, *India's China War* (New York: Columbia University Press, 1970), 357–58.

17. Sorensen, *Kennedy,* 663.

18. Michael Brecher, "Non-Alignment under Stress: The West and the India-China Border War," *Pacific Affairs* 52, no. 4 (Winter 1979–80): 615; John Kenneth Galbraith, *Letters to Kennedy,* ed. James Goodman (Cambridge, MA: Harvard University Press, 1998), 114; Ralph J. Retzlaff, "India: A Year of Stability and Change," *Asian Survey* 3, no. 2 (February 1963): 98.

19. Department of State, telegram to the Embassy in India, October 25, 1962, *FRUS, 1961–1963,* 19:352–53; Embassy in India, telegram to the

Department of State, October 29, 1962, *FRUS, 1961–1963,* 19:361; Carl Kaysen, memorandum to John F. Kennedy, November 3, 1962, *FRUS, 1961–1963,* 19:363; Editorial Note, *FRUS, 1961–1963,* 19:384.

20. Robert W. Komer, memorandum to Phillips Talbot, October 24, 1962, Box 420, NSF/Komer/India, JFKL; Alastair Lamb, *The Kashmir Problem* (New York: Frederick A. Praeger, 1968), 101.

21. Schlesinger, *Thousand Days,* 531.

22. Akbar, *Nehru,* 560–61.

23. Editorial Note, *FRUS, 1961–1963,* 19:384.

24. Robert W. Komer, memorandum to Carl Kaysen, November 16, 1962, Box 420, NSF/Komer/India, JFKL.

25. Robert W. Komer, memorandum to Carl Kaysen, November 2, 1962, Box 420, NSF/Komer/India, JFKL; Robert W. Komer, memorandum to McGeorge Bundy, November 5, 1963, Box 420, NSF/Komer/India, JFKL.

26. Robert W. Komer, memorandum to Phillips Talbot, November 9, 1962, Box 420, NSF/Komer/India, JFKL.

27. "Presidential Meeting on Sino-India Conflict," memorandum for the record, November 19, 1962, *FRUS, 1961–1963,* 19:394–96; Roger Hilsman, *To Move a Nation: The Politics of Foreign Policy in the Administration of John F. Kennedy* (Garden City, NY: Doubleday, 1967), 327, 329–30.

28. Chester Bowles, *Promises to Keep: My Life in Public Service, 1941–1969* (New York: Harper & Row, 1971), 474; Galbraith, *Ambassador's Journal,* 423–26; Komer, Fourth Oral History Interview, JFKL, 5–6; Robert W. Komer, memorandum to McGeorge Bundy, November 13, 1962; Robert W. Komer, memorandum to Phillips Talbot, draft cable attached, November 27, 1962; Robert W. Komer, memorandum to McGeorge Bundy, November 27, 1962; Robert W. Komer, memorandum to McGeorge Bundy, November 29, 1962; Robert W. Komer, memorandum to John F. Kennedy, November 30, 1962, all in Box 420, NSF/Komer/India, JFKL; Galbraith, *Letters to Kennedy,* 115–18.

29. Robert W. Komer, memorandum to McGeorge Bundy, November 24, 1962, Box 420, NSF/Komer/India, JFKL.

30. Robert W. Komer, memorandum to McGeorge Bundy, November 29, 1962, Box 420, NSF/Komer/India, JFKL.

31. Robert W. Komer, memorandum to John F. Kennedy, November 12, 1962, Box 420, NSF/Komer/India, JFKL.

32. Robert W. Komer, memorandum to Carl Kaysen, November 20, 1962, Box 420, NSF/Komer/India, JFKL.

33. Tharoor, *Nehru,* 212; Stephen P. Cohen, "India's China War and After: A Review Article," *Journal of Asian Studies* 30, no. 4 (August 1971): 854–55.

34. Robert W. Komer, Fourth Oral History Interview, JFKL, 17–18; Galbraith, *Ambassador's Journal,* 439; Embassy in India, telegram to the Department of State, November 30, 1962, *FRUS, 1961–1963,* 19:417.

35. Department of State, telegram to the Embassy in India, December 8, 1962, *FRUS, 1961–1963,* 19:428; Sorensen, *Kennedy,* 665.

36. Joint Chiefs of Staff, "Air Defense for India," memorandum to Robert McNamara, December 14, 1962, *FRUS, 1961–1963,* 19:443–44.

37. Robert W. Komer, memorandum to McGeorge Bundy and Carl Kaysen, December 12, 1962, Box 420, NSF/Komer/India, JFKL; Galbraith, *Letters to Kennedy,* 118–21.

38. Robert W. Komer, memorandum to John F. Kennedy, December 16, 1962, Box 420, NSF/Komer/India, JFKL.

39. Robert W. Komer, draft memorandum to McGeorge Bundy, December 7, 1962, Box 420, NSF/Komer/India; Robert W. Komer, memorandum to McGeorge Bundy, January 7, 1963, Box 421, NSF/Komer/India, JFKL.

40. Robert W. Komer, draft memorandum to McGeorge Bundy, December 7, 1962, Box 420, NSF/Komer/India; Robert W. Komer, memorandum to McGeorge Bundy, January 7, 1963, Box 421, NSF/Komer/India, JFKL.

41. Robert W. Komer, draft memorandum to McGeorge Bundy, December 7, 1962, Box 420, NSF/Komer/India, JFKL; Robert W. Komer, memorandum to McGeorge Bundy, January 7, 1963, Box 421, NSF/Komer/India, JFKL.

42. Robert W. Komer, letter to John Kenneth Galbraith, January 18, 1963, Box 421, NSF/Komer/India, JFKL.

43. Robert W. Komer, memorandum to John F. Kennedy, January 12, 1963, *FRUS, 1961–1963,* 19:468–70; Robert W. Komer, memorandum to John F. Kennedy, February 16, 1963, *FRUS, 1961–1963,* 19:494–97; Galbraith, *Letters to Kennedy,* 121–23.

44. John F. Kennedy, "President's News Conference," February 21, 1963, *American Presidency Project,* ed. Gerhard Peters and John T. Woolley, http://www.presidency.ucsb.edu/ws/index.php?pid=9573.

45. Bowles, *Promises to Keep,* 439, 473.

46. Pakistani Ambassador (Ahmed), letter to Dean Rusk, February 18, 1963, *FRUS, 1961–1963,* 19:502–3.

47. Robert W. Komer, memorandum to John F. Kennedy, March 23, 1963, *FRUS, 1961–1963,* 19:524–26. See also Komer, Third Oral History Interview, JFKL, 19.

48. Walt W. Rostow, memorandum to John F. Kennedy, April 8, 1963, *FRUS, 1961–1963,* 19:538–41.

49. Robert W. Komer, memorandum to John F. Kennedy, April 24, 1963, *FRUS, 1961–1963,* 19:553–54.

50. "President's Meeting on India," memorandum for the record, April 25, 1963, *FRUS, 1961–1963,* 19:561–65.

51. Ibid.

52. Robert W. Komer, memorandum to John F. Kennedy, May 8, 1963, doc. #CK3100305966, Declassified Documents Reference System, Farmington Hills, MI; Robert W. Komer, "Should We Stop Pushing Kashmir?" memorandum to John F. Kennedy, May 14, 1963, doc. #CK3100040345, Declassified Documents Reference System; Robert W. Komer, memorandum to John F. Kennedy, May 20, 1963, Box 419, NSF/Komer/India, JFKL.

53. Robert W. Komer, memorandum to McGeorge Bundy, May 7, 1963, Box 418, NSF/Komer/India, JFKL.

54. Robert W. Komer, letter to John Kenneth Galbraith, May 4, 1963, Box 418, NSF/Komer/India, JFKL; Robert W. Komer, memorandum to McGeorge Bundy, May 7, 1963, Box 418, NSF/Komer/India, JFKL.

55. "President's Meeting on India," memorandum for the record, May 17, 1963, *FRUS, 1961–1963,* 19:593–96.

56. Ibid; Komer, Fourth Oral History Interview, JFKL, 6.

57. Robert W. Komer, memorandum to John F. Kennedy, June 19, 1963, *FRUS, 1961–1963,* 19:614–15.

58. Komer, Fourth Oral History Interview, JFKL, 6; Embassy in Portugal, telegram to the Department of State, September 6, 1963, *FRUS, 1961–1963,* 19:675; Walter P. McConaughy, memorandum of conversation between Gen. Maxwell D. Taylor and President Mohammad Ayub Khan, December 20, 1963, *FRUS, 1961–1963,* 19:712; Robert W. Komer, memorandum to Averell Harriman, August 10, 1963, Box 421, NSF/Komer/India, JFKL.

59. Robert W. Komer, memorandum to McGeorge Bundy, September 6, 1963, Box 418, NSF/Komer/India, JFKL.

60. Robert McNamara, "Feasibility of Deployment of a Carrier Task Force in the Indian Ocean," memorandum to the chairman of the Joint Chiefs of Staff, August 6, 1963, *FRUS, 1961–1963,* 19:641; Robert W. Komer, memorandum to Averell Harriman, August 10, 1963, Box 421, NSF/Komer/India, JFKL.

61. Robert W. Komer, memorandum to John F. Kennedy, July 10, 1963, Box 422, NSF/Komer/India, JFKL; Robert W. Komer, memorandum to McGeorge Bundy, October 17, 1963, *FRUS, 1961–1963,* 19:681–83.

62. Howard B. Schaffer, *Chester Bowles: New Dealer in the Cold War* (Cambridge, MA: Harvard University Press, 1993), 246; Robert W. Komer, memorandum to John F. Kennedy, June 21, 1963, Box 418, NSF/Komer/India, JFKL.

63. Brecher, "Non-Alignment under Stress," 626.

64. Robert W. Komer, memorandum to McGeorge Bundy, July 16, 1963, Box 418, NSF/Komer/India, JFKL.

65. Robert W. Komer, memorandum to John F. Kennedy, November 12, 1963, *FRUS, 1961–1963,* 19:689–90.

66. Kux, *Estranged Democracies,* 215; Robert W. Komer, memorandum to McGeorge Bundy, October 5, 1963, Box 418, NSF/Komer/India, JFKL.

67. Margaret W. Fisher, "India in 1963: A Year of Travail," *Asian Survey* 4, no. 3 (March 1964): 740–41; Robert P. McMahon, *Cold War on the Periphery: The United States, India and Pakistan* (New York: Columbia University Press, 1994), 297; Schaffer, *Chester Bowles,* 245.

68. Robert W. Komer, memorandum to John F. Kennedy, November 12, 1963, *FRUS, 1961–1963,* 19:689–90; John F. Kennedy, "Special Message to the Congress on the Free World Defense and Assistance Programs," April 2, 1963, *American Presidency Project,* http://www.presidency.ucsb.edu/ws/index.php?pid=9136; John F. Kennedy, "President's News Conference," September 12, 1963, *American Presidency Project,* http://www.presidency.ucsb.edu/ws/index.php?pid=9405; Kux, *Estranged Democracies,* 210–11, 215–18; McMahon, *Cold War on the Periphery,* 297; Schaffer, *Chester Bowles,* 245; Steven A. Hoffman, *India and the China Crisis* (Berkeley: University of California Press, 1990), 224–30; Robert W. Komer, memorandum to McGeorge Bundy, October 5, 1963, Box 418, NSF/Komer/India, JFKL; Lamb, *Kashmir Problem,* 105.

69. Robert W. Komer, memorandum to William Bundy, November 14, 1963, *FRUS, 1961–1963,* 19:690–91.

70. McMahon, *Cold War on the Periphery,* 272–304; Robert P. McMahon, "Choosing Sides in South Asia," in *Kennedy's Quest for Victory,* 198–222; Satu P. Limaye, *U.S.-Indian Relations: The Pursuit of Accommodation* (Boulder, CO: Westview Press, 1993), 5–23; Chary, *Eagle and the Peacock,* 118–19.

71. McMahon, *Cold War on the Periphery,* 303–4.

72. Ibid., 275.

73. Robert W. Komer, memorandum to Phillips Talbot, October 24, 1962, Box 420, NSF/Komer/India, JFKL; Steven A. Hoffman, "Rethinking the Linkage between Tibet and the China-India Border Conflict: A Realist Approach," *Journal of Cold War Studies* 8, no. 3 (Summer 2006): 167.

74. Robert W. Komer, memorandum to Carl Kaysen, November 2, 1962, Box 420, NSF/Komer/India, JFKL.

75. Robert W. Komer, memorandum to McGeorge Bundy, October 5, 1963, Box 418, NSF/Komer/India, JFKL.

76. Stephen J. Blank, *Natural Allies? Regional Security in Asia and the Prospects for Indo-American Strategic Cooperation* (Carlisle, PA: Strategic Studies Institute, U.S. Army War College, 2005), 3. See Ashley J. Tellis, *India as*

a New Global Power: An Action Agenda for the United States (Washington, DC: Carnegie Endowment for International Peace, 2005), 9.

77. Tellis, *India as a New Global Power,* 9. See Amit Gupta, *The U.S.-India Relationship: Strategic Partnership or Complementary Interests?* (Carlisle, PA: Strategic Studies Institute, U.S. Army War College, 2005), v.

78. Limaye, *U.S.-Indian Relations,* 16–18; Chary, *Eagle and the Peacock,* 118; Gopal Krishna, "India and the International Order," in *The Expansion of International Society,* ed. Hedley Bull and Adam Watson (Oxford, UK: Clarendon Press, 1984), 276.

79. Kux, *Estranged Democracies,* 182; Anderson, "U.S.-India Relations," 66, 74–75, 78; Gupta, *U.S.-India Relationship,* 12.

80. Sorensen, *Kennedy,* 719.

81. Ibid., 717.

CHAPTER 5. PACIFICATION CZAR

1. Doris Kearns Goodwin, *Lyndon Johnson and the American Dream* (New York: St. Martin's Press, 1991), 247. Johnson's remarks were made in an interview with Goodwin.

2. For a description of the Johnson Oval Office and a press conference, see Jim Bishop, *A Day in the Life of President Johnson* (New York: Random House, 1967), 71, 103. The March 21, 1966, press conference is in the *Public Papers of the Presidents of the United States, Lyndon B. Johnson,* book I, *January 1 to June 30, 1966* (Washington, DC: USGPO, 1967), 343–51.

3. Robert Komer, *Organization and Management of the "New Model" Pacification Program—1966–1969* (Santa Monica, CA: RAND, 1970), 27.

4. John W. Macy Jr., memorandum for the record, March 18, 1966, Box 317, Robert W. Komer Personnel File, John W. Macy Files, LBJL.

5. Excerpt from Robert Komer's trial testimony, item #0251114002, Virtual Vietnam Archive, http://www.vietnam.ttu.edu/virtualarchive/items.php?item=0251114002. In the trial transcript, Komer provides his version of this conversation between Johnson and himself.

6. Emmette S. Redford and Richard T. McCulley, *White House Operations: The Johnson Presidency* (Austin: University of Texas Press, 1986), 13, 15, 100–101, 104–6.

7. Francis M. Bator, "No Good Choices: LBJ and the Vietnam/Great Society Connection" (Cambridge, MA: American Academy of Arts and Sciences, 2007), 3, http://www.amacad.org/publications/nogoodChoices.aspx.

8. Robert W. Komer, quoted in Merle Miller, *Lyndon: An Oral Biography* (New York: G. P. Putnam's Sons, 1980), 291–93. See also Komer, Oral History Interview I, LBJL, 3–9.

9. Komer, Oral History Interview I, LBJL, 16, 26, 46.

10. Ibid., 14–17; Komer, *Blowtorch,* chap. IX, 8–9.

11. Ronald Steel, *In Love with Night: The American Romance with Robert Kennedy* (New York: Simon & Schuster, 2000), 110.

12. Komer, Oral History Interview I, LBJL, 18–19: Robert W. Komer, interview by Joe P. Franz, August 18, 1970, Oral History Interview II, LBJL, 65.

13. Komer, First Oral History Interview, JFKL, 2.

14. Harold H. (Hal) Saunders (NSC staff member in the Kennedy and Johnson administrations), interview by author, October 18, 2007. See also Office of the Historian, *History of the National Security Council, 1947–1997* (Washington, DC: Bureau of Public Affairs, U.S. Department of State, 1997), http://www.fas.org/irp/offdocs/NSChistory.htm; Preston, *War Council,* 49–50; Daalder and Destler, *In the Shadow of the Oval Office,* 41–42; George C. Herring, *LBJ and Vietnam: A Different Kind of War* (Austin: University of Texas Press, 1994), 6–8, 13.

15. Francis M. Bator, "Lyndon Johnson and Foreign Policy: The Case of Western Europe and the Soviet Union," in *Presidential Judgment: Foreign Policy Decision Making in the White House,* ed. Aaron Lobel (Hollis, NH: Hollis Publishers, 2001), 63.

16. Francis M. Bator (deputy special assistant to the president for national security affairs in the Johnson administration), interview by the author, May 14, 2008.

17. Komer, Berman, and Ball, "Lyndon Johnson's War."

18. Rowland Evans and Robert Novick, *Lyndon B. Johnson: The Exercise of Power* (New York: New American Library, 1966), 329; Rowland Evans and Robert Novak, "Inside Report: Pacification Czar," *Washington Post,* April 29, 1967.

19. Robert Komer, interview by Neil Sheehan, April 10, 1968, Box 70, Neil Sheehan Papers, Library of Congress, Washington, DC.

20. McGeorge Bundy, quoted in Prados, *Keepers of the Keys,* 119.

21. Ibid.

22. Ibid., 158. See also Bundy, "Bob Komer's Future."

23. Prados, *Keepers of the Keys,* 157.

24. James C. Thomson Jr., "Ambassadorial Appointments," memorandum to John Macy, February 13, 1965; "List of Suggested Candidates for Ambassador to Pakistan," n.d., both in Box 17, Komer Personnel File, John W. Macy Files, LBJL.

25. Golda Meir, *My Life* (New York: G. P. Putnam's Sons, 1975), 313.

26. Milne, *America's Rasputin,* 161.

27. Komer, Oral History Interview I, 42–43.

28. Robert W. Komer, "Forestalling a Crisis in South Vietnam," February 1, 1961, Box 447, NSF/Komer/Vietnam, 1961–1963, JFKL.

29. Ibid.

30. Robert W. Komer, memorandum to Walt W. Rostow, April 28, 1961, Box 447, NSF/Komer/Vietnam, 1961–1963, JFKL.

31. Joint Chiefs of Staff, quoted in Gaddis, *Strategies of Containment,* 244.

32. Robert W. Komer, memorandum to McGeorge Bundy, October 31, 1961, quoted in Gaddis, *Strategies of Containment,* 244–45.

33. Preston, *War Council,* 72.

34. Robert W. Komer, memorandum to McGeorge Bundy, quoted in Milne, *America's Rasputin,* 135.

35. Rakove, "Genuine Departure," 471.

36. Preston, *War Council,* 217.

37. Thomson, "How Could Vietnam Happen?" 19. Thomson does not mention Komer by name, but the description fits only him. Thomson thought highly of Komer's judgment, and thus it is conceivable that Thomson would confide in him. Thomson also mentions that he was under "the friendly tutelage" of Komer early in his tenure on the NSC staff. See James C. Thomson, interview by Paige E. Mulhollan, July 22, 1971, Interview I, transcript, Oral History Collection, LBJL.

38. Robert W. Komer, quoted in Miller, *Lyndon,* 465; Richard A. Hunt, *Pacification: The American Struggle for Vietnam's Hearts and Minds* (Boulder, CO: Westview Press, 1995), 2–3.

39. U.S. Department of Defense, "Re-Emphasis on Pacification, 1965–1967," in *History of United States Decisionmaking in Vietnam,* ed. Senator Gravel (Boston: Beacon Press, 1971), 2:554; Hunt, *Pacification,* 3, 70.

40. Robert W. Komer, quoted in Miller, *Lyndon,* 465.

41. U.S. Department of Defense, "Re-Emphasis on Pacification," 2:539.

42. McGeorge Bundy, "Non-Military Organization for Vietnam—in Saigon and Washington," memorandum to Lyndon B. Johnson, February 16, 1966, *FRUS, 1964–1968,* vol. 4, *Vietnam, 1966* (Washington, DC: USGPO, 1998), 231–35; "Notes of Meeting with the President on Vietnam," February 26, 1966, *FRUS, 1964–1968,* 4:260–62; "Notes on Meeting," February 26, 1966, *FRUS, 1964–1968,* 4:263–66.

43. Robert W. Komer, memorandum to Lyndon B. Johnson, March 8, 1966, *FRUS, 1964–1968,* 4:274–76. The attachment to this memorandum is a memorandum from Chester Cooper to President Johnson.

44. Jack Valenti, *A Very Human President* (New York: W. W. Norton, 1975), 250–53.

45. Hunt, *Pacification,* 72.

46. Robert W. Komer, memorandum to Lyndon B. Johnson, March 2, 1966, *FRUS, 1964–1968,* vol. 33, *Organization and Management of Foreign Policy; United Nations* (Washington, DC: USGPO, 2004), 130–31.

47. Komer, *Organization and Management,* 27.

48. "Johnson Administration and Pacification in Vietnam: The Guide Introduction," Robert Komer–William Leonhart File, LBJL. http://www.cisupa.proquest.com/ksc_assets/catalog/3218_LBJPacificationVietnam.pdf

49. Komer, *Organization and Management,* 239.

50. Komer, Oral History Interview II, LBJL, 23.

51. "Appointment of Special Assistant to the President for Peaceful Construction in Vietnam," National Security Action Memorandum No. 343, March 28, 1966, LBJL, http://www.lbjlib.utexas.edu/johnson/archives.hom/nsams/nsam343.asp. McNamara also contributed language to the directive. See Robert W. Komer, memorandum to Robert McNamara, March 29, 1967, Box 5, NSF/Komer/Rostow, LBJL; and Department of Defense, "Evolution of the War—Re-emphasis on Pacification: 1965–1967," Part IV.C.8 in *U.S.-Vietnam Relations, 1945–1967,* 62, http://www.archives.gov/research/pentagon-papers/.

52. "Appointment of Special Assistant to the President."

53. Ibid.

54. Walter Guzzardi Jr., "Management of the War: A Tale of Two Capitals," *Fortune,* April 1967, 136.

55. Komer, *Organization and Management,* 29; Robert W. Komer, interview by Neil Sheehan, April 10, 1968, Box 70, Neil Sheehan Papers, Library of Congress, Washington, DC.

56. Robert B. Semple Jr., "3 Johnson Aides to Go to Vietnam," *New York Times,* March 23, 1966; Box 317, Komer Personnel Files, John W. Macy Files, LBJL.

57. Robert W. Komer, telegram to Lyndon B. Johnson, April 13, 1966, *FRUS, 1964–1968,* 4:120.

58. Robert W. Komer, "Report on Saigon Trip," memorandum to Lyndon B. Johnson, April 19, 1966, Box 9, NSF/Komer/First Trip Report [4/66], LBJL.

59. Robert W. Komer, Letter No. 3 to William Porter, April 15, 1966, Box 4, NSF/Komer/Porter-Komer Numbered Letters, LBJL. These letters are private, back-channel correspondence from Komer to Porter.

60. Robert W. Komer, Letter No. 5 to William Porter, April 27, 1966; Robert W. Komer, Letter No. 6 to William Porter, April 29, 1966; Robert W. Komer, Letter No. 7 to William Porter, May 5, 1966, all in Box 4, NSF/RWK/Porter-Komer Numbered Letters, LBJL.

61. Komer, Letter No. 6.

62. Robert W. Komer, telegram to Lyndon B. Johnson, May 9, 1966, *FRUS, 1964–1968,* 4:374–76; Komer, Letter No. 7.

63. "Summary Notes of the 557th Meeting of the National Security Council," May 10, 1966, *FRUS, 1964–1968,* 4:381–83.

64. Lyndon B. Johnson, "Remarks to Reporters at the Conclusion of a Security Council Meeting on Vietnam," May 10, 1966, American Presidency Project, http://www.presidency.ucsb.edu/ws/?pid=27587.

65. "Meeting with the President on Viet-Nam," memorandum for the record, May 16, 1966, *FRUS, 1964–1968,* 4:388–89; Hunt, *Pacification,* 73.

66. Department of State, telegram to the Embassy in Vietnam, May 19, 1966, *FRUS, 1964–1968,* 4:390–91.

67. Robert W. Komer, memorandum to Lyndon B. Johnson, May 24, 1966, *FRUS, 1964–1968,* 4:398; Robert W. Komer, "Moving the Vietnam Civil Side," memorandum to Lyndon B. Johnson, May 30, 1966, Box 6, NSF/Komer/General Maxwell Taylor, LBJL.

68. Komer, *Organization and Management,* 4–5; Komer, Oral History Interview II, LBJL, 21–22; Komer, interview by Paige E. Mulhollan, November 15, 1971, Oral History Interview III, LBJL, 31, 34.

69. William Leonhart, "Report on Visit to Vietnam: May 17–29, 1966," memorandum to Lyndon B. Johnson, May 30, 1966, *FRUS, 1964–1968,* 4:405–8.

70. Thomas W. Scoville, *Reorganizing for Pacification Support* (Washington, DC: U.S. Army Center of Military History, 1999), 26.

71. Lyndon B. Johnson, quoted in Robert Dallek, *Flawed Giant: Lyndon Johnson and His Times, 1961–1973* (New York: Oxford University Press, 1998), 382.

72. Lewis Sorley, "To Change a War: General Harold K. Johnson and the PROVN Study," *Parameters* 28, no. 1 (Spring 1998): 94–97.

73. Ibid., 99–101; Hunt, *Pacification,* 75.

74. Lewis Sorley, *Honorable Warrior: General Harold K. Johnson and the Ethics of Command* (Lawrence: University Press of Kansas, 1998), 241.

75. Volney F. Warner, interview by Dean M. Owen, February 2, 1983, Senior Officer Oral History Program, Project 83–3, U.S. Army Military History Institute (MHI), Carlisle, PA, 71.

76. Robert W. Komer, quoted in Hunt, *Pacification,* 75.

77. Robert W. Komer, Letter No. 8 to William Porter, May 11, 1966, Box 4, NSF/Komer/Komer-Porter Numbered Letters, LBJL; Dallek, *Flawed Giant,* 382.

78. Robert W. Komer, memorandum to the Lyndon B. Johnson, May 20, 1966, Box 6, NSF/Komer/General Maxwell Taylor, LBJL.

79. Robert W. Komer, memorandum to Lyndon B. Johnson, June 14, 1966, *FRUS, 1964–1968,* 4:419. See also William R. Peers, message to William Westmoreland, June 1966, Box 3, William C. Westmoreland Papers, MHI.

80. Komer, Letter No. 8.

81. Robert W. Komer, "Second Komer Trip to Vietnam, 23–29 June 1966," memorandum to Lyndon B. Johnson, July 1, 1966, item #0240423005, Virtual Vietnam Archive, http://www.vietnam.ttu.edu/virtualarchive/items .php?item=0240423005; William Conrad Gibbons, *The U.S. Government and the Vietnam War: Executive and Legislative Roles,* part 4, *July 1965– January 1968* (Princeton, NJ: Princeton University Press, 1995), 354–55; Philip B. Davidson, *Secrets of the Vietnam War* (Novato, CA: Presidio, 1990), 6–7.

82. Komer, Oral History Interview III, LBJL, 40.

83. Jack Foisie, "Allies in Vietnam Have Started to Win, Westmoreland Says," *Los Angeles Times,* July 3, 1966.

84. Gibbons, *U.S. Government and the Vietnam War,* part 4, 355.

85. George A. Carver, "Comments on Mr. Komer's Report to the President on His 28–29 June Trip to Vietnam," memorandum to Richard Helms, July 7, 1966, *FRUS, 1964–1968,* 4:486–88.

86. Richard Helms, "Report to the President on Your Recent Trip to Vietnam, 1 July 1966," memorandum to Robert W. Komer, July 18, 1966, *FRUS, 1964–1968,* 4:505–7.

87. Robert W. Komer, Letter No. 10 to William Porter, July 27, 1966, Box 4, NSF/Komer/Porter-Komer Numbered Letters, LBJL; Embassy in Vietnam, telegram to the Department of State, July 27, 1966, *FRUS, 1964–1968,* 4:533–38; Department of State, telegram to the Embassy in Vietnam, August 3, 1966, *FRUS, 1964–1968,* 4:554–55; Embassy in Vietnam, telegram to the Department of State, August 10, 1966, *FRUS, 1964– 1968,* 4:568–77; Komer, *Organization and Management,* 36–37; Hunt, *Pacification,* 36–37; Komer, Letter No. 9.

88. Jack Valenti, memorandum to Lyndon B. Johnson, March 1, 1966, *FRUS, 1964–1968,* 33:374; Hunt, *Pacification,* 72.

89. H. W. Brands, *The Wages of Globalism: Lyndon Johnson and the Limits of American Power* (New York: Oxford University Press, 1995), vii.

90. Guzzardi, "Management of the War," 137.

91. Hunt, *Pacification,* 72. Komer's personality fit well with LBJ's style, but as Daalder and Destler point out, this was not the case with Bundy, and ultimately, Johnson saw Bundy as "threatening his capacity to govern as he wished to." See *In the Shadow of the Oval Office,* 56.

CHAPTER 6. A NEW THRUST TO PACIFICATION

1. Department of Defense, "Evolution of the War," 45.

2. Hunt, *Pacification*, 6.

3. Komer, *Organization and Management*, 32–33.

4. Hunt, *Pacification*, 76.

5. Scoville, *Reorganizing for Pacification Support*, 31.

6. Robert W. Komer, memorandum to John Paul Vann, August 6, 1966, with draft 3, August 7, 1966, "Giving a New Thrust to Pacification" attached, Box 1, 1966 File, John Paul Vann Papers, MHI; "Giving a New Thrust to Pacification," draft 3, August 7, 1966, Box 7, NSF/Komer/Pacification, LBJL; Hunt, *Pacification*, 77.

7. Mark Moyar, *Phoenix and the Birds of Prey: The CIA's Secret Campaign to Destroy the Viet Cong* (Annapolis, MD: Naval Institute Press, 1997), 49.

8. Komer, *Organization and Management*, 33–36.

9. Memorandum to John Paul Vann, August 6, 1966, MHI; Komer, *Organization and Management*, 33.

10. Komer, interview by Sheehan, April 8, 1975, Box 70, Sheehan Papers. See also Neil Sheehan, *A Bright Shining Lie* (New York: Random House, 1988), 655.

11. Komer, *Organization and Management*, 36; Dallek, *Flawed Giant*, 382; Gibbons, *U.S. Government and the Vietnam War*, part 4, 468–69.

12. Robert W. Komer, "Re-Evaluation of VC (non-NVA) Strength," letter to Robert McNamara, September 2, 1966, Box 5, NSF/Komer/McNamara-Vance-McNaughton, LBJL.

13. John Hart, memorandum to Henry Cabot Lodge, March 6, 1967, Box 6, NSF/Komer/Vice President, LBJL.

14. Komer, *Organization and Management*, 38–39; Hunt, *Pacification*, 77; Robert W. Komer, memorandum to Robert McNamara, September 29, 1966, Box 5, NSF/Komer/McNamara-Vance-McNaughton, LBJL; Department of Defense, "Evolution of the War," 92.

15. Robert W. Komer, note to Richard Helms, September 29, 1966, Box 5, NSF/Komer/Helms, LBJL.

16. Komer, *Organization and Management*, 39–40; Hunt, *Pacification*, 77–78; Department of Defense, "Evolution of the War," 92–93.

17. Robert W. Komer, "Sir R. G. K. Thompson on Pacification," memorandum for the record, September 23, 1966, Visits (1967–1968) File, Deputy for Civil Operations and Revolutionary Development, U.S. Military Assistance Command, Vietnam (DEPCORDSMACV) Files, U.S. Army Center of Military History, Fort Lesley J. McNair, Washington, DC; "Sir R. G. K. Thompson on Pacification," memorandum for the record, September 23, 1966, Box 12, Komer-Leonhart File, LBJL; Robert W. Komer, Letter

No. 17 to William Porter, September 21, 1966, Box 4, NSF/Komer/Porter-Komer Numbered Letters, LBJL; Robert W. Komer, letters to Charles Mohr, September 19, 1966, and September 26, 1966, Box 4, NSF/Komer/Porter-Komer Numbered Letters, LBJL.

18. Charles Mohr, "Vietnam's 'Pacification' Is Tougher Than It Looked at Honolulu," *New York Times,* September 25, 1966; William Porter, letter to Robert W. Komer, September 27, 1966, Box 4, NSF/Komer/Porter-Komer Numbered Letters, LBJL.

19. Dallek, *Flawed Giant,* 382–83.

20. Ibid., 383. See also Earle Wheeler, message to U. S. G. Sharp and William Westmoreland, October 1966, Box 4, Westmoreland Papers.

21. Walt W. Rostow, memorandum to Lyndon B. Johnson, October 3, 1966, *FRUS, 1964–1968,* 4:690; George A. Carver, "McNamara's Pacification Reorganization Proposal Activity," memorandum to Richard Helms, October 6, 1966, *FRUS, 1964–1968,* 4:712–16.

22. Lyndon B. Johnson, quoted in Dallek, *Flawed Giant,* 383.

23. Ibid., 388.

24. Robert W. Komer, Letter No. 17 to William Porter, September 21, 1966, Box 4, NSF/Komer/Porter-Komer Numbered Letters, LBJL; Komer, Oral History Interview III, LBJL, 56.

25. Robert W. Komer, memorandum to Lyndon B. Johnson, October 5, 1966, *FRUS, 1964–1968,* 4:707–11; Hunt, *Pacification,* 74–75; William C. Westmoreland, *A Soldier Reports,* rev. ed. (New York: Da Capo Press, 1989), 190.

26. Robert W. Komer, memorandum to Lyndon B. Johnson, October 5, 1966, *FRUS, 1964–1968,* 4:707–11; Richard A. Hunt, e-mail message to author, June 20, 2005.

27. Robert W. Komer, memorandum to Lyndon B. Johnson, October 5, 1966, *FRUS, 1964–1968,* 4:710n4.

28. Carver, "McNamara's Pacification Reorganization Proposal Activity," 712–16; Hunt, *Pacification,* 78; Gibbons, *U.S. Government and the Vietnam War,* 450–60; Department of Defense, "Evolution of the War, part 4" 99–104.

29. Joint Chiefs of Staff, "Actions Recommended for Vietnam," memorandum to Robert McNamara, October 14, 1966, *FRUS, 1964–1968,* 4:738–42.

30. Carver, "McNamara Pacification Reorganization Proposal Activity," 712–16; Komer, Oral History Interview II, LBJL, 31.

31. Earle Wheeler, telegram to William Westmoreland, October 17, 1966, *FRUS, 1964–1968,* 4:756–58.

32. Nicholas Katzenbach, "Administration of Revolutionary Development," memorandum to Lyndon B. Johnson, October 15, 1966, *FRUS, 1964–1968,* 4:746–52.

33. Komer, *Organization and Management,* 40–46; Department of State, telegram to the Embassy in Vietnam, November 4, 1966, *FRUS, 1964–1968,* 4:798–99; Komer, Letter No. 18; Scoville, *Reorganizing for Pacification Support,* 40; Gibbons, *U.S. Government and the Vietnam War,* part 4, 471; Department of Defense, "Evolution of the War," 106–8.

34. Hunt, *Pacification,* 80; Westmoreland, *Soldier Reports,* 212; Scoville, *Reorganizing for Pacification Support,* 40–42; Harold K. Johnson, message to William Westmoreland, November 1966, Box 4, Westmoreland Papers.

35. Komer, *Organization and Management,* 40; Lyndon B. Johnson, letter to Henry Cabot Lodge Jr., November 16, 1966, *FRUS, 1964–1968,* 4:848–49.

36. Komer, Letter No. 18.

37. Richard Holbrooke, "Vietnam Trip Report: October 26–November 18, 1966," memorandum to Robert W. Komer, December 1, 1966, Box 5, NSF/Komer/Gaud, LBJL.

38. Department of Defense, "Evolution of the War," 119.

39. Robert W. Komer, memorandum to Dean Rusk, December 1, 1966, Box 7, NSF/Komer/Manila, LBJL.

40. Richard Holbrooke, "What Is 'the Other War' Anyway?" memorandum to Robert W. Komer, December 10, 1966, Box 8, NSF/Komer/Report to the President [8/66] [1], LBJL.

41. Komer, Oral History Interview II, LBJL, 38–41; Gibbons, *U.S. Government and the Vietnam War,* part 4, 479; Komer, Oral History Interview III, LBJL, 30–32.

42. Komer, Oral History Interview II, LBJL, 38–41; Gibbons, *U.S. Government and the Vietnam War,* part 4, 479–80.

43. Robert N. Ginsburgh, interview by John E. VanDuyn and R. B. Clement, May 26, 1971, Oral History Interview #477, Albert F. Simpson Historical Research Center, Air University, Maxwell Air Force Base, AL, 65–70; Gibbons, *U.S. Government and the Vietnam War,* part 4, 480. Nicholas Katzenbach, in his memoir, claims the Non-Group as his idea. See Katzenbach, *Some of It Was Fun: Working with RFK and LBJ* (New York: W. W. Norton, 2008), 263–64.

44. Ginsburgh interview, 67; Gibbons, *U.S. Government and the Vietnam War,* part 4, 480–81.

45. Katzenbach, *Some of It Was Fun,* 265.

46. Gibbons, *U.S .Government and the Vietnam War,* part 4, 483; Walt W. Rostow and Robert W. Komer, "A Strategy for the Next Phase in Vietnam," September 20, 1966, *FRUS, 1964–1968,* 4:650–52.

47. Gibbons, *U.S .Government and the Vietnam War,* part 4, 484.

48. Ibid., 485–86. See also Department of Defense, "U.S. Ground Strategy and Force Deployments: 1965–1967, Volume II: Program 5," Part IV.C.6(b)

in *U.S.-Vietnam Relations, 1945–1967,* 4–7, http://www.archives.gov/research/pentagon-papers/; and Robert W. Komer, memorandum to Robert McNamara, November 29, 1966, *FRUS, 1964–1968,* 4:867–72.

49. Gaddis, *Strategies of Containment,* 260.

50. Gibbons, *U.S .Government and the Vietnam War,* part 4, 487–88.

51. Ibid., 488.

52. Ibid., 488–90.

53. Ibid., 488–94; Department of Defense, *History of United States Decisionmaking in Vietnam,* 4:400.

54. Richard Holbrooke, "Vietnam Trip Report, 26 October–18 November 1966," memorandum to Robert W. Komer, December 1, 1966, *FRUS, 1964–1968,* 4:321; William Leonhart, "Visit to Vietnam—December 1966," memorandum to Lyndon B. Johnson, December 30, 1966, *FRUS* 4:353; Hunt, *Pacification,* 82–87; Robert W. Komer, letter to Robert McNamara, January 21, 1967, Box 5, NSF/Komer/McNamara-Vance-McNaughton, LBJL.

55. Holbrooke, "What Is 'the Other War' Anyway?"

56. Gibbons, *U.S. Government and the Vietnam War,* part 4, 487n19.

57. Robert W. Komer, memorandum for Lyndon B. Johnson, January 23, 1967, Box 5, NSF/Komer/Rostow, LBJL.

58. Robert W. Komer, letter to Robert McNamara, January 21, 1967, Box 5, NSF/Komer/McNamara-Vance-McNaughton, LBJL.

59. Robert W. Komer, "Transmittal of CAS Saigon Memorandum to Ambassador Lodge," memorandum for Hubert Humphrey, March 18, 1967, with attached memorandum from the CIA, March 10, 1967, Box 6, NSF/Komer/Vice President, LBJL.

60. Lyndon Johnson, "Remarks at a Press Briefing by David Lilienthal and Robert Komer Following Their Return from Vietnam," February 27, 1967, *American Presidency Project,* http://www.presidency.ucsb.edu/ws/?pid=28664; Gibbons, *U.S. Government and the Vietnam War,* part 4, 608–9n19; "Westmoreland Says Enemy Intensifies Terrorism," *New York Times,* March 21, 1967.

61. Richard Holbrooke, memorandum to Robert W. Komer, February 27, 1967, Box 8, NSF/Komer/Report to the President [8/66] [1], LBJL.

62. Robert W. Komer, "Change for the Better—Latest Impressions from Vietnam," memorandum for Lyndon B. Johnson, February 28, 1967; Richard Holbrooke, memorandum to Robert W. Komer, February 27, 1967, both in Box 9, NSF/Komer/Vietnam Trip Reports, LBJL.

63. Komer, "Transmittal of CAS Saigon Memorandum to Ambassador Lodge."

64. Robert Montague, "Briefing on CORDS," unpublished and undated paper, Box 2, Robert Montague Papers, MHI, 24–25; Gibbons, *U.S. Government*

and the Vietnam War, part 4, 575–76n43; Hunt, *Pacification,* 76; Lyndon Johnson, "Address on U.S. Policy in Vietnam Delivered before a Joint Session of the Tennessee State Legislature," March 15, 1967, *American Presidency Project,* http://www.presidency.ucsb.edu/ws/?pid=28664.

65. *Public Papers of the Presidents of the United States, Lyndon B. Johnson,* Book I, 381; Lyndon Baines Johnson, *The Vantage Point: Perspectives on the Presidency, 1963–1969* (New York: Holt, Rinehart and Winston, 1971), 259; R. W. Apple, "Difficult Phase in Saigon," *New York Times,* March 17, 1967; Max Frankel, "Johnson Plans to Repeat Vietnam Strategy Parley," *New York Times,* March 26, 1967; Larry Berman, *Lyndon Johnson's War: The Road to Stalemate in Vietnam* (New York: W. W. Norton, 1989), 32.

66. Komer, *Organization and Management,* 52–53.

67. Robert W. Komer, letter to Robert I. Channon, June 20, 1974, item #0440423030, Virtual Vietnam Archive, http://www.vietnam.ttu.edu/virtual archive/items.php?item=0440423030.

68. Hunt, *Pacification,* 87; Robert W. Komer, memorandum to Lyndon B. Johnson, March 18, 1967, in *Lyndon B. Johnson's Vietnam Papers: A Documentary Collection,* ed. David M. Barrett (College Station: Texas A&M University Press, 1997), 402–3; Lyndon Johnson, "The President's News Conference in Guam Following the Conference," March 21, 1967, *American Presidency Project,* http://www.presidency.ucsb.edu/ws/?pid=28153; R. W. Apple Jr., "Unanswered Questions, Guam Parley Unable to Determine Future of the Pacification Program," *New York Times,* March 22, 1967; George W. Ashworth, "Senators Term 'Other War' Vital," *Christian Science Monitor,* April 4, 1967; John Osborne, "Fantasy in Vietnam," *New Republic,* May 27, 1967, 14–15.

69. Komer, *Organization and Management,* 52–56; Robert W. Komer, memorandum to Walt W. Rostow, March 27, 1967, Box 5, NSF/Komer/Rostow, LBJL; Robert W. Komer, memorandum to Robert McNamara, March 29, 1967, Box 5, NSF/Komer/Rostow, LBJL; Westmoreland, *Soldier Reports,* 214.

70. Richard A. Hunt, e-mail message to the author, June 20, 2005.

71. Robert W. Komer, memorandum to Robert McNamara, March 29, 1967, Box 5, NSF/Komer/Rostow, LBJL.

72. Ibid., 53.

73. Gibbons, *U.S. Government and the Vietnam War,* part 4, 610–11, 619n19, 629; Department of Defense, *History of United States Decisionmaking in Vietnam,* 4:154.

74. Gibbons, *U.S. Government and the Vietnam War,* part 4, 621–22; Komer, *Organization and Management,* 57–58. See also Department of Defense, "U.S. Ground Strategy and Force Deployments: 1965–1967," 79–82.

75. Department of Defense, *History of United States Decisionmaking in Vietnam,* 4:463–67.

76. Komer, *Organization and Management,* 57.

77. Lyndon Baines Johnson, letter to Robert W. Komer, May 1, 1967, Box 4, NSF/Komer/ Moyers/Christianson, LBJL.

78. Department of Defense, "Evolution of the War," 63–65, 73.

79. Gregory A. Daddis, "No Sure Victory: Measuring U.S. Army Effectiveness and Progress in the Vietnam War" (PhD diss., University of North Carolina–Chapel Hill, 2009), 184.

80. Robert W. Komer, "The Civil Side of the War in Vietnam" (lecture, National War College, Washington, DC, March 29, 1967). Document declassified by the Department of Defense at the author's request, January 2009.

81. Ibid.

82. Ibid.

83. Ibid.

84. Komer, interview by Sheehan, April 8, 1975.

85. Carl von Clausewitz, *On War,* ed. and trans. Michael Howard and Peter Paret (Princeton, NJ: Princeton University Press, 1989), 88.

CHAPTER 7. IN COUNTRY

1. Neil Sheehan, *After the War Was Over: Hanoi and Saigon* (New York: Random House, 1992), 57.

2. Hilsman, *To Move a Nation,* 328–29.

3. John Balaban, *Remembering Heaven's Face: A Moral Witness in Vietnam* (New York: Poseidon Press, 1991), 33.

4. Walter T. Kerwin Jr., interview by D. A. Doehle, Senior Officer Oral History Program, Project 80–2, vol. 2, Walter T. Kerwin Papers, MHI, 350.

5. Ibid.

6. Daniel Ellsberg, *Secrets* (New York: Viking, 2002), 177–78.

7. Ward Just, *A Dangerous Friend* (Boston: Houghton Mifflin, 1999), 8.

8. Philip B. Davidson, *Vietnam at War* (Novato, CA: Presidio Press, 1988), 409.

9. Hunt, *Pacification,* 86–87.

10. "Responsibility for U.S. Role in Pacification (Revolutionary Development)," National Security Action Memorandum No. 362, http://www.lbjlib.utexas.edu/johnson/archives.hom/nsams/nsam362.asp; Hunt, *Pacification,* 87–88.

11. William Westmoreland, quoted in Zalin Grant, *Facing the Phoenix* (New York: W. W. Norton, 1991), 292.

12. William Westmoreland, quoted in Dale Andrade, *Ashes to Ashes: The Phoenix Program and the Vietnam War* (Lexington, MA: Lexington Books, 1990), 56.

13. Ward Just, "U.S. Army Role Dismays U.S. Civilians in Vietnam," *Washington Post,* May 12, 1967; Ward Just, "Komer: Key Civilian in 'Pacification,'" *Washington Post,* May 15, 1967.

14. Robert M. Montague, "Tactics," memorandum to Robert W. Komer, May 6, 1967, Box 3, Montague Papers.

15. Scoville, *Organizing for Pacification Support,* 60.

16. Robert W. Komer, quoted in Hunt, *Pacification,* 99.

17. David Halberstam, "Return to Vietnam," *Harper's,* December 1967, 47.

18. Davidson, *Vietnam at War,* 458.

19. Sheehan, *Bright Shining Lie,* 653–54.

20. Davidson, *Vietnam at War,* 454.

21. Just, "Komer: Key Civilian."

22. R. W. Apple Jr., "Bunker Transfers Pacification Drive to Westmoreland," *New York Times,* May 11, 1967; Jonathan Randal, "The Shake-Up in Saigon," *New York Times,* May 13, 1967; Johnson, *Vantage Point,* 260.

23. Ellsworth Bunker, "Report No. 3," back-channel report to Lyndon B. Johnson, May 17, 1967, item #1790101003, Virtual Vietnam Archive, http://www.vietnam.ttu.edu/virtualarchive/items.php?item=1790101003.

24. John Mecklin, "The Struggle to Rescue the People," *Fortune,* April 1967, 127, 242; Colby and Forbath, *Honorable Men,* 251; Peter Braestrup, *Big Story: How the American Press and Television Reported and Interpreted the Crisis of Tet 1968 in Vietnam and Washington* (Boulder, CO: Westview Press, 1977), 1:539. James K. McCollum reports that CORDS peak strength under Komer was 5,500 American personnel. See McCollum, "The CORDS Pacification Organization in Vietnam," *Armed Forces and Society* 10, no. 1 (Fall 1983): 113. As to the budget figures, Guenther Lewy uses a figure of $850 million for the expenditure on pacification in fiscal year 1968. See his book *America in Vietnam* (New York: Oxford University Press, 1978), 89.

25. Scoville, *Organizing for Pacification Support,* 60–61.

26. Ellsworth Bunker, Report No. 5, back-channel report to Lyndon B. Johnson, May 31, 1967, item #2120805019, Virtual Vietnam Archive, http://www.vietnam.ttu.edu/virtualarchive/items.php?item=2120805019.

27. Just, "Komer: Key Civilian."

28. Just, "U.S. Army Role Dismays."

29. Just, "Komer: Key Civilian."

30. Ibid.

31. William C. Westmoreland, interview by Martin L. Ganderson, Senior Officer Oral History Project, 1982-F, vol. 1, Westmoreland Papers, 147, 149.

32. Just, "Komer: Key Civilian."

33. Komer, *Organization and Management,* 65; "CORDS Organization," MACCORDS briefing, July 1, 1967, 1967–1973 File, MACV/MACCORDS File, MHI.

34. R. W. Komer, interview by Richard H. Moorsteen and Thomas W. Scoville, Section II, n.d., Box 6, Montague Papers, 81; Hunt, *Pacification,* 88; "CORDS Organization"; Bunker, "Report No. 5."

35. Robert W. Komer, memorandum to Ellsworth Bunker, May 26, 1967, Bunker Memos, R. W. Komer Files, DEPCORDSMACV Files.

36. Hunt, *Pacification,* 89–90, 93, 99; "CORDS Organization."

37. Davidson, *Vietnam at War,* 455, 458–59; Hunt, *Pacification,* 87, 90; Graham A. Cosmas, *MACV: The Joint Command in the Years of Escalation, 1962–1967* (Washington, DC: U.S. Army Center of Military History, 2006), 360.

38. W. Scott Thompson and Donaldson D. Frizzell, eds., *The Lessons of Vietnam* (New York: Crane, Russak, 1977), 214.

39. George I. Forsythe, interview by Frank L. Henry, 1974, Senior Officer Oral History Program, Project 74–1, vol. 2, George I. Forsythe Papers, MHI, 418–19.

40. William R. Corson, *The Betrayal* (New York: W. W. Norton, 1968), 213; Robert W. Komer, "DEPCORDS Trip to I FFORCEV," memorandum to William Westmoreland, June 5, 1967, Westmoreland Memos, R. W. Komer Files (1967–1968), DEPCORDSMACV Files. William Colby would later remark about Corson's views: "He's one of these guys that [thinks that] his solution is the only solution and the whole world is either venal or stupid if it doesn't apply to them. There are a lot of people like that around." See William E. Colby, interview by Ted Gittinger, March 1, 1982, Interview II, transcript, Oral History Collection, LBJL.

41. Robert W. Komer, "DepCORDS Visit to IV Corps," memorandum to William Westmoreland, June 7, 1967, Westmoreland Memos, R. W. Komer (1967–1968), DEPCORDSMACV Files; Ellsworth Bunker, "Report No. 6," back-channel report to Lyndon B. Johnson, June 7, 1967, item #2120805019, Virtual Vietnam Archive, http://www.vietnam.ttu.edu/virtualarchive/items.php?item=2120805019.

42. Robert W. Komer, "Attack on the Vietcong Infrastructure," memorandum to William Westmoreland, June 19, 1967, DEPCORDSMACV Files; Robert W. Komer, "Organization for Attack on VC Infrastructure," memorandum to Ellsworth Bunker, June 14, 1967, Box 11, Komer-Leonhart File (1966–1968)/ICEX, LBJL; Andrade, *Ashes to Ashes,* 58.

43. Robert W. Komer, letter to Lyndon B. Johnson, June 3, 1967, item #0240702016, Virtual Vietnam Archive, http://www.vietnam.ttu.edu/virtualarchive/items.php?item=0240702016.

44. Robert W. Komer, "How to Get Our Case across to McNamara," memorandum to William Westmoreland, June 19, 1967, DEPCORDSMACV Files.

45. William Gaud, "Responsibility for U.S. Support of Revolutionary Development," memorandum to Nicholas Katzenbach, June 22, 1967; Robert W. Komer, "Responsibility for U.S. Support of Revolutionary Development," memorandum to William Westmoreland, June 30, 1967, both in DEPCORDSMACV Files.

46. "Vietnam: Change in Pacification," *New York Times,* June 4, 1967.

47. Hunt, *Pacification,* 91; Scoville, *Reorganizing for Pacification Support,* 62, 66; Forsythe interview, 413–16; Robert Montague, letter to George I. Forsythe, May 12, 1967, Box 3, 1967 File (Papers-Pacification Program), Montague Papers; "CORDS Organization"; Harold K. Johnson, message to William Westmoreland, May 1967, Box 5, Westmoreland Papers.

48. Robert W. Komer, memorandum to Walt W. Rostow, April 8, 1967, Box 5, NSF/Komer/Rostow, LBJL.

49. Richard Holbrooke, "Warning Flags on the Saigon Political Front," memorandum to Robert W. Komer, April 11, 1967, Box 4, NSF/Komer/Bunker, LBJL.

50. Charles Maechling, "Camelot, Robert Kennedy, and Counter-Insurgency—A Memoir," *Virginia Quarterly Review* 75, no, 3 (Summer 1999): 440; Ellsworth Bunker, "Report No. 8," back-channel report to Lyndon B. Johnson, June 21, 1967, item #2120807025, Virtual Vietnam Archive, http://www.vietnam.ttu.edu/virtualarchive/items.php?item=2120807025.

51. Bunker, "Report No. 8."

52. Ibid.

53. Komer, *Organization and Management,* 65.

54. Robert W. Komer, "Organization for Attack on VC Infrastructure," memorandum to William Westmoreland, June 14, 1967, doc. #CK3100062692, Declassified Documents Reference System; R. W. Komer, Interview, n.d., CD #6328, U.S. Marine Corps Historical Center, Quantico, VA; Moyar, *Phoenix and the Birds of Prey,* 50–52; Robert W. Komer, memorandum to Ellsworth Bunker, June 18, 1967, Komer Personal File, DEPCORDSMACV Files; Hunt, *Pacification,* 113; Komer, *Organization and Management,* 160–61; Graham A. Cosmas, *The Joint Chiefs of Staff and the War in Vietnam, 1960–1968,* Part 3 (Washington, DC: Office of Joint History, Office of the Chairman of the Joint Chiefs of Staff, 2009),

109; Andrade, *Ashes to Ashes,* 59; Thomas L. Ahern Jr., *The CIA and Rural Pacification in South Vietnam* (Washington, DC: Center for the Study of Intelligence, CIA, 2001), 288, http://www.foia.cia.gov/vietnam.asp; Douglas Valentine, *The Phoenix Program* (New York: William Morrow, 1990), 127–31.

55. Joseph A. McChristian, *The Role of Military Intelligence, 1965–1967,* Vietnam Studies (Washington, DC: Department of the Army, 1974), 78; Davidson, *Secrets of the Vietnam War,* 8.

56. Joseph A. McChristian, Westmoreland v. CBS (court proceedings), item #0250512001, Virtual Vietnam Archive, http://www.vietnam.ttu.edu/vir tualarchive/items.php?item=0250512001; Davidson, *Secrets of the Vietnam War,* 8.

57. Daniel O. Graham, interview by Ted Gittinger, May 14, 1982, Interview I, LBJL.

58. Davidson, *Secrets of the Vietnam War,* 8.

59. Ibid.; Cosmas, *MACV: The Joint Command in the Years of Escalation,* 362; Scoville, *Reorganizing for Pacification Support,* 78–79; Komer, *Organization and Management,* 60, 160–61.

60. Davidson, *Secrets of the Vietnam War,* 8–9; Komer, *Organization and Management,* 60, 160–61.

61. L. Wade Lathram, "Action Program for Attack on VC Infrastructure, 1967–1968," memorandum to Robert W. Komer, n.d., item #2234306061, Virtual Vietnam Archive, http://www.vietnam.ttu.edu/virtualarchive/ items.php?item=2234306061; Komer, "Organization for Attack on VC Infrastructure."

62. Komer, *Organization and Management,* 161.

63. Ibid., 158–60.

64. Robert W. Komer, quoted in Ahern, *CIA and Rural Pacification,* 287.

65. Komer, *Organization and Management,* 162–63; Ahern, *CIA and Rural Pacification,* 288.

66. Ahern, *CIA and Rural Pacification,* 288–89; Andrade, *Ashes to Ashes,* 61; Headquarters, U.S. Military Assistance Command, Vietnam, "Military Intelligence: Intelligence Coordination and Exploitation for Attack on VC Infrastructure (C) Short Title: ICEX (U)," Directive #381–41, July 9, 1967, Box 5, Vietnam/Southeast Asia, National Security Archive, Gelman Library, George Washington University, Washington, DC.

67. Richard Helms, "Transmittal of Vietnam Report," memorandum to Lyndon B. Johnson, July 27, 1967, item #0010128012, Virtual Vietnam Archive, http://www.vietnam.ttu.edu/virtualarchive/items.php?item=0010128012.

68. Ibid.

69. R. W. Apple Jr., "Komer's Critics Concede Gain in Vietnam Pacification Drive," *New York Times,* July 10, 1967; Robert W. Komer, letter to Charles Percy and Hugh Scott, May 17, 1967, DEPCORDSMACV Files.

70. Ellsworth Bunker, "Report No. 13," back-channel report to Lyndon B. Johnson, July 13, 1967, item #2120810002, Virtual Vietnam Archive, http://www.vietnam.ttu.edu/virtualarchive/items.php?item=2120810002.

71. Notes of Meeting, July 12, 1967, *FRUS, 1964–1968,* vol. 5, *Vietnam 1967* (Washington, DC: USGPO, 2002), 601.

72. Ibid.

73. Robert W. Komer, television interview, July 16, 1967, transcript, item #2130908033, Virtual Vietnam Archive, http://www.vietnam.ttu.edu/virtualarchive/items.php?item=2130908033.

74. Johnson, *Lyndon B. Johnson's Vietnam Papers,* 445.

75. James L. Trainor, "What Business Does the Military Have in Pacification/Nation-Building?" *Armed Force Management,* August 1967, 32–33, 71–72.

76. Scoville, *Reorganizing for Pacification Support,* 70–71.

77. Samuel Zaffiri, *Westmoreland: A Biography of General William C. Westmoreland* (New York: William Morrow, 1994), 211.

78. Robert W. Komer, letter to Robert I. Channon, June 20, 1974, item #0440423030, Virtual Vietnam Archive, http://www.vietnam.ttu.edu/virtualarchive/items.php?item=0440423030.

79. Ahern, *CIA and Rural Pacification,* 252.

80. Hunt, *Pacification,* 105.

CHAPTER 8. TAKING OFF

1. Walt W. Rostow, telegram to Lyndon B. Johnson, July 9, 1967, *FRUS, 1964–1968,* 5:585.

2. Walt W. Rostow, memorandum to Lyndon B. Johnson, August 1, 1967, *FRUS, 1964–1968,* 5:653.

3. Ellsworth Bunker, "Report No. 13," back-channel report to Lyndon B. Johnson, July 13, 1967, item #2120810002, Virtual Vietnam Archive, http://www.vietnam.ttu.edu/virtualarchive/items.php?item=2120810002.

4. Walt W. Rostow, telegram to Lyndon B. Johnson in Texas, July 9, 1967, *FRUS, 1964–1968,* 5:585; Robert W. Komer, "How to Get Our Case across to Washington," memorandum to William Westmoreland, June 19, 1967, *FRUS, 1964–1968,* 5:524.

5. Robert W. Komer, memorandum to William Westmoreland, August 9, 1967, DEPCORDSMACV Files.

6. R. W. Komer, "Impact of Pacification on Insurgency in Vietnam," Report P-4443 (Santa Monica, CA: RAND, 1970), 4.

7. William Colby, *Lost Victory: A Firsthand Account of America's Sixteen-Year Involvement in Vietnam,* with James McCarger (Chicago: Contemporary Books, 1989), 208.

8. Robert W. Komer, quoted in Ted Gittinger, ed., *The Johnson Years: A Vietnam Roundtable* (Austin: University of Texas, 1993), 82.

9. Bunker, "Report No. 9."

10. Komer, "Impact of Pacification," 4.

11. Ibid., 4–6; Ellsworth Bunker, "Report No. 11," back-channel report to Lyndon B. Johnson, July 12, 1967, item #2120809017, Virtual Vietnam Archive, http://www.vietnam.ttu.edu/virtualarchive/items.php?item=212 0809017.

12. Ellsworth Bunker, "Report No. 16," back-channel report to Lyndon B. Johnson, August 16, 1967, item #2120813010, Virtual Vietnam Archive, http://www.vietnam.ttu.edu/virtualarchive/items.php?item=2120813010.

13. Ibid.

14. Department of Defense, "Re-Emphasis on Pacification," 569.

15. Assistant Chief of Staff, CORDS, "Government Operations Subcommittee Meeting with ACofS CORDS," memorandum for the record, July 3, 1967, Congressional File (1967–1968), DEPCORDSMACV Files.

16. Walt W. Rostow, note with attachments to Lyndon B. Johnson, September 27, 1967, item #0010208010, Virtual Vietnam Archive, http://www.viet nam.ttu.edu/virtualarchive/items.php?item=0010208010.

17. Walt W. Rostow, note with attachment to Lyndon B. Johnson, August 28, 1967, item #0010134005, Virtual Vietnam Archive, http://www.vietnam. ttu.edu/virtualarchive/items.php?item=0010134005.

18. Walt W. Rostow, note with attachments to Lyndon B. Johnson, September 27, 1967, item #0010208010, Virtual Vietnam Archive, http://www.viet nam.ttu.edu/virtualarchive/items.php?item=0010208010.

19. Robert W. Komer, letter to Richard Holbrooke, October 1, 1967, DEPCORDSMACV Files.

20. Walt W. Rostow, memorandum to Lyndon B. Johnson, October 7, 1967, item #0010205013, Virtual Vietnam Archive, http://www.vietnam.ttu.edu/ QuickSearch.php?srch=0010205013; James P. Grant, "Review of Refugee Problem in South Vietnam," letter to Robert W. Komer, September 25, 1967, DEPCORDSMACV Files.

21. Douglas Kinnard, *The War Managers* (Hanover, NH: University Press of New England, 1977), 104; Komer, *Organization and Management,* 197; Westmoreland, *Soldier Reports,* 215.

22. Robert W. Komer, letter to Walt W. Rostow, October 4, 1967, doc. #CK3100101793, Declassified Documents Reference System; James McAllister, "What Can One Man Do? Nguyen Duc Thang and the Limits

of Reform in South Vietnam," *Journal of Vietnamese Studies* 4, no. 2 (Summer 2009): 118.

23. Robert W. Komer, letter to Lyndon B. Johnson, October 4, 1967, doc. #CK3100104160, Declassified Documents Reference System.

24. Philip Goodhart, "Vietnam: Autumn Reflections," 1968, item #2131006001, Virtual Vietnam Archive, http://www.vietnam.ttu.edu/vir tualarchive/items.php?item=2131006001.

25. Ellsworth Bunker, "Report No. 21," back-channel report to Lyndon B. Johnson, September 20, 1967, item #2120902010, Virtual Vietnam Archive, http://www.vietnam.ttu.edu/virtualarchive/items.php?item=2120902010.

26. Richard Helms, "Measuring Pacification Progress," memorandum to Nicholas Katzenbach, November 2, 1966, Box 18, Pacification [5], Komer-Leonhart File, LBJL; CIA Headquarters, message to CIA Station, Saigon, December 8, 1966, Box 18, Pacification [4], Komer-Leonhart File, LBJL; Chester Cooper and Richard Moorsteen, "CIA's Pacification Indicator," memorandum to Robert W. Komer and William Leonhart, November 4, 1966, Box 18, Pacification [5], Komer-Leonhart File, LBJL; George W. Allen, *None So Blind: A Personal Account of the Intelligence Failure in Vietnam* (Chicago: Ivan R. Dee, 2001), 222; Albert C. Bole Jr. and K. Kobata, "An Evaluation of the Measurements of the Hamlet Evaluation System," Project No. 118 (Newport, RI: Naval War College Center for Advanced Research, 1975), 198.

27. Helms, "Measuring Pacification Progress"; CIA Headquarters, message to CIA Station, Saigon, December 8, 1966, Box 18, Pacification [4], Komer-Leonhart File, LBJL; Cooper and Moorsteen, "CIA's Pacification Indicator"; Allen, *None So Blind,* 219–22; Bole and Kobata, "Evaluation of the Measurements of the Hamlet Evaluation System," 198; Hunt, *Pacification,* 95–96; Komer, *Organization and Management,* 199.

28. Braestrup, *Big Story,* 1:540.

29. Wade Lathram, interview by William E. Knight, June 2, 1993, Association for Diplomatic Studies and Training, Foreign Affairs Oral History Project, Special Collections Room, Lauinger Library, Georgetown University, Washington, DC.

30. Bunker, "Report No. 21."

31. Braestrup, *Big Story,* 540.

32. Komer, *Organization and Management,* 198–203.

33. Robert W. Komer, memorandum to Ellsworth Bunker, October 1, 1967, Box 43, Westmoreland Papers.

34. Hunt, *Pacification,* 95–96.

35. Townsend Hoopes, *The Limits of Intervention* (New York: David McKay, 1969), 71–72.

36. Robert W. Komer, "Removal of Corrupt and/or Incompetent Province Officials," memorandum to Ellsworth Bunker and William Westmoreland, September 20, 1967; Robert W. Komer, "Reassignment of Corrupt and Incompetent GVN Officials," memorandum to William Westmoreland, October 18, 1967, both in DEPCORDSMACV Files.

37. Ellsworth Bunker, "Report No. 22," back-channel report to Lyndon B. Johnson, September 27, 1967, item #2120902016, Virtual Vietnam Archive, http://www.vietnam.ttu.edu/virtualarchive/items.php?item=212 0902016; Ellsworth Bunker, "Report No. 24," back-channel report to Lyndon B. Johnson, October 12, 1967, item #1790105002, Virtual Vietnam Archive, http://www.vietnam.ttu.edu/virtualarchive/items.php?item=179 0105002.

38. Robert W. Komer, "Conversation with Chief of State Thieu," memorandum for the record, October 6, 1967; Robert W. Komer, "Lunch with Truong Tai Ton (Minister of State in Prime Minister's Office)," memorandum for the record, September 22, 1967; Robert W. Komer, memorandum to George Forsythe and John Calhoun, November 14, 1967; George Forsythe, "Meeting with Brigadier General Nguyen Van Kiem," memorandum for the record, November 30, 1967; Robert W. Komer, "Meeting with Minister of Interior (Linh Quang Vien)," memorandum for the record, December 11, 1967, all in the GVN Liaison (1967–1968) File, DEPCORDSMACV Files.

39. Ellsworth Bunker, "Report No. 26," back-channel report to Lyndon B. Johnson, October 25, 1967, item #2120905016, Virtual Vietnam Archive, http://www.vietnam.ttu.edu/virtualarchive/items.php?item=2120905016.

40. R. W. Komer, letter to the editor, *Washington Post,* November 23, 1967.

41. Carroll Kilpatrick, "Gains Gradual in Pacification, Komer Reports," *Washington Post,* November 22, 1967.

42. Braestrup, *Big Story,* 55–56.

43. Ellsworth Bunker, "Report No. 29," back-channel report to Lyndon B. Johnson, November 29, 1967, item #2120908034, Virtual Vietnam Archive, http://www.vietnam.ttu.edu/virtualarchive/items.php?item=212 0908034.

44. Komer, *Organization and Management,* 72–73.

45. Ellsworth Bunker, "Report No. 31," back-channel report to Lyndon B. Johnson, December 13, 1967, item #2120911004, Virtual Vietnam Archive, http://www.vietnam.ttu.edu/virtualarchive/items.php?item=2120911004.

46. Bole and Kobata, "Evaluation of the Hamlet Evaluation System," 8–20, 198–99; Robert W. Komer, transcript of news conference on the Hamlet Evaluation System, December 1, 1967, item #2234306047, Virtual Vietnam Archive, http://www.vietnam.ttu.edu/virtualarchive/items.php?item=223 4306047.

336 NOTES TO PAGES 164–167

47. Robert W. Komer, memorandum to Ellsworth Bunker, December 16, 1967, DEPCORDSMACV Files.

48. William J. Lederer, "Vietnam: Those Computer Reports," *New Republic,* December 23, 1967, 14.

49. Robert W. Barnett, note to William Leonhart, December 28, 1967, with *New Republic* article attached, Box 12, Komer-Leonhart File, LBJL.

50. American Embassy Saigon, message to Secretary of State, January 1968, Box 12, Komer-Leonhart File, LBJL.

51. Ellsworth Bunker, "Report No. 32," back-channel report to Lyndon B. Johnson, December 28, 1967, item #2120911016, Virtual Vietnam Archive, http://www.vietnam.ttu.edu/virtualarchive/items.php?item=2120911016; Hunt, *Pacification,* 116; Andrade, *Ashes to Ashes,* 72–73.

52. Ellsworth Bunker, "Report No. 30," back-channel report to Lyndon B. Johnson, December 7, 1967, item #1790107001, Virtual Vietnam Archive, http://www.vietnam.ttu.edu/virtualarchive/items.php?item=1790107001; Ellsworth Bunker, "Report No. 31," back-channel report to Lyndon B. Johnson, December 13, 1967, item #2120911004, Virtual Vietnam Archive, http://www.vietnam.ttu.edu/virtualarchive/items.php?item=2120911004; Bunker, "Report No. 32."

53. Robert W. Komer, quoted in *Johnson Years,* 81; Colby and Forbath, *Honorable Men,* 245–46, Richard Helms, memorandum for Walt W. Rostow, January 22, 1968, doc. #CK3100141559, Declassified Documents Reference System. See Notes of Meeting, November 21, 1967, *FRUS, 1964–1968,* 5:1058–59, for a different account of Komer's request.

54. Robert W. Komer, letter to John Paul Vann, December 27, 1967, Box 28, John Paul Vann correspondence with Robert W. Komer, Sheehan Papers.

55. Robert W. Komer, memorandum to George Forsythe and L. Wade Lathram, November 14, 1967; George Forsythe, memorandum for the record, November 30, 1967; Komer, "Lunch with Truong Tai Ton"; Robert W. Komer, "Conversation with Chief of State Thieu," all in DEPCORDSMACV Files; Colby, *Lost Victory,* 211.

56. Robert W. Komer, memorandum for the record, December 23, 1967, DEPCORDSMACV Files.

57. Bunker, "Report No. 32."

58. Department of State, Presidential Visits Abroad, http://www.state.gov/r/pa/ho/trvl/pres/12796.htm; Lyndon B. Johnson, "Remarks to Service Personnel and Award of Distinguished Service Medal and Medal of Freedom to Military and Civilian Leaders, Can Rahn Bay, Vietnam," December 23, 1967, *American Presidency Project,* http://www.presidency.ucsb.edu/ws/index.php?pid=28635. See also Lyndon B. Johnson, "The President's Daily Diary," December 23, 1967, LBJL, 8, http://www.lbjlib.utexas.edu/johnson/archives.hom/diary/1967/671223–08.asp;

59. Komer, *Organization and Management,* 74.
60. Ward Just, "The Heart-Mind Gap in Vietnam War," *Washington Post,* November 19, 1967.
61. Ibid.
62. Gregory A. Cosmas, *MACV: The Joint Command in the Years of Withdrawal, 1968–1973* (Washington, DC: U.S. Army Center of Military History, 2007), 439.
63. Charles A. Joiner, "South Vietnam: Political, Military and Constitutional Arenas in Nation Building," *Asian Survey* 9, no. 1 (January 1968): 70–71.
64. John E. Mueller, "The Search for the 'Breaking Point' in Vietnam: The Statistics of a Deadly Quarrel," *International Studies Quarterly* 24, no. 4 (December 1980): 503.
65. Halberstam, "Return to Vietnam," 58.
66. Chester L. Cooper, Judith E. Corson, Laurence J. Legere, David E. Lockwood, and Donald M. Weller, *The American Experience with Pacification in Vietnam,* Report R-185 (DAHC 15 67 C 0011, ARPA-20, Special Studies) (Arlington, VA: Institute for Defense Analysis, International and Social Sciences Division, 1972), 3:249–50.
67. Ibid., 250.
68. Thomas C. Thayer, ed., *A Systems Analysis View of the Vietnam War, 1965–1972,* vol. 10, *Pacification and Civil Affairs* (Washington, DC: OASD(PA&E)RP, Asia Division, 1975), 19, 28. See also Thomas C. Thayer, *War without Fronts: The American Experience in Vietnam* (Boulder, CO: Westview Press, 1985), 143, 169.
69. U.S. Military Assistance Command, Vietnam, *Command History,* vol. 2, *1967* (Saigon: U.S. Military Assistance Command, Vietnam, 1968), 594.
70. Just, "Heart-Mind Gap."
71. Lewis Sorley, *Thunderbolt: General Creighton Abrams and the Army of His Times* (New York: Simon & Schuster, 1992), 196.
72. Cosmas, *MACV: The Joint Command in the Years of Withdrawal,* 362; Kerwin interview, 353, 362–63; Montague, "Briefing on CORDS," 27.
73. MACV, *Command History,* 2:1967, 594.
74. Joiner, "South Vietnam," 71.
75. Ibid.; Just, "Heart-Mind Gap."

CHAPTER 9. THE YEAR OF THE MONKEY

1. Joiner, "South Vietnam," 71.
2. Edward M. Kennedy, speech before the International Rescue Committee, New York City, October 31, 1967, DEPCORDSMACV Files; Louis A. Wiesner, *Victims and Survivors: Displaced Persons and Other War Victims in Viet-Nam, 1954–1975* (Westport, CT: Greenwood Press, 1988), 96.

3. "Briefing for Senator Edward M. Kennedy," memorandum, DEPCORDSMACV Files; Wiesner, *Victims and Survivors,* 97–98.

4. Hunt, *Pacification,* 103; Robert W. Komer, "Comments on Senator Kennedy's Speech," memorandum, n.d., DEPCORDSMACV Files; Ellsworth Bunker, "Report No. 33," back-channel report to Lyndon B. Johnson, January 2, 1968, item #2121004012, Virtual Vietnam Archive, http://www.vietnam.ttu.edu/virtualarchive/items.php?item=2121004012; Robert W. Komer, cable to Lyndon B. Johnson, January 13, 1968, doc. #CK3100187782, Declassified Documents Record System.

5. "Conversations with Ambassador Komer and Major General Forsythe—CORDS MACV," memorandum for the record, January 17, 1968, *FRUS, 1964–1968,* vol. 6, *Vietnam, January–August 1968* (Washington, DC: USGPO, 2002), 37–40; Ahern, *CIA and Rural Pacification,* 307. Komer and Forsythe enumerated these problems, but signs of optimism were also discussed. See John C. Donnell, "Pacification Reassessed," *Asian Survey* 7, no. 8 (August 1967): 573–76. For a trenchant analysis of the inability of Komer and other U.S. officials to halt corruption and rein in "warlord" tendencies, see Halberstam, "Return to Vietnam," 47–58.

6. "Conversations with Ambassador Komer and Major General Forsythe," 37–40. See also McAllister, "What Can One Man Do?" 138–39.

7. "Conversations with Ambassador Komer and Major General Forsythe," 37–40.

8. Ibid.

9. Robert W. Komer, "Policy Statement on Leverage," memorandum with enclosure to Ellsworth Bunker and William Westmoreland, January 30, 1968, Box 45, Westmoreland Papers.

10. Ibid.

11. Ibid.

12. Hunt, *Pacification,* 134–35; Ellsworth Bunker, "Report No. 36," back-channel report to Lyndon B. Johnson, January 24, 1968, item #2121005018, Virtual Vietnam Archive, http://www.vietnam.ttu.edu/virtualarchive/items.php?item=2121005018.

13. Robert W. Komer, memorandum to Ellsworth Bunker, January 15, 1968, DEPCORDSMACV Files; Ellsworth Bunker, "Report No. 34," back-channel report to Lyndon B. Johnson, January 13, 1968, item#2121005011, Virtual Vietnam Archive, http://www.vietnam.ttu.edu/virtualarchive/items.php?item=2121005011.

14. George C. Wilson, "Viet Defection Drive Slipping," *Washington Post,* January 14, 1968.

15. Robert Thompson, "Will We Win?" *Newsweek,* January 1, 1968, 28; George M. Brooke III, "A Matter of Will: Sir Robert Thompson, Malaya,

and the Failure of American Strategy in Vietnam" (PhD diss., Georgetown University, 2004), 281.

16. Brooke, "Matter of Will," 283; Robert Thompson, *Make for the Hills: Memories of Far Eastern Wars* (London: Leo Cooper, 1989), 152.

17. Robert W. Komer, news conference, transcript, January 24, 1968, item #2131010011, Virtual Vietnam Archive, http://www.vietnam.ttu.edu/virtualarchive/items.php?item=2131010011.

18. Braestrup, *Big Story,* 1:541.

19. "Vietcong's Truce Plans Unchanged," *Washington Post,* January 16, 1968.

20. Ralph William Johnson, "Phoenix/Phung Hoang: A Study of Wartime Intelligence Management" (PhD diss., American University, 1985), 205–6; Westmoreland, *Soldier Reports,* 261–62.

21. "VC Truce Begins, but War Goes On," *Washington Post,* January 27, 1968; Johnson, "Phoenix/Phung Hoang," 206.

22. Lee Lescaze, "Saigon Takes on Holiday Air as Tet Arrives," *Washington Post,* January 29, 1968.

23. Lathram interview, 23–24.

24. Don Oberdorfer, *Tet!* (Garden City, NY: Doubleday, 1971), 15; Robert Komer, interview by Neil Sheehan, April 8, 1975, Folder 36, Tape Summaries, Robert Komer, 1–5, Box 121, Sheehan Papers.

25. "Vietcong Seize Part of U.S. Embassy," *Washington Post,* January 31, 1968; Westmoreland, *Soldier Reports,* 324–25; Zaffiri, *Westmoreland,* 283. The reporting by the *Washington Post* is inaccurate regarding the Viet Cong sappers. Westmoreland told the press "none of the Viet Cong had gotten inside the Chancery."

26. "Ho Chi Minh Pleased," *New York Times,* January 31, 1968.

27. Peter Braestrup, "Heavy Fighting Persists; General Warns of Big Thrust," *Washington Post,* February 2, 1968.

28. Hunt, *Pacification,* 136.

29. Ibid., 136–37.

30. Oberdorfer, *Tet!* 15; Braestrup, *Big Story,* 1:64; Halberstam, "Return to Vietnam," 47.

31. Robert W. Komer, quoted in Miller, *Lyndon,* 501.

32. Hunt, *Pacification,* 137–38.

33. Don Oberdorfer, interview by Ted Gittinger, September 17, 1981, Oral History Interview II, LBJL, 19.

34. Ibid., 138.

35. Westmoreland, *Soldier Reports,* 332.

36. Robert W. Komer, quoted in Kim Willenson, *The Bad War: An Oral History of the Vietnam War* (New York: New American Library, 1987), 95.

37. Philip B. Davidson, interview by Ted Gittinger, March 30, 1982, Oral History Interview I, transcript, LBJL.

38. Komer, *Organization and Management,* 83.

39. Embassy in Vietnam, telegram to the Department of State, February 2, 1968, *FRUS, 1964–1968,* 6:102–4; Ellsworth Bunker, "Report No. 37," back-channel report to Lyndon B. Johnson, February 4, 1968, item #2121007006, Virtual Vietnam Archive, http://www.vietnam.ttu.edu/vir tualarchive/items.php?item=2121007006; "Project Recovery," information paper with enclosures, n.d., Box 45, Westmoreland Papers.

40. Embassy in Vietnam, telegram to the Department of State, February 2, 1968, *FRUS, 1964–1968,* 6:102.

41. Embassy in Vietnam, telegram to the Department of State, February 8, 1968, *FRUS, 1964–1968,* 6:147–52.

42. Jeffrey J. Clarke, *Advice and Support: The Final Years, 1965–1973* (Washington, DC: U.S. Army Center of Military History, 1988), 311.

43. Komer, *Organization and Management,* 79.

44. Westmoreland, *Soldier Reports,* 330, 333; Johnson, "Phoenix/Phung Hoang," 210–12; Ronald H. Spector, *After Tet: The Bloodiest Year in Vietnam* (New York: Free Press, 1993), 283–84; Colby, *Lost Victory,* 241–43.

45. Komer, *Organization and Management,* 81–82.

46. William Westmoreland, telegram to the chairman of the Joint Chiefs of Staff and the commander in chief, Pacific, February 9, 1968, *FRUS, 1964– 1968,* 6:153–58; Notes of meeting, February 9, 1968, *FRUS, 1964–1968,* 6:158–68; Notes of meeting, *FRUS, 1964–1968,* 6:168–72; Notes of meeting, *FRUS, 1964–1968,* 6:175–82.

47. Robert W. Komer, "Trip to Southern Long Thanh, Phuc Tuy, near Baria Village," record of COMUSMACV fonecon, February 11, 1968, Box 28, Westmoreland Papers.

48. Spector, *After Tet,* ix; Oberdorfer, *Tet!* 250–51.

49. Frank C. Porter, "Pacification Work 'Did Stop,'" *Washington Post,* February 20, 1968.

50. Murray Marder, "Ky, Thang Quit Recovery Unit; U.S. Officials 'Disappointed,'" *Washington Post,* February 21, 1968.

51. Robert W. Komer, quoted in Willenson, *Bad War,* 95.

52. Ibid., 96. Westmoreland indicates the meeting occurred on February 23, 1968. See *Soldier Reports,* 353.

53. Robert W. Komer, quoted in Willenson, *Bad War,* 96.

54. Robert W. Komer, quoted in ibid., 96–97.

55. Westmoreland, *Soldier Reports,* 352–53.

56. Andrew J. Birtle, "PROVN, Westmoreland, and the Historians: A Reappraisal," *Journal of Military History* 72, no. 4 (October 2008): 1226.

57. Zaffiri, *Westmoreland,* 304.

58. Westmoreland, *Soldier Reports,* 353, 358–59

59. Braestrup, *Big Story,* 1:557.

60. Ibid., 1:455, 518; Komer, *Organization and Management,* 79; William Westmoreland, message to All Province Senior Advisors [drafted by Robert W. Komer], February 1968, Box 26, Westmoreland Papers; Ellsworth Bunker, "Report No. 40," back-channel report to Lyndon B. Johnson, February 22, 1968, item #1790109004, Virtual Vietnam Archive, http://www.vietnam.ttu.edu/virtualarchive/items.php?item=1790109004.

61. "U.S. Admits Blow to Pacification," *New York Times,* February 25, 1968.

62. "Supreme Test," *Newsweek,* February 26, 1968, 34–38.

63. Embassy in Vietnam, telegram to the Department of State, February 29, 1968, *FRUS, 1964–1968,* 6:282–86; Komer, *Organization and Management,* 79; Ward Just, "Guerrillas Wreck Pacification Plan," *Washington Post,* February 4, 1968.

64. L. Wade Lathram, letter to Maurice D. Roush, February 28, 1968, Documents 1968–1970, 1973, Various CORDS Reports Box, MACV Command Historian's Collection, MHI.

65. Komer, *Organization and Management,* 79.

66. Carroll Kilpatrick, "LBJ Sees Komer on Pacification," *Washington Post,* March 8, 1968; John Prados, *Lost Crusader: The Secret Wars of CIA Director William Colby* (New York: Oxford University Press, 2003), 200.

67. Rowland Evans and Robert Novak, "President Grows More Aggressive, Sounds Like a Commander-in-Chief," *Washington Post,* February 26, 1968.

68. Embassy in Vietnam, telegram to the Department of State, March 18, 1968, *FRUS, 1964–1968,* 6:403–5.

69. Bunker, "Report No. 40."

70. Allan E. Goodman, Randolph Harris, and John C. Wood, "South Vietnam and the Politics of Self-Support," *Asian Survey* 11, no. 1 (January 1971): 10–11. See also Ellsworth Bunker, "Report No. 59," back-channel report to Lyndon B. Johnson, July 11, 1968, item #1790114002, Virtual Vietnam Archive, http://www.vietnam.ttu.edu/virtualarchive/items.php?item=1790114002. Bunker's message is a mid-1968 assessment of progress on U.S. efforts in Vietnam.

71. Braestrup, *Big Story,* 1:544–50. Sir Robert Thompson would later concede that he had failed to understand how the Viet Cong's substantial losses during the Tet offensive had created a vacuum in the countryside. See his memoir, *Make for the Hills,* 155. It would not be until Thompson visited South Vietnam in February–March 1968, at Komer's behest and under a RAND contract, that he agreed the pacification program was not "in ruins"; it was still in its early stages, and thus the damage from the Tet offensive was minimal. See Brooke, "Matter of Will," 287.

72. Braestrup, *Big Story,* 1:545, 550–51.

73. "Supreme Test," *Newsweek,* February 26, 1968, 36.

CHAPTER 10. THE OLD FOX GETS FIRED

1. Colby and Forbath, *Honorable Men,* 236–38.

2. Colby, *Lost Victory,* 233–35.

3. Ibid., 235–38.

4. Colby and Forbath, *Honorable Men,* 250.

5. John Paul Vann, quoted in Spector, *After Tet,* 283.

6. Ibid.

7. Colby, *Lost Victory,* 241.

8. Ellsworth Bunker, "Report No. 43," back-channel report to Lyndon B. Johnson, March 14, 1968, item #2121012001, Virtual Vietnam Archive, http://www.vietnam.ttu.edu/virtualarchive/items.php?item=2121012001.

9. Ellsworth Bunker, "Report No. 44," back-channel report to Lyndon B. Johnson, March 20, 1968, item #2121012005, Virtual Vietnam Archive, http://www.vietnam.ttu.edu/virtualarchive/items.php?item=2121012005; Ellsworth Bunker, "Report No. 45," back-channel report to Lyndon B. Johnson, March 28, 1968, item #2121012013, Virtual Vietnam Archive, http://www.vietnam.ttu.edu/virtualarchive/items.php?item=2121012013; Cosmas, *Joint Chiefs of Staff and the War in Vietnam,* part 3, 146–47; William Westmoreland, "Post-Tet Pacification Assessment," message to U. S. G. Sharp [drafted by Robert W. Komer], March 1968, Box 26, Westmoreland Papers; "MACV Commanders' Conference," memorandum for the record, March 31, 1968, Box 46, Westmoreland Papers; American Embassy Saigon, cable to Secretary of State, March 1968, doc. #CK3100121699, Declassified Documents Reference System.

10. Don Oberdorfer, "An Ending of His Own," in *Reporting Vietnam: American Journalism 1959–1969* (New York: Library of America, 1998), 1:594, 596–97.

11. Ibid.

12. Ellsworth Bunker, "Report No. 46," back-channel report to Lyndon B. Johnson, April 4, 1968, item #2121101016, Virtual Vietnam Archive, http://www.vietnam.ttu.edu/virtualarchive/items.php?item=2121101016.

13. Notes of Meeting, Camp David, Maryland, April 9, 1968, *FRUS, 1964–1968,* 6:155n8. See also Robert W. Komer, back-channel memorandum to Ellsworth Bunker, Pacification Assessment, doc. #CK3100145051, Declassified Document Reference System.

14. Robert W. Komer, letter to Nguyen Van Thieu, April 14, 1968; Robert W. Komer, letter to Nguyen Van Thieu, April 29, 1968, both in DEPCORDSMACV Files.

15. Ellsworth Bunker, "Report No. 47," back-channel report to Lyndon B. Johnson, April 19, 1968, item #1790111002, Virtual Vietnam Archive, http://www.vietnam.ttu.edu/virtualarchive/items.php?item=1790111002.

16. Peter Braestrup, "Pacification 'Back on Track,'" *Washington Post,* April 19, 1968.

17. "Report Charges War Setback," *Washington Post,* May 26, 1968.

18. Ellsworth Bunker, "Report No. 50," back-channel report to Lyndon B. Johnson, May 9, 1968, item #2121107013, Virtual Vietnam Archive, http://www.vietnam.ttu.edu/virtualarchive/items.php?item=2121107013.

19. Embassy in Vietnam, telegram to the Department of State, May 23, 1968, *FRUS, 1964–1968,* 6:704–9; "Meeting with Prime Minister Tran Van Huong," memorandum for the record, May 31, 1968, *FRUS, 1964–1968,* 6:740–43.

20. "Meeting with Prime Minister Tran Van Huong," memorandum for the record, May 31, 1968, *FRUS, 1964–1968,* 6:740–43.

21. Ellsworth Bunker, "Report No. 54," back-channel report to Lyndon B. Johnson, June 8, 1968, item #2121109010, Virtual Vietnam Archive, http://www.vietnam.ttu.edu/virtualarchive/items.php?item=2121109010.

22. Bunker, "Report No. 50."

23. Robert Shaplen, "Letter from Saigon," *New Yorker,* June 29, 1968, 50, 59.

24. Bunker, "Report No. 54."

25. Ibid.; Ellsworth Bunker, "Report No. 57," back-channel report to Lyndon B. Johnson, June 27, 1968, item #2121109020, Virtual Vietnam Archive, http://www.vietnam.ttu.edu/virtualarchive/items.php?item=2121109020.

26. "Historical Sketch of CORDS, 1967–1969," MACCORDS 1967–1971, MACV Command Historian's Collection, MHI.

27. Johnson, "Phoenix/Phung Hoang," 203–4, 214; Ellsworth Bunker, "Report No. 58," back-channel report to Lyndon B. Johnson, July 4, 1968, item #1790114001, Virtual Vietnam Archive, http://www.vietnam.ttu.edu/virtualarchive/items.php?item=1790114001.

28. Andrade, *Ashes to Ashes,* 89, 90.

29. Robert W. Komer, letter to Tran Van Huong, June 10, 1968; Robert W. Komer, letter to Huynh Van Dao, June 11, 1968; Robert W. Komer, letter to Huyhn Van Dao, October 10, 1968, all in DEPCORDSMACV Files.

30. Robert W. Komer, "RF/PF Improvement Action Program," letter to Nguyen Van La, June 15, 1968; Robert W. Komer, "RF/PF Improvement," letter to Nguyen Van La, June 16, 1968; Robert W. Komer, "RF Training," letter to Nguyen Van La, June 30, 1968; Robert W. Komer, letter to Nguyen Van La, July 10, 1968; Robert W. Komer, "RF/PF Desertion," letter to Nguyen Van La, July 22, 1968, all in DEPCORDSMACV Files.

31. Clark Clifford, "Trip to South Vietnam," memorandum to Lyndon B. Johnson, July 13–18, 1968, *FRUS, 1964–1968,* 6:875–82; Colby, *Lost Victory,* 259.

32. Colby, *Lost Victory,* 259; Robert W. Komer, memorandum to Ellsworth Bunker and Creighton Abrams, July 16, 1968, DEPCORDSMACV Files.

33. Ellsworth Bunker, "Report No. 60," back-channel report to Lyndon B. Johnson, August 1, 1968, item #1790115001, Virtual Vietnam Archive, http://www.vietnam.ttu.edu/virtualarchive/items.php?item=1790115001.

34. Zeb B. Bradford Jr., quoted in Lewis Sorley, *A Better War* (New York: Harcourt, Brace, 1999), 61–62.

35. Robert W. Komer, letter to Creighton Abrams, July 28, 1968, DEPCORDSMACV Files.

36. Robert W. Komer, letter to Nguyen Van La, August 16, 1968, DEPCORDSMACV Files; Ellsworth Bunker, "Report No. 61," back-channel report to Lyndon B. Johnson, August 7, 1968, item #2121113012, Virtual Vietnam Archive, http://www.vietnam.ttu.edu/virtualarchive/items.php?item=2121113012.

37. Ellsworth Bunker, "Report No. 62," back-channel report to Lyndon B. Johnson, August 15, 1968, item #1790115003, Virtual Vietnam Archive, http://www.vietnam.ttu.edu/virtualarchive/items.php?item=1790115003; Ellsworth Bunker, "Report No. 64," back-channel report to Lyndon B. Johnson, August 29, 1968, item #2121114006, Virtual Vietnam Archive, http://www.vietnam.ttu.edu/virtualarchive/items.php?item=2121114006; "Historical Sketch of CORDS, 1967–1969."

38. Komer, *Organization and Management,* 88; COMUSMACV, message to CINCPAC, August 1968, 1966 File, Vann Papers. See also Colby and Forbath, *Honorable Men,* 254; Clay McManaway, interview by Charles Stuart Kennedy, June 29, 1993, transcript, Foreign Affairs Oral History Collection, Association for Diplomatic Studies and Training, Library of Congress, Washington, DC. There are discrepancies regarding who was actually involved in drawing up the detailed plans, depending on the source. However, one element is clear, the Accelerated Pacification Campaign was Komer's idea; this is made evident in the recent official history: Cosmas, *Joint Chiefs of Staff and the War in Vietnam,* part 3, 247. See also James Hubert Embrey, "Reorienting Pacification: The Accelerated Pacification Campaign of 1968" (PhD diss., University of Kentucky, 1997), 44. Embrey also interviewed McManaway, who confirmed that the pacification offensive that would form the groundwork for the Accelerated Pacification Campaign was Komer's alone. Embrey also notes that Komer had raised the same concept in July 1968, but Abrams, the new MACV commander, had tabled it for consideration.

39. Komer, *Organization and Management,* 86.

40. Embrey, "Reorienting Pacification," 45–48, 52.

41. "Historical Sketch of CORDS, 1967–1969"; Peter Braestrup, "VC Thrust Hurts Allies Little," *Washington Post,* September 17, 1968.

42. Colby and Forbath, *Honorable Men,* 257–58; Colby, *Lost Victory,* 251–54.

43. Colby, *Lost Victory,* 254–55.

44. Komer, *Organization and Management,* 86–87.

45. Ibid., 87–88.

46. Peter Braestrup, "Thieu Finally Puts Pacification First," *Washington Post,* September 8, 1968.

47. Ibid.

48. Ibid.

49. Robert W. Komer, letter to Nguyen Van La, September 11, 1968, DEPCORDSMACV Files.

50. Braestrup, "VC Thrust Hurts Allies Little."

51. "Komer Sees Long Road for Pacification Effort," *Washington Post,* September 24, 1968.

52. Robert Montague, note to Robert W. Komer, September 28, 1968, Accelerated Pacification Campaign (March–September 1968) File, DEPCORDSMACV Files.

53. Embassy in Vietnam, telegram to the Department of State, October 2, 1968, *FRUS, 1964–1968,* vol. 7, *Vietnam, September 1968–January 1969* (Washington, DC: USGPO, 2003), 115–19.

54. Robert W. Komer, "Third Quarter Report on Pacification (July–September 1968)," memorandum to Ellsworth Bunker, October 16, 1968, DEPCORDSMACV Files.

55. Nels A. Parson Jr., memorandum to Acting Chief, P and P Division, October 5, 1968, Accelerated Pacification Campaign (March–September 1968) File, DEPCORDSMACV Files.

56. Ahern, *CIA and Rural Pacification.*

57. Ellsworth Bunker, "Report No. 71," back-channel report to Lyndon B. Johnson, October 19, 1968, item #1790117003, Virtual Vietnam Archive, http://www.vietnam.ttu.edu/virtualarchive/items.php?item=1790117003; Ahern, *CIA and Rural Pacification,* 350.

58. Robert W. Komer, letter to McGeorge Bundy, September 15, 1968, DEPCORDSMACV Files.

59. Robert W. Komer, letter to Dean Rusk, August 22, 1968, DEPCORDSMACV Files.

60. Robert W. Komer, letter to Leonard Marks, September 15, 1968, DEPCORDSMACV Files.

61. Robert W. Komer, letter to Harry McPherson, September 21, 1968, DEPCORDSMACV Files.

62. Komer, Oral History Interview II, LBJL, 60–61.

63. Komer, *Blowtorch,* chap. XV, 6, and chap. XVI, 1.

64. Sorley, *Better War,* 63.

65. "Komer Leaving Pacification Job in Vietnam to Be Envoy to Turkey," *Washington Post,* October 29, 1968; Robert W. Komer, memorandum to Ellsworth Bunker, October 31, 1968, Komer-Abrams (1968) File, DEPCORDSMACV Files.

66. Robert W. Komer, letter to George Carver, October 30, 1968, Accelerated Pacification Campaign (March–September 1968) File, DEPCORDSMACV Files.

67. U.S. Military Assistance Command, Vietnam, *Command History,* vol. 3, *1968* (Saigon: U.S. Military Assistance Command, Vietnam, 1969), 521–22; Ellsworth Bunker, "Report No. 72," back-channel report to Lyndon B. Johnson, October 30, 1968, item #1790117004, Virtual Vietnam Archive, http://www.vietnam.ttu.edu/virtualarchive/items.php?item=1790117004; Colby, *Lost Victory,* 254.

68. American Embassy Saigon, message to Secretary of State, November 1968, Box 12, Komer-Leonhart File, LBJL; Peter Braestrup, "Peace Debate Can't Stir Saigon's Sunday," *Washington Post,* November 4, 1968.

69. Memorandum for the record, November 5, 1968, *FRUS, 1964–1968,* 7:569–70.

70. Prados, *Lost Crusader,* 206.

71. Dave Warsh, "Hamlet Counts Seen Important Viet Sign," *Pacific Stars and Stripes,* November 10, 1968.

72. Andrade, *Ashes to Ashes,* 55.

73. Sorley, *Better War,* 62. Gregory A. Daddis, in his study of the Vietnam War, writes that this is an unfair characterization of Komer's role. See Daddis, "No Sure Victory," 247–48.

74. Braestrup, *Big Story,* 1:533, 541.

75. Gabriel Kolko, *Anatomy of a War: Vietnam, the United States, and the Modern Historical Experience* (New York: New Press, 1994), 237.

76. John Prados, *Vietnam: The History of an Unwinnable War, 1945–1975* (Lawrence: University Press of Kansas, 2009), 321.

77. Braestrup, *Big Story,* 1:540.

78. Frank G. Wisner, interview by Richard L. Jackson, March 22, 1998, Foreign Affairs Oral History Project, Association for Diplomatic Studies and Training, Special Collections Room, Lauinger Library, Georgetown University, Washington, DC.

79. Kinnard, *War Managers,* 104.

80. Brooke, "Matter of Will," 287–89.

81. Guzzardi, "Management of the War," 135.

82. Cooper et al., *American Experience with Pacification in Vietnam,* 1:22–24.

83. Thayer, *War without Fronts,* 137.

84. Davidson, *Vietnam at War,* 457.

85. Arthur Daley, "Sports of the Times: The Mahatma," *New York Times,* November 17, 1965. This maxim is attributed to Branch Rickey, "The Mahatma." The full quote: "Things worthwhile generally don't just happen. Luck is a fact, but should not be a factor. Good luck is what is left over after intelligence and effort have combined at their best. Negligence or indifference are [sic] usually reviewed from an unlucky seat. The law of cause and effect and causality both work the same with inexorable exactitudes. Luck is the residue of design."

86. Davidson, *Vietnam at War,* 457.

87. Clarke, *Advice and Support,* 235–36, 507.

88. Braestrup, *Big Story,* 1:540; Cooper et al., *American Experience with Pacification in Vietnam,* 2:302.

89. Cooper et al., *American Experience with Pacification in Vietnam,* 3:295.

90. Ibid., 298.

CHAPTER 11. A NEW TRANSATLANTIC BARGAIN

1. Edward Walsh, "Hey, Prime Minister, Get Out of the Way! We Want to See Jimmy," *Washington Post,* May 7, 1977; Edward Walsh, "Callaghan on Carter: 'He's a Knockout,'" *Washington Post,* May 9, 1977; Jimmy Carter, "Remarks at the Newcastle Civic Centre, Newcastle-Upon-Tyne, England," May 6, 1977, *American Presidency Project,* http://www.presidency.ucsb.edu/ws/index.php?pid=7472.

2. Jimmy Carter, "NATO Ministerial Meeting Text of Remarks at the First Session of the Meeting," May 10, 1977, *American Presidency Project,* http://www.presidency.ucsb.edu/ws/index.php?pid=7492; Jimmy Carter, "Meetings in London and Geneva Question-and-Answer Session with Reporters following the Meetings," May 10, 1977, *American Presidency Project,* http://www.presidency.ucsb.edu/ws/index.php?pid=7494; Jimmy Carter, "The President's News Conference," May 12, 1977, *American Presidency Project,* http://www.presidency.ucsb.edu/ws/index.php?pid=7495; Zbigniew Brzezinski, *Power and Principle: Memoirs of the National Security Adviser, 1977–1981* (New York: Farrar, Straus, and Giroux, 1983), 292–93; Robert M. Gates, *From the Shadows: The Ultimate Insider's Story of Five Presidents and How They Won the Cold War* (New York: Simon & Schuster, 1996), 111.

3. "Rusk Honors Komer," *New York Times,* November 26, 1968.

4. Sorley, *Better War,* 63.

5. Komer, *Blowtorch,* chap. XV, 6, and chap. XVI, 1.

6. "Turkish Students Protest Arrival of U.S. Ambassador," *New York Times,* November 29, 1968; "More Protests on Komer," *New York Times,* December 1, 1968; Sam Cohen, "Turk Leftists Step Up Drive against Komer," *Washington Post,* December 4, 1968; "Envoy Komer's Car Burned in Turkey by Anti-U.S. Student Demonstrators," *Washington Post,* January 7, 1969; "Turkey Apologizes to U.S. for Attack on Komer's Car," *New York Times,* January 8, 1969; "Around the World," *Washington Post,* March 15, 1969; "Charges by Leftists in Turkey Refuted by Nation's Gains," *Washington Post,* April 3, 1968; Komer, *Blowtorch,* chap. XVI, 3.

7. Komer, *Blowtorch,* chap. XVI, 5–6.

8. "Nixon, Advisors Discuss Fate of Domestic Plans," *Washington Post,* April 5, 1969.

9. "Eroded Relations Seen by Komer," *Washington Post,* May 7, 1968.

10. Anthony Lewis, "Turks' New Mood Is Puzzling," *New York Times,* February 17, 1969; "Extreme Leftists in Turkey Voicing Pleasure over Nixon's Decision to Replace Komer as Ambassador," *New York Times,* April 10, 1969.

11. Robert W. Komer, "Clear, Hold and Build," *Army,* May 1970, 17–24; Robert W. Komer, "Pacification: A Look Back and Ahead," *Army,* June 1970, 20–29.

12. Mai Elliott, *RAND in Southeast Asia: A History of the Vietnam War Era* (Santa Monica, CA: RAND, 2010), 383–87. There is a discrepancy regarding the dates of this visit and at whose behest it occurred between Elliott's account and that of Thomas L. Ahern Jr., *Vietnam Declassified: The CIA and Counterinsurgency* (Lexington: University Press of Kentucky, 2010), 338. However, it seems clear that Komer wrote two reports or a two-section report resulting from his visit. One element was a RAND document and the other was on the Phoenix Program, which appears to have been provided to the CIA.

13. Elliott, *RAND in Southeast Asia,* 386, 388, 391.

14. Ahern, *Vietnam Declassified,* 338–41; Prados, *Lost Crusader,* 229; Valentine, *Phoenix Program,* 184, 321–23.

15. U.S. House of Representatives, *U.S. Assistance Programs in Vietnam: Hearings Before a Subcommittee of the Committee on Government Operations,* 92nd Cong., 289 (1971) (letter by R. W. Komer).

16. Prados, *Lost Crusader,* 237.

17. Ibid., 235; James William Gibson, *The Perfect War: Technowar in Vietnam* (Boston: Atlantic Monthly Press, 1986), 299; Moyar, *Phoenix and the Birds of Prey,* 181.

18. Moyar, *Phoenix and the Birds of Prey,* 53–54. See also Gen. Bruce Palmer's remark that Colby revitalized Phoenix when he became CORDS chief.

Bruce Palmer Jr., *U.S. Intelligence and Vietnam* (Washington, DC: Central Intelligence Agency, 1984), 70.

19. Austin Long, *On "Other War": Lessons from Five Decades of RAND Counterinsurgency Research* (Santa Monica, CA: RAND, 2006), 40–41.

20. Komer, "Impact of Pacification on Insurgency," 1–19; Komer, *Blowtorch,* chap. XVII, 1–2.

21. Robert W. Komer, "Impact of Pacification on Insurgency in South Vietnam," in *Revolutionary War: Western Response,* ed. David S. Sullivan and Martin J. Sattler (New York: Columbia University Press, 1971), 48–72.

22. Ibid.; Eqbal Ahmad, "Revolutionary War and Counter-Insurgency," in *Revolutionary War,* 44, 70–73.

23. R. W. Komer, *The Malayan Emergency in Retrospect: Organization of a Successful Counterinsurgency Effort* (Santa Monica, CA: RAND, 1972).

24. R. W. Komer, *Bureaucracy Does Its Thing: Institutional Constraints on U.S.-GVN Performance in Vietnam* (Santa Monica, CA: RAND, 1972), v–xiii; Long, *On "Other War,"* 41–42.

25. Long, *On "Other War,"* 9.

26. Richard L. Kugler, *Commitment to Purpose: How Alliance Partnership Won the Cold War* (Santa Monica, CA: RAND, 1993), 291–92; Robert W. Komer, interviewed by Alfred Goldberg, Roger R. Task, and Stuart I. Rochester, March 25, 1981, Historian's Office, Office of the Secretary of Defense, Arlington, VA, 2–3 (hereafter cited as OSD Interview); Robert W. Komer, "The Origins and Objectives," *NATO Review* 26, no. 3 (June 1978): 10, 12; Brian J. Auten, *Carter's Conversion: The Hardening of American Defense Policy* (Columbia: University of Missouri Press, 2008), 153; John S. Duffield, *Power Rules: The Evolution of NATO's Conventional Force Posture* (Stanford, CA: Stanford University Press, 1995), 213.

27. R. W. Komer, "Treating NATO's Self-Inflicted Wound," Paper P-5092 (Santa Monica, CA: RAND, 1973), 1–2.

28. Ibid., 2–8.

29. Ibid., 8–15. The RAND paper was subsequently published in *Foreign Policy* no. 13 (Winter 1973–74): 34–48.

30. Robert W. Komer et al., *Rationalizing NATO's Defense Posture,* Report R-1657-ARPA/ISA/PAE (Santa Monica, CA: RAND, 1975); Robert W. Komer, "Preparation for Coalition War," Paper P-5707 (Santa Monica, CA: RAND, 1976), 1–10.

31. Bernard Weinraub, "Pacification Chief in Vietnam Now a Top Pentagon Adviser," *New York Times,* March 14, 1978; Komer, "Origins and Objectives," 10.

32. Brzezinski, *Power and Principle,* 51; National Security Council, "Comprehensive Review of European Issues," Presidential Review

Memorandum/NSC-9, February 1, 1977, http://www.fas.org/irp/offdocs/prm/prm09.pdf.

33. Brzezinski, *Power and Principle,* 52. See also Raymond A. Moore, "The Carter Administration and Foreign Policy," in *The Carter Years: The President and Policy Making,* ed. M. Glenn Abernathy, Dilys M. Hill, and Phil Williams (New York: St. Martin's Press, 1984), 60–61.

34. Phil Williams, "Carter's Defense Policy," in *Carter Years,* 88; James A. Linger, "Europe and the Superpowers," in *Defense Policy and the Presidency: Carter's First Years,* ed. Sam C. Sarkesian (Boulder, CO: Westview Press, 1979), 279.

35. Komer, OSD Interview, 3.

36. Ibid., 3–6; Komer, "Origins and Objectives," 9–10; Auten, *Carter's Conversion,* 153–54; James C. Wendt and Nanette Brown, *Improving the NATO Force Planning Process: Lessons from Past Efforts,* Report R-3383-USDP (Santa Monica, CA: RAND, 1986), 16.

37. Robert W. Komer, "Ten Suggestions for Rationalizing NATO," *Survival* 19, no. 2 (March/April 1977): 67–72.

38. Gregory F. Treverton, "PRC Meeting on Europe," memorandum to Zbigniew Brzezinski, April 13, 1977, doc. #CK3100516992, Declassified Documents Reference System.

39. Auten, *Carter's Conversion,* 154n63.

40. Komer, "Origins and Objectives," 11.

41. Linger, "Europe and the Superpowers," 256.

42. Komer, OSD Interview, 6–7; Kugler, *Commitment to Purpose,* 317.

43. Komer, OSD Interview, 6–7; Kugler, *Commitment to Purpose,* 327; Kenneth H. Bacon, "NATO Program to Call for More Money and a Bolstering of European Defenses," *Wall Street Journal,* May 18, 1977.

44. Auten, *Carter's Conversion,* 155, 155n67.

45. Komer, OSD Interview, 4–5, 8–9.

46. Kugler, *Commitment to Purpose,* 313.

47. Komer, OSD Interview, 10; Simon Lunn, *Burden-Sharing in NATO,* Chatham House Papers 18 (London: Royal Institute of International Affairs/Routledge & Kegan Paul, 1983), 16.

48. Kugler, *Commitment to Purpose,* 318; Simon Duke, *The Burdensharing Debate: A Reassessment* (New York: St. Martin's Press, 1993), 73.

49. Robert W. Komer, quoted in Duke, *Burdensharing Debate,* 75.

50. National Security Council, "U.S. National Strategy," Presidential Directive/NSC-18, August 26, 1977, http://www.fas.org/irp/offdocs/pd/pd18.pdf.

51. Benjamin F. Schemmer, "Haig Now Says NATO Can Expect 8–14 Days Warning, Not 48 Hours," *Armed Forces Journal International,* October 1977, 16.

52. Harold Brown, *Thinking about National Security: Defense and Foreign Policy in a Dangerous World* (Boulder, CO: Westview Press, 1983), 102.

53. Komer, OSD Interview, 26–29; Robert Komer, "Looking Ahead," *International Security* 4, no. 1 (Summer 1979): 111–13; U.S. House of Representatives, Committee on International Relations, *Western Europe in 1977: Security, Economic and Political Issues: Hearings Before the Subcommittee on Europe and the Middle East,* 95th Cong. (1977).

54. U.S. Senate, Committee on Armed Services, NATO and the New Soviet Threat, S. Rep. 95–1 at 1 (1977).

55. Auten, *Carter's Conversion,* 150, 152.

56. U.S. Senate, *NATO Posture and Initiatives: Hearings Before the Subcommittee on Manpower and Personnel,* 95th Cong., 1–8, 45–48, 55 (1977).

57. Duffield, *Power Rules,* 210, 342n61, 342n62.

58. U.S. House, *Western Europe in 1977,* 200–202.

59. Ibid., 219, 221, 223.

60. Komer, OSD Interview, 11.

61. Ibid., 12–13.

62. Ibid., 13.

63. Ibid., 14–17.

64. U.S. Senate, *First Concurrent Resolution on the Budget, FY79, Vol. 1: Hearings before the Committee on the Budget,* 95th Cong., 400–402 (1978); Bernard Weinraub, "Higher Outlay Emphasizes Buildup in Aid to NATO," *New York Times,* January 24, 1978, 17.

65. George C. Wilson, "Carter's 'NATO Budget' Indicates Shift of Military Focus," *Washington Post,* January 15, 1978.

66. Komer, OSD Interview, 17–18.

67. Richard Burt, "U.S. Presses NATO to Approve Ambitious Programs for Defense," *New York Times,* May 29, 1978; Kenneth H. Bacon, "NATO Members Agree on Defense Plan, Differ on Approach to African Situation," *Wall Street Journal,* June 1, 1978; Joseph M. A. H. Luns, "The Washington Summit Meeting in Perspective," *NATO Review* 26, no. 4 (August 1978): 3–7.

68. George C. Wilson, "Arms: Theory into Practice," *Washington Post,* May 18, 1978; "Ambassador Robert W. Komer," *Armed Forces Journal International,* September 1978, 47; "A Hamlet's Ghost for NATO," *Wall Street Journal,* May 31, 1978.

69. U.S. Comptroller General, *NATO's New Defense Program: Issues for Consideration,* Report to Congress of the United States, ID-79–1A (Washington, DC: U.S. General Accounting Office, 1979); Drew Middleton, "NATO Extends 3% Rise in Annual Spending to '85," *New York Times,* May 16, 1979.

70. Lunn, *Burden-Sharing in NATO,* 29.
71. Duffield, *Power Rules,* 218.

CHAPTER 12. PENTAGON POLICYMAKER

1. Richard Burt, "Pentagon Seeks to Give Policy Post to Vietnam War Pacification Chief," *New York Times,* August 11, 1979; Paul K. Davis, "Observations on the Rapid Deployment Joint Task Force: Origins, Direction, and Mission," Paper P-6751 (Santa Monica, CA: RAND, 1982), iii, http://www.rand.org/pubs/papers/2005/P6751.pdf. Davis served in the Department of Defense between August 1977 and August 1981 as director of regional studies and as acting deputy assistant secretary of defense (regional programs). In this capacity, he directed studies and programs that contributed to the Defense Department's establishment of what became the RDJTF.
2. Robert Komer, *Blowtorch,* chap. XIX, 1–2.
3. Jimmy Carter Library archivist, e-mail message to the author, March 2, 2005; Komer, OSD Interview, 34–35; Kenneth E. Morris, *Jimmy Carter: American Moralist* (Athens: University of Georgia Press, 1996), 241.
4. Burt, "Policy Post to Vietnam War Pacification Chief"; Komer, *Blowtorch,* chap. XIX, 2; Jimmy Carter, "Department of Defense Nomination of Robert W. Komer to Be Under Secretary for Policy," September 27, 1979, *American Presidency Project,* http://www.presidency.ucsb.edu/ws/?pid=31431.
5. U.S. Senate, Committee on Armed Services, *Hearing on the Nominations of Robert W. Komer to Be Under Secretary of Defense for Policy, Honorable Edward Hidalgo to Be Secretary of the Navy, and Dennis P. McAuliffe to Be Administrator of the Panama Canal Commission,* 99th Cong., 3–6 (1979); "Navy Secretary Confirmed," *New York Times,* October 20, 1979.
6. Komer, *Blowtorch,* chap. XIX, 2–5.
7. "Who Lost Iran?" *Time,* December 4, 1979, http://www.time.com/time/magazine/article/0,9171,912266,00.html.
8. Maxwell Orme Johnson, *The Military as an Instrument of U.S. Policy in Southwest Asia: The Rapid Deployment Joint Task Force, 1979–1982* (Boulder, CO: Westview Press, 1983), 9, 64; Brzezinski, *Power and Principle,* 446.
9. William E. Odom, "The Cold War Origins of the U.S. Central Command," *Journal of Cold War Studies* 8, no. 2 (Spring 2006): 57–58.
10. Ibid.; Hargrove, *Jimmy Carter as President,* 148.
11. Jed C. Snyder, *Defending the Fringe: NATO, the Mediterranean, and the Persian Gulf,* SAIS Papers in International Affairs, Number 11 (Boulder, CO: Westview Press, 1987), 116; National Security Council, "Comprehensive

Net Assessment and Military Force Posture Review," Presidential Review Memorandum/NSC-10, February 18, 1977; Department of Defense, "PRM-10 Force Posture Study," June 5, 1977, both available at http://www.jimmycarterlibrary.gov/documents/prmemorandums/prm10.pdf.

12. Odom, "Cold War Origins," 56, 58.

13. David Newsom, interview by author, May 30, 2007.

14. Olav Njølstad, "The Carter Legacy: Entering the Second Era of the Cold War," in *The Last Decade of the Cold War: From Conflict Escalation to Conflict Transformation,* ed. Olav Njølstad (London: Frank Cass, 2004), 203; Michael Sheridan, telephone interview by author, April 17, 2007.

15. U.S. House of Representatives, Committee on Foreign Affairs, Subcommittee on Europe and the Middle East, *Hearings on NATO After Afghanistan,* 96th Cong., 7 (1980).

16. Jimmy Carter, *Keeping Faith: Memoirs of a President* (New York: Bantam Books, 1982), 471–72; Dennis Ross, "Considering Soviet Threats to the Persian Gulf," *International Security* 6, no. 2 (Autumn 1981): 164. Ross was the assistant to the director of net assessment (ONA) in the Office of the Secretary of Defense when he wrote this essay. Previously, he had he worked in Office of the Secretary of Defense's Office of Program Analysis and Evaluation, where he focused on Middle East military issues. Both offices produced studies of U.S.-Soviet military capabilities during the 1970s.

17. Hargrove, *Jimmy Carter as President,* 155; Carter, *Keeping Faith,* 473; "My Opinion of the Russians Has Changed Most Dramatically . . ." *Time,* December 4, 1979, http://www.time.com/time/magazine/article/0,9171,921764,00.html.

18. Brzezinski, *Power and Principle,* 430.

19. Melvyn P. Leffler, "From the Truman Doctrine to the Carter Doctrine: Lessons and Dilemmas of the Cold War," *Diplomatic History* 7, no. 4 (October 1983): 245–46; Brzezinski, *Power and Principle,* 444.

20. Don Oberdorfer, "Evolution of a Decision," *Washington Post,* January 24, 1980.

21. Hendrick (Rick) Hertzberg, "Exit Interview," interview by Marie Allen, December 10, 1980, Jimmy Carter Library, Atlanta, Georgia, 19–22, 24.

22. Jimmy Carter, "The State of the Union Address Delivered before a Joint Session of the Congress," January 23, 1980, *American Presidency Project,* http://www.presidency.ucsb.edu/ws/?pid=33079.

23. Hargrove, *Jimmy Carter as President,* 114, 153–54, 156; Leffler, "From the Truman Doctrine," 255.

24. Zbigniew Brzezinski with Madeleine K. Albright, Leslie G. Denend, and William Odom, interview by Inis Claude, February 18, 1982, Carter

Presidency Project, Miller Center for Public Affairs, University of Virginia, Charlottesville, 40. (Hereafter cited as "Interview of Brzezinski et al.")

25. Kugler, *Commitment to Purpose,* 341–42, 345.

26. Harold Brown, *Department of Defense Annual Report, Fiscal Year 1981* (Washington, DC: Department of Defense, 1980), 115.

27. Hargrove, *Jimmy Carter as President,* 149.

28. U.S. Senate, *U.S. Security Interests and Policies in Southwest Asia: Hearings Before the Committee on Foreign Relations,* 96th Cong., 297–302 (1980) (testimony of Robert W. Komer, under secretary of policy, Department of Defense); C. Paul Bradley, *Recent United States Policy in the Persian Gulf* (Grantham, NH: Tompson and Rutter, 1982), 99–101; James H. Noyes, *The Clouded Lens: Persian Gulf Security and U.S. Policy,* 2nd ed. (Stanford, CA: Hoover Institution Press, 1982), 126–27; David A. Quinlan, *The Role of the Marine Corps in Rapid Deployment Forces* (Washington, DC: National Defense University Press, 1983), 4–5; Organization of the Joint Chiefs of Staff, *United States Military Posture for FY 1982* (Washington, DC: Department of Defense, 1981), 50; U.S. Senate, *Department of Defense Authorization for Appropriations for Fiscal Year 1981: Hearings on S. 2294 before the Senate Committee on Armed Services,* 96th Cong., 1233 (1980); Michael Getler, "Persian Gulf: Little Debate on Buildup," *Washington Post,* August 10, 1980.

29. Kugler, *Commitment to Purpose,* 342.

30. William E. Odom, interview by the author, May 29, 2007.

31. Davis, "Observations on the Rapid Deployment Joint Task Force," iii, 15–16; Brzezinski, *Power and Principle,* 444, 450.

32. Komer, OSD Interview, 49.

33. Joint Chiefs of Staff, *United States Military Posture,* 55–56; *A Discussion of the Rapid Deployment Force with Lieutenant General P. X. Kelley,* Special Analysis No. 80–4 (Washington, DC: American Enterprise Institute for Public Policy Research, 1980), 3–4; Bradley, *Recent United States Policy,* 98–99; E. Asa Bates, "The Rapid Deployment Force—Fact or Fiction," *RUSI: Journal of the Royal United Services Institute for Defence Studies* 126, no. 2 (June 1981): 24; Robert P. Haffa Jr., *The Half War: Planning U.S. Rapid Deployment Forces to Meet a Limited Contingency, 1960–1983* (Boulder, CO: Westview Press, 1984), 126.

34. Komer, OSD Interview, 49.

35. Ross, "Soviet Threats," 177–78.

36. Leffler, "From the Truman Doctrine," 258, 263. For Komer's testimony, see U.S. Senate, *Department of Defense Authorization,* 436, 445, 478; and U.S. Senate, *U.S. Security Interests and Policies in Southwest Asia,* 299.

37. Chryss Galassi, "'Blowtorch Bob' Is Back on Top," with David C. Martin, *Newsweek,* March 24, 1980, 54.

38. Komer, *Blowtorch,* chap. XIX, 14–15; Bates, "Rapid Deployment Force," 24.

39. U.S. Senate, *Department of Defense Authorization,* 1243–44; Komer, OSD Interview, 50; Davis, "Observations," 8, 10.

40. Harold Brown, "What the Carter Doctrine Means to Me," *MERIP Reports,* no. 90 (September 1980): 22–23.

41. William Odom, "MILCON: M-B-B Luncheon Item," memorandum to Zbigniew Brzezinski, July 30, 1980, doc. #CK3100487560, Declassified Documents Reference System.

42. Komer, OSD Interview, 81–82; Robert W. Komer, memorandum to Lyndon B. Johnson, March 16, 1964, *FRUS, 1964–1968,* vol. 21, *Near East Region* (Washington, DC: USGPO, 2000), 89; Dean Rusk, "Indian Ocean Facilities," memorandum to Lyndon B. Johnson, July 15, 1964, *FRUS, 1964–1968,* 21:91–93; John McNaughton, "Indian Ocean Islands," letter to Robert McNamara, June 12, 1965, *FRUS, 1964–1968,* 21:94–96; Robert W. Komer, memorandum to McGeorge Bundy, October 15, 1965, *FRUS, 1964–1968,* 21:98; Robert W. Komer, memorandum to McGeorge Bundy, *FRUS, 1964–1968,* 21:99–100; Paul Nitze, "Proposed Limited Support Facility on Diego Garcia," memorandum to Robert McNamara, February 24, 1967, *FRUS, 1964–1968,* 21:103–5; Commander Navy Installations Command (CNIC), "U.S. Navy Support Facility Diego Garcia History," http://www.cnic.navy.mil/DiegoGarcia/About/History/index.htm.

43. CNIC, "U.S. Navy Support Facility Diego Garcia History"; "Diego Garcia 'Camp Justice' 7°20'S 72°25'E," GlobalSecurity.org, May 7, 2011, http://www.globalsecurity.org/military/facility/diego-garcia.htm.

44. Komer, OSD Interview, 45–45, 48; Davis, "Observations," 16; Sheridan interview.

45. Sheridan interview.

46. Davis, "Observations," 16–18.

47. Sheridan interview; Davis, "Observations," 16–18.

48. Komer, OSD Interview, 82, 86–87; Snyder, *Defending the Fringe,* 117.

49. Komer, OSD Interview, 88.

50. Ibid., 88–89.

51. Getler, "Persian Gulf: Little Debate on Buildup."

52. Paul Jabber, "U.S. Interests and Regional Security in the Middle East," *Daedulus* 109 (Fall 1980): 80; Jeffrey Record, *The Rapid Deployment Force and U.S. Military Intervention in the Persian Gulf* (Cambridge, MA: Institute for Foreign Policy Analysis, 1981), 34–35, 54; James R. Schlesinger, "Rapid (?) Deployment (?) Force (?)," *Washington Post,* September 24, 1980.

53. Bradley, *Recent United States Policy,* 99.

54. "Security Assistance for Southwest Asia," summary of a Special Coordinating Committee Meeting, October 28, 1980, doc. #CK3100472777, Declassified Documents Reference System.

55. Assistant National Intelligence Officer for Near East and South Asia, "SCC Meeting of 7 November 1980: Security Framework," memorandum to Director of Central Intelligence, November 7, 1980, http://www.foia.cia.gov/docs/DOC_0000200682/DOC_0000200682.pdf.

56. Interview of Brzezinski et al., 41. See also National Intelligence Officer for Near East and South Asia, "SCC Meeting of 16 December 1980—Security Framework," memorandum to Director of Central Intelligence, December 17, 1980, http://www.foia.cia.gov/docs/DOC_0000200681/DOC_0000200681.pdf.

57. Brzezinski, *Power and Principle,* 468.

CHAPTER 13. THE SIN OF UNILATERALISM

1. George C. Wilson, "Farewell Broadside Unloaded on the Military Mossbacks," *Washington Post,* February 14, 1981.

2. George Mason University, *Security Challenges in the 1980's,* Miscellaneous Publications of George Mason University, No. 2 (Fairfax, VA: George Mason University, 1983), vii; Robert W. Komer, "The President, the NSC and the Secretary of Defense," in *Four Virginia Papers Presented at the Miller Center Forums, 1981, Part V,* ed. Kenneth W. Thompson (Washington, DC: University Press of America, 1982), 50.

3. George Mason University, *Security Challenges,* 45–47.

4. Ibid., 47–50.

5. Komer, "President, the NSC and the Secretary of Defense," 41–60.

6. Ibid., 49–53.

7. George C. Wilson, "In Policy Shift, Pentagon Seeks Naval Superiority," *Washington Post,* December 14, 1971.

8. George C. Wilson, "U.S. Has Lost Naval Superiority over Soviets, Leaders Tell Hill Panel," *Washington Post,* February 6, 1981.

9. Ibid.

10. Richard Halloran, "Navy Secretary Seeks More Strength to Balk Soviets," *New York Times,* May 17, 1981.

11. Wilson, "In Policy Shift."

12. Ibid.

13. Ibid.

14. Ibid.

15. Ibid.

16. Robert W. Komer, "The High Cost of Ruling the Seas," *Washington Post,* February 7, 1982.

17. Ibid.

18. Ibid.

19. Michael Getler, "Carter Team Likes Defense Outlays but Not Priorities," *Washington Post,* February 12, 1982.

20. Ibid.

21. Robert W. Komer, "Maritime Strategy vs. Coalition Defense, *Foreign Affairs* 60, no. 5 (Summer 1982): 1124–42.

22. Ibid., 1143–44.

23. Stansfield Turner and George Thibault, "Preparing for the Unexpected: The Need for a New Military Strategy," *Foreign Affairs* 60, no. 6 (Fall 1982): 122–35.

24. Robert W. Komer, "To the Editor," *Foreign Affairs* 61, no. 2 (Winter 1982–83): 453–54.

25. John Lehman, "To the Editor," *Foreign Affairs* 61, no. 2 (Winter 1982–83): 455–56.

26. "Mr. Komer Replies, Admiral Turner Replies," *Foreign Affairs* 61, no. 3 (Winter 1982–83): 456–57.

27. Michael Getler, "'Too Late to Stop' Fleet Buildup, Says Navy Secretary," *Washington Post,* December 2, 1982; Helen Dewar, "Pentagon Diet Appears to Be a Slim Hope," *Washington Post,* April 30, 1983.

28. Dewar, "Pentagon Diet."

29. George C. Wilson, "Navy Is Preparing for Submarine Warfare beneath Coastal Ice," *Washington Post,* May 19, 1983.

30. Richard Halloran, "What the Navy Should Spend: A Classic Washington Clash," *New York Times,* August 24, 1983.

31. George C. Wilson, "Lehman Wins a Budget Battle," *Washington Post,* September 8, 1983.

32. Halloran, "What the Navy Should Spend," *New York Times,* August 24, 1983.

33. Fred Hiatt, "Feud Erupts on Navy's Future," *Washington Post,* October 11, 1983.

34. Fred Hiatt, "Weinberger Asked to Mediate," *Washington Post,* October 12, 1983.

35. Fred Hiatt and T. R. Reid, "Congress Shows Its Distrust of Pentagon's Arms Buying," *Washington Post,* November 20, 1983.

36. Caspar Weinberger, *Fighting for Peace: Seven Critical Years in the Pentagon* (New York: Warner Books, 1990), 57.

37. Fred Hiatt, "Military Buildup Still Secure," *Washington Post,* December 17, 1983.

38. Jeffrey Record, "Jousting with Unreality: Reagan's Military Strategy," *International Security* 8, no. 3 (Winter 1983–84): 3–14.

39. John Glenn, Barry E. Carter, and Robert W. Komer, *Rethinking Defense and Conventional Forces* (Washington, DC: Center for National Policy, 1983), 43–52.

40. Robert W. Komer, "Carrier-Heavy Navy Is Waste-Heavy," *Los Angeles Times,* May 16, 1984.

41. Thomas D. Watkins, "Current Strategy of the U.S. Navy," letter to the *Los Angeles Times,* June 21, 1984.

42. Fred Hiatt, "Lehman's 'Forward Strategy' Is Challenged in Navy Journal," *Washington Post,* August 26, 1984.

43. Peter Nailor, "*Maritime Strategy or Coalition Defense?* A Review," *International Affairs* 60, no. 4 (Autumn 1984): 735.

44. Steven E. Miller, "Defense Misspending, a Review," *New York Times,* November 25, 1984.

45. Dov S. Zakheim, "Review of *Maritime Strategy or Coalition Defense?*" *Political Science Quarterly* 99, no. 4 (Winter 1984–85): 721–22.

46. Fred Hiatt, "Weinberger Faces Cuts Optimistically," *Washington Post,* January 20, 1985.

47. Fred Hiatt, "The Weinberger Counterattack," *Washington Post,* February 3, 1985.

48. Ibid.

49. Bill Keller, "Former Officials Call Arms Budget 'Unbalanced,'" *New York Times,* February 8, 1985.

50. James Linville, "Richard Price, The Art of Fiction No. 144," *Paris Review,* no. 138 (Spring 1996), http://www.theparisreview.org/interviews/1431/the-art-of-fiction-no-144-richard-price.

51. Hiatt, "Weinberger Counterattack."

52. Robert W. Komer, "What Decade of Neglect?" *International Security* 10, no. 2 (Autumn 1985): 70–83.

53. Peter Swartz, interview by author, February 27, 2007.

CHAPTER 14. THE WISDOM OF HINDSIGHT

1. Robert W. Komer, *Bureaucracy at War: U.S. Performance in the Vietnam Conflict* (Boulder, CO: Westview Press, 1986), xiv.

2. Richard J. Walton, "The Laundering of McGeorge Bundy," *The Nation,* April 12, 1980, 429.

3. Fox Butterfield, "The New Vietnam Scholarship," *New York Times,* February 13, 1983; Peter Braestrup, ed., "Background Books: Vietnam," in *Vietnam as History: Ten Years after the Paris Peace Accords* (Washington,

DC: Woodrow Wilson International Center for Scholars and the University Press of America, 1984).

4. Robert W. Komer, review of *On Strategy: A Critical Analysis of the Vietnam War,* by Harry G. Summers Jr., *Survival* 27, no. 2 (March/April 1985): 94.

5. Ibid.

6. Russell F. Weigley, "Reflections on 'Lessons' from Vietnam," in *Vietnam as History,* 115–24; Russell F. Weigley, "Vietnam, What Manner of War?" *Air University Review* 34, no. 2 (January/February 1983): 114–20; Kenneth J. Alnwick, "Strategic Choice, National Will, and the Vietnam Experience," *Air University Review* 34, no. 2 (January/February 1983): 133–36; John M. Gates, "Vietnam: The Debate Goes On," *Parameters* 14, no. 1 (Spring 1984): 15–25; John M. Gates, "If at First You Don't Succeed, Try to Rewrite History: Revisionism and the Vietnam War," in *Looking Back on the Vietnam War: A 1990s Perspective on the Decisions, Combat, and Legacies,* ed. William Head and Lawrence E. Grinter (Westport, CT: Praeger, 1993), 177–89. See also Col. Stuart Herrington's introduction to Orrin DeForest and David Chanoff, *Slow Burn: The Rise and Bitter Fall of American Intelligence in Vietnam* (New York: Simon & Schuster, 1990), 13. Herrington states, "Those who suggest that the United States erred by focusing its power on the Vietcong when we should have known all along that Hanoi was the enemy and 'gone for Hanoi's jugular' simply do not understand the nature of revolutionary warfare and the key role played by Hanoi's Southern organization."

7. George C. Herring, "American Strategy in Vietnam: The Postwar Debate," *Military Affairs* 46, no. 2 (April 1982): 57–58.

8. Ibid., 60–61.

9. Robert E. Osgood, *Limited War Revisited* (Boulder, CO: Westview Press, 1979), 37.

10. Herring, "American Strategy in Vietnam," 60–61.

11. Ibid., 59–60. See also Guenter Lewy, "Some Political-Military Lessons of the Vietnam War," in *Assessing the Vietnam War: A Collection from the Journal of the U.S. Army War College,* ed. Lloyd J. Matthews and Dale E. Brown (Washington, DC: Pergamon-Brassey's International Defense Publishers, 1987), 141–57.

12. Komer, *Bureaucracy at War,* xiv.

13. Ibid, xiv–xv.

14. Ibid., 1–6, 9–12.

15. Ibid., 12.

16. Ibid., 12–13, 21–40

17. Ibid., 13–17.

18. Ibid., 17–18.

19. Ibid., 111–31.

20. Ibid., 133–34, 159.

21. Ibid., 147–50.

22. Ibid., 150–54.

23. Thomas M. Huber, "Compound Warfare: A Conceptual Framework," in *Compound Warfare: That Fatal Knot,* ed. Thomas M. Huber (Fort Leavenworth, KS: U.S. Army Command and General Staff College Press, 2002), 1–10. See also Randall N. Briggs, "Compound Warfare in the Vietnam War," in the same book.

24. Komer, *Bureaucracy at War,* 165–66.

25. Ibid., 159–72.

26. Ibid., 172–73.

27. Eliot A. Cohen, "Constraints on America's Conduct of Small Wars," *International Security* 9, no. 2 (Autumn 1984): 180.

28. Richard A. Hunt, "On Our Conduct of the Vietnam War: A Review Essay of Two New Works," *Parameters* 16, no. 3 (Autumn 1986): 54–57.

29. Andrew J. Pierre, review of *Bureaucracy at War: U.S. Performance in the Vietnam Conflict,* by Robert W. Komer, *Foreign Affairs* 64, no. 5 (Summer 1986): 1110.

30. Stanley Karnow, "Commentary: The Two Vietnams," in *Vietnam as History,* 82.

31. Stephen W. Twing, *Myths, Models, and U.S. Foreign Policy: The Cultural Shaping of Three Cold Warriors* (Boulder, CO: Lynne Rienner, 1998), 38–44.

32. Thompson and Frizzell, *Lessons of Vietnam,* 187.

33. Richard H. Shultz Jr., "The Vietnamization-Pacification Strategy of 1969–1972: A Quantitative and Qualitative Reassessment," in *Lessons from an Unconventional War: Reassessing U.S. Strategies for Future Conflicts,* ed. Richard A. Hunt and Richard H. Shultz Jr. (New York: Permagon Press, 1982), 54–55, 107–9.

34. Herbert Y. Schandler, "America and Vietnam: The Failure of Strategy, 1964–67," in *Vietnam as History,* 30.

35. Donald Vought, "American Culture and American Arms: The Case of Vietnam," in *Lessons from an Unconventional War,* 174.

36. Bruce Palmer Jr., *The 25-Year War: America's Military Role in Vietnam* (New York: Simon & Shuster, 1985), 115–16.

37. Colby, *Lost Victory,* 206, 211, 356.

38. Tran Dinh Tho, *Pacification* (Washington, DC: U.S. Army Center of Military History, 1980), 161–82.

39. David Kilcullen, "Report of Counterinsurgency Seminar 07," comp. David Dilegge (seminar, Small Wars Center of Excellence, Wargaming Division,

Marine Corps Warfighting Laboratory, Quantico, VA, September 26, 2007).

CONCLUSION

1. Komer, CIA Personnel File.
2. Komer, *Blowtorch,* ch. XX, 3–4.
3. Fred Charles Iklé, "The Role of Character and Intellect in Strategy," in *On Not Confusing Ourselves: Essays on National Security Strategy in Honor of Albert and Roberta Wohlstetter,* ed. Andrew W. Marshall, J. J. Martin, and Henry S. Rowen (Boulder, CO: Westview Press, 1991), 315.
4. John M. Collins, *Grand Strategy: Principles and Practices* (Annapolis, MD: Naval Institute Press, 1973), 224–25.
5. Thomas J. Peters and Robert H. Waterman, *In Search of Excellence: Lessons from America's Best-Run Companies* (New York: Harper & Row, 1982), 202, 206. The quote is from James Brian Quinn, "Technological Innovation, Entrepreneurship and Strategy," *Sloan Management Review* 21, no. 3 (Spring 1979): 206.
6. Theodore Levitt, "Ideas Are Useless Unless Used," *Inc.,* February 1981, quoted in Peters and Waterman, *In Search of Excellence,* 206–7.
7. Peter B. Vaill, *Spirited Leading and Learning: Process Wisdom for a New Age* (San Francisco: Jossey-Bass, 1998), 239–45.
8. Cecil V. Crabb, *American Diplomacy and the Pragmatic Tradition* (Baton Rouge: Louisiana State University Press, 1989).
9. Bostdorff and Goldzwig, "Idealism and Pragmatism in American Foreign Policy Rhetoric," 517.
10. Hans J. Morgenthau, "Kennedy and Foreign Policy," in *Truth and Power: Essays of a Decade, 1960–1970* (New York: Praeger, 1970), 143.
11. Russell L. Ackoff, *Redesigning the Future* (New York: Wiley, 1974), 24.
12. Vaill, *Spirited Leading and Learning,* 74–76, 81.
13. Komer, "Factors Bearing on U.S. Policies and Plans for the Middle East."
14. Collins, *Grand Strategy,* 223.
15. Vaill, *Spirited Leading and Learning,* 200.
16. Ibid., 204.
17. Ibid.
18. Ibid., 62.
19. Ibid., 37, 42.
20. Several published articles discuss the value of CORDS. As examples, see Kurt Amend, "Counterinsurgency Principles for the Diplomat," *Orbis* 54, no. 2 (Spring 2010): 215–31; Hans Binnendijk and Patrick M. Cronin, "Through the Complex Operations Prism," *Prism* 1, no. 1 (December

2009): 9–20; William B. Caldwell IV and Steven M. Leonard, "FM 3–07, Stability Operations: Uplifting the Engine of Change," *Military Review* 88, no. 4 (July/August 2008): 6–13; Robert B. Oakley and Michael Casey Jr., "The Country Team: Restructuring America's First Line of Engagement," *Joint Force Quarterly* no. 47 (4th Quarter 2007): 146–54; Dale Andrade and James H. Willbanks, "CORDS/Phoenix: Counterinsurgency Lessons from Vietnam for the Future," *Military Review* 86, no. 2 (March/April 2006): 9–23; and Ross Coffey, "Revisiting CORDS: The Need for Unity of Effort to Secure Victory in Iraq," *Military Review* 86, no. 2 (March/April 2006): 24–34.

21. U.S. Department of the Army, *Counterinsurgency,* Field Manual 3–24 (Washington, DC: U.S. Department of the Army, 2006), 2–12, 2–13.

22. Nathan Freier and Donald G. Rose, "Strike Two: *Bureaucracy Does Its Thing* Reprised," in *Hope Is Not a Plan: The War in Iraq from Inside the Green Zone,* ed. Thomas Mowle (Westport, CT: Praeger Security International, 2007), 107–31, 161n1.

23. Richard K. Betts, "Blowtorch Bob in Baghdad," *American Interest* 1, no. 4 (Summer 2006): 33–40.

24. Robert M. Gates, "Speech at the National Defense University" (Washington, DC, September 29, 2008), http://www.defense.gov/Speeches/Speech.aspx?SpeechID=1279.

25. Vaill, *Spirited Leading and Learning,* 81.

26. Richard Immerman, "The Intellectual and Emotional Qualities Needed by Strategists Working the Current National Security Environment" (address, "Teaching Strategy Workshop," U.S. Army War College, Carlisle Barracks, PA, April 9, 2010).

27. Ibid.

28. Ibid.

29. Philip A. Crowl, "The Strategist's Short Catechism: Six Questions without Easy Answers," in *Military Strategy,* comp. Anthony W. Gray Jr. and Eston T. White (Washington, DC: National Defense University, 1983), 94–103.

30. Hilary Austen Johnson, "Artistry for the Strategist," *Journal of Business Strategy* 28, no. 4 (2007): 15, 19–20. See also Bernard Brodie, "Strategy as an Art and a Science," *Naval War College Review* 51, no. 1 (Winter 1998): 26–38.

BIBLIOGRAPHY

ARCHIVES AND OTHER REPOSITORIES

Amory, Robert, Jr. Oral history. John F. Kennedy Library, Boston, MA.

Brzezinski, Zbigniew, with Madeleine Albright, Leslie G. Denend, and William Odom. Oral history. Carter Presidency Project. Miller Center for Public Affairs, University of Virginia, Charlottesville.

Colby, William E. Oral history. Lyndon Baines Johnson Library, Austin, TX.

Davidson, Philip B. Oral history. Lyndon Baines Johnson Library, Austin, TX.

Deputy for Civil Operations and Revolutionary Development, U.S. Military Assistance Command, Vietnam. Files. U.S. Army Center of Military History, Fort Lesley J. McNair, Washington, DC.

Forsythe, George I. Papers. U.S. Army Military History Institute, Carlisle, PA.

Ginsburgh, Robert N. Oral history. Albert F. Simpson Historical Research Center, Air University, Maxwell Air Force Base, AL.

Graham, Daniel O. Oral history. Lyndon Baines Johnson Library, Austin, TX.

Hertzberg, Hendrick (Rick). Exit Interview. Jimmy Carter Library, Atlanta, GA.

Kerwin, Walter T. Papers. U.S. Army Military History Institute, Carlisle, PA.

———. Oral history. U.S. Army Military History Institute, Carlisle, PA.

Komer, Robert. Interview. Neil Sheehan Papers. Library of Congress, Washington, DC.

———. Lectures. Special Collections, National Defense University Library, Fort Lesley J. McNair, Washington, DC.

———. National Security Files. John F. Kennedy Library, Boston, MA.

———. National Security Files. Lyndon Baines Johnson Library. Austin, TX.

———. Oral history. John F. Kennedy Library. Boston, MA.

———. Oral history. Lyndon Baines Johnson Library. Austin, TX.

———. Oral history. Historian's Office, Office of the Secretary of Defense, Arlington, VA.

Komer, Robert, and William Leonhart. Papers (Komer-Leonhart File). Lyndon Baines Johnson Library, Austin, TX.

Lathram, Wade. Oral history. Special Collections Room, Lauinger Library, Georgetown University, Washington, DC.

MACV Command Historian's Collection. U.S. Army Military History Institute, Carlisle, PA.

MACV/MACCORDS File. U.S. Army Military History Institute, Carlisle, PA.

Macy, John W. Files (Personnel Files). Lyndon Baines Johnson Library. Austin, TX.

Montague, Robert. Papers. U.S. Army Military History Institute, Carlisle, PA.

National Security Files. Meetings and Memoranda/Staff Memoranda. John F. Kennedy Library, Boston, MA.

National Security Files. Policy Planning/General. John F. Kennedy Library, Boston, MA.

Oberdorfer, Don. Oral history. Lyndon Baines Johnson Library, Austin, TX.

Sheehan, Neil. Papers. Library of Congress, Washington, DC.

Talbott, Phillips. Oral history. John F. Kennedy Library, Boston, MA.

Thomson, James C. Oral history. Lyndon Baines Johnson Library, Austin, TX.

Vann, John Paul. Papers. U.S. Army Military History Institute, Carlisle, PA.

Vietnam/Southeast Asia Papers. National Security Archive, Gelman Library, George Washington University, Washington, DC.

Virtual Vietnam Archive. Texas Tech University, Lubbock, TX. http://www.vietnam.ttu.edu/virtualarchive/

Warner, Volney F. Oral history. U.S. Army Military History Institute, Carlisle, PA.

Westmoreland, William C. Oral history. U.S. Army Military History Institute, Carlisle, PA.

———. Papers. U.S. Army Military History Institute, Carlisle, PA.

Wisner, Frank G. Oral history. Special Collections Room, Lauinger Library, Georgetown University, Washington, DC.

BOOKS AND MONOGRAPHS

Abernathy, M. Glenn, Dilys M. Hill, and Phil Williams, eds. *The Carter Years: The President and Policy Making.* New York: St. Martin's Press, 1984.

Ackoff, Russell L. *Redesigning the Future.* New York: Wiley, 1974.

Ahern, Thomas L., Jr. *Vietnam Declassified: The CIA and Counterinsurgency.* Lexington: University Press of Kentucky, 2010.

Akbar, M. J. *Nehru: The Making of India.* New York: Viking, 1988.

Allen, George W. *None So Blind: A Personal Account of the Intelligence Failure in Vietnam.* Chicago: Ivan R. Dee, 2001.

Andrade, Dale. *Ashes to Ashes: The Phoenix Program and the Vietnam War.* Lexington, MA: Lexington Books, 1990.

Auten, Brian J. *Carter's Conversion: The Hardening of American Defense Policy.* Columbia: University of Missouri Press, 2008.

Badeeb, Saeed M. *The Saudi-Egyptian Conflict over North Yemen, 1962–1970.* Boulder, CO: Westview Press, 1986.

Balaban, John. *Remembering Heaven's Face: A Moral Witness in Vietnam.* New York: Poseidon Press, 1991.

Barnett, Richard J. *Roots of War.* New York: Atheneum, 1972.

Bartholomees, J. Boone, Jr., ed. *The U.S. Army War College Guide to National Security Issues.* Vol. 1, *Theory of War and Strategy,* 5th ed. Carlisle, PA: Strategic Studies Institute, U.S. Army War College, 2012.

Bass, Warren. *Support Any Friend: Kennedy's Middle East and the Making of the U.S.-Israel Alliance.* New York: Oxford University Press, 2003.

Ben-Zvi, Abraham. *Lyndon B. Johnson and the Politics of Arms Sales to Israel: In the Shadow of the Hawk.* Portland, OR: Frank Cass, 2004.

Berman, Larry. *Lyndon Johnson's War: The Road to Stalemate in Vietnam.* New York: W. W. Norton, 1989.

Bird, Kai. *The Color of Truth: McGeorge Bundy and William Bundy, Brothers in Arms: A Biography.* New York: Simon & Schuster, 1998.

Bishop, Jim. *A Day in the Life of President Johnson.* New York: Random House, 1967.

Blank, Stephen J. *Natural Allies? Regional Security in Asia and the Prospects for Indo-American Strategic Cooperation.* Carlisle, PA: Strategic Studies Institute, U.S. Army War College, 2005.

Blaufarb, Douglas S. *The Counterinsurgency Era: U.S. Doctrine and Performance.* New York: Free Press, 1977.

Bole, Albert C., Jr., and K. Kobata. "An Evaluation of the Measurements of the Hamlet Evaluation System." Project No. 118. Newport, RI: Naval War College Center for Advanced Research, 1975.

Bose, Meena. *Shaping and Signaling Presidential Policy: The National Security Decision Making of Eisenhower and Kennedy.* College Station: Texas A&M University Press, 1998.

Bowles, Chester. *Promises to Keep: My Life in Public Service, 1941–1969.* New York: Harper & Row, 1971.

Bradley, C. Paul. *Recent United States Policy in the Persian Gulf.* Grantham, NH: Tompson and Rutter, 1982.

Braestrup, Peter. *Big Story: How the American Press and Television Reported and Interpreted the Crisis of Tet 1968 in Vietnam and Washington,* Vol. 1. Boulder, CO: Westview Press, 1977.

———, ed. *Vietnam as History: Ten Years after the Paris Peace Accords.* Washington, DC: Woodrow Wilson International Center for Scholars and the University Press of America, 1984.

Brands, H. W., Jr. *Cold Warriors: Eisenhower's Generation and American Foreign Policy.* New York: Columbia University Press, 1988.

———. *The Wages of Globalism: Lyndon Johnson and the Limits of American Power.* New York: Oxford University Press, 1995.

Brodie, Bernard. *War and Politics.* New York: Macmillan, 1973.

Brown, Harold. *Thinking about National Security: Defense and Foreign Policy in a Dangerous World.* Boulder, CO: Westview Press, 1983.

Brzezinski, Zbigniew. *Power and Principle: Memoirs of the National Security Adviser, 1977–1981.* New York: Farrar, Straus, and Giroux, 1983.

Bull, Hedley, and Adam Watson, eds. *The Expansion of International Society.* Oxford, UK: Clarendon Press, 1984.

Carter, Jimmy. *Keeping Faith: Memoirs of a President.* New York: Bantam Books, 1982.

Chary, M. Srinivas. *The Eagle and the Peacock: U.S. Foreign Policy toward India since Independence.* Westport, CT: Greenwood Press, 1995.

Chilcoat, Richard A. *Strategic Art: The New Discipline for 21st Century Leaders.* Carlisle, PA: Strategic Studies Institute, U.S. Army War College, 1995.

Clark, Lloyd. *Anzio: Italy and the Battle for Rome—1944.* New York: Atlantic Monthly Press, 2006.

Clarke, Jeffrey J. *Advice and Support: The Final Years, 1965–1973.* Washington, DC: U.S. Army Center of Military History, 1988.

Clausewitz, Carl von. *On War.* Edited and translated by Michael Howard and Peter Paret. Princeton, NJ: Princeton University Press, 1989.

Cline, Ray S. *The CIA under Reagan, Bush, and Casey.* Washington, DC: Acropolis Books, 1981.

Colby, William. *Lost Victory: A Firsthand Account of America's Sixteen-Year Involvement in Vietnam.* With James McCarger. Chicago: Contemporary Books, 1989.

Colby, William, and Peter Forbath. *Honorable Men: My Life in the CIA.* New York: Simon & Schuster, 1978.

Collins, John M. *Grand Strategy: Principles and Practices.* Annapolis, MD: Naval Institute Press, 1973.

Conn, Stetson. *Historical Work in the United States Army 1862–1954.* Washington, DC: U.S. Army Center of Military History, 1980.

Cooper, Chester L., Judith E. Corson, Laurence J. Legere, David E. Lockwood, and Donald M. Weller. *The American Experience with Pacification in Vietnam.* 3 vols. Report R-185 (DAHC 15 67 C 0011, ARPA-20, Special Studies). Arlington, VA: Institute for Defense Analysis, International and Social Sciences Division, 1972.

Corson, William R. *The Betrayal.* New York, W. W. Norton, 1968.

Cosmas, Graham A. *The Joint Chiefs of Staff and the War in Vietnam, 1960–1968.* Part 3. Washington, DC: Office of Joint History, Office of the Chairman of the Joint Chiefs of Staff, 2009.

———. *MACV: The Joint Command in the Years of Escalation, 1962–1967.* Washington, DC: U.S. Army Center of Military History, 2006.

———. *MACV: The Joint Command in the Years of Withdrawal, 1968–1973.* Washington, DC: U.S. Army Center of Military History, 2007.

Crabb, Cecil V., Jr. *The American Approach to Foreign Policy: A Pragmatic Perspective.* Lanham, MD: University Press of America, 1985.

———. *American Diplomacy and the Pragmatic Tradition.* Baton Rouge: Louisiana State University Press, 1989.

———. *Policy-Makers and Critics: Conflicting Theories of American Foreign Policy.* 2nd ed. New York: Praeger, 1986.

Daalder, Ivo H., and I. M. Destler. *In the Shadow of the Oval Office: Profiles of the National Security Advisers and the Presidents They Served—From JFK to George W. Bush.* New York: Simon & Schuster, 2009.

Dallek, Robert. *Flawed Giant: Lyndon Johnson and His Times, 1961–1973.* New York: Oxford University Press, 1998.

Darling, Arthur B. *The Central Intelligence Agency: An Instrument of Government to 1950.* University Park: Pennsylvania State University Press, 1990.

Davidson, Philip B. *Secrets of the Vietnam War.* Novato, CA: Presidio, 1990.

———. *Vietnam at War.* Novato, CA: Presidio Press, 1988.

Dean, Robert D. *Imperial Brotherhood: Gender and the Making of Cold War Foreign Policy.* Amherst: University of Massachusetts Press, 2001.

Dear, I. C. B., ed. *The Oxford Companion to World War II.* Oxford, UK: Oxford University Press, 1995.

Dearborn, Mary. *Mailer: A Biography.* Boston: Houghton Mifflin, 2001.

DeForest, Orrin, and David Chanoff. *Slow Burn: The Rise and Bitter Fall of American Intelligence in Vietnam.* New York: Simon & Schuster, 1990.

D'Este, Carlo. *World War II in the Mediterranean, 1942–1945.* Chapel Hill, NC: Algonquin Books, 1990.

Donovan, John C. *The Cold Warriors: A Policy-Making Elite.* Lexington, MA: D. C. Heath, 1974.

Duffield John S. *Power Rules: The Evolution of NATO's Conventional Force Posture.* Stanford, CA: Stanford University Press, 1995.

Duke, Simon. *The Burdensharing Debate: A Reassessment.* New York: St. Martin's Press, 1993.

Eccles, Henry E. *Military Power in a Free Society.* Newport, RI: Naval War College Press, 1979.

Elliott, Mai. *RAND in Southeast Asia: A History of the Vietnam War Era.* Santa Monica, CA: RAND, 2010.

Ellsberg, Daniel. *Secrets.* New York: Viking, 2002.

Evans, Rowland, and Robert Novick. *Lyndon B. Johnson: The Exercise of Power.* New York: New American Library, 1966.

Fain, W. Taylor. *American Ascendance and British Retreat in the Persian Gulf Region.* New York: Palgrave Macmillan, 2008.

Fairlie, Henry. *The Kennedy Promise: The Politics of Expectation.* Garden City, NY: Doubleday, 1973.

Fisher, Nigel. *Harold Macmillan.* New York: St. Martin's Press, 1982.

Fitzsimmons, Louise. *The Kennedy Doctrine.* New York: Random House, 1972.

Ford, Harold P. *Estimative Intelligence.* Lanham, MD: University Press of America, 1993.

Fuller, Helen. *Year of Trial: Kennedy's Crucial Decisions.* New York: Harcourt, Brace and World, 1962.

Gaddis, John Lewis. *Strategies of Containment: A Critical Appraisal of Postwar American National Security Policy.* New York: Oxford University Press, 1982.

Galbraith, John Kenneth. *Ambassador's Journal: A Personal Account of the Kennedy Years.* Boston: Houghton Mifflin, 1969.

———. *Letters to Kennedy.* Edited by James Goodman. Cambridge, MA: Harvard University Press, 1998.

Gardner, Paul F. *Shared Hopes, Separate Fears: Fifty Years of U.S.-Indonesian Relations.* Boulder, CO: Westview Press, 1997.

Gates, Robert M. *From the Shadows: The Ultimate Insider's Story of Five Presidents and How They Won the Cold War.* New York: Simon & Schuster, 1996.

George, Alexander L. *Presidential Decisionmaking in Foreign Policy: The Effective Use of Information and Advice.* Boulder, CO: Westview Press, 1980.

George Mason University. *Security Challenges in the 1980's.* Miscellaneous Publications of George Mason University. No. 2. Fairfax, VA: George Mason University, 1983.

Gibbons, William Conrad. *The U.S. Government and the Vietnam War: Executive and Legislative Roles.* Part 4, *July 1965–January 1968.* Princeton, NJ: Princeton University Press, 1995.

Gibson, James William. *The Perfect War: Technowar in Vietnam.* Boston: Atlantic Monthly Press, 1986.

Gittinger, Ted, ed. *The Johnson Years: A Vietnam Roundtable.* Austin: University of Texas, 1993.

Glenn, John, Barry E. Carter, and Robert W. Komer. *Rethinking Defense and Conventional Forces.* Washington, DC: Center for National Policy, 1983.

Goodhart, Philip. *Vietnam: Autumn Reflections.* n.p., N.d.

Goodwin, Doris Kearns. *Lyndon Johnson and the American Dream.* New York: St. Martin's Press, 1991.

Gould, Harold A., and Sumit Ganguly, eds. *The Hope and the Reality: U.S.-Indian Relations from Roosevelt to Reagan.* Boulder, CO: Westview Press, 1992.

Grant, Zalin. *Facing the Phoenix.* New York: W. W. Norton, 1991.

Gray, Anthony W., Jr., and Eston T. White, comp. *Military Strategy.* Washington, DC: National Defense University, 1983.

Gray, Colin S. *Strategic Studies: A Critical Assessment.* Contributions in Political Science, Number 70. Westport, CT: Greenwood Press, 1982.

Gupta, Amit. *The U.S.-India Relationship: Strategic Partnership or Complementary Interests?* Carlisle, PA: Strategic Studies Institute, U.S. Army War College, 2005.

Haffa, Robert P., Jr. *The Half War: Planning U.S. Rapid Deployment Forces to Meet a Limited Contingency, 1960–1983.* Boulder, CO: Westview Press, 1984.

Halberstam, David. *The Best and the Brightest.* New York: Random House, 1972.

Hargrove, Erwin C. *Jimmy Carter as President: Leadership and the Politics of the Public Good.* Baton Rouge: Louisiana State University Press, 1988.

Harper, Paul, and Joann P. Kreig, eds. *John F. Kennedy: The Promise Revisited.* New York: Greenwood Press, 1988.

Harvard Class of 1942. *Twenty-Fifth Anniversary Report.* Cambridge, MA: Harvard College, 1967.

Head, William, and Lawrence E. Grinter, eds. *Looking Back on the Vietnam War: A 1990s Perspective on the Decisions, Combat, and Legacies.* Westport, CT: Praeger, 1993.

Heclo, Hugh, and Lester M. Salamon, eds. *The Illusion of Presidential Government.* Boulder, CO: Westview Press, 1981.

Herring, George C. *LBJ and Vietnam: A Different Kind of War.* Austin: University of Texas Press, 1994.

Hersh, Burton. *The Old Boys: The American Elite and the Origins of the CIA.* New York: Charles Scribner's Sons, 1992.

Hershberg, James G. *James B. Conant: Harvard to Hiroshima and the Making of the Nuclear Age.* New York: Alfred A. Knopf, 1993.

Hilsman, Roger. *To Move a Nation: The Politics of Foreign Policy in the Administration of John F. Kennedy.* Garden City, NY: Doubleday, 1967.

Hoffman, Steven A. *India and the China Crisis.* Berkeley: University of California Press, 1990.

Hogan, Michael J., ed. *The End of the Cold War: Its Meaning and Implications.* New York: Cambridge University Press, 1992.

Hogan, Michael J., and Thomas G. Paterson, eds. *Explaining the History of American Foreign Relations.* 2nd ed. New York: Cambridge University Press, 2004.

Hoopes, Townsend. *The Limits of Intervention.* New York: David McKay, 1969.

Horne, Alistair. *Harold Macmillan.* Vol. 2, *1957–1966.* New York: Viking, 1986.

Huber, Thomas M., ed. *Compound Warfare: That Fatal Knot.* Fort Leavenworth, KS: U.S. Army Command and General Staff College Press, 2002.

Hunt, Richard A. *Pacification: The American Struggle for Vietnam's Hearts and Minds.* Boulder, CO: Westview Press, 1995.

Hunt, Richard A., and Richard H. Schultz Jr., eds. *Lessons from an Unconventional War: Reassessing U.S. Strategies for Future Conflicts.* New York: Permagon Press, 1982.

Jentleson, Bruce W., and Thomas G. Paterson, eds. *Encyclopedia of U.S. Foreign Relations.* 4 vols. New York: Oxford University Press, 1997.

Johnson, Loch K. *Strategic Intelligence.* Vol. 1, *Understanding the Hidden Side of Government.* Westport, CT: Praeger Security International, 2007.

Johnson, Lyndon Baines. *Lyndon B. Johnson's Vietnam Papers: A Documentary Collection.* Edited by David M. Barrett. College Station: Texas A&M University Press, 1997.

———. *The Vantage Point: Perspectives on the Presidency, 1963–1969.* New York: Holt, Rinehart and Winston, 1971.

Johnson, Maxwell Orme. *The Military as an Instrument of U.S. Policy in Southwest Asia: The Rapid Deployment Joint Task Force, 1979–1982.* Boulder, CO: Westview Press, 1983.

Jones, Howard Palfrey. *Indonesia: The Possible Dream.* New York: Harcourt Brace Jovanovich, 1971.

Just, Ward. *A Dangerous Friend.* Boston: Houghton Mifflin, 1999.

Karalekas, Anne. *History of the Central Intelligence Agency.* Laguna Hills, CA: Aegean Park Press, 1977.

Katzenbach, Nicholas deB. *Some of It Was Fun: Working with RFK and LBJ.* New York: W. W. Norton, 2008.

Keller, Morton, and Phyllis Keller. *Making Harvard Modern: The Rise of America's University.* New York: Oxford University Press, 2001.

Kennan, George F. *American Diplomacy, 1900–1950.* New York: Mentor Books, 1951.

Kennedy, John F. *The Strategy of Peace.* Edited by Allen Nevins. New York: Popular Library, 1960.

Kent, Sherman. *Strategic Intelligence for American World Policy.* Princeton, NJ: Princeton University Press, 1949.

Kinnard, Douglas. *The War Managers.* Hanover, NH: University Press of New England, 1977.

Kissinger, Henry. *Diplomacy.* New York: Simon & Schuster, 1994.

Kivimaki, Timo. *US-Indonesian Hegemonic Bargaining: Strength of Weakness.* Aldershot, UK: Ashgate Publishing, 2003.

Kolko, Gabriel. *Anatomy of a War: Vietnam, the United States, and the Modern Historical Experience.* New York: New Press, 1994.

———. *Confronting the Third World: United States Foreign Policy, 1945–1980.* New York: Pantheon Books, 1988.

Komer, Robert W. *Bureaucracy at War: U.S. Performance in the Vietnam Conflict.* Boulder, CO: Westview Press, 1986.

————. *Bureaucracy Does Its Thing: Institutional Constraints on U.S.-GVN Performance in Vietnam.* Santa Monica, CA: RAND, 1972.

————. *Civil Affairs and Military Government in the Mediterranean Theater.* Washington, DC: Office of the Chief of Military History, n.d.

————. *The Malayan Emergency in Retrospect: Organization of a Successful Counterinsurgency Effort.* Santa Monica, CA: RAND, 1972.

————. *Maritime Security or Coalition Defense?* Cambridge, MA: Abt Books, 1984.

————. *Organization and Management of the "New Model" Pacification Program—1966–1969.* Santa Monica, CA: RAND, 1970.

————. *Rationalizing NATO's Defense Posture.* Report R-1657-ARPA/ISA/PAE. Santa Monica, CA: RAND, 1976.

Kugler, Richard L. *Commitment to Purpose: How Alliance Partnership Won the Cold War.* Santa Monica, CA: RAND, 1993.

Kuklick, Bruce. *Blind Oracles: Intellectuals and War from Kennan to Kissinger.* Princeton, NJ: Princeton University Press, 2006.

Kux, Dennis. *India and the United States: Estranged Democracies.* Washington, DC: National Defense University Press, 1993.

Lamb, Alastair. *The Kashmir Problem.* New York: Frederick A. Praeger, 1968.

Langer, William L. *In and Out of the Ivory Tower.* New York: Neale Watson Academic Publications, 1977.

Lebow, Richard Ned. *The Tragic Vision of Politics: Ethics, Interests, and Orders.* New York: Cambridge University Press, 2003.

Lewy, Guenther. *America in Vietnam.* New York: Oxford University Press, 1978.

Limaye, Satu P. *U.S.-Indian Relations: The Pursuit of Accommodation.* Boulder, CO: Westview Press, 1993.

Lobel, Aaron, ed. *Presidential Judgment: Foreign Policy Decision Making in the White House.* Hollis, NH: Hollis Publishers, 2001.

Long, Austin. *On "Other War": Lessons from Five Decades of RAND Counterinsurgency Research.* Santa Monica, CA: RAND, 2006.

Lord, Carnes. *The Presidency and the Management of National Security.* New York: Free Press, 1988.

Lunn, Simon. *Burden-Sharing in NATO.* Chatham House Papers 18. London: Royal Institute of International Affairs/Routledge and Kegan Paul, 1983.

Mackay, Sandra. *The Saudis.* Boston: Houghton Mifflin, 1987.

Mackintosh-Smith, Tim. *Yemen: The Unknown Arabia.* Woodstock, NY: Overlook Press, 2000.

Macmillan, Harold. *At the End of the Day, 1961–1963.* New York: Harper and Row, 1973.

Marshall, Andrew W., J. J. Martin, and Henry S. Rowen, eds. *On Not Confusing Ourselves: Essays on National Security Strategy in Honor of Albert and Roberta Wohlstetter.* Boulder, CO: Westview Press, 1991.

Matthews, Lloyd J., and Dale E. Brown, eds. *Assessing the Vietnam War: A Collection from the Journal of the U.S. Army War College.* Washington, DC: Pergamon-Brassey's International Defense Publishers, 1987.

Maxwell, Neville. *India's China War.* New York: Columbia University Press, 1970.

McChristian, Joseph A. *The Role of Military Intelligence, 1965–1967.* Vietnam Studies. Washington, DC: Department of the Army, 1974.

McMahon, Robert P. *Cold War on the Periphery: The United States, India and Pakistan.* New York: Columbia University Press, 1994.

McMullen, Christopher J. *Resolution of the Yemen Crisis, 1963: A Case Study in Mediation.* Washington, DC: Institute for the Study of Diplomacy, Georgetown University, 1980.

Meir, Golda. *My Life.* New York: G. P. Putnam's Sons, 1975.

Miller, Merle. *Lyndon: An Oral Biography.* New York: G. P. Putnam's Sons, 1980.

Miller, Nathan. *Spying for America: The Hidden History of U.S. Intelligence.* New York: Paragon House, 1989.

Milne, David. *America's Rasputin: Walt Rostow and the Vietnam War.* New York: Hill and Wang, 2008.

Miroff, Bruce. *Pragmatic Illusions: The Presidential Politics of John F. Kennedy.* New York: David McKay, 1976.

Morgenthau, Hans J. *Truth and Power: Essays of a Decade, 1960–70.* New York: Praeger Publishers, 1970.

Morris, Kenneth E. *Jimmy Carter: American Moralist.* Athens: University of Georgia Press, 1996.

Mowle, Thomas, ed. *Hope Is Not a Plan: The War in Iraq from Inside the Green Zone.* Westport, CT: Praeger Security International, 2007.

Moyar, Mark. *Phoenix and the Birds of Prey: The CIA's Campaign to Destroy the Viet Cong.* Annapolis, MD: Naval Institute Press, 1997.

National War College. *Academic Year 1956–1957 Course.* Washington, DC: Fort Lesley J. McNair, 1956.

Njølstad, Olav, ed. *The Last Decade of the Cold War: From Conflict Escalation to Conflict Transformation.* London: Frank Cass, 2004.

Noyes, James H. *The Clouded Lens: Persian Gulf Security and U.S. Policy.* 2nd ed. Stanford, CA: Hoover Institution Press, 1982.

Nuechterlein, Donald E. *America Recommitted: United States National Interests in a Restructured World.* Lexington: University Press of Kentucky, 1991.

———. *United States Interests in a Changing World.* Lexington: University Press of Kentucky, 1973.

Nutting, Anthony. *Nasser.* New York: E. P. Dutton, 1972.

Oberdorfer, Don. *Tet!* Garden City, NY: Doubleday, 1971.

Osgood, Robert E. *Limited War Revisited.* Boulder, CO: Westview Press, 1979.

Palmer, Bruce, Jr. *The 25-Year War: America's Military Role in Vietnam.* New York: Simon & Shuster, 1985.

Parker, Richard. *John Kenneth Galbraith: His Life, His Politics, His Economics.* New York: Farrar, Straus, and Giroux, 2005.

Paterson, Thomas, ed. *Kennedy's Quest for Victory: American Foreign Policy, 1961–1963.* New York: Oxford University Press, 1989.

Peters, Thomas J., and Robert H. Waterman. *In Search of Excellence: Lessons from America's Best-Run Companies.* New York: Harper and Row, 1982.

Prados, John. *The Blood Road: The Ho Chi Minh Trail and the Vietnam War.* New York: Wiley, 1998.

———. *Keepers of the Keys: A History of the National Security Council from Truman to Bush.* New York: William Morrow, 1991.

———. *Lost Crusader: The Secret Wars of CIA Director William Colby.* New York: Oxford University Press, 2003.

———. *Vietnam: The History of an Unwinnable War, 1945–1975.* Lawrence: University Press of Kansas, 2009.

Preston, Andrew. *The War Council: McGeorge Bundy, the NSC, and Vietnam.* Cambridge, MA: Harvard University Press, 2006.

Quinlan, David A. *The Role of the Marine Corps in Rapid Deployment Forces.* Washington, DC: National Defense University Press, 1983.

Quirk, John Patrick, David Atlee Phillips, Ray Cline, and Walter Pforzheimer. *The Central Intelligence Agency, A Photographic History.* Guilford, CT: Foreign Intelligence Press, 1986.

Ranelagh, John. *The Agency: The Rise and Decline of the CIA.* New York: Simon & Schuster, 1986.

Raskin, Marcus G., and Bernard Fall, eds. *The Viet-Nam Reader.* New York: Vintage Books, 1967.

Record, Jeffrey. *The Rapid Deployment Force and U.S. Military Intervention in the Persian Gulf.* Cambridge, MA: Institute for Foreign Policy Analysis, 1981.

Redford, Emmette S., and Richard T. McCulley. *White House Operations: The Johnson Presidency.* Austin: University of Texas Press, 1986.

Reporting Vietnam: American Journalism 1959–1969. Vol. 1. New York: Library of America, 1998.

Rostow, Walt W. *The Diffusion of Power: An Essay in Recent History.* New York: Macmillan, 1972.

———. *View from the Seventh Floor.* New York: Harper and Row, 1964.

Rudgers, David F. *Creating the Secret State: The Origins of the Central Intelligence Agency, 1943–1945.* Lawrence: University Press of Kansas, 2000.

Sarkesian, Sam C., ed. *Defense Policy and the Presidency: Carter's First Years.* Boulder, CO: Westview Press, 1979.

Schaffer, Howard B. *Chester Bowles: New Dealer in the Cold War.* Cambridge, MA: Harvard University Press, 1993.

———. *Ellsworth Bunker: Global Troubleshooter, Vietnam Hawk.* Chapel Hill: University of North Carolina Press, 2003.

Schlesinger, Arthur M., Jr. *A Thousand Days: John F. Kennedy in the White House.* Boston: Houghton Mifflin, 1965.

Schmidt, Dana Adams. *Yemen: The Unknown War.* New York: Holt, Rinehart, and Winston, 1968.

Scoville, Thomas W. *Reorganizing for Pacification Support.* Washington, DC: U.S. Army Center of Military History, 1999.

Selznick, Philip. *Leadership in Administration: A Sociological Interpretation.* New York: Harper & Row, 1957.

Sheehan, Neil. *After the War Was Over: Hanoi and Saigon.* New York: Random House, 1992.

———. *A Bright Shining Lie.* New York: Random House, 1988.

Sidey, Hugh. *John F. Kennedy, President.* New York: Atheneum, 1964.

Simpson, Christopher, ed. *Universities and Empire: Money and Politics in the Social Sciences during the Cold War.* New York: New Press, 1998.

Smith, Joseph Burkholder. *Portrait of a Cold Warrior.* New York: G. P. Putnam's Sons, 1976.

Smith, Russell Jack. *The Unknown CIA: My Three Decades with the Agency.* Washington, DC: Pergamon-Brassey's International Defense Publishers, 1989.

Snyder, Jed C. *Defending the Fringe: NATO, the Mediterranean, and the Persian Gulf.* SAIS Papers in International Affairs, Number 11. Boulder, CO: Westview Press, 1987.

Sorensen, Theodore C. *Kennedy.* New York: Harper and Row, 1965.

Sorley, Lewis. *A Better War.* New York: Harcourt, Brace, 1999.

———. *Honorable Warrior: General Harold K. Johnson and the Ethics of Command.* Lawrence: University Press of Kansas, 1998.

———. *Thunderbolt: General Creighton Abrams and the Army of His Times.* New York: Simon & Schuster, 1992.

Spector, Ronald H. *After Tet: The Bloodiest Year in Vietnam.* New York: Free Press, 1993.

Steel, Ronald. *In Love with Night: The American Romance with Robert Kennedy.* New York: Simon & Schuster, 2000.

Steury, Donald P., ed. *Sherman Kent and the Board of National Estimate.* Washington, DC: Center for the Study of Intelligence, Central Intelligence Agency, 1994.

Stookey, Robert. *Yemen: The Politics of the Yemen Arab Republic.* Boulder, CO: Westview Press, 1978.

Strober, Gerald S., and Deborah H. Strober. *"Let Us Begin Anew": An Oral History of the Kennedy Presidency.* New York: HarperCollins, 1993.

Summitt, April R. *John F. Kennedy and U.S.-Middle East Relations: A History of American Foreign Policy in the 1960s.* Lewiston, NY: Edward Mellen Press, 2008.

Tanzer, Lester, ed. *The Kennedy Circle.* Washington, DC: Robert B. Luce, 1961.

Taylor, Maxwell D. *Swords and Plowshares.* New York: W. W. Norton, 1972.

Tellis, Ashley J. *India as a New Global Power: An Action Agenda for the United States.* Washington, DC: Carnegie Endowment for International Peace, 2005.

Tharoor, Shashi. *Nehru: The Invention of India.* New York: Arcade Publishing, 2003.

Thayer, Thomas C. *War without Fronts: The American Experience in Vietnam.* Boulder, CO: Westview Press, 1985.

Thesiger, Wilfred. *The Last Nomad.* New York: E. P. Dutton, 1980.

Thompson, Kenneth W., ed. *Four Virginia Papers Presented at the Miller Center Forums, 1981, Part V.* Washington, DC: University Press of America, 1982.

———. *The Kennedy Presidency.* Lanham, MD: University Press of America, 1985.

Thompson, Robert. *Make for the Hills: Memories of Far Eastern Wars.* London: Leo Cooper, 1989.

Thompson, W. Scott, and Donaldson D. Frizzell, eds. *The Lessons of Vietnam.* New York: Crane, Russak, 1977.

Tran Dinh Tho. *Pacification.* Washington, DC: U.S. Army Center of Military History, 1980.

Twing, Stephen W. *Myths, Models, and U.S. Foreign Policy: The Cultural Shaping of Three Cold Warriors.* Boulder, CO: Lynne Rienner, 1998.

U.S. Army Center of Military History. *Anzio Beachhead, 22 January–25 May 1944.* 1949. Reprint, Washington, DC: U.S. Army Center of Military History, 1990.

U.S. Department of State. *History of the National Security Council, 1947–1997.* Washington, DC: U.S. Department of State.

Vaill, Peter B. *Spirited Leading and Learning: Process Wisdom for a New Age.* San Francisco: Jossey-Bass, 1998.

Valenti, Jack. *A Very Human President.* New York: W. W. Norton, 1975.

Valentine, Douglas. *The Phoenix Program.* New York: William Morrow, 1990.

Walcott, Charles E., and Karen M. Hult. *Governing the White House: From Hoover through LBJ.* Lawrence: University Press of Kansas, 1995.

Washington University Studies. *New Series: Literature and Language.* No. 23. St. Louis: Washington University Press, 1953.

Weber, Ralph E. *Spymasters: Ten CIA Officers in Their Own Words.* Wilmington, DE: SE Books, 1999.

Weinberger, Caspar. *Fighting for Peace: Seven Critical Years in the Pentagon.* New York: Warner Books, 1990.

Weintel, Edward, and Charles Bartlett. *Facing the Brink: An Intimate Study of Crisis Diplomacy.* New York: Charles Scribner's Sons, 1967.

Weisner, Louis A. *Victims and Survivors: Displaced Persons and Other War Victims in Viet-Nam, 1954–1975.* Westport, CT: Greenwood Press, 1988.

Wendt, James C., and Nanette Brown. *Improving the NATO Force Planning Process: Lessons from Past Efforts.* Report R-3383-USDP. Santa Monica, CA: RAND, 1986.

Westmoreland, William C. *A Soldier Reports.* Rev. ed. New York: Da Capo Press, 1989.

Willenson, Kim. *The Bad War: An Oral History of the Vietnam War.* New York: New American Library, 1987.

Winks, Robin W. *Cloak and Gown.* New York: William Morrow, 1987.

Wofford, Harris. *Of Kennedys and Kings: Making Sense of the Sixties.* Pittsburgh, PA: University of Pittsburgh Press, 1992.

Yarger, Harry R. *Strategy and the National Security Professional.* Westport, CT: Praeger Security International, 2008.

Zaffiri, Samuel. *Westmoreland: A Biography of General William C. Westmoreland.* New York: William Morrow, 1994.

ARTICLES, BOOK CHAPTERS, AND PAPERS

Aboul-Enein, Youssef. "The Egyptian-Yemen War (1962–1967): Egyptian Perspectives on Guerrilla Warfare." *Infantry,* January/February 2004. http://www.army.mil/professionalWriting/volumes/volume2/march_2004/3_04_3.html.

Ahmad, Eqbal. "Revolutionary War and Counter-Insurgency." In *Revolutionary War: Western Response.* Edited by David S. Sullivan and Martin J. Sattler. New York: Columbia University Press, 1971.

Alnwick, Kenneth J. "Strategic Choice, National Will, and the Vietnam Experience." *Air University Review* 34, no. 2 (January/February 1983): 133–36.

Alsop, Stewart. "Vietnam: The President's Next Big Decision." *Saturday Evening Post,* March 25, 1967, 25–28.

"Ambassador Robert W. Komer." *Armed Forces Journal International,* September 1978, 47–52.

Amend, Kurt. "Counterinsurgency Principles for the Diplomat." *Orbis* 54, no. 2 (Spring 2010): 215–31.

Anderson, Walter K. "U.S.-Indian Relations, 1961–1963: Good Intentions and Uncertain Results." In *The Hope and the Reality: U.S.-Indian Relations from Roosevelt to Reagan*. Edited by Harold A. Gould and Sumit Ganguly. Boulder, CO: Westview Press, 1992.

Andrade, Dale, and James H. Willbanks. "CORDS/Phoenix: Counterinsurgency Lessons from Vietnam for the Future." *Military Review* 86, no. 2 (March/April 2006): 9–23.

Barnes, Trevor. "The Secret Cold War: The CIA and American Foreign Policy in Europe, 1946–1956, Part II." *Historical Journal* 25, no. 3 (September 1982): 649–70.

Bartholomees, J. Boone, Jr. "A Survey of the Theory of Strategy." In *The U.S. Army War College Guide to National Security Issues*. Vol. 1, *Theory of War and Strategy*, 5th ed. Edited by J. Boone Bartholomees Jr. Carlisle, PA: Strategic Studies Institute, U.S. Army War College, 2012.

Bates, E. Asa. "The Rapid Deployment Force—Fact or Fiction." *RUSI: Journal of the Royal United Services Institute for Defence Studies* 126, no. 2 (June 1981): 23–33.

Bator, Francis M. "Lyndon Johnson and Foreign Policy: The Case of Western Europe and the Soviet Union." In *Presidential Judgment: Foreign Policy Decision Making in the White House*. Edited by Aaron Lobel. Hollis, NH: Hollis Publishers, 2001.

———. "No Good Choices: LBJ and the Vietnam/Great Society Connection." Cambridge, MA: American Academy of Arts and Sciences, 2007. http://www.amacad.org/publications/nogoodChoices.aspx.

Beschloss, Michael R. "A Tale of Two Presidents." *Wilson Quarterly* 88, no. 1 (Winter 2000): 60–70.

Betts, Richard K. "Blowtorch Bob in Baghdad." *American Interest* 1, no. 4 (Summer 2006): 33–40.

Binnendijk, Hans, and Patrick M. Cronin. "Through the Complex Operations Prism." *Prism* 1, no. 1 (December 2009): 9–20.

Birtle, Andrew J. "PROVN, Westmoreland, and the Historians: A Reappraisal." *Journal of Military History* 72, no. 4 (October 2008): 1213–247.

Bostdorff, Denise M., and Steven R. Goldzwig. "Idealism and Pragmatism in American Foreign Policy Rhetoric: The Case of John F. Kennedy and Vietnam." *Presidential Studies Quarterly* 24, no. 3 (Summer 1994): 515–30.

Brecher, Michael. "Non-Alignment under Stress: The West and the India-China Border War." *Pacific Affairs* 52, no. 4 (Winter 1979–80): 612–30.

Briggs, Randall N. "Compound Warfare in the Vietnam War." In *Compound Warfare: That Fatal Knot*. Edited by Thomas M. Huber. Fort Leavenworth, KS: U.S. Army Command and General Staff College Press, 2002.

Brinkley, Douglas. "Dean Gooderham Acheson." In *Encyclopedia of U.S. Foreign Relations*, Vol. 1. Edited by Bruce W. Jentleson and Thomas G. Paterson. New York: Oxford University Press, 1997.

Brodie, Bernard. "General André Beaufré on Strategy: A Review of Two Books." Paper P-3157. Santa Monica, CA: RAND, June 1965.

———. "Strategy as an Art and a Science." *Naval War College Review* 51, no. 1 (Winter 1998): 26–38.

Brown, Harold. "What the Carter Doctrine Means to Me." *MERIP Reports*, no. 90 (September 1980): 1–32.

Caldwell, William B., IV, and Steven M. Leonard. "FM 3-07, Stability Operations: Uplifting the Engine of Change." *Military Review* 88, no. 4 (July/August 2008): 6–13.

Churba, Joseph. "Arabia Felix." *Air University Review* 20, no. 5 (July/August 1969): 107–9. http://www.airpower.maxwell.af.mil/airchronicles/aureview/1969/jul-aug/churba.html.

Coffey, Ross. "Revisiting CORDS: The Need for Unity of Effort to Secure Victory in Iraq." *Military Review* 86, no. 2 (March/April 2006): 24–34.

Cohen, Eliot A. "Constraints on America's Conduct of Small Wars." *International Security* 9, no. 2 (Autumn 1984): 151–81.

Cohen, Stephen P. "India's China War and After: A Review Article." *Journal of Asian Studies* 30, no. 4 (August 1971): 847–57.

Crowl, Philip A. "The Strategist's Short Catechism: Six Questions without Easy Answers." In *Military Strategy*. Compiled by Anthony W. Gray Jr. and Eston T. White. Washington, DC: National Defense University, 1983.

Cullather, Nick. "Modernization Theory." In *Explaining the History of American Foreign Relations*, 2nd ed. Edited by Michael J. Hogan and Thomas G. Paterson. New York: Cambridge University Press, 2004.

Cutler, Robert. "The Development of the National Security Council." *Foreign Affairs* 34, no. 3 (April 1956): 441–58.

Daalder, Ivo, and I. M. Destler. "In the Shadow of the Oval Office: The Next National Security Adviser." *Foreign Affairs* 88, no. 1 (January/February 2009): 114–29.

Davis, Jack. "The Kent-Kendall Debate of 1949." *Studies in Intelligence* 35, no. 2 (Summer 1991): 91–103.

———. "Sherman Kent and the Profession of Intelligence Analysis." *Occasional Papers* 1, no. 5 (November 2002). https://www.cia.gov/library/kent-center-occasional-papers/vol1no5.htm.

Davis, Paul K. "Observations on the Rapid Deployment Joint Task Force: Origins, Direction, and Mission." Paper P-6751. Santa Monica, CA: RAND, 1982. http://www.rand.org/pubs/papers/2005/P6751.pdf.

Destler, I. M. "National Security Management: What Presidents Have Wrought." *Political Science Quarterly* 95, no. 4 (Winter 1980–81): 573–88.

———. "National Security II: The Rise of the Assistant (1961–1981)." In *The Illusion of Presidential Government*. Edited by Hugh Heclo and Lester M. Salamon. Boulder, CO: Westview Press, 1981.

A Discussion of the Rapid Deployment Force with Lieutenant General P. X. Kelley. Special Analysis No. 80-4. Washington, DC: American Enterprise Institute for Public Policy Research, 1980.

Donnell, John C. "Pacification Reassessed." *Asian Survey* 7, no. 8 (August 1967): 567–76.

Earle, Edward Mead. "American Military Policy and National Security." *Political Science Quarterly* 53, no. 1 (March 1938): 1–13.

Fisher, Margaret W. "India in 1963: A Year of Travail." *Asian Survey* 4, no. 3 (March 1964): 737–45.

Ford, Harold P. "A Tribute to Sherman Kent." In *Sherman Kent and the Board of National Estimates*. Edited by Donald P. Steury. Washington, DC: Center for the Study of Intelligence, Central Intelligence Agency, 1994.

Freier, Nathan, and Donald G. Rose. "Strike Two: *Bureaucracy Does Its Thing* Reprised." In *Hope Is Not a Plan: The War in Iraq from Inside the Green Zone*. Edited by Thomas Mowle. Westport, CT: Praeger Security International, 2007.

Galassi, Chryss. "'Blowtorch Bob' Is Back on Top." With David C. Martin. *Newsweek,* March 24, 1980, 54.

Galvin, John R. "What's the Matter with Being a Strategist?" *Parameters* 19 (March 1989): 2–10.

Gates, John M. "If at First You Don't Succeed, Try to Rewrite History: Revisionism and the Vietnam War." In *Looking Back on the Vietnam War: A 1990s Perspective on the Decisions, Combat, and Legacies*. Edited by William Head and Lawrence E. Grinter. Westport, CT: Praeger, 1993.

———. "Vietnam: The Debate Goes On." *Parameters* 14, no. 1 (Spring 1984): 15–25.

Gerges, Fawaz A. "The Kennedy Administration and the Egyptian-Saudi Conflict in Yemen: Co-opting Arab Nationalism." *Middle East Journal* 49, no. 2 (Spring 1995): 292–311.

Goodman, Allan E., Randolph Harris, and John C. Wood. "South Vietnam and the Politics of Self-Support." *Asian Survey* 11, no. 1 (January 1971): 1–25.

Gray, Colin. "The Strategist as Hero." *Joint Force Quarterly*, no. 63 (3rd Quarter 2011): 37–45.

Greenberg, Harold M. "Intelligence of the Past; Intelligence for the Future." In *Strategic Intelligence*. Vol. 1, *Understanding the Hidden Side of Government*.

Edited by Loch K. Johnson. Westport, CT: Praeger Security International, 2007.

"The Guam Gambit." *National Review,* April 4, 1967, 334.

Guzzardi, Walter, Jr. "Management of the War: A Tale of Two Capitals." *Fortune,* April 1967, 134–39.

Halberstam, David. "Return to Vietnam." *Harper's,* December 1967, 47–58.

———. "The Very Expensive Education of McGeorge Bundy." *Harper's,* July 1969, 21–41.

Hartley, Anthony. "John Kennedy's Foreign Policy." *Foreign Policy,* no. 4 (Fall 1971): 77–87.

Herring, George C. "American Strategy in Vietnam: The Postwar Debate." *Military Affairs* 46, no. 2 (April 1982): 57–63.

Herrington, Stuart. Introduction to *Slow Burn: The Rise and Bitter Fall of American Intelligence in Vietnam.* By Orrin DeForest and David Chanoff. New York: Simon & Schuster, 1990.

Hodgson, Godfrey. "The Establishment." *Foreign Policy,* no. 10 (Spring 1973): 3–40.

Hoffman, Steven A. "Rethinking the Linkage between Tibet and the China-India Border Conflict: A Realist Approach." *Journal of Cold War Studies* 8, no. 3 (Summer 2006): 165–94.

Huber, Thomas M. "Compound Warfare: A Conceptual Framework." In *Compound Warfare: That Fatal Knot.* Edited by Thomas M. Huber. Fort Leavenworth, KS: U.S. Army Command and General Staff College Press, 2002.

Hunt, Richard A. "On Our Conduct of the Vietnam War: A Review Essay of Two New Works." *Parameters* 16, no. 3 (Autumn 1986): 54–57.

Iklé, Fred Charles. "The Role of Character and Intellect in Strategy." In *On Not Confusing Ourselves: Essays on National Security Strategy in Honor of Albert and Roberta Wohlstetter.* Edited by Andrew W. Marshall, J. J. Martin, and Henry S. Rowen. Boulder, CO: Westview Press, 1991.

Jabber, Paul. "U.S. Interests and Regional Security in the Middle East." *Daedulus* 109 (Fall 1980): 67–80.

Jeffreys-Jones, Rhodri. "The Socio-Educational Composition of the CIA Elite: A Statistical Note." *Journal of American Studies* 19, no. 3 (1985): 421–24.

Johnson, Hilary Austen. "Artistry for the Strategist." *Journal of Business Strategy* 28, no. 4 (2007): 13–21.

Joiner, Charles A. "South Vietnam: Political, Military and Constitutional Arenas in Nation Building." *Asian Survey* 9, no. 1 (January 1968): 58–71.

Karnow, Stanley. "Commentary: The Two Vietnams." In *Vietnam as History: Ten Years after the Paris Peace Accords.* Edited by Peter Braestrup. Washington, DC: Woodrow Wilson International Center for Scholars and the University Press of America, 1984.

Kennedy, Paul. "History from the Middle: The Case of the Second World War." *Journal of Military History* 74, no. 1 (January 2010): 35–51.

Kent, Sherman. "The First Year of the Office of National Estimates: The Directorship of William L. Langer." In *Sherman Kent and the Board of National Estimates.* Edited by Donald P. Steury. Washington, DC: Center for the Study of Intelligence, Central Intelligence Agency, 1994.

———. "The Law and Custom of the National Intelligence Estimate." In *Sherman Kent and the Board of National Estimates.* Edited by Donald P. Steury. Washington, DC: Center for the Study of Intelligence, Central Intelligence Agency, 1994.

Kissinger, Henry. "Reflections on a Partnership: British and American Attitudes to Postwar Foreign Policy." *International Affairs* 58, no. 4 (Autumn 1982): 571–87.

Komer, Robert W. "Clear, Hold and Build." *Army*, May 1970, 16–24.

———. "The Establishment of Allied Control in Italy." *Military Affairs* 13, no. 1 (Spring 1949): 20–28.

———. "Impact of Pacification on Insurgency in South Vietnam." In *Revolutionary War: Western Response.* Edited by David S. Sullivan and Martin J. Sattler. New York: Columbia University Press, 1971.

———. "Impact of Pacification on Insurgency in Vietnam." Report P-4443. Santa Monica, CA: RAND, August 1970.

———. "Looking Ahead." *International Security* 4, no. 1 (Summer 1979): 108–16.

———. "Maritime Strategy vs. Coalition Defense." *Foreign Affairs* 60, no. 5 (Summer 1982): 1124–44.

———. "The Origins and Objectives." *NATO Review* 26, no. 3 (June 1978): 9–12.

———. "Pacification: A Look Back and Ahead." *Army*, June 1970, 20–29.

———. "Preparation for Coalition War." Paper P-5707. Santa Monica, CA: RAND, 1976.

———. "The President, the NSC and the Secretary of Defense." In *Four Virginia Papers Presented at the Miller Center Forums, 1981, Part V.* Edited by Kenneth W. Thompson. Washington, DC: University Press of America, 1982.

———. Review of *On Strategy: A Critical Analysis of the Vietnam War*, by Harry G. Summers Jr. *Survival* 27, no. 2 (March/April 1985): 94–95.

———. "Ten Suggestions for Rationalizing NATO." *Survival* 19, no. 2 (March/April 1977): 67–72.

———. "To the Editor." *Foreign Affairs* 61, no. 2 (Winter 1982–83): 453–54.

———. "Treating NATO's Self-Inflicted Wound." Paper P-5092. Santa Monica, CA: RAND, October 1973.

———. "What Decade of Neglect?" *International Security* 10, no. 2 (Autumn 1985): 70–83.

Krishna, Gopal. "India and the International Order." In *The Expansion of International Society*. Edited by Hedley Bull and Adam Watson. Oxford, UK: Clarendon Press, 1984.

Lederer, William J. "Vietnam: Those Computer Reports." *New Republic*, December 23, 1967, 13–14.

Lehman, John. "To the Editor." *Foreign Affairs* 61, no. 2 (Winter 1982–83): 455–56.

Leffler, Melvyn P. "From the Truman Doctrine to the Carter Doctrine: Lessons and Dilemmas of the Cold War." *Diplomatic History* 7, no. 4 (October 1983): 245–66.

Levi, Werner. "Ideology, Interests, and Foreign Policy." *International Studies Quarterly* 14, no. 1 (March 1970): 1–31.

Lewy, Guenter. "Some Political-Military Lessons of the Vietnam War." In *Assessing the Vietnam War: A Collection from the Journal of the U.S. Army War College*. Edited by Lloyd J. Matthews and Dale E. Brown. Washington, DC: Pergamon-Brassey's International Defense Publishers, 1987.

Linger, James A. "Europe and the Superpowers." In *Defense Policy and the Presidency: Carter's First Years*. Edited by Sam C. Sarkesian. Boulder, CO: Westview Press, 1979.

Linville, James. "Richard Price, The Art of Fiction No. 144." *Paris Review*, no. 138 (Spring 1996). http://www.theparisreview.org/interviews/1431/the-art-of-fiction-no-144-richard-price.

Lippmann, Walter. "The Rivalry of Nations." *Atlantic Monthly*, February 1948, 17–20.

Little, Douglas. "From Even-Handed to Empty-Handed: Seeking Order in the Middle East." In *Kennedy's Quest for Victory: American Foreign Policy, 1961–1963*. Edited by Thomas G. Paterson. New York: Oxford University Press, 1989.

———. "The New Frontier on the Nile: JFK, Nasser, and Arab Nationalism." *Journal of American History* 75, no. 2 (September 1988): 501–27.

Luns, Joseph M. A. H. "The Washington Summit Meeting in Perspective." *NATO Review* 26, no. 4 (August 1978): 3–7.

MacKaye, William. "Bundy in the White House." *Saturday Evening Post*, March 10, 1962, 82–85.

Maechling, Charles, Jr. "Camelot, Robert Kennedy, and Counterinsurgency—A Memoir." *Virginia Quarterly Review* 75, no. 3 (Summer 1999): 438–58.

McAllister, James. "What Can One Man Do? Nguyen Duc Thang and the Limits of Reform in South Vietnam." *Journal of Vietnamese Studies* 4, no. 2 (Summer 2009): 117–53.

McCollum, James K. "The CORDS Pacification Organization in Vietnam." *Armed Forces and Society* 10, no. 1 (Fall 1983): 105–22.

McFadzean, Andrew. "The Bigger Picture: Biography and/or History? Robert Bowie." *Australasian Journal of American Studies* 22, no. 2 (December 2003): 41–63.

———. "Interviews with Robert Bowie: The Use of Oral Testimony in Writing the Biography of Professor Robert Richardson Bowie, Washington Policy Planner and Harvard University Professor." *Oral History Review* 26, no. 2 (Summer/Fall 1999): 29–46.

McLellan, David S. "The 'Operational Code' Approach to the Study of Political Leaders: Dean Acheson's Philosophical and Instrumental Beliefs." *Canadian Journal of Political Science* 4, no. 1 (March 1971): 52–75.

McMahon, Robert P. "Choosing Sides in South Asia." In *Kennedy's Quest for Victory: American Foreign Policy, 1961–1963*. Edited by Thomas G. Paterson. New York: Oxford University Press, 1988.

McNamara, Robert. "Britain, Nasser and the Outbreak of the Six Day War." *Journal of Contemporary History* 35, no. 4 (October 2000): 619–39.

Mearsheimer, John J. Review of *Promise and Power: The Life and Times of Robert McNamara,* by Deborah Shapley. *Bulletin of Atomic Scientists* 49, no. 6 (July/August 1993). http://mearsheimer.uchicago.edu/pdfs/A0020x1.pdf.

Mecklin, John. "The Struggle to Rescue the People." *Fortune,* April 1967, 126–33.

Merrill, Dennis. "Walt Whitman Rostow." In *Encyclopedia of U.S. Foreign Relations*, Vol. 4. Edited by Bruce W. Jentleson and Thomas G. Patterson. New York: Oxford University Press, 1997.

Millikan, Max, and Walt W. Rostow. "Notes on Foreign Economic Policy." In *Universities and Empire: Money and Politics in the Social Sciences during the Cold War.* Edited by Christopher Simpson. New York: New Press, 1998.

Milne, David. "America's Intellectual Diplomacy." *International Affairs* 86, no. 1 (2010): 49–68.

———. "A Hawk among Hawks." *Vietnam,* August 2007, 55–60.

———. "'Our Equivalent of Guerrilla Warfare': Walt Rostow and the Bombing of North Vietnam, 1961–1968." *Journal of Military History* 71, no. 1 (January 2007): 169–203.

Moore, Raymond A. "The Carter Administration and Foreign Policy." In *The Carter Years: The President and Policy Making.* Edited by M. Glenn Abernathy, Dilys M. Hill, and Phil Williams. New York: St. Martin's Press, 1984.

Morgenthau, Hans J. "Kennedy and Foreign Policy." In *Truth and Power: Essays of a Decade, 1960–1970.* New York: Praeger, 1970.

"Mr. Komer Replies, Admiral Turner Replies." *Foreign Affairs* 61, no. 3 (Winter 1982–83): 456–57.

Mueller, John E. "The Search for the 'Breaking Point' in Vietnam: The Statistics of a Deadly Quarrel." *International Studies Quarterly* 24, no. 4 (December 1980): 497–519.

"My Opinion of the Russians Has Changed Most Dramatically . . . " *Time*, January 14, 1980. http://www.time.com/time/magazine/article/0,9171,921764,00.html.

Nadelmann, Ethan. "Setting the Stage: American Policy toward the Middle East, 1961–1966." *International Journal of Middle East Studies* 14, no. 4 (November 1982): 435–57.

Nailor, Peter. "*Maritime Strategy or Coalition Defense? A Review.*" *International Affairs* 60, no. 4 (Autumn 1984): 735.

Oakley, Robert B., and Michael Casey Jr. "The Country Team: Restructuring America's First Line of Engagement." *Joint Force Quarterly,* no. 47 (4th Quarter 2007): 146–54.

Oberdorfer, Don. "An Ending of His Own." In *Reporting Vietnam: American Journalism 1959–1969*, Vol. 1. New York: Library of America, 1998.

Odom, William E. "The Cold War Origins of the U.S. Central Command." *Journal of Cold War Studies* 8, no. 2 (Spring 2006): 52–82.

Osborne, John. "Fantasy in Vietnam." *New Republic,* May 27, 1967, 13–15.

Paterson, Thomas G. "Introduction: John F. Kennedy's Quest for Victory and Global Crisis." In *Kennedy's Quest for Victory: American Foreign Policy, 1961–1963.* Edited by Thomas G. Paterson. New York: Oxford University Press, 1989.

Pierre, Andrew J. Review of *Bureaucracy at War: U.S. Performance in the Vietnam Conflict,* by Robert W. Komer. *Foreign Affairs* 64, no. 5 (Summer 1986): 1110.

Pugliaresi, Lucian, and Diane T. Berliner. "Policy Analysis at the Department of State: The Policy Planning Staff." *Journal of Policy Analysis and Management* 8, no. 3 (Summer 1989): 379–94.

Quinn, James Brian. "Technological Innovation, Entrepreneurship and Strategy." *Sloan Management Review* 21, no. 3 (Spring 1979): 19–30.

Record, Jeffrey. "Jousting with Unreality: Reagan's Military Strategy." *International Security* 8, no. 3 (Winter 1983–84): 3–18.

Retzlaff, Ralph J. "India: A Year of Stability and Change." *Asian Survey* 3, no. 2 (February 1963): 96–106.

Rosen, Stephen Peter. "Vietnam and the American Theory of Limited War." *International Security* 7, no. 2 (Autumn 1982): 83–113.

Ross, Dennis. "Considering Soviet Threats to the Persian Gulf." *International Security* 6, no. 2 (Autumn 1981): 159–80.

Rostow, Walt W. "Guerrilla Warfare in Underdeveloped Areas." In *The Viet-Nam Reader*. Edited by Marcus G. Raskin and Bernard Fall. New York: Vintage Books, 1967.

Schandler, Herbert Y. "America and Vietnam: The Failure of Strategy, 1964–67." In *Vietnam as History: Ten Years after the Paris Peace Accords*. Edited by Peter Braestrup. Washington, DC: Woodrow Wilson International Center for Scholars and the University Press of America, 1984.

Schemmer, Benjamin F. "Haig Now Says NATO Can Expect 8–14 Days Warning, Not 48 Hours." *Armed Forces Journal International*, October 1977, 16–17.

Schlesinger, Arthur, Jr. "A Biographer's Perspective." In *The Kennedy Presidency*. Edited by Kenneth W. Thompson. Lanham, MD: University Press of America, 1985.

———. "Effective National Security Advising: A Most Dubious Precedent." *Political Science Quarterly* 113, no. 3 (Autumn 2000): 347–51.

———. "Some Lessons from the Cold War." In *The End of the Cold War: Its Meaning and Implications*. Edited by Michael J. Hogan. New York: Cambridge University Press, 1992.

Shaplen, Robert. "Letter from Saigon." *New Yorker*, June 29, 1968, 37–40.

Shultz, Richard H., Jr. "The Vietnamization-Pacification Strategy of 1969–1972: A Quantitative and Qualitative Reassessment." In *Lessons from an Unconventional War: Reassessing U.S. Strategies for Future Conflicts*. Edited by Richard A. Hunt and Richard H. Shultz Jr. New York: Permagon Press, 1982.

Sorensen, Theodore C. "Kennedy: Retrospect and Prospect." In *The Kennedy Presidency*. Edited by Kenneth W. Thompson. Lanham, MD: University Press of America, 1985.

Sorley, Lewis. "To Change a War: General Harold K. Johnson and the PROVN Study." *Parameters* 28, no. 1 (Spring 1998): 93–109.

Steury, Donald P. Introduction to *Sherman Kent and the Board of National Estimates*. Edited by Donald P. Steury. Washington, DC: Center for the Study of Intelligence, Central Intelligence Agency, 1994.

Suganami, Hidemi. "Narrative Explanation and International Relations: Back to Basics." *Millennium—Journal of International Studies* 37, no. 2 (2008): 327–56.

"Supreme Test." *Newsweek*, February 26, 1968, 34, 36.

Suri, Jeremi. "Henry Kissinger, the American Dream, and the Jewish Immigrant Experience in the Cold War." *Diplomatic History* 31, no. 2 (November 2008): 719–47.

Thompson, Kenneth W. "Kennedy's Foreign Policy: Activism versus Pragmatism." In *John F. Kennedy: The Promise Revisited*. Edited by Paul Harper and Joann P. Kreig. New York: Greenwood Press, 1988.

Thompson, Robert. "Will We Win?" *Newsweek*, January 1, 1968, 92–94.

Thomson, James C., Jr. "How Could Vietnam Happen? An Autopsy." *Atlantic Monthly*, April 1968, 47–53.

Trainor, James L. "What Business Does the Military Have in Pacification/Nation-Building?" *Armed Force Management*, August 1967, 32–33, 71–72.

Turner, Stansfield, and George Thibault. "Preparing for the Unexpected: The Need for a New Military Strategy." *Foreign Affairs* 60, no. 6 (Fall 1982): 122–35.

Vought, Donald. "American Culture and American Arms: The Case of Vietnam." In *Lessons from an Unconventional War, Reassessing U.S. Strategies for Future Conflicts*. Edited by Richard A. Hunt and Richard H. Shultz Jr. New York: Permagon Press, 1982.

Walton, Richard J. "The Laundering of McGeorge Bundy." *The Nation,* April 12, 1980, 428.

Weber, Eugen. "Nationalism, Socialism, and National Socialism." In *My France: Politics, Culture, Myth.* Cambridge, MA: Belknap Press of the Harvard University Press, 1991.

Webster, David. "Regimes in Motion: The Kennedy Administration and Indonesia's New Frontier, 1960–1962." *Diplomatic History* 33, no. 1 (January 2009): 95–123.

Weigley, Russell F. "Reflections on 'Lessons' from Vietnam." In *Vietnam as History: Ten Years after the Paris Peace Accords.* Edited by Peter Braestrup. Washington, DC: Woodrow Wilson International Center for Scholars and the University Press of America, 1984.

———. "Vietnam, What Manner of War?" *Air University Review* 34, no. 2 (January/February 1983). http://www.airpower.au.af.mil/airchronicles/aure view/1983/jan-feb/weigley.html.

"Who Lost Iran?" *Time*, December 4, 1978. http://www.time.com/time/maga zine/article/0,9171,912266,00.html.

Williams, Phil. "Carter's Defense Policy." In *The Carter Years: The President and Policy Making.* Edited by M. Glenn Abernathy, Dilys M. Hill, and Phil Williams. New York: St. Martin's Press, 1984.

Wise, David. "Scholars of the Nuclear Age." In *The Kennedy Circle.* Edited by Lester Tanzer. Washington, DC: Robert B. Luce, 1961.

Wish, Naomi Bailin. "Foreign Policy Makers and Their National Role Conceptions." *International Studies Quarterly* 24, no. 4 (December 1980): 532–54.

Wright, Jonathan. "George Frost Kennan and the Study of American Foreign Policy: Some Critical Comments." *Western Political Quarterly* 20, no. 1 (March 1967): 149–60.

Zakheim, Dov S. "Review of *Maritime Strategy or Coalition Defense?*" *Political Science Quarterly* 99, no. 4 (Winter 1984–85): 721–22.

DISSERTATIONS AND THESES

Brooke, George M., III. "A Matter of Will: Sir Robert Thompson, Malaya, and the Failure of American Strategy in Vietnam." PhD diss., Georgetown University, 2004.

Daddis, Gregory A. "No Sure Victory: Measuring U.S. Army Effectiveness and Progress in the Vietnam War." PhD diss., University of North Carolina–Chapel Hill, 2009.

Embrey, James Hubert. "Reorienting Pacification: The Accelerated Pacification Campaign of 1968." PhD diss., University of Kentucky, 1997.

Johnson, Ralph William. "Phoenix/Phung Hoang: A Study of Wartime Intelligence Management." PhD diss., American University, 1985.

Komer, Robert W. "Civilian Strategists in the Great War: Lloyd George and Churchill and the Conduct of the War." AB honors thesis, Harvard University, 1942. Harvard Archives, Cambridge, MA.

Rakove, Robert Benjamin. "A Genuine Departure: Kennedy, Johnson, and the Nonaligned World." PhD diss., University of Virginia, 2008.

LECTURES AND SPEECHES

Gates, Robert M. "Speech at the National Defense University." Washington, DC, September 29, 2008. http://www.defense.gov/Speeches/Speech.aspx?SpeechID=1279.

Immerman, Richard. "The Intellectual and Emotional Qualities Needed by Strategists Working in the Current National Security Environment." Address, "Teaching Strategy Workshop," U.S. Army War College, Carlisle Barracks, PA, April 9, 2010.

Kilcullen, David. "Report of Counterinsurgency Seminar 07." Compiled by David Dilegge. Seminar, Small Wars Center of Excellence, Wargaming Division, Marine Corps Warfighting Laboratory, Quantico, VA, September 26, 2007.

Komer, Robert W. "The Civil Side of the War in Vietnam." Lecture, National War College, Washington, DC, March 29, 1967.

———. "Factors Bearing on U.S. Policies and Plans for the Middle East." Lecture, National War College, Washington, DC, May 18, 1964.

Nuechterlein, Donald. "National Interests and Foreign Policy Formulation." Lecture, Naval Air Executive Seminar on National Security, University of Virginia, Charlottesville, November 7, 2000. http://donaldnuechterlein.com/2000/major.html.

———. "U.S. National Interests and Policies in the Middle East." Lecture, Military Officers' Association of America, Charlottesville, VA, March 24, 2011. http://donaldnuechterlein.com/2011/2011.03.lecture.html.

SOUND RECORDINGS

Komer, Robert W. Interview. CD #6328. U.S. Marine Corps Historical Center, Quantico, VA.

Komer, Robert, Larry Berman, and Moya Ann Ball. "Lyndon Johnson's War." Panel discussion, moderated by Douglas Brinkley. In *Vietnam 1954–1965 Conference*, sponsored by the U.S. Naval Institute and McCormick Tribune Foundation, CD 1. Elkridge, MD: A.V.E.R. Associates, 1996.

INTERVIEWS

Bator, Francis M. (deputy special assistant to the president for national security affairs in the Johnson administration). May 14, 2008.

Newsom, David (ambassador, U.S. Department of State, retired). May 30, 2007.

Odom, William E. (lieutenant general, U.S. Army, retired). May 29, 2007.

Saunders, Harold H. (Hal) (NSC staff member in the Kennedy and Johnson administrations). October 18, 2007.

Sheridan, Michael (brigadier general, U.S. Marine Corps, retired), April 17, 2007.

Swartz, Peter (captain, U.S. Navy, retired). February 27, 2007.

UNPUBLISHED MANUSCRIPT

Komer, Robert W. *Blowtorch*. Unpublished manuscript, 6th draft. n.d.

PUBLIC DOCUMENTS

Congressional Documents

U.S. Comptroller General. *NATO's New Defense Program: Issues for Consideration*. Report to the Congress of the United States ID-79-1A. Washington, DC: U.S. General Accounting Office, 1979.

U.S. House of Representatives. *U.S. Assistance Programs in Vietnam: Hearings Before a Subcommittee of the Committee on Government Operations*. 92nd Cong. (1971).

U.S. House of Representatives, Committee on Foreign Affairs, Subcommittee on Europe and the Middle East. *Hearings on NATO after Afghanistan*. 96th Cong. (1980).

U.S. House of Representatives, Committee on International Relations. *Western Europe in 1977: Security, Economic and Political Issues: Hearings Before the Subcommittee on Europe and the Middle East*. 95th Cong. (1977).

U.S. Senate. *Department of Defense Authorization for Appropriations for Fiscal Year 1981: Hearings on S. 2294 before the Senate Committee on Armed Services*. 96th Cong. (1980).

———. *First Concurrent Resolution on the Budget, FY79, Vol. 1: Hearings before the Committee on the Budget.* 95th Cong. (1978).

———. *NATO Posture and Initiatives: Hearings Before the Subcommittee on Manpower and Personnel.* 95th Cong. (1977).

———. *U.S. Security Interests and Policies in Southwest Asia: Hearings Before the Committee on Foreign Relations.* 96th Cong. (1980). (Testimony No. 9.)

U.S. Senate, Committee on Armed Services. *Hearing on the Nominations of Robert W. Komer to Be Under Secretary of Defense for Policy, Honorable Edward Hidalgo to Be Secretary of the Navy, and Dennis P. McAuliffe to Be Administrator of the Panama Canal Commission.* 99th Cong. (1979).

———. NATO and the New Soviet Threat, S. Rep. 95-1 at 1 (1977).

Presidential Documents

Carter, Jimmy. *Public Papers of the President: Jimmy Carter.* Online by Gerhard Peters and John T. Woolley. *The American Presidency Project.* http://www.presidency.ucsb.edu/.

Johnson, Lyndon B. *Public Papers of the President: Lyndon Baines Johnson.* Online by Gerhard Peters and John T. Woolley. *The American Presidency Project.* http://www.presidency.ucsb.edu/.

Kennedy, John F. *Public Papers of the President: John F. Kennedy.* Online by Gerhard Peters and John T. Woolley. *The American Presidency Project.* http://www.presidency.ucsb.edu/.

DOCUMENTS OF U.S. DEPARTMENTS AND AGENCIES

Ahern, Thomas L., Jr. *The CIA and Rural Pacification in South Vietnam.* Washington, DC: Center for the Study of Intelligence, Central Intelligence Agency, 2001. http://www.foia.cia.gov/vietnam.asp.

Brown, Harold. *Department of Defense Annual Report, Fiscal Year 1981.* Washington, DC: Department of Defense, 1980.

Organization of the Joint Chiefs of Staff. *United States Military Posture for FY 1982.* Washington, DC: Department of Defense, 1981.

Palmer, Bruce, Jr. *U.S. Intelligence and Vietnam.* Washington, DC: Central Intelligence Agency, 1984.

Thayer, Thomas C., ed. *A Systems Analysis View of the Vietnam War, 1965–1972.* Vol. 10, *Pacification and Civil Affairs.* Washington, DC: OASD(PA&E)RP, Asia Division, 1975.

U.S. Department of the Army. *Counterinsurgency.* Field Manual 3-24. Washington, DC: U.S. Department of the Army, 2006.

U.S. Department of Defense. "Evolution of the War—Re-emphasis on Pacification: 1965–1967." Part IV.C.8 in *U.S.-Vietnam Relations, 1945–1967.* http://www.archives.gov/research/pentagon-papers/.

———. "Re-Emphasis on Pacification, 1965–1967." *History of United States Decisionmaking in Vietnam*, ed. Senator Gravel, vol. 2. Boston: Beacon Press, 1971.

———. "U.S. Ground Strategy and Force Deployments: 1965–1967, Volume II: Program 5." Part IV.C.6(b) in *U.S.-Vietnam Relations, 1945–1967*. http://www.archives.gov/research/pentagon-papers/.

U.S. Department of State. *Foreign Relations of the United States, 1961–1968*. Vols. 1–34. Washington, DC: USGPO, 1991–2005.

U.S. Military Assistance Command, Vietnam. *Command History*. Vol. 2, *1967*. Saigon: U.S. Military Assistance Command, Vietnam, 1968.

———. *Command History*. Vol. 3, *1968*. Saigon: U.S. Military Assistance Command, Vietnam, 1969.

FRANK LEITH JONES is the professor of security studies at the U.S. Army War College in Carlisle, Pennsylvania, where he holds the Gen. Dwight D. Eisenhower Chair of National Security. A retired member of the Senior Executive Service, he served in several high-level policy and strategy positions in the Office of the Secretary of Defense.